Worlds to
EXPLORE

Another world to explore: A member of a 1917 expedition to Alaska's Valley of Ten Thousand Smokes marvels at a mud canyon, one feature in a range of volcanic phenomena so astonishing that it was like watching a new planet being formed.

Worlds to
EXPLORE

✶

CLASSIC TALES OF
TRAVEL & ADVENTURE
FROM NATIONAL GEOGRAPHIC

✶

EDITED BY MARK JENKINS

 NATIONAL GEOGRAPHIC

WASHINGTON, D.C.

Library of Congress Cataloging-in-Publication Data

Worlds to explore: classic tales of travel and adventure from National Geographic/ edited by Mark Jenkins
    p.cm
    Includes index.
    ISBN 0-7922-5487-2
    1. Voyages and travels. 2. Jenkins, Mark, 1960 July 12-. II. National Geographic Society (U.S.)

G465.W665 2006
910'—dc22   2005058392

ISBN-10: 0-7922-5487-2
ISBN-13: 978-0-7922-5487-4

One of the world's largest nonprofit scientific and educational organizations, the National Geographic Society was founded in 1888 "for the increase and diffusion of geographic knowledge." Fulfilling this mission, the Society educates and inspires millions every day through its magazines, books, television programs, videos, maps and atlases, research grants, the National Geographic Bee, teacher workshops, and innovative classroom materials. The Society is supported through membership dues, charitable gifts, and income from the sale of its educational products. This support is vital to National Geographic's mission to increase global understanding and promote conservation of our planet through exploration, research, and education.

For more information, please call 1-800-NGS LINE (647-5463) or write to the following address:

National Geographic Society
1145 17th Street N.W.
Washington, D.C. 20036-4688 U.S.A.

Visit the Society's Web site at www.nationalgeographic.com.

Designed by Cameron Zotter

Contents

✶

8/06

FOREWORD

HUMAN BEINGS TRAVEL FOR MANY REASONS. NOMADS TRAVEL BECAUSE they have to. The curious travel because they think they need to. Traders travel because money tempts them to. Imperialists and their soldiers travel because great powers order them to. Religious zealots travel because they believe a deity requires them to. The imprisoned travel because the idea of escape motivates them to.

But I travel—as do many around the world, and quite probably most of you who are reading this—for a much less obvious set of reasons. I travel to satisfy two elemental and compelling yearnings, both of which were in my case, and are in the case of many, conceived in youth—and in a time of life which, in my own case at least, was long before I in fact ever travelled anywhere at all.

The first of these yearnings became clear to me when I was about ten years old. It was always on an evening, always cold with a yellow curling fog, seemingly always November, when my parents would indulge me in my favourite London routine, the treat I was given whenever we visited the big city. My father would park the Ford Popular at the lower end of Haymarket, hurry across Pall Mall to the far side of Cockspur Street—and I would promptly be transported into a state of schoolboy rapture. For this is where the head offices of all the shipping lines were, and in each of their glowing windows were enormous scale models, made of oak and teak and iron and finely chased brass, of the great ocean liners that would and could in those days take one to ports at the farthest ends of the Earth.

"*Oh where are you going to, all you Big Steamers*," wrote Kipling, wondering at the treasure they were bringing in their holds:

> *And where will you fetch it from, all you Big Steamers,*
> *And where shall I write you when you are away?"*
> "*We fetch it from Melbourne, Quebec, and Vancouver—*
> *Address us at Hobart, Hong-kong, and Bombay."*

I would spend what seemed like hours gazing at these ships, and dreaming. The offices of the Peninsular & Oriental Lines were there, with their big India-bound steamships, and the White Star lines had extravagant models of old four-masters, and probably there were the Union Castle ships that went to

St. Helena and the Cape, and there were models of banana boats owned by Bibby and the Ellerman Lines and designed for scuttling to the Caribbean—and perhaps, though my memory is a little hazy, even Cunard had an office somewhere nearby, with its huge blue-and-white models of the three-funneled *Queen Mary* in one great bow window, and beside her a newer rendering, at a scale of ten feet to an inch, of her smaller, sleeker sister, the *Elizabeth*.

I had the most wonderful fantasies, standing there in the West End fog. I imagined what might occur were I ever rich enough to march in to the clerk at his high desk and have him handwrite a long-sea ticket for me, just as he had done for Gladys Aylward in *The Inn of the Sixth Happiness*, or for Adela Quested in *A Passage to India*. I dreamed—and only now have I come to realise where those dreams came from—of all the myriad delights of sea travel. But back in these days of my youth it was only the journey that I imagined: The destinations themselves were almost too exotic to contemplate; my mind was perfectly content to linger on the minutiae of the rituals of passage.

So I dreamed of endless, slow-unrolling long-sea wakes, of pursers and stewards and navigating officers, of morning bouillon on the boat deck, of dressing for dinner in Red Sea Rig, of straw hats or topees bought from Simon Artz in Port Said, and watching the gully-gully men performing their tricks on the wharfs beside Suez. I imagined seeing the first flying fish off Tenerife, or the first albatross in the Southern Ocean, or of slumbering sweatily through the Doldrums, of being terrified in the big seas of the Roaring Forties, of seeing the heat shimmering over the sandhills of Aden, of the cloth of cloud on Table Mountain, or of staying up to spy the first icebergs in the cold Atlantic near Greenland. And I imagined calling at ports that were not our destination, places that offered the temporary fascination of merely being waystations, places of easy unattachment.

And then my parents, who had meanwhile been looking at the more ordinary shops on Piccadilly, broke my reverie. We had to go, barked my father, and soon I was back in the rear seat of the car, driving north to the suburbs, and all my evening dreams became obscured by the greasy London fog as it swallowed up the visions of still glowing ships, much as a thick winter sea-fret might do as the steamer thrashes away into the ocean.

I was 17 when I took my first journey by sea, and in doing so happened to confront the second of the compulsions.

It was on the *Empress of Britain*, a 25,000-ton liner, all white, with the red-checked funnel mark of Canadian Pacific Lines. I had saved up for two years for the £80 needed to buy a tiny berth in a four-person windowless cabin on Six Deck, down near the bilges, and though the room was tiny and the food unmemorable, everything else about the five-day Atlantic crossing between Liverpool and Montreal was just as I had imagined.

My ticket—I was off to go exploring with friends who had promised to "show me Canada"—had indeed been handwritten by a man in a Cockspur Street head office; there was indeed morning bouillon, great steaming mugs of it served to keep out April's boat-deck chill; there would have been shuffleboard had the seas not been running so high; and I was welcomed onto the bridge for each forenoon watch to pore over the charts and check our steadily westward progress. There came a brief excitement one afternoon, a few hours south of Cape Farewell, when we damaged our rudder on a piece of drifting brash ice; but the crew jury-rigged another, and we limped into the St. Lawrence estuary at half speed, arriving a little late, but with an additional sea story to tell.

And then there was my first sight of the North American continent. By this time in my life—it was now a full decade after my ship-model dreams—I had become every bit as enraptured by destinations as by the simple mechanics of journeying, and I had now in particular become enchanted with the geography of the New World. So, perhaps not unreasonably, I wanted to savor the first moment of my arrival there.

There was thick fog in the Cabot Strait, so I never saw Cape Breton Island in daylight, nor did I spy the southern tip of Newfoundland. Our rudder-slowed progress meant that we would now sight Quebec at about five in the morning, and so I stayed up all night, and was standing by the bowsprit in the freezing dark when suddenly I saw the glinting flash of the light on Cape Gaspé. I could barely move: I watched and watched until I could make out the mass of land behind—American land, I kept reminding myself—and then, to my utter delight, made out the first firefly trail of a car's headlamps on a cliff-top road. A farmer delivering the milk, I thought. Or the Poste Canada carrier, or the boy with the *Montreal Gazette*. It was all so deliciously foreign, so utterly romantic, so full of strange wonder.

And then the banks of the river closed in on us, and the strange slowly became familiar, and by lunchtime we were sliding under the great cantilever bridge at Québec City with the Chateau Frontenac looming large on the starboard side, and by evening we were tying up in Montreal, and there on the quayside were my friends, and the adventure for which I had come to America was about to begin—and it was a very long and varied adventure, which took me thousands of miles and led to the telling of hundreds of stories.

These two essential elements, which have underpinned all of my subsequent travels, had their first airings, I like to think, in those two episodes—first during the foggy evenings before the glowing storefronts in London, and then at the moment of that long anticipated shipboard arrival in Montreal. I can sum it up this way: In the very early years my notion of travel was guided, quite simply, by romance, by fantasy, and by dreams. And by the time I had become a student, this sense had been transmuted, moderated, and mediated by a new need, the second element: the entirely practical need I felt to have adventure, to suffer experiences, and to enjoy and endure memorable happenings.

And I would suggest that this twin-track approach, if I can call it that, is what should perhaps underpin everybody's longing for travel. I would like to hope that the dual yearnings for romance on the one hand and adventure on the other should be the prime motivating forces that drive all of us, at least once in a while, to get away from the comfort of our living rooms and into the wild outdoors.

If one accepts this argument—and by no means all travelers do—then one has to wonder at the source, the *fons et origo*, of all this romance and this aspiration to adventure. And the answer, which was perhaps more obvious half a century ago than it is today, is that such things are born, quite simply, in reading and in *writing*. They are born in the kind of writing that is found in the pages that follow—of plain and unaffected accounts of astonishing adventures undertaken in the remotest corners of the planet, by men and women—largely men, it has to be conceded, but not exclusively—who were impelled by a sense of dash, brio, derring-do, and romance, to go out and tell the world's story to those who were obliged to stay home. And it was the reading of this kind of writing that promoted legions to get up from their armchairs and follow, quite literally, in the footsteps of those who had gone before.

Kipling's poetry worked its magic, of course, as his verses about steamships did for me as a ten-year-old boy. Then later came the novels of John Buchan, Somerset Maugham, Graham Greene, E. M. Forster, and Erskine Childers. The writings of Robert Byron, T. E. Lawrence, Wilfred Thesiger, Thor Heyerdahl (who appears in these pages), Richard Burton, James Cameron, Robert Louis Stevenson—the stories of all of these travelers and a thousand more we—those of my generation, that is—imbibed from childhood, becoming thereby accustomed to yarns about endless ocean passages and immense train journeys and arrivals at exotic jungle cities and forgotten civilizations and the enduring of privations on the remotest steppes and in faraway and forgotten island kingdoms.

The NATIONAL GEOGRAPHIC was the most powerful influence of all, perhaps. We read the kind of essays that appear in this collection—we read George Kennan on Dagestan and Joseph Rock on Chaulmoogra Oil. We read and remembered the essays by Eliza Scidmore—the lady who gave Washington its cherry trees—on both Benares and on Japanese tsunamis. We took as gospel the accounts by Shackleton and Peary and Richard Byrd of the awful powers of ice and cold. We went contentedly with Beebe and Cousteau under the oceans, and with Lindbergh and Piccard high above the clouds. The GEOGRAPHIC gave us all of this, month by yellow-bordered month, year after year, and those of us who read these essays in real time, or who were born close enough to their day to be aware of the writings still, were privileged indeed.

And from all these writers we caught the same incurable infections: We were lured by the romance of their storytelling, and we were caught in the web of adventures that they so deftly spun. And we travelled, too, and though we went perhaps never so far or so high or so deep as these travelers had, we went out with much the same spirit, and when we came back from our peregrinations, we found we had reaped much the same reward.

And we did so because we were lucky, because travel then—travel that took place while the shadow of these writers loomed large, as it does not loom still— was so very, very different from the travel that is undertaken today.

The ship models are all gone from Cockspur Street. No clerks on high chairs will hand write a passage ticket for you. There are no liners to the Cape any more, nor are there banana boats bound for the Caribbean. And the *Empress of Britain* creaks around the world as the *Topaz* now, full of peace activists and politicians, having ceased (as "uneconomic") her trans-Atlantic voyaging just six months after I went on my first journey with her.

But travel has changed in other ways as well. My own experience of Egypt suggests just how. I first went to Luxor in 1966, taking the train from Cairo Central and drinking Egyptian date wine in an observation car overlooking the desert. I stayed in an immense and gloomy suite in the Winter Palace Hotel, kept awake by the clicking of a rickety fan on the ceiling. I drank *karkady*, hibiscus tea, out on the terrace, while I waited for my felucca to take me, slowly and steadily, across the Nile to the Valley of the Kings. On the far side was a horse tonga, and in it we clopped steadily up to the tomb of Tutankhamen, where I paid a few piastres to a blind guard eating a watermelon and went in, out of the heat, to see the sarcophagus and marvel at what Lord Carnarvon had discovered (as Maynard Williams writes, so vividly, in the pages that follow) back in 1922.

I was back in Luxor a year ago. The Winter Palace now has an immense glass tower next door, for the package tourists. Karkady is barely available, and never *offered*, as they say, on the air-conditioned terrace. The feluccas have been replaced by hydrofoils which zoom across the Nile in moments. The horse tongas have been replaced by diesel motor coaches. Gravel roads have given way to metalled highways. And at the tomb there is a rota system: I had to wait an hour while three tour buses from Bulgaria, Japan, and Taiwan disgorged their passengers; and was then thought eccentric and unhelpful to be wanting to view the king alone, and not in the company of hundreds. To avoid confusion I was herded among a party of Germans, and told that this was by far the better way to see what I had come to see.

I have no wish to bemoan the state of modern travel, other than to note the reality that with half the world perpetually on the move—with, as an instance, a hundred million Chinese middle-class travelers now jockeying to be let out of their country to view the Eiffel Tower, Pisa, the Crown Jewels, and Venice—the planet is becoming supersaturated with displaced humanity. The romance, so powerful a motivation not long ago, has as a result long been entirely stripped from the process of today's travel. Adventure is also, and to a very large extent, no longer an element in all but the most wayward of wandering. The two compulsions that prompted those of us who read the books and the articles and were lured by what they told us, have, in other words, long since evaporated as the most potent motivations for the kind of travel most of us can and do undertake today.

And what makes the situation so curiously alarming is that this change has happened within half a century, within much less than a single lifetime.

When I was a youngster, and on to when I became a young man, the essays of the kind that appear here still had great relevance to the kind of travel that I and the rest of the world performed: The shadow of Joseph Rock and Ellsworth Huntington and Maj. Edward Keith-Roach fell upon us and our wanderings. It influenced us, it persuaded us, it gave us ideas and inspiration.

But then, in my middle age, when I had moved well beyond the shadow and the influence of these same men and women, travel itself suddenly changed to the point where it could hardly be influenced by what these writers had to say anyway—since romance and adventure played so little a part in motivating the travelers who undertook it.

So, one might ask: what possible effect could the writings of Joseph Rock have now on a modern traveler going to his beloved Szechuan in a tourist bus? How might Virginia Hamilton's writings have an impact on Korean golfers teeing off in her beloved Borneo? What might the tennis player with whom I once traveled to the Ross Ice Shelf—where he set up a net and had his picture taken for the club back home—learn from the writings of one such as Richard Byrd?

And yet. And yet I admit, in spite of all this, to feeling a stirring of optimism. I do not like how we travel today, and I hanker, I must confess, for the manner we explored our carefree way around the planet half a century ago and more. And what is more, I suspect that many thinking travelers of today feel much the same, and that a rebellion of sorts is at hand. A movement to restore travel, if it all possible, to some semblance of what it was.

Of course it never will be possible, progress being what it is. But if just the yearning for this restoration is there, then perhaps the writings that are presented here will become of more consequence than as a mere curiosity, presenting us with more than just a genteel reminder of the eccentricity and wanderlust of earlier times. Maybe these essays and these voices will serve anew as a clarion call: A call to urge that travel as it used to be—travel prompted by both a romantic view of our world and by a pressing need to enjoy adventuring through and across it—should, can, and must in some shape or form be revived. In which case this book will be of even more inestimable a value than, on first reading, it appears to be.

—Simon Winchester

INTRODUCTION

In 1983 Richard Guindon published a cartoon depicting an elderly couple at their kitchen table, with the caption "The ceremony to renew the subscription to the National Geographic is no small matter at the Foster household."

Only it's not a subscription they're renewing. It's a membership. There is a subtle but important difference, for membership in the National Geographic Society meant more than just receiving a magazine. It implied a kind of participation, too, which Guindon's drawing recognizes: In preparation for another year of armchair adventures, the couple has dressed for the occasion. Mr. Foster is wearing his pith helmet.

Similar cartoons were a staple of the 1930s, when we may imagine the Fosters first enlisted in the Society. Comical explorers—eccentric, absent-minded, mad as hoots—were shown blundering about in jungles or being carried to cooking pots by cannibals, meanwhile making facetious comments about the National Geographic. Bearded and burdened with magnifying glasses, butterfly nets, binoculars, and cameras, they were always togged out in the requisite safari clothes topped, again, by pith helmets.

You will meet no such amusing caricatures in this book. Many of the men and women here represented may have indeed worn pith helmets, widely believed to ward off sunstroke in tropical countries. But others wore the wide-brimmed terai hat popular in India and East Africa, or military-style campaign hats, sailors' caps, aviator goggles, turbans, and even, on one memorable occasion, leather football helmets. And all escaped with their heads, although it was a close shave in some cases.

But both the genuine thing and the caricature spring from the same source: those old NATIONAL GEOGRAPHICS now piled carefully in attics, still sporting their classically dignified oak-and-laurel-framed covers. That border of vegetation did not spring into being with the publication; it was planted there in 1910 and today has withered completely away. But it flourished throughout the first half of the 20th century, characterizing an era at the magazine, one from which this anthology of travel and adventure narratives has been drawn.

The original GEOGRAPHIC did not boast much of a cover, merely a terracotta wrapper emblazoned with its name and the Society's seal. Only one of the 33 scholars, scientists, and explorers who assembled in Washington's Cosmos Club on the night of January 13, 1888, where in the glow of the hearth fire they founded an association "for the increase and diffusion of geographic knowledge," had any claim to being a journalist or writer. That was George Kennan, an expert on Russia (and great uncle of the George Kennan who during the Cold War devised the "containment" doctrine to counter Soviet expansionism). Yet even he wrote but one story for the magazine, recounting a trip to the Caucasus Mountains, and that was only many years later. Travel narrative simply wasn't an important component of the sporadically published journal of a small, scientifically inclined organization. Even in the 1890s, when travel writer Eliza Scidmore became one of its associate editors, the magazine remained dry and technical, although she spiced things up with such articles as her piece on the devastation caused by a Japanese tsunami.

It was the multitalented Alexander Graham Bell, the Society's second president, who, faced with a declining membership and an empty bank account, concluded that the way to plump the membership rolls was to transform NATIONAL GEOGRAPHIC from a journal of technical geography into a periodical with broad popular appeal. That task he entrusted to his future son-in-law, Gilbert Hovey Grosvenor, who in the course of his long tenure—he arrived in 1899 and retired in 1954—remade the stiff little publication into one of the most durably popular magazines in the world, with Society membership growing from less than two thousand to more than two million. His success was due to his pioneering use of photographs and to the emphasis he placed on the idea of community. Armchair travelers might, in return for annual membership dues, not merely receive a magazine that brought them, in Bell's phrase, "the world and all that is in it," but also share in dispatching explorers to the globe's far corners. So seriously was this idea of community taken that one elderly lady, offered membership in the Society, reportedly declined on the grounds that she was "too advanced in years to participate in expeditions."

The idea of participation naturally led to that of contribution. As a result, the early decades of the century were a golden age for amateurs at the GEOGRAPHIC, as travelers, explorers, diplomats, naturalists, professors, archaeologists, tourists, and ex-Presidents saw not just an opportunity to get published but also a chance to share their adventures with a responsive audience and so "promote the work of the Society." They contributed articles and photographs in such numbers that for many years they filled more of the magazine's pages than did professional journal-ists, with the result that travel narrative became an important part of the overall mix. Inevitably, their number included some remarkable charac-ters. Gilbert Grosvenor may have looked stolidly Victorian, but he was born and reared in exotic Constantinople, and knew how to pull into his orbit the likes of Robert E. Peary of North Pole fame, Hiram Bingham of Machu Picchu renown, and the strange, tormented Joseph Rock, a plant hunter who haunted China's far provinces. In gratitude for his support, these characters strewed his name all over the world, from the Grosvenor Mountains in Antarctica, to Grosvenor Lake in Alaska, to Grosvenor Arch in Utah. Several birds, a fish, a Chinese medicinal plant, and even a fossil shell are also his namesakes.

By the 1930s the GEOGRAPHIC had its own foreign editorial staff as well, a corps of roving writer-photographers who spent most of their careers on far-flung assignments abroad. Its dean was the gregarious, out-going Maynard Owen Williams. "Ours is a job of courting friendship, not adventure," he would say, and it was a task he pursued with the happy zeal of the missionary he once was. With a hand in one hundred published articles, Williams opened the world for GEOGRAPHIC readers. His usual beat was the broad swath of countries from Greece to Afghanistan to the Far East. As we shall see, he was among the first journalists to peer into the tomb of Tutankhkamun, and he accompanied the dauntless Citroen-Haardt Expedition as it drove across Asia from the shores of the Mediterranean all the way to those of the Yellow Sea.

It was his colleague, Luis Marden, however, who would be called the "epitome" of the GEOGRAPHIC man. A polymath with an incredibly wide range of talents and interests, Marden was an excellent writer, a superb photographer, and both a scholar and a man of action. The article detailing his quest for the remains of the famous ship *Bounty* forms the concluding selection in this volume, for he found those remains in January 1957, on nearly the day a new era arrived at the Society, the day when Melville Bell Grosvenor, son of the pioneering editor, took charge, soon introducing tel-evision documentaries, globes, atlases, and many other exciting changes, including the placement of pictures on the magazine's cover. Cover pho-tographs, of course, brought the oak-and-laurel-framed era at the NATIONAL GEOGRAPHIC to a close. By that time, however, the journal and its cast of colorful contributors had so pervaded popular culture that car-toonists, ever subversive, could make fun of it.

The following selections represent not only an era at the NATIONAL
GEOGRAPHIC but also the twilight of a golden age of travel, before the
advent of mass tourism. Again the significant date is 1957, when the
Boeing 707, the first jumbo jet, rolled off the assembly lines, due to enter
commercial service the following year. Propeller planes could carry
several dozen passengers; jumbo jets initially carried upward of 170 people
and cut travel times in half. Within a few years, no place was as far away as
it once might have seemed.

Thus the era preceding the jet age has a peculiar appeal to today's jaded
tourists. It was a time, after all, when there was just enough modern transportation—trains or ocean liners, for instance—to permit greater ease of travel than ever before, yet neither so fast nor so omnipresent as to annihilate
distance. It still took time to get any place really interesting, and the journey
was as important as the arrival. Instead of flying from Hong Kong over the
Pacific and North America to London in just 22 hours, as a modern jet has
done, a passenger embarked on a 1930s Pan Am Clipper would depart from
San Francisco and spend days crossing the ocean, stopping at Honolulu,
Midway, Wake Island, Guam, and Manila before arriving in Hong Kong's
junk-crowded harbor. From there to London by ship it took weeks, the liners touching at Singapore, Colombo, Bombay, or Suez, allowing the passengers to take in each port's situation and sights before dressing for dinner.

It was also an age before the world was homogenized by global-
ization. Peoples and places still looked culturally distinctive, and the farther away from the West they were, the more men and women lived
according to immemorial tradition. In some remote places xenophobia
reigned, and Afghanistan, Tibet, and Nepal were in some sense "forbidden"
or "closed" to protect their still medieval societies. (Such barriers were
selectively permeable, and we shall see that motorcars preceded Western
explorers into the stifling valleys of Arabia's isolated Hadhramaut region.)

Nevertheless, old ways of life were beginning to erode and disappear,
so the more adventurous travelers deliberately sought them out before
they had vanished forever. In this volume, for instance, are stories on the
camel caravans that once plodded across the Sahara and along the Silk
Route; on the waning days of the age of sail, when great square-riggers
shouldered the seas; and on the pilgrimage to Mecca, before modernization changed its ancient patterns.

Still, if travel was more interesting, it was also more restricted than it is
today, which explains the avidity with which stay-at-home dreamers

devoured the GEOGRAPHIC. During the oak-and-laurel era, more than 90 percent of the Society's members lived in the United States, and most had never left the country. When even routine travelogues seemed exotic, how much more so were articles on what were called the "out places" or "far places." Plant hunter Joseph Rock did not feel like sharing the magazine with such staples as gondola trips through Venice or tours of old Poland. Traveling in the out places was altogether different, as he makes abundantly clear in what follows. In deference, so to speak, to this great favorite of generations of GEOGRAPHIC readers, the present volume features neither gondola trips nor tourist itineraries. For that reason, neither are the familiar sights and landscapes of North America and Europe here represented.

The stories in the following pages inevitably reflect the attitudes of a bygone era. Big game hunting was still widely viewed as high adventure, although Felix Shay's narrative of a lion hunt, written during the golden age of African safaris, seems unexpectedly modern. Living as they did in the fading light of empire, our authors might seem patronizing to non-Europeans; yet that is not the case in Ida Treat's fine story about sailing the forbidden Dankali coast. Readers in search of an "orientalist" bias, meaning the acceptance of that complex of stereotypes portraying Asia as the Inscrutable East, will probably find what they seek. The GEOGRAPHIC was a mirror of its times.

This book also reflects a transitional era in the history of exploration. The men gathered about the Cosmos Club fireplace that 1888 evening bathed also in the sunset glow of what is now called the second great age of discovery (the first being that associated with Magellan and Columbus). Spanning the late 17th to early 20th centuries, and including the voyages of James Cook and others who finished mapping the globe, the second age ended with the attainment of the Poles and, by extension, with the 1953 conquest of Mount Everest (often called Earth's "Third Pole"), the last great feat of exploration that depended more on men than machines. Among the Society's founders that long-ago night were survivors of two ill-fated Arctic expeditions, joined by pioneers in oceanography and explorers of the American West, such as Israel Russell, whose 1890 attempt to climb Mount St. Elias in Alaska, then believed to be the highest peak in North America, was the National Geographic Society's first field expedition. Russell's vivid narrative is the earliest published article to be included in this book.

The second age of discovery saw the flowering of great explorer-naturalists, among them that romantic breed, the plant hunters. In the early 20th century Frank Kingdon-Ward and Joseph Rock combed the rich botanical refugia of Asia, introducing many new species into Western cultivation while also, as we shall see, dodging bandits, warlords, and earthquakes. At the same time, natural history expeditions were fanning out across Africa, Asia, and South America, collecting specimens the old-fashioned way, by shooting them and, whether large elephant or tiny bird, mounting them for museum displays. It was an era when tropical explorers wore pith helmets against the sun, took quinine to ward off malaria, and pushed into jungles that seemed both interminable and inexhaustible.

Though the Poles had been attained, there were still new worlds to explore. New possibilities and fresh perspectives opened up thanks to new tools, chief among them the airplane. The NATIONAL GEOGRAPHIC grew up with flight, charting each new stage in the development of aviation. Anyone perusing the rhapsodic accounts by Sir Ross Smith or Anne Morrow Lindbergh in the following pages, for instance, will glimpse something of the rapture that then attended flying. The airplane's ability to surmount jungle, desert, mountain, and ocean sped the long overdue exploration of such places as the Amazon, New Guinea, and Antarctica.

Whether or not he was first to fly over the North Pole (historians disagree), Richard E. Byrd's feats in the Antarctic were unquestionably brilliant. When in 1929 he commanded the first flight over the South Pole, he became one of the last men on Earth ever to take in with a single glance range after range of previously unseen mountains. Byrd's massive, military-style assaults on the frozen continent marked the prelude to the third great age of discovery, the highly technological thrust into such alien realms as space and the ocean deeps. This third age is generally dated from 1957—that year again—with the beginning of the International Geophysical Year, when 5,000 scientists studied Earth as one functioning system and when the Soviets launched Sputnik, Earth's first artificial satellite.

William Beebe, Albert Stevens, and Jacques-Yves Cousteau pioneered the reach into the seas and the heavens. For courage and vision, and for colorful personality, these men were every bit the equal of the explorer-heroes of old. Cousteau, of course, became world famous; Beebe's bathysphere dives went a record half-mile deep into the abyss; and Stevens's balloon *Explorer* II rose a record 13.7 miles up into the stratosphere. All three neatly mirrored each other's Jules Verne–like achievements. In supporting this reach upward to the heights, downward into the depths, and out toward the ends of the Earth, the National Geographic Society shared in these (at the time) ultimate feats in exploration.

As the Egyptian explorer Ahmed Hassanein tells us in his article included in this volume, caravan tea, brewed far out in the desert, is strong stuff. Imparting vitality, exhilaration, and eagerness for the journey, we may think of it, metaphorically, as the elixir of adventure, consumed only by men and women able to stomach it. Everyone in this book partook of this stimulating draft, whether they only sipped it or slurped it with relish. Their resulting tales are full of discomfort and danger, loneliness and exile, but also humor, rapture, and enchantment. Caravan tea is clearly a potent brew, and some among us might incline more toward the "pallid tea of civilization," enjoyed in a comfortable armchair with a book of oak-and-laurel-framed adventure stories at hand.

Whichever the cup preferred, both types of imbiber compose one society, as the novelist Joseph Conrad knew. In one of his last published essays, "Geography and Some Explorers," which appeared in the March 1924 NATIONAL GEOGRAPHIC, he wrote: "Of all the sciences, geography finds its origin in action, and, what is more, in adventurous action, of the kind that appeals to sedentary people, who like to dream of arduous adventure in the manner of prisoners dreaming behind their bars of all the hardships and hazards of liberty, dear to the heart of man."

Whether you head for the armchair, or to the line of waiting camels, don't forget that pith helmet.

MARK JENKINS
WASHINGTON, D.C.
FEBRUARY, 2006

PART ONE:

The world of africa

WILD MAN & WILD BEAST IN AFRICA
January 1911

THEODORE ROOSEVELT (1858–1919)

SOLDIER, AUTHOR, BIG GAME HUNTER, AND PRESIDENT OF THE United States, Theodore Roosevelt lived at a pitch of intensity few others could hope to match. But after eight years in the White House, he felt he was passing the peak of his powers. He was pushing 50, nearly blind in one eye, afflicted with gout, and he carried a paunch that later gave rise to his Swahili nickname, bwana tumbo, or, roughly, "Sir Belly." So he persuaded himself that a rigorous, dangerous hunting trip to the game-rich savannas of East Africa was just the thing to round out the strenuous life he had always preached. Characteristically, though, he envisioned it as a natural history expedition as well, and so he arranged to collect specimens for the Smithsonian Institution in Washington.

The resulting 1909–10 safari still remains the biggest ever mounted in East Africa. For 11 months a small army of naturalists, taxidermists, guides, and porters snaked through the bush and savanna of Kenya, Uganda, and Sudan. Thousands of mammals, birds, reptiles, amphibians, fish, insects, and even shells were collected, crated, and shipped to Washington—the largest such collection ever brought out of Africa by a single party.

Roosevelt on safari burned with exuberant vitality. He seemed never to sleep. When not testing his mettle against lions or elephants, he was studying birds or examining stomach contents with boyish glee. During lulls, while others napped, he would reach for one of the 60 volumes specially bound and cased for the trip, from the Bible to Shakespeare to Mark Twain. At evening he would relish dinners of elephant trunk soup, oryx tongue, and ostrich liver, then settle back and, with customary zest, talk far into the night—an ordeal for some of his guides because, to their horror, the teetotaling ex-President had forbidden spirits on the safari.

Roosevelt's progress through the African bush was followed closely by the press and the public, and after returning to the United States, his first popular lecture was delivered in Washington under the auspices of the National Geographic Society. A vividly anecdotal address, it was printed in the January 1911 issue of NATIONAL GEOGRAPHIC, from which the following selections are taken.

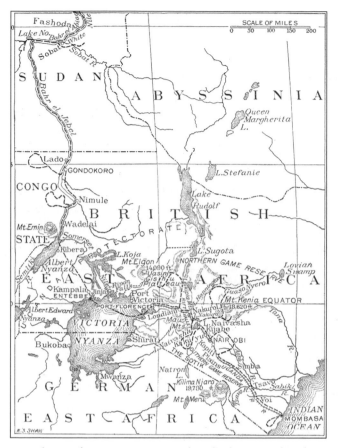

British East Africa as it was in 1910, when Theodore Roosevelt's safari,
the largest ever mounted in the region, snaked its way
across Kenya and Uganda into the Sudan.

I CAN SAY THAT NO OTHER EXPEDITION OF THE KIND HAS EVER
come back from Africa or Asia with a better collection of specimens than
we brought back, the collection being especially good in the large game
animals. The series of skins, and in many cases of skeletons, of the square-
mouthed rhinoceros, reticulated giraffe, giant eland, bongo, northern sable
antelope, white-withered lechwe antelope, and Vaughn's kob, for instance,
are unrivaled in any European museum. We brought back, I think, all told,
some 14,000 specimens of mammals, birds, reptiles, fishes, etc.

Let me repeat, that I cannot overemphasize the part my companions
played in the expedition. The chief value of the expedition came not from
what I shot, but from what the naturalists, under the direction of Mr.
Walcott, who were with me, did in preserving and collecting specimens. It

is not a very hard thing to go off into the wilderness and kill an elephant, or a white rhino, or a reticulated giraffe, or giant eland; but it is a very hard thing to get good photographs of them, and a still harder thing to cure and transport the skins and skulls of a number of such specimens. I can give you, perhaps, an idea of the amount of work done when I mention that we used on the trip ten tons of salt (all at times carried by native porters) in order to cure the skins; that when we killed elephants, for instance, we would have to use 20 men to carry each elephant's skull....

I shall always keep in my mind the memory of one evening when I had killed a lioness. The porters with me were, as they always are, very much excited over the killing of a lion, for the lions are often man-eaters, and kill many of the natives, so that the natives like to recipro-cate and see the lions killed. I had killed this lioness quite late in the evening, and the men asked permission to carry it in whole to camp. I did not think they could do it, but I let them try. They started carrying the lioness in relays. It was a very heavy load. After a while they found that it was heavier than they had thought. We went about ten miles from camp, and we had gone only about a mile when darkness set in. There was an element of interest in going through that part of Africa at night, because then all the wild beasts were abroad. On the occasion in question we were accompanied on one side by a lion for one-half an hour. I do not think he could quite make us out. He could smell the dead lioness and he also smelt us; but I do not think he knew quite what had happened; and so he walked along side us for a couple of miles, moaning or yawning as he went. Of course we had to keep a lookout for him. I had another white man with me, and either he would go ahead and I behind, or vice versa, so as to keep the porters closed up; because, in a case like that, if a lion does attack a party of travelers, he is most like-ly to seize the one behind. We still had the lion on one side of us when suddenly on the other side there was a succession of snorts like a steam-engine blowing off steam. It was a rhinoceros, I think two rhinoceros-es, up on that side.

While a rhinoceros's short suit is brains, his long suit is courage, and he is a particularly exasperating creature to deal with, because he has not sense enough to know that you can harm him, and he has enough bad temper to want to harm you, so that there is often no way of keeping rid of him except by killing him. Of course we did not want to kill anything we could help—anything we did not use—and we still more strongly objected to being killed ourselves. It was almost pitch dark and there was no moon, although there was star-light. We could hear this rhinoceros snort, and then we would run forward and kneel down or lay down on the ground and try to catch the loom of the rhinoceros against the sky-line, so that we would have a chance to shoot him if he came on. I sometimes had to adjure the porters—I use a mild word when I say "adjure"—in order that they might not break and scatter, when one or more would probably have been killed. Finally we left both the lion and the rhino and came to a Masai corral, which was about three miles from our camp. The men carrying the lioness were very tired and I thought it best to stop and skin her. So we called to the people inside of the corral to let us come inside and skin the lioness. At night the cattle are put in the middle of those corrals—those big fenced inclosures with square huts around the edge. The Masai replied that we could not come in because the smell of the lioness would make the cattle stampede. I think they were a little suspicious of us. My companion offered to give them his rifle to hold as a proof of our good intentions; but they said no; that they didn't want that. They handed us torches; we started a fire. They finally became convinced that we were peaceable, and then they came out to witness the skinning. The porters crouched near the blazing fire and our gun-bearers started to skin the lioness. Tarlton, the Australian who was with me, and I stood behind, holding the bridles of our horses. Masai warriors and girls came out and, forming a circle around the porters, chaffed and jested with them....

I really doubt if there is a railroad trip in the world as well worth taking as that railroad trip up to the little British East African capital of Nairobi. The British government has made a great game preserve of part of that country. On the trip from the coast, Governor Jackson, who had very courteously come down to meet me at Mombasa, and the great English hunter Selous and I passed our time on the cowcatcher of the engine, and it was much like going through the garden of Eden with Adam and Eve absent. At one spot we could see suddenly six or eight giraffe going off at their peculiar rocking canter. Then we would see a herd of brightly colored hartebeestes, which would pay no attention to the train at all. Then we would come around a curve and the engineer would have to pull his whistle frantically to get the zebras off the track. The last of the herd would kick and buck and gallop off 50 yards and turn around and again look at the train. Then we would see a rhinoceros off to one side; and so on indefinitely.

Nairobi itself is a town of perhaps 5,000 or 6,000 people. To my mind it is a very attractive little town. It is very much scattered out, and the wild beasts come right up to the edge of the town. A friend, Mr. McMillan, lent us the use of his house in town while we were staying there, and a leopard came up to the piazza one night after one of the dogs. On another occasion one of the local officials, a district commissioner, going out to dinner on his bicycle in a dress suit, and naturally unarmed, almost ran over a lion. Fortunately the lion was much frightened and went away. On two evenings in succession I dined at houses. The dinner was much as it would be in Washington, London, or anywhere else, the ladies in pretty soft dresses and the men in the usual evening garb of civilization. The houses were about a quarter of a mile apart, and a few days previous a young lady, in the early evening, while bicycling from one to the other to take part in a rehearsal of "Trial by Jury," was knocked off her bicycle by a stampede of zebras, and was really quite hurt and had to give up the rehearsal....

The two beasts that are the most interesting to my mind, as indeed they are to most hunters, are the elephant and the lion. A really successful effort is being made to preserve the elephant in East Africa. The bulls are only allowed to be shot after they have reached a certain point in the development of their tusks, and the cows and young stock are not allowed to be killed at all. The result is that, while of course there has been a diminution in the number of elephants, I think that they are now holding their own in many parts of East and Central Africa. Elephants are always interesting. It is rather exciting to study them in their haunts, because you have to watch them carefully, and there is some risk if you are discovered. I do not myself think that an elephant is quite as dangerous as a buffalo, and I think it considerably less dangerous than a lion. Still, many of them are wicked, and they kill a good many people. When you get close to them and watch them for a time you will note that they are perpetually in motion. I have never seen an elephant entirely still. He will flap one ear; then he will suddenly put up his trunk and curl it and try to see if he can smell anything; then he will shift from one foot to another. They never seem to stand entirely still. When we were camping in the Lado, hunting white rhinoceroses, there were a good many elephants around. We had obtained our elephant series and did not want to molest them. Once, when walking about a mile and a half from camp, we suddenly saw a herd of 50 or 60 elephants accompanied by a flock of

Theodore Roosevelt in typical pose, standing beside the carcass of a large dead animal.
The bull elephant was sacrificed for science, as Roosevelt's safari was also
a natural history expedition, collecting specimens for the Smithsonian Institution.

a couple of hundred white cow herons. When we first saw the elephants they were in an open flat, where the long grass had been burned. As the elephants walked through the short grass the herons marched alongside, catching the grasshoppers put up. As soon as they came to long grass all the herons flew up and lit on the backs of the elephants. There was one little pink elephant calf and two herons perched on its back. The elephants evidently did not mind the birds; otherwise they could have removed them with their trunks. Those elephants were quite indifferent to our presence if we did not come too near. While looking at them we heard Dr. Mearns shooting birds around camp; but it did not disturb the elephants. They stayed two days in the neighborhood, and we got as close a look at them as we wished. We did not want to have to shoot any of them; and, as an elephant cow will often attack a man if it thinks he is menacing her calf, we had to be cautious about going too close.

The elephant is the most intelligent of game. The rhinoceroses were not as interesting as the elephants, because they were not as intelligent. After we had completed our collection of rhinoceroses it became quite a problem how to avoid them and get the other things we wanted. It is amusing to realize how soon we got to accepting our difficulties with rhinos as a matter of course. Here in civilization, if you asked a man to kindly go down and scare off a rhinoceros for you, the man would look at you with a certain surprise; in Africa it was a matter-of-course incident. When near a rhino there is always a chance that he will charge, whether through stupidity, or fright, or anger. The trouble is that one never knows whether he will or will not charge home. It often happens that after he has come to a distance of about 25 yards he will wheel and run off; but, not being a mind-reader, a man cannot tell whether a particular rhino does or does not intend to charge home. Cuninghame, who was handling the safari for us, would now and then send me off to scare away rhinos who were too near the line of march, and I would perform the task with gingerly caution. Once Cuninghame and I were hunting buffalo on the Guaso Nairo. We were on the trail of a herd, when suddenly Cuninghame stopped, and, turning around with his air of patient dejection, said: "Oh, Mr. Roosevelt, look at that rhino." I answered, "Yes, look at him." He continued, "I do not want to lose this spoor. Would you mind going down and frightening him off? But do not make much noise, because we do not want to frighten the buffalo." So I strolled down, trying to make up my mind how much noise I could make that would frighten the rhino but not the buffalo. I struck just about the happy medium; and, after meditating a little, with his ears and tail up, the rhino trotted away in zigzags until it was safe for us to pass. About half a mile on we sighted the buffalo and started to stalk them. We were just finishing the stalk when there arose a yelling like that of lost souls behind us, and away went the buffalo. Back we went, to find that one of the porters, when we halted to drive off the rhino, had lost his knife; and he and two others took advantage of our stalking the buffalo to run back to see if they could find the knife. By that time the rhino had returned. Evidently he thought that his dignity had been offended, and he went for the porters and tossed one of them. So we had to give up the buffalo for the time being and go back and give first aid to the injured porter.

The most interesting thing I saw in Africa was a feat that was infinitely greater than anything we performed with our rifles... It was one of the really most notable feats I have ever known to be performed in hunting.

We saw the Nandi spearmen kill a lion with their spears, and I shall close my lecture by telling you about it. These people are a northern branch of the Masai. They are a splendid race physically—tall, sinewy fellows. The warriors carry ox-hide shields and very heavy spears, seven or eight feet long, the long-bladed head of soft iron kept with a razor edge and the iron of the rear half of the spear ending in a spike, the only wood that is bare being just about enough to give a grip for the hand. The brightly burnished head is about four feet in length. These Nandi came over on purpose to show me how they killed a lion with their spears.

Several of us went out with them on horseback to round up a lion for them. We traveled three or four hours—half a dozen horsemen and 30 or 40 stalwart naked savages with ox-hide shields and spears. Then we roused a big lion with a fine mane, and, after running a mile or two, rounded him up under a bush, and the spearmen came trotting up. It was as fine a sight as I ever saw. The first spearman that came up halted about 60 yards from the lion. (We were watching him with our rifles to see that he did not attack the first spearmen.) Then this man knelt down with his ox-hide shield in front of him, looking over the shield at the lion; and, as man after man came up, they formed a ring around the lion, all kneeling. The lion stood under the bush. As they closed in on him he began to grow more and more angry, roaring, and looking first to one side and then to the other and lashing his tail furiously. It was a fine sight to see these men make the ring, with their spears and their eager, intent faces, and the great, murderous, man-eating beast in the middle, ever growing more and more angry. As soon as the ring was completed they all got up and started to close in. The lion charged straight for the weakest part of the ring. The man in front braced himself; we could see his muscles all stand out as if he were a bronze statue. There were five or six men who took part in the fight. From each side the two or three nearest men sprang in to see if they could not get the lion as he came straight on toward the man in his immediate front. When he was about not more than six feet from him the man lobbed the spear; that is, he did not take his arm back and throw it, but simply cast it loose with a little motion of the wrist and trusted to the weight of the spear to go in.

As the lion came forward the spear struck him on the left shoulder, and came out diagonally through him in front of his right hip. The lion reared like a rearing horse and bore the shield down, burying his teeth and claws in the man. At the same moment another man leaped in on one side and threw his spear; the spear-head glimmered like white fire in the sunlight, and, entering transversely, came out through the lion on the hither side. The lion turned on that man, but could not bite him, only clawing him a little. Another spear struck the lion, and he went down; he took one spear in his mouth and bit it, twisting it so that it looked like a horseshoe; the next moment the men were on him and it was all over. I do not suppose the thing lasted ten seconds, but it was as remarkable a spectacle for those ten seconds as any human being could wish to see.

In the nine years he had left to live, Roosevelt made another bid for the Presidency and undertook a harrowing, exhausting journey down Brazil's River of Doubt. But he always recalled his African adventure with a glow of enthusiasm. Never, he would ebulliently declare, had he taken a trip so well worth the taking. As his friend, Carl Akeley, put it, "Few men could get so much out of a trip to Africa ... because few men could take so much to it."

ELEPHANT HUNTING
IN EQUATORIAL AFRICA

August 1912

CARL AKELEY (1864–1926)

FEAR DID NOT COME QUICKLY TO SOMEONE LIKE CARL AKELEY. The quiet man with a pipe, who chuckled as he told a good story, was a well-known African big-game hunter once mauled by a leopard he killed with his bare hands. "Ake" had made his name as a museum taxidermist, the first to pose animals realistically in dioramas depicting natural settings. He was also an exquisite animal sculptor and a superb wildlife photographer who invented his own movie camera.

Yet fear was his constant companion throughout a grueling 1910–1911 East African safari. Together with his wife, Delia, he was collecting elephants for an American Museum of Natural History exhibit in New York. Elephants might be captivating, but they did not like being shot at, which made them extremely dangerous at close quarters. Day after day spent creeping through the bush with hostile elephants around proved so nerve-racking that the couple nearly broke down several times. Close calls piled up one after another until, a few months before the events in this excerpt, Ake was severely mauled by a bull elephant on the slopes of Mount Kenya. He survived with broken ribs, punctured lungs, a scalp nearly torn off, and a cheek slashed open to reveal his teeth. Returning to the field, he finished the job, although the following account of his continued elephant stalking hints at the fear still lurking beneath the surface, however much it is downplayed with that characteristic chuckle.

Today Carl Akeley lies buried on the saddle between Mounts Mikeno and Karisimi in the Virunga Mountains, where he was the first to study gorillas systematically and where he died of disease in 1926. The Akeley Hall of African Mammals, a major attraction at the American Museum of Natural History, is his most lasting legacy. Its centerpiece is the marvelous elephant group that he and Delia collected on that exhausting safari in 1910–1911.

ONE EVENING IN UGANDA, WHEN RATHER DISCOURAGED AFTER a day of unsuccessful effort to locate elephants, we suddenly heard the squeal of an elephant far to the east. The squealing and trumpeting increased in frequency and distinctness until in an hour's time we realized that a large herd was drifting slowly in our direction. By eleven o'clock they had come very close, some within two hundred yards of camp, and on three sides of us. The crashing of trees and the squealing and trumpeting as the elephants fed, quarreling over choice morsels, resulted in a din such as we had never before heard from elephants.

Our men kept innumerable fires going for fear that the elephants might take a notion to raid the plantain grove in which we were camped, and at daylight I was off for the day's hunt. The herd had drifted down to the forest side, forty minutes from camp; in fact many of them had entered the forest. For a couple of miles we traveled through a scene of devastation such as a cyclone leaves in its wake: 8-foot grass trampled flat except for here and there an "island" that had been spared; half of the scattering trees twisted off and stripped of bark, and of all branches and leaves.

We approached within a few hundred yards of the forest, where the grass was undisturbed except for trails showing how the elephants at daybreak had trekked through in small bands, single file. When about to cross a little wooded gulley, we thought it wise to stop and look over the situation. From the top of a mass of rocks we discovered a cow feeding only 20 yards away and others all about in the high grass between us and the timber.

There was clear passage to a rocky elevation 100 yards to the left, for which we made, and while standing there, 75 feet above the level, I received an impression of Africa that must remain with me to the last.

There was not a breath of wind, and the forest, glistening in the morning sunlight, stretched away for miles to the east and to the west and up the slope to the north. Here and there in the high grass that intervened between our perch and the forest edge, 300 yards away, were scattered elephants singly and in groups feeding and loafing along, to be swallowed by the dark shadows of the dense forest side.

From the gulley which I had started to cross a little time before there stalked 25 or 30 of the great beasts, their bodies shining with a fresh coating of mud and water from the pool where they had drunk and bathed. As is usual with big herds, they had broken up into small bands on entering the forest, and now, as the last of them disappeared into the cover of the trees, a fuller appreciation of the surroundings suddenly dawned upon me.

From a mile or more in either direction there came a reverberating roar and crash as the great hordes of monsters ploughed their way through the tangles of vegetation, smashing trees as they quarreled, played, and fed, all regardless of forestry regulations.

Where the little stream, at the bottom of the gulley entered the forest, troops of black and white Colobus monkeys were racing about the trees, swearing at the elephants. From the tree tops deeper in the forest two or three troops of chimpanzees yelled and shouted at one another or everything in general, baboons barked, and great hornbills did their best to drown all other noises with their discordant rasping chatter.

Suddenly a cow elephant at the edge of the forest just in front of us uttered her peculiar shrill scream of warning. Not only the elephants, but all the other forest folk, paid heed and instantly were silent; a moment before the noise had been appalling; the silence now was even more so. Then there came a gentle rustling sound like that of leaves stirred by a breeze, increasing in volume until it sounded like a mighty windstorm in the trees.

I looked about to see whence it came. With my glasses I scoured the forest far and near, but not a visible leaf seemed to stir. Then I realized that the sound was made by elephants on the move, hastening away from danger—the scuffling of their feet among the dry leaves on the ground and the scraping of their sides against the equally dry leaves of the bushes. In a way this was even more impressive than the great din or the death-like silence preceding.

The old cow had caught a whiff of air tainted by man and all obeyed her warning. In a few moments the rustling subsided; the monkeys and birds returned to their normal state. The elephants had evidently settled down without going far; but only at rare intervals during the rest of the day did we hear the squeal of a chastised youngster or the breaking of a tree.

With my gun bearers I went down into the forest. Trails crisscrossed in all directions, so that it was impossible to follow a given trail any distance. A band of a dozen or so got our wind and passed us in confusion at close range, but the bush was so dense that I had but small glimpses of them. A mile into the forest brought us to an irregular clearing, 200 by 500 yards in extent, almost bisected by a "peninsula" of forest.

At the base of this peninsula I nearly ran against a young bull, one of a considerable number, as I soon discovered. The whole herd began working toward the point of the peninsula and I ran along the outer edge to head them off. Just as the leader emerged from the point, they saw or winded us—shifty, uncertain breezes had sprung up—and they turned back. I ran into the timber to try for a better view of them. I soon found myself facing a cow who, solicitous for her very young calf, had wheeled about, all attention and menacing.

Fortunately, at the moment we were partially screened behind a clump of small trees, and as we remained motionless the cow's fears were soon allayed, and, turning, she gave the calf a boost with her trunk and followed the herd, which was moving off toward the clearing on the other side.

Hurrying out and around the point, I found the herd in the clearing, rounded up in close formation, conscious of the presence of an unseen enemy. There were about 25 elephants, mostly cows, and just as I was on the point of backing off to a safer distance, thinking there were no big bulls in the lot, a fine pair of tusks appeared at the near side. A clump of bushes offered cover for a near approach and I went in quickly to within 20 yards of him, and as his front leg was thrust forward offering a good opportunity for a heart shot, I fired both barrels of the double rifle in quick succession.

All was commotion as I seized my second rifle and, seeing that there was no direct charge, retreated some 50 yards to the top of an ant hill, from which I could see what was going on. I then witnessed a scene such as I had heard described and which I had been keen to verify. A number of cows were clustered about the bull, for he had fallen 30 yards from where he was shot, and with their tusks and trunks were doing their best to get him upon his feet; the remainder of the cows were doing patrol duty, rushing about in an increasing circle, searching for the source of trouble. That meant me, so I retired to a safe distance and waited for the atmosphere to clear.

This bull stood 11 feet 4 inches high at the shoulders, and the tusks weighed 95 and 110 pounds respectively, while the circumference of the front foot around the sole was $67^1/_2$ inches, the largest recorded, I believe.

The following day I went into the forest again and soon came up with a herd, but in cover so dense that an inspection could not be made. We worked with them for hours, and finally succeeded in driving them out into the open, but unfortunately the grass was high and I had not succeeded in gaining a point of vantage, when with angry grunts they doubled back to the forest.

Delia Akeley, framed by tusks from elephants she had killed, was the wife of naturalist Carl Akeley. Throughout their 1910–11 safari for the American Museum of Natural History, she led the expedition in the field during the weeks he was sick or injured.

As I turned to follow, my attention was called to a commotion in the bush at the edge of the forest some 400 yards to the left. Another herd was coming out into the grasslands, and from the top of an ant hill I saw them distinctly as they passed over a rise 50 yards away. There were 11 cows. I waited a few moments, thinking that, as often happens, a bull might follow in their wake. The cows had passed on to a distance of 300 or 400 yards, and I was about to leave the ant hill and return to camp when from the direction of the cows there came a low, ominous rumble like distant thunder. It was not very unlike the angry rumbling sounds we had so frequently heard when with elephants, but it was plain talk and meant trouble.

A hasty glance around convinced us that there was but one thing to do, to stand and meet the charge from the elevation where we were and from which we could see. If we tried to escape to one side or to the forest we could not see them over the high grass before they were upon us.

The rumbling was repeated two or three times, increasing in volume, and was then followed by the wild shriek of one angry cow and immediately taken up by 10 others as they charged toward us. They came half way and stopped for a moment. They had lost the wind, but immediately caught it again, and roaring and screaming with redoubled energy came into view over a slight rise. It was a disconcerting spectacle. Their great ears at full spread, trunks thrashing wildly, a roaring, screaming mass, 40 tons of frantic female elephant vengeance. I remember that I felt homesick.

Were they to continue in a straight course they would pass at 40 yards; then a dash on our part to one side and we could lose them and be safe. When they were nearly opposite us, however, they either saw or winded us afresh and wheeled straight in, with a burst of shrieks. A shot from the big cordite rifle stopped the leader, but, encouraged by the others, she came on, only to be knocked down by the second shot. The others crowded about her, sniffed and—bolted. The old cow slowly regained her feet and staggered away, while we in deep gratitude returned to camp.

AT THE TOMB OF
TUTANKHAMEN
May 1923

MAYNARD OWEN WILLIAMS (1888–1963)

WHEN MAYNARD OWEN WILLIAMS FIRST VISITED EGYPT'S *Valley of the Kings, it was 1912, and he was a young teacher and newspaper correspondent based in the Near East. Like the thousands of other tourists who had tramped past the ransacked tombs honeycombing the cliffs, he may have strolled right over the sleeping pharaoh and his hoard of hidden treasure. Williams, who once befriended a sometime archaeologist named T. E. Lawrence, famous for another line of work, may also have brushed past a bristly, little known Egyptologist named Howard Carter, who spent years in the valley searching for undiscovered tombs.*

With what amounted to storybook flourish—and just before his patron, the Earl of Carnarvon, cut him off—Carter found what he had been seeking. Beneath a pile of overlooked ancient debris, he discovered a sunken staircase. The stairs led to doors still sealed with the cartouche of the obscure New Kingdom pharaoh Tutankhamen. On November 4, 1922—the "day of days," as he called it— the seal was broken. Carter peered inside and, when asked if he saw anything, could only babble, "Yes, wonderful things."

It was one of the most exciting finds of the century, and hordes of clamorous journalists and curious tourists soon crowded into the Luxor hotels just across the Nile River. To their disappointment, Carter closely guarded the site. But in February 1923 he staged an official opening of the tomb, welcoming among other guests the Queen of Belgium and Lord Allenby, the British High Commissioner in Egypt. That event is what brought Maynard Owen Williams back to the Valley of the Kings.

Big, cheerful, and gregarious, 34-year-old Williams was by then a veteran foreign correspondent and a superb photographer who in 1919 had become the NATIONAL GEOGRAPHIC's first staff field man. He was one of the first journalists allowed a glimpse of the sarcophagus, and his surprisingly candid account of his experiences at and in the tomb of Tutankhamen throws an interesting sidelight on this most famous of all archaeological discoveries.

THE NOONDAY SUN WAS HOT AND GETTING HOTTER. I SHOULDERED my heavy camera and started up the steep path. Thus should one approach that hell-hole in the hills where the greatest Pharaohs hid themselves and where not more than two or three still lie undisturbed by modern man.

As I passed the tomb of Seti I and turned toward the lower entrance of the valley, I saw below me a small white tent, a wooden shelter for the armed guard, the clutter of lumber which archeologists use, and the new wall of irregular stones which hid the entrance to Tutankhamen's mausoleum.

Two correspondents sat there and another roamed about waiting for news. For weeks they had waited under the glare of the sun, compelled by the force of circumstances to be detectives rather than scribes. Suddenly and without warning some wondrous treasure would be brought forth in its rough but easy-riding ambulance, to be rushed to another tomb which was used as storehouse and preserving laboratory.

Now and then some rumor would escape the portals, to be weighed and considered before it was put upon the telegraph wire or in the discard.

A press photographer was there, wearing a tarboosh to render himself less conspicuous among Moslem crowds. If it had not been so bright he could have used his nose for a red light in the dark room, and on his cheeks he was raising skin as the farmers of Szechuan raise crops, with new growth showing between the older ones, which were nearly ready to harvest.

These were the men who were trying to give the news of this great discovery to the world.

This superheated graveyard, which was to become a picnic ground and levee for royalty on the morrow, was a silent place. The correspondents spoke in whispers, as though the secrets of the spot would be violated by loud talk. Mystery hung as heavy on the place as mystery ever can in the full light of day.

One of the bosses quietly called two white-robed natives, who removed the curtain and the wooden hatch-work which closed the outer portal and carried two limp boards down into the shadowy depths.

Conjecture at once began. It wanted only a "My dear Watson" to make the scene complete. "They're too weak for shorings and not stiff enough to carry anything on." But the photographer looked once more at his shutter and once more judged the well-known distance to the gate through which anything removed from the tomb must pass.

It was late when I left, and the third correspondent rode beside me as I walked; but the two men I had first met and the tarbooshed press photographer hung there at the mouth of the silent tomb, hoping that some secret would yet be revealed that day.

After dinner I sat in the lobby of the big tourist hotel at Luxor and watched the serio-comedy on the eve of the official opening, where the gaiety of Brussels on the eve of Waterloo was combined with a tenseness that was evident to all.

This tenseness was not all on the side of the anxious reporters who had for so long put up a nerve-racking fight to get the news; for they had beaten the diggers themselves in telling the world that the wall into the inner chamber had been pierced the day before and that the hoped-for sarcophagus had been seen.

Now and then some one went to speak to Lord Carnarvon and his charming daughter. But few seemed to care to announce their bridge scores or their opinions of the League of Nations, and the subject about which all were thinking was taboo.

Early Sunday morning I rode out to the scene of the official opening. There were only a few visitors as yet, but the stage was all set for the big event of the day. To the left was the tomb of Rameses IX, in whose shady corridor the Sultana and the Egyptian officials would later await the coming of the Belgian Queen. Just beyond, a steep stairway led to the unimportant tomb to which the mummy of the heretic king Akhenaton, whom Manetho [an ancient Egyptian chronicler] refused to mention, was brought from Tell-el-Amarna.

If the spirit of this ruler who sought to release his people from priestly forms and outworn conventions and to establish monotheism throughout his empire still hovered in the place, what feelings it must have had! For this tomb was being utilized as a dark room for the official photographer, and under his red light developed strange pictures of the treasures that were being found across the way—finds of such magnificence as Akhenaton never knew.

Overhanging the new entrance was the tomb of Rameses VI, one of those weak rulers of the XXth dynasty under whom the priests of Ammon seized an increasing amount of temporal power.

As the day grew hot, small companies of visitors arrived; but there had been no attempt to make this a popular holiday and the crowd could never have numbered more than 200.

About noon there arrived a squad of camels laden with food and drink for the distinguished guests. The last of them seemed to be sweating from heat, an unusual phenomenon, made plain when one noticed that his load was ice in gunny sacks.

None of this feast was eaten by the guests, for the train which brought Her Majesty and Lord and Lady Allenby to Luxor was so late that lunching out there in the graveyard of royalty was not to be thought of. Those who had come early had already eaten their lunches in the tunnel leading to the tomb of Amenmesse, as one eats in a railway lunchroom, with one eye on the clock and the other on the door. The age-old walls of stone echoed to the rattle of the portable typewriter operated by a press association man.

Then came Lord Allenby in his motorcar, to wait near the barrier to welcome the Queen.

A motor rolled up; a white-clad figure alighted; there were numerous introductions, especially to those Egyptian officials present, and the Queen, with Mr. Carter leading the way, with Lord Carnarvon on her left and with Lord Carnarvon's daughter just behind, went down the incline that leads to the tomb mouth. Within a moment Her Majesty had entered the shadowy portal behind which Tutankhamen, if indeed his mummy actually be under that huge gilt canopy, silently awaited her coming.

The next item of real interest was the dust on Lord Allenby's back when he came out, perhaps a half hour later. A man doesn't come out here in the desert with an unwilted carnation in his buttonhole and then get his back dusty by accident. The sarcophagus fills the inner chamber so tightly that the distinguished Englishman had to brush the wall to get by the corner.

On Monday, the day after the official opening, I entered the tomb, together with the first small group of correspondents.

It was a stamp-collector in Beirut who made me understand the precautions taken by the excavators on the first day when the inner opening was revealed to the correspondents. I started to pick up one of his treasures in my bare hand and he almost cried with pain. He quickly passed me some delicate tweezers with which I could examine the stamp at leisure. He realized that I could not understand his care, but he forced me to be careful.

There were those among us who were able to understand much from what we observed; but my study of Egyptian treasures had been made hurriedly more than ten years before.

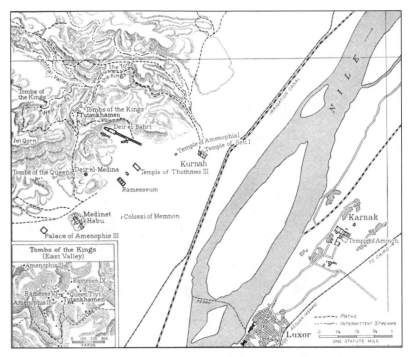

The Valley of the Kings (top left), across the Nile from Luxor and 450 miles upriver from Cairo, is honeycombed with tombs of ancient Egyptian pharaohs, including that of Tutankhamen, discovered in 1922.

This is what I saw:

Steep steps led down to an incline which ended at a new iron gate, beyond which there was a strong light. In these days the Valley of the Kings' Tombs could almost advertise, "All modern improvements," as several of the tombs have long been lighted for the convenience of visitors, and Mr. Burton had, for the benefit of his official photographic work, a high-power electric bulb which made the first chamber we entered as light as day.

Just behind the light, which was shielded by a rough board, there was one of the nearly life-size figures of the king, stricken stiff by the artist and standing helpless in its vain attempt to guard the royal tomb, a gilt mace in one hand, a long gilt staff in the other, with a palm-leaf guard below the hand. The portions of this statue which represented skin were the dark, almost black, color which distinguishes the male figure from the female in Egyptian art.

The official photographs of this statue and its twin on the other side of the doorway, at the right end of the transverse chamber, make description

Gilded chariot wheels are brought up from the tomb of Pharaoh Tutankhamen, discovered by Egyptologist Howard Carter (hatless, on left), who, upon first gazing into its depths, saw "wonderful things" in there.

of these guardian figures futile. Their decorations are in gilt, if not in gold, and the feet—long, flat and shapeless—stand upon what may be gold sandals. In the face and one leg of the right-hand statue there are deep cracks, which do not lessen the uncanny effect of the sculpture.

Facing each other across the space to which they were supposed to form a barrier, these statues have far-away look—gazing down from the fourteenth century before Christ. Their carefully creased kilts, which stand out in front of them like elevated snow-plows, are said to be unlike any others found, although similar ones are frequently represented in paintings and bas-reliefs.

Between these two statues was the entrance to the inner chamber, blocked by new timbers, so that one could not pass into the chamber itself.

The distance between the huge sarcophagus and the rough walls is so small that one would have to pass with care. New boards separated from the sarcophagus by soft buffers protected this corner of the huge case in which it is hoped Tutankhamen reposes. It was evident that after Lord Allenby got his back dusty greater precautions had been taken to protect this matchless relic of the past.

Words cannot give any impressions of the decorations of this great box, of which only a corner could be seen. The secret eyes looked out reproachfully at one from half-way down the right-hand edge and a serpent helplessly vibrated his coils at convenient folds up near the top.

The structure appears to be wood, covered with gold leaf or thicker gold, which is quite bright and has across it a fine frieze in lapis lazuli or faience enamel. It seemed to me to be about nine feet high, and by looking in to the left, in which direction the sarcophagus extends, it appeared to be about eighteen or twenty feet long. Its breadth could only be judged by the size of the chamber, but might be eleven feet.

If the view of the inner chamber, on whose right-hand wall there is a small but brightly colored mural decoration, was as disappointing in extent as it was satisfying in quality, the view of the chamber in which we stood was a source of equal disappointment.

The great mass of treasure which had packed this chamber had been removed, leaving it almost bare. At the right, the two guardian statues of the king, which could not protect his withered form; at the left, a few treasures, including two alabaster vases, which appeared to me more beautiful than the marvelous specimens which had been removed and which I knew through photographs. The pet goose of one of the superintendents was there, a small wooden figure, about which he was far more willing to joke than he was to describe the hidden wonders of the inner chamber.

Near the lower left corner of the back wall a small barrier of thin boards shut off all view of a chamber beyond, which rumor says is filled to the roof with funeral offerings.

Further references to the "Christmas goose" did not help my understanding of Egyptology, and I reluctantly departed. But before I went away I overhead two remarks. A press association man was discussing the decorations on the sarcophagus with the superintendent:

"It's awfully nouvel art," said the news writer.

"Yes, quite Louis Quatorze," replied the superintendent.

"I suppose, if the mummy is in there, he will be wearing some fine jewelry," said a lady present.

"If he's intact, he'll be ragged out like a bloomin' Maharaja," was the reply. And as I went out into the blinding sunlight, some one said something about sharing the Christmas goose if the press photographer would furnish the lard....

Back I rode toward Luxor. The *ghaffirs*, who yesterday stood so straight when the Queen went by, now squatted in the dust. The camel corps, whose picturesque forms had so fittingly guarded that ribbon of road through this Khyber Pass of Egypt, were no longer to be seen. A train of sugar cane whistled its departure for Armant; and the very girl who two days ago offered to share her sugar cane with a wanderer on foot now came out to beg baksheesh of me, mounted on "Marconi" [a donkey], whose wave-length was short and irregular.

Up the Nile there swept an ugly hull with butterfly sails of purest white. The bougainvilleas across the water, a vivid mass of purple against the yellow walls of the big hotel, contrasted with the dusty colonnades of the Temple of Luxor across the river. As I came to the boat landing, I could smell the coffee which the donkey-drivers were making in their rude reed shelters.

We crossed the Nile in that slanting fashion which sets the distant hills in motion around each point upon its bank, and came in the glory of late afternoon to the gray bund of Luxor, alive with tourists from the big hotels and from three steamers which had just arrived.

I stepped into a shop to leave my films and realized that the sway of Tutankhamen still grips the world, for a woman in white was speaking:

"I do hope that we can get a pass, because I'm just crazy over mummies, and they say this one will be the best of all."

ADVENTURES IN EASTERN DARFUR

January 1924

MAJ. EDWARD KEITH-ROACH (1885-1954)

IN THE EARLY 1920s, GILBERT H. GROSVENOR, THE EDITOR OF NATIONAL GEOGRAPHIC, chanced to meet a British diplomat at a Washington luncheon and discovered that Edward Keith-Roach had stories to tell.

During the First World War, the semi-independent Sultan of Darfur, ruler of the wildest and most remote corner of the Anglo-Egyptian Sudan, revolted against the British, who governed that country from distant Khartoum. Eventually he was defeated and killed, and Britain stretched out her long arm and imposed direct rule on the rebellious province. That led in 1916 to the appointment of Major Keith-Roach, then serving in the British-officered Egyptian Army, as the district commissioner for Eastern Darfur. He was respon-sible for administering a vast tract of thorny grassland the size of Ireland, peopled by tribes over whom the Mahdi, the fanatical anti-Western jihadist of the 1880s, once held sway. And he would do so largely alone. There was not another European within a week's camel journey.

If he quailed at the prospect, the 31-year-old vicar's son and former banker was not the kind to show it. Keith-Roach clamped his pipe in his teeth and in the best British tradition got down to business. For nearly four years, 1916 to 1920, his headquarters was but a straw tukl *[hut] where two tracks in the sand met, tracks along which for untold generations caravans carrying ivory, ostrich feathers, slaves, and Mecca-bound pilgrims had passed. The people were Arabic-speaking black Africans so little known to the West they were sometimes called "the Lost Tribes of Islam." Among them, Keith-Roach was ruler, judge, doctor, and cartographer. The area was not only unmapped but virtually unexplored.*

Fascinated by Keith-Roach's anecdotes, Gilbert Grosvenor published an article written by the major in the January 1924 GEOGRAPHIC, *from which the following extracts are taken. With ongoing reports of genocide ravaging Darfur, they make poignant reading today.*

FROM PORT SAID I RAILED TO KHARTUM, AND AFTER TWO DAYS spent in getting provisions for my long solitude, which was to last more than three years, I took the train to El Obeid, about 350 miles southwest, where camels were purchased to carry me and my baggage some 300 miles to my future home. Um Kedada was the name of my headquarters, and after three weeks' trekking I was told early one morning we were approaching the place; so, pushing my camel on ahead of the escort, I mounted the last sandy hill and found—a few native soldiers and a well.

The journey was long and tiring. We marched practically all and every night except for a couple of hours at midnight to rest the camels. We tried, while the camels grazed, to sleep during the day under what shade could be found from a tree, but continually had to move the position of the camp bed as the relentless sun mounted higher in the heavens. The heat at midday varied between 110 and 120 degrees Fahrenheit in the shade, but was much more intense in the sun.

At varying intervals the track was strewn with grim relics of former camel caravans. Supercilious in life, the camel is even more so in death. Lying on his side, his upper lip drawn back, his head thrown up until it almost touches the hump, he shows by every attitude his utter contempt for the world he has left behind.

Marching at night has a fascination all its own. My camel, being lightly laden and speedier than the others, generally outstripped them all, and I was alone in the beauty of the African night. A full moon gave light enough to read by, and a breeze from the north would blow across the sandy plains, making every blade of grass bow its rustling head. Here a cricket chirped, there a ringdove cooed to its mate, and beyond an owl hooted as he transferred his quarters from one tree to another. And so on for mile after mile, the soft pad of the camel was scarcely perceptible, even in the silence of the night. Occasionally I passed native caravans and the courtesies of the road were exchanged: "*Keif halak? Taiybin! El hamd el Allah. Masa-salaamih.*" (How are you? Well! Praise be to God. Go with safety.) Ghostly voices coming out of the night!

Early in the small hours the moon disappeared, leaving momentarily a red glow in a haze of palest lilac. For the next hour or so, there being no competitor, the stars shone with renewed splendor on the darkened world, and once or twice a meteor shot half across the heavens, leaving a trail of fire. Toward 6 o'clock the east was flooded by palest rose pink, and a few minutes later the sun was up. The spell was over, life became real again, and I instinctively felt for my helmet and looked round for a place to camp.

Um Kedada, which was a military base for our army on the march up to El Fasher early in the year, stands on high ground with a fair outlook, surrounded by escarpments of low-lying hills. Its chief call to fame is a most excellent water supply—an invaluable asset! The well, broad and fairly deep, is lined with rough stone halfway down, and was dug many years ago at the instigation of an old sultan, who made a chain of wells leading into Kordofan to assist his raiding parties, which periodically sallied forth after his neighbors' cattle. The old method of lining is now, alas, a lost art among these people.

It is difficult adequately to picture what a well means until one has lived near the Sahara. In my 300 miles I passed two places only where there were any, and on my arrival at Um Kedada I had been for six days subsisting on what water I could carry on my own camels; they had been all that time without a drink.

Greetings made to all assembled at the well, animals watered, and men rested, I looked round for a convenient place to build a temporary house.

In a land of opposites, where one writes from right to left, takes off one's shoes and leaves the hat on when entering a house, we naturally begin building at the roof and build downward. Native *tukls*, or huts, are made from dried millet stalks and are shaped like straw beehives, but are finished at the top with little tufts.... Eight long branches are placed with ends on the ground, tied together in the center, and laced round with smaller branches until the structure looks like an army bell tent. This is the roof, which is then thatched with millet straw from the bottom upward and tied together tightly at the top into the little tuft.

This superstructure is then raised up on poles set in a circle with a V at the top, standing about four feet out of the ground. The sides are then thatched and the palace is ready for occupancy. Doors and windows are a trouble, owing to the constant wind that blows in the sand at all times of the day and night; so windows are dispensed with, and a kind of hurdle, placed on the windward side, serves for a door....

The official in charge of Eastern Darfur has to be administrator, magistrate, collector of revenue, estimator of crops for tithes, commandant of police, veterinary surgeon, surveyor, doctor, and all the other things that go to make up a well-ordered community. Consequently many months were spent in setting up the system of organization. Sheiks were appointed in charge of villages, and *omdas* placed in authority over groups of villages and given limited powers, sufficient to enforce their orders. Police had to be recruited and trained. Roads had to be cut through the scrub or tracks widened. All this entailed many weeks' touring by camel from place to place.

Villages were few and far between, there being only about 300 in the whole district, containing about 30 to 200 people each. The country is mostly bush scrub and covered with a grass called *haskaneet*, the seeds of which have innumerable little spikes that get into everything—food, clothes, hair, and skin—setting up nasty irritations. The natives all carry homemade tweezers to extract the spikes from their legs. This grass springs up during the rains, and a month afterward is burned brown, when the seed pods start flying about....

I generally trekked fifteen days a month, but one long tour took me over two months. At harvest time I frequently rode enormous distances on my camels to pay surprise visits to estimators who were assessing the crops for revenue purposes.

Practically the whole of the district was unmapped, and so when I traveled by day a man pushed a cyclometer in front while I took bearings with a prismatic compass, checking the distance traveled by the cyclometer, and plotted it on map paper while I camped at midday....

The children attract attention. The babies are carried on the mothers' backs. A child is caught by the wrist and adroitly swung around to the mother's back, a leg on either side of her waist, and is tied by a piece of her raiment, with its arms inside. There the infant stays for hours, with its little head sticking out, looking wonderingly at the world, while the mother does her work. Its hands being tied in, its poor little eyes often are covered with flies. When sun and flies become too much for its patience, it whimpers meekly and the mother throws the other end of the *tobe* [a cotton garment] over its head and waggles it to sleep.

Both boys and girls have their tribal marks cut on their cheeks at an early age, salt being rubbed in to keep the slits open. Little girls wear a *rahad*, a short skirt of strings of leather hanging from a belt, which swings picturesquely like a kilt as they walk. If there is enough rough cotton cloth to go round, the boys have a sacklike skirt with holes for their arms; otherwise they go as God made them....

The principal occupation of a native man of Darfur is killing time, and his average daily round is as follows: An early riser, he is up betimes to send his women off, either to the well or to the tebeldi tree [a hollow baobab that serves as a rain reservoir] to get water. If he owns a fair number of animals, he accompanies the women and assists them. He then sees the animals driven out to pasture by a small boy, who is responsible for bringing them back at night. That furnished, his day's work is done.

His wife returns and at once busies herself preparing grain for the thick, fermented beer, like pea soup, which is the principal means of sustenance. She thus occupies practically her entire day. Meanwhile her lord and master sleeps until sunset, recuperating his strength. If he is feeling very energetic, he perhaps spins a little cotton or weaves some cloth, squatting outside his tukl so that he can keep an eye on his women and see that they do not slack off.

As soon as the first rains come, the man goes off with his wife or wives and escorts each to her own patch, because each has her own seed supply, just as each has a separate house. Holding in both hands a branch of a tree that is bent at nearly a right angle, with sometimes a small iron hoe at the end, he ambles at a jog trot down the cultivated plot. Each time the left foot comes to the ground he gives a jab at the soil at his left side, which displaces the sand a little. When he has gone about fifty paces he turns again and makes a fresh line parallel to the other. His faithful helpmate walks behind him with the millet seed in a dried watermelon rind, and, without bending, drops a few seeds into the hole, brushes it over with her foot, and passes on to the next. In a day they can plant an extensive area.

As soon as all is planted, he and she wait until the seeds begin to sprout, unless he has planted when the rains are due. This he frequently does in feverish anxiety—the only time he ever exhibits this trait. Then it often happens that there is a dry spell for a month, in which case the grain dies and the work has to be done over again....

Batikhs, or watermelons, do not grow wild, but are sown in large areas of cleared ground. When the fruits are ripe they are stored away under low-thatched shanties. Toward sunset the ever-patient donkey is driven down to the field, and enough melons brought back for the next day's use.

A woman brings an earthen vessel with perforated bottom from the smoke-begrimed tukl and squats beside it. Taking a melon, she breaks it with her clenched fist, and, with a hand that is far from clean, scoops out the inside, throwing the rind into the sand again. When all the pulp has been extracted it is teased and squeezed to break up the fiber. The vessel is placed on another and the liquid percolates through straws at the bottom.

The rind is then broken up and pounded in a vessel fashioned out of a tree trunk. All possible moisture is withdrawn and the residue becomes food and drink for donkey, goat, and fowl. Once, when touring to complete my map, I lived for six weeks, using these melons for my sole water supply,

A thatched tukl, or hut, served as Maj. Keith-Roach's headquarters during the years he administered an unmapped chunk of Africa the size of Ireland. Gathered for a rare official reception are village headmen, sheiks, and uniformed Egyptian or Sudanese staff.

and beyond being unable to shave, suffered little ill-effect; but for sheer nastiness, I commend you to tea made from strained watermelon juice....

There is much sameness about visits of ceremony. The following is typical of many. The headman of the village received me with great ceremony outside his tukl, conducted me inside, and put me to sit on his native bed, the only thing to sit upon in the dwelling. A large watermelon was produced from under the bed, and from this he cut me an enormous slice, then sat at my feet, watching every mouthful.

A mysterious but heated argument which had been going on for some time outside ceased, and the man's two bearded sons brought in the meal—big flat cakes made of millet flour, a mess of eggs and sour milk beaten together, and a pot of beautifully cooked chickens. The chickens the father pulled to pieces with his hands and presented to me on a small grass mat. This course was followed by excellent coffee, served in little cups without handles. I had three cups, thinking the meal finished, but an ancient teapot was brought forth, and I capped my repast with a cup of strong, bitter tea, sweetened to a nauseating degree.

The omda and I talked of many things, and after inspecting his water supply, live stock, and fields, I turned to leave. His two sons were mounted, ready to see me on my way. The old man signed to me to stop. Then the two younger men cantered off some distance, turned suddenly around and, thrashing their horses with their *kurbags* (rhinoceros hide whips), dashed straight at me at a full gallop, pulling their foaming horses back on their haunches about six inches from me. The nearer the visitor, the greater the compliment....

One morning an oldish man walked into my office and said that a lion and a lioness were molesting the peace of his village, about 15 miles away. He wished me to come and destroy the beasts. I promised to go the following day, but unfortunately the investigation of a case of murder occupied my attention and I could not go.

The day after, the old man came before me, dangling at the end of a piece of rope what I at first thought was a skin of honey, but a second glance showed it was the head of a lioness. He told a story which I corroborated the same afternoon when I went to the village to dress the wounds of the chief actors. Three boys of about 15 or 16 years—no Arab knows his exact age, but calculates by the time of some striking incident—went out to their field, each carrying a small throwing spear, and they saw the lion and his mate under a bush. The first lad threw his spear and missed, and the quarry bounded off under another bush. The next boy hurled his spear and also missed. A third spear hurtled through the air from the arm of the youngest lad and struck the lioness in the side. She immediately turned and, with one spring, seized the thrower round the shoulders, threw him to the ground, and began gnawing at his neck.

One of the boys took off the long garment he was wearing, bound it swiftly around his right arm, and, grasping the animal's left ear with his left hand, drove his right arm down her throat. As her teeth closed on his arm, the third Arab picked up his small hatchet and rained blows on the head of the lioness until she fell dead at their feet.

The boys soon recovered from their wounds, and for weeks afterward all the girls of the village wore little pieces of lion meat in their hair as a tribute to the prowess of the young men....

CROSSING THE LIBYAN DESERT
September 1924

A. M. HASSANEIN BEY (1889–1946)

DURING THE FIRST WORLD WAR, WHILE NEGOTIATING A PEACE agreement with the warlike Senussi sect of Libya, a young Egyptian army officer heard rumors that deep in the Libyan Desert, remote from any known caravan route, mysterious unmapped oases supposedly existed. Intrigued, he began laying plans to seek them out.

Ahmed Mohammed Hassanein Bey was a handsome, high born Egyptian of Bedouin ancestry who was educated at Oxford at a time when the British still governed his native country. Graceful in movement as well as manner, he represented Egypt in fencing at the 1920 Antwerp Olympics and was entering upon a diplomatic career when wanderlust interrupted. Because he was a Muslim and had proved his friendship, the wary Senussi chieftains granted him permission to explore the Libyan Desert, which they controlled.

In 1923, at the age of 33, the dashing Hassanein Bey mounted a six-month, 2,200-mile expedition that crept by camel caravan from the Mediterranean across the Libyan Desert into the Anglo-Egyptian Sudan. Mapping and surveying as he went, he finally found those rumored oases, named Arkenat and Ouenat, pinpointing them near the rugged southwest corner of Egypt. In doing so he gained glory, receiving among other distinctions a gold medal from the Royal Geographical Society. The director of Egypt's Desert Survey, in a curious phrasing, declared it "an almost unique achievement in the annals of geographic exploration."

No question, however, that he was a unique man. Sir Ahmed Mohammed Hassanein Pasha, as he finally came to be called, was equally at home in the khaki of Anglo-Egyptian officialdom or the flowing robes of a Bedouin sheik. This rare ability to bridge two worlds led to his becoming the most important advisor to Egypt's royal house before his untimely death in a Cairo automobile accident. It also gives interest to the following extracts, describing immemorial customs of the Sahara caravans, from his NATIONAL GEOGRAPHIC article, reflecting the perspective of one trained in the West while remaining at heart a loyal son of the desert.

TWO DAY'S JOURNEY FROM JAGHBUB, ON THE WAY TO JALO, WE CAME across a petrified forest. The big bits of petrified trees are still used as landmarks on the way, set up according to an age-old practice of the desert.

It is customary when a caravan finds small pieces of stone lying about along the route to heap them up, to show that some one has passed. Of course, tracks in the sand are obliterated by the wind. It is a wonderful sight sometimes, when one has been trekking for five or six days without seeing any sign of the hand of man, to come across a pile of two or three stones on the ground. It straightway encourages one. The body of a camel or even the skeleton of an unfortunate traveler, though an awful sight, at least shows that a caravan has passed that way....

The most interesting feature of the trip to Jalo was eight days of sandstorm.

The desert is usually very calm, with an occasional breeze, which becomes stronger and stronger; then gradually the land looks as if it has been fitted with pipes emitting steam. The fine sand first rises, but as the velocity of the wind increases heavier grains rise. When the sand gets as high as one's head, it becomes distressing, and perhaps dangerous if the traveler has to face it. Now he is obliged to go very slowly, and if he is not careful and vigilant he may miss the way. But if the wind is blowing from the right or left, it is not so difficult, because the sand can be warded off with the Bedouin clothes.

One day we had to advance in the teeth of the storm, and I saw how it could destroy a caravan. Of course, one has to keep moving slowly. To stop means to be drowned by the sand. The camels instinctively know this and continue to advance in spite of the tormenting blast. On the other hand, the moment the rain comes they stop or even kneel down....

Sometimes, however, toward sunset, when we had been battling for hours against the seemingly interminable bombardment, the wind would stop dead, as if a master hand had given a signal. For an hour or more the fine sand and dust would settle slowly, like a falling mist. Afterward the moon would rise, and under the pale magic of its flooding light the desert would assume a new aspect. Had there been a sandstorm? Who could remember? Could this peaceful expanse of loveliness ever be cruel? Who could believe it?...

The arms for the trip were a motley assortment—9 rifles, 4 revolvers, and 3,000 rounds of ammunition. Three of the rifles were old Egyptian army weapons. The others were Italian, Russian, and German guns smuggled into the Senussi country by the German submarine gun runners during the World War, and used in the Senussi attacks against the western frontiers of Egypt under the leadership of Sayed Ahmed, cousin of Sayed Idris, who was under the influence of Turkish and German officers.

During the desert journey these guns were seldom used except upon our approach to a Bedouin settlement in an oasis, on which occasions I ordered each man of the caravan to fire three rounds, ostensibly as a salute, but in reality to impress the possibly hostile natives with our armed strength...

In addition to our 15 men and 37 camels, an important member of the expedition was Baraka, my chestnut Arabian horse, which made the entire journey and endured the hardships astonishingly well. Day after day, in midsummer, he stood tethered near my tent, in the broiling sun, with the temperature sometimes registering 113°F. He is in Cairo now enjoying for life a well-earned rest.

The mascot of the caravan was Bibo, an unimpressive-looking non-descript dog. He was one of the marvels of the expedition. There were days when he must have traveled 60 or 75 miles while we were covering 25 or 30, for he had an insane propensity for chasing birds over the desert.

His vitality was amazing, but he also had a certain canny instinct, for when weary he plainly indicated the fact and appealed, in a manner almost akin to speech, to one of the boys, who would lift him aboard a camel. Here he would perch upon a sheepskin water bag, the coolest spot in the desert. As the day progressed, he would move around to the water bag slung on the other side; so that, like the Kentucky colonel of whom I have heard, who with his mint-julep glass "followed the shade around the house," Bibo followed his around the hump....

From the time we left Sollum until our arrival in El Obeid, we had not one glass of clear water for drinking purposes. In cases where we were using new sheepskin water bags, the water absorbed the tar with which the bags were lined, and where we used old containers the liquid invariably carried in suspension particles of the hair of the hide, as well as other impurities.

On the long treks between water wells, our water camels each carried four sheepskins with an aggregate capacity of 24 gallons.

There is considerable misconception as to the amount of water required by the desert traveler. In winter we found it possible to subsist on an ordinary glassful in the morning and another in the evening. Occasionally, on the daylight marches, a third glass was taken at midday, but this was looked upon as more or less of an effeminate weakness. When it became hot we tried to save water by resting during the day and trekking by night.

My horse required a third of a sheepskin of water daily, or half a sheepskin every other day, when the supply was scant. Our food consisted chiefly of rice, flour, dates, and Bedouin butter, the latter almost invariably in liquid form, made from sheep's milk and usually rancid because of its containers—old hide bags.

The stand-by of the desert traveler, however, is tea—not the emasculated and emaciated beverage of civilization, but a potent black brew made from one handful of tea and sugar in equal proportions, placed in a small pot having a capacity of perhaps a pint of water. This is boiled and the bitter-sweet liquid is served in tiny glasses holding about two ounces.

Two glasses of this drink will imbue the user with remarkable vitality. He becomes wakeful, watchful, and eager for the journey. The effect is exhilarating without being intoxicating. This desert tea is an acquired taste; but once the Bedouin beverage habit is formed, it is very difficult to go back to the pallid tea of civilization....

When an oasis is reached, a feast may be tendered to the leader by the sheik, or head man, and less pretentious entertainment provided for the men of the caravan. No resentment is felt at such discrimination; but out in the sands each must subsist as every other man in the caravan and do his share of the day's work, without regard to rank.

As a matter of fact, a greater tax was placed upon my endurance than upon that of any other member of the organization; for, in addition to the work of inspecting each camel load and taking a hand at breaking and establishing camp, when all others were through for the day or the night, as the case might be, it was then my responsibility to enter the scientific data in my diary, wind and compare the six watches which I carried (four of which, unfortunately, went out of commission before the end of the journey), label and store the geological specimens collected, and record the films used.

The theodolite [a surveying telescope] was one of my chief cares on the journey, for the Bedouins are extremely suspicious of this instrument. They had had sufficient experience with European nations to deduce the fact that where surveys of their country had been made armed forces generally followed for purposes of conquest. It therefore became necessary for me to practice pardonable deception in order to utilize the instrument.

Readings were taken principally late in the afternoon, and I always made my observations at some distance from native settlements, explaining to the inquisitive Bedouins that the theodolite was in reality a camera, which could be taken out of its box in twilight or dawn. I had to explain that the camera and the theodolite worked alike, *attracting* pictures to them.

"How could a camera attract a picture far away from it?" asked a Bedouin of the Nubian head man of my caravan, who was very good at concocting harmless inaccuracies. Abdullah threw his hands in the air: "Ask the magnet how he attracts the iron!" was the simple and, to the Bedouin, convincing reply....

It is a trek of nine days from Buttafal well to Zieghen, across one of the most desolate parts of the world. Birds migrating northward to Europe, some of them small robins, fly 250 miles without a drink of water. Sometimes these intrepid travelers, apparently mistaking us for trees, would alight upon our heads or shoulders. We would give them a drink, and off they would fly again. They never made a mistake and started south. As we went along we saw remnants of wings which told their own story.

During this stage of the journey I used to ask the guide in the morning to indicate the line of march for the day. He would trail a line with his stick. I would take bearings on it and check him ten or fifteen times in an hour with my compass, and he would not waver a yard, walking half a mile ahead of the caravan. It was extraordinary to watch him, to see that beautiful straight line.

In daylight trekking, the Bedouin uses his shadow for a compass, and so experienced has he become that his course alters imperceptibly as his shadow moves in sundial fashion. About midday he would get in trouble, because traveling by his shadow, this would then be between his feet!

I caught him at the end of one day in just one mistake. The stars had not come out, and he was going absolutely due west when he should have been going south. If I asked him in the daytime, "Are we going in the right direction?" he would wave his hand and say, "God knows best!" Of course, "God knows best," said with an air of assurance, is all right, but if a Bedouin guide tells you "God knows best" in a hazy way, after you have seen him wobble, it means he has gone astray....

Near Zieghen there have been tragedies, because if the traveler happens to go a little to the right or the left he will miss the well and find no water, for here, as in some other places in the desert, the well is not walled in with masonry, but is merely a water hole. Often only a patch of damp sand indicates the presence of water, and the guide will dig a little and find the well.

Three days from Zieghen there is an old landmark called Garet El Fadeel. In the desert, whenever anything is named for a man it means a bit of tragedy. This man, El Fadeel, was one of the finest guides between

Hassanein Bey assembled his caravan in the date groves of Siwa, a famed oasis in northern Egypt. The ancient fortress-like buildings were originally erected as protection against marauders sweeping up out of the Libyan Desert.

Jalo and Kufra. On his final journey he was leading his caravan when a little sandstorm arose. He had trouble with his eyes, so asked a companion to describe all the landmarks. They mistook one, went to the west instead of to the east, and missed their well.

They realized their mistake too late. They tried to go to Kufra, but fell exhausted on the way. One camel escaped and finally reached Kufra, where it had been accustomed to graze. When it arrived the natives saw a mark on its neck and knew it was El Fadeel's camel. A search was begun for the party, but it was of no avail. The men had died of thirst.

Curiously enough, fifteen years later this party's luggage was found untouched, preserved by the sand....

The camel-driver on march is an interesting subject of study. There is between him and his beast of burden a bond of affection hardly less strong than that which exists between the Arab horseman and his steed. The camel is the essential of life in the sands. Travel and trade are dependant upon him.

On march the camel goes best when his driver sings. These songs, or chants, almost invariably concern the virtues of the ungainly but intrepid beast. His praises are sounded in most extravagant terms, and the animal seems to like it.

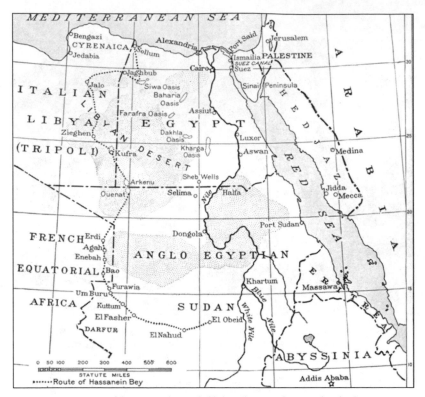

Hassanein Bey's camel-borne expedition plodded south across the unexplored Libyan Desert, mapping, surveying, and proving the existence of long-rumored oases.

The camel-driver knows his charge so well that he is able instantly to identify the beast by its footprints in the sands; and not only is he able to do this, but also to identify the son of that camel; in other words, it would seem that each camel family has its own footprint peculiarities.

The average animal will carry a burden of from 250 to 300 pounds, but it is the duty of the astute explorer to supervise the loading at the beginning of each march, seeing always that the camel which carried a heavy load yesterday is given a light burden to-day.

Where supplies are plentiful, the animals are given grass and barley, but in desert trekking, when these are not obtainable, they are fed twice a day on dried dates, a meal consisting of as much fruit as can be gathered together twice in two hands. The animals are serviceable up to 23 or 25 years of age and are valued at from $50 to $100.

It is recorded that, when water supplies have been exhausted, caravan leaders have slain their weaker camels and the drivers have then extracted all the moisture possible from the stomachs of the animals. In the final extremity, the frothy pink blood has, in some instances, been drunk; but this practice inevitably means the end, for such a draught is comparable to the drinking of sea water by shipwrecked persons.

In winter, in case of necessity, a camel in good condition can go for 15 days without water; in summer, from 10 to 12 days is the limit.

If an animal becomes completely exhausted on a trek, it must be killed. This is one of the saddest experiences of the desert, for a camel is really a member of a caravan and not merely a beast of burden.

There is a tremendous advantage in night traveling, for one never fails to march less than 12 hours and frequently the time stretches to 13 and even 14, our highest continuous trek being for 14$^1/_2$ hours (between Ouenat and Erdi), covering a distance of a little more than 40 miles.

The reason for the longer period of travel at night is that, once a caravan gets under way after the intense heat of the day is over—that is to say, between 4 and 6 o'clock in the afternoon—the advance continues without respite until sunrise.

From 10 to 1 o'clock at night is the most trying period of desert travel. It is then that the vitality of both men and animals seems to be at lowest ebb, and there have been times between these hours when I have felt that nothing would be quite so welcome as death, with its accompanying eternal sleep.It becomes almost impossible to drag one foot after the other, and only through the exercise of most rigid watchfulness can sleep be fought off as fatigue increases.

But if night marches have their advantages, they also have their disadvantages, such as difficult, rocky ground—bad going for the feet of men and camels—and when there is no moon, danger of missing one's way in crossing sand dunes, for the guiding star may be lost.

But with the first break of dawn and the appearance of light in the east, the desert traveler seems to take a miraculous new lease on life. It is as if he had been suddenly rejuvenated. Miles seem fairly to reel from beneath his feet, and there comes a jubilation of spirit which is indescribable.

After this rebirth of energy, no desert traveler would consent to halt. He is spurred on by an irresistible force, and this urge continues until the sun has appeared above the horizon, giving warning that the time of heat and suffering has arrived.

It is now that camp must be quickly made, tents raised, food cooked and eaten; then a quick drop into the oblivion of sleep, which can last at most only for three or four hours. After that the heat becomes so intense that there is no opportunity for real relaxation and comfort. It often happened that within 15 or 20 minutes from the time that halt was called in the morning our entire camp would be slumbering.

The manner in which a Bedouin guide finds his way across the desert at night is a source of wonder to the uninitiated. In a region which provides no familiar landmarks, he depends solely upon the stars.

As we were proceeding in a southwesterly direction during most of our night trekking, the polestar was at the guide's back. He would glance over his shoulder, face so that the polestar would be behind his right ear, then take a sight on a star to the south in that line. He would march for perhaps five minutes with his eye riveted on this star, then turn and make a new observation of the polestar; for, of course, the star to south was constantly progressing westward. He would then select a new star for guidance and continue.

One of the possibilities of losing one's way in the desert, even when accompanied by a capable guide, may be due to the fact that, after a long series of treks, when days are so hot as to provide insufficient rest for the party, the guide may doze as he walks and thus keep his eye fixed too long on the same star. His bearing in this way shifts westward, out of the true line of march.

Knowing the method by which the Bedouin keeps his direction, one is not surprised that, between sundown and the appearance of the stars, he is completely lost and is a helpless figure in the desert. At that hour of the evening, and also in the early morning, when the stars had disappeared but the sun had not risen, it was necessary for me to take the lead, following my compass bearings....

CAIRO TO CAPE TOWN, OVERLAND
February 1925

FELIX SHAY

SINCE FELIX SHAY FREELY ADMITTED TO BEING UTTERLY IGNORANT *about Africa before ever setting foot there, he certainly hadn't heard of Ewart Grogan, who in 1900 was the first person ever to walk from Cape Town to Cairo, hoping thereby to win the hand of his beloved.*

Shay was a successful advertising man who, in 1923, together with his wife, Porter, made a long voyage around the world. Africa wasn't originally on the itinerary, yet seized by a whim, "merely seeking an unusual adventure," the Shays did debark in Cairo, and 135 days later had made their way via river steamer, train, automobile, and at least 400 miles of shanks' mare to Cape Town. They had the time of their lives, and were quite possibly the first American couple ever to retrace that romantic route Ewart Grogan had pioneered.

Shay then pulled off another improbable feat: He persuaded the editors at NATIONAL GEOGRAPHIC to look at his unsolicited manuscript—an elephantine 20,000 words long—and they not only published it, they devoted the entire February 1925 issue to it. "You give the average reader a better mental picture of Africa," one of them wrote Shay, "than can be obtained in any other narrative of equal length."

It still remains vivid, although its open, guileless style reveals as much about Shay as about Africa. Ebullient, enthusiastic, occasionally short-tempered, with a self-deprecating sense of humor, Shay was the shrewd man of affairs who nevertheless displayed an almost childish wonder at new worlds of experience. In the following episode, a comic lion hunt in Kenya, he marvels at the great game-rich savannas as they were in the twilight of East Africa's golden age.

Adventure implies danger; it is the whiff of danger that sharpens the experience. Yet it's not always the lion that gets you. Throughout this article it is clear how much Felix and Porter ("two amateur, and somewhat foolhardy, adventurers") enjoyed each other's company. By the late 1930s, however, their bright day was done. Felix Shay was in the Washington Home for Incurables, ravaged by an illness that doctors could not identify: sleeping sickness, "chronic encephalitis," or some other deadly thing picked up in Africa.

WHEN FIRST WE TALKED WITH THE WHITE HUNTER [A PROFESSIONAL guide in East Africa], he asked us what we wished to shoot. "Oh, we wish to shoot lions." Up until that minute I had not thought of what I wanted to shoot. Never in my life had I gone hunting.

"Righto! I think we can find lions," he replied. Thus, casually and irresponsibly, were we committed to a lion hunt.

We left Nairobi at 7 a.m., in a little American-made car, to cover some 75 miles, to where the lion has his haunts.

One mile outside Nairobi the road degenerated into a wagon track across low lush meadows, simply soft mud. We had chains on the wheels all day. We got stuck innumerable times. We had to get out and push. We skidded at every turn. We had three punctures.

This is the principal road in Kenya Colony.

The Masai are still the most warlike and most feared of all the African tribes. They are a cattle-owning people. They live on cows' milk and cows' blood. They consider agricultural work disgraceful. The little flour and such which they require they get by trade.

Incidentally, they have cattle tick and cattle fever rampant among their vast herds; so there is a quarantine station on the edge of the Masai country to keep their cattle and the consequent contamination out of Kenya. This quarantine station, a one-room shed on stilts, was to be our headquarters while we hunted lions. This saved buying and carrying a tent.

More or less, I have seen the sights of the world, but I shall never forget the thrill as we came into the Kedong Valley, five miles from this quarantine station. I expected to see big game in Africa; I had seen some. But my idea of hunting (purely academic) was to go out and search around till an animal appeared on the horizon; then take a quick shot at it and trust to luck. Imagine, then, the spectacle of *thousands* of animals within the radius of a few hundred yards of our car, grazing peacefully, such animals as one usually sees in the zoo. We were amazed and delighted.

We stopped the car for a better view and to hold conversation with two naked braves, who, all dressed up, were journeying toward some trysting place. Their hair, raised in pompon fashion, was matted with an oily red mud and braided into little ropes. Their bodies were painted with eccentric spirals in white. They wore rings in their noses and ears. They were very grand and very polite and very curious, especially about Porter.

The Kedong Valley consists of a series of gently undulating plains with pocketlike grazing grounds intruding into the foothills. Occasional shaggy outcroppings of rocks, hummocks and ledges provide shelter for the game and points of vantage for the hunter.

Next morning we turned out at daybreak. The grass, four feet high, was wet. Before we walked 100 yards we were soaked to the waist. No one cared for that, because the most interesting sport in all the world was before us. The golf mania is as nothing compared to the big-game mania.

That first morning the rising sun found the plains full of elands, kongoni, antelopes, Grant's gazelle, Thomson's gazelle, zebras, ostriches, giraffes, hyenas, foxes, wild dogs, jackals - literally, thousands of animals. We forgot that we were there to shoot and stopped in wonder to admire.

A mile or more from the camp we came on a herd of zebras, say 70 yards away, that stood stock-still and stared.

The White Hunter suggested, "Go ahead, take a shot."

I dropped to one knee and let go.

The zebra at which I aimed kicked his heels into the air and fled to parts unknown.

One is neither discouraged nor disconcerted when one expects to miss—aye, prefers to miss—for I have not the stomach of a hunter. I hate to kill things.

On we went again, and the "honor" was now Porter's.

We turned the corner of a rocky abutment. Down below us, on the plain, 200 yards away, was a herd of kongoni, a variety of horned beast which weighs at maturity about 300 pounds. Porter sat down like a professional, leveled her gun on her knee, and promptly knocked over a large male.

First blood to Porter. We arranged the beast and photographed her and it, she trying vainly to conceal her elation. She is a Canadian and something of a big-game hunter; she gets a thrill out of it.

"Well," suggested our mentor and guide, "shall we have some breakfast?" We were all agreeable.

Across the plains Porter explained to me the defect in my stance, and how my gun should not have wiggle-waggled. She insinuated that I lacked poise. Of necessity I was meek enough. One must face the facts.

Then the hunter questioned, "What is that over under that tree?" He put his field glasses on it. It was a dead zebra!

I never looked at Porter while we walked over. I was hoping against hope. Sure enough, there, dead under the tree, shot five inches behind the shoulder, was *my* zebra! Right on the center of the target!

Did I gloat? No! I said only one sentence to Porter. Quietly, when the White Hunter was not listening, I mentioned that pertinent phrase, "Woman's place is in the home."...

Two Kuku natives turned up at the shack. We engaged them as gun-bearers, skinners, and general all-round helpers, at a shilling a day each. This business of hunting was becoming complicated.

To understand a "hunt" in Central Africa, one must understand the condition of a man's pocketbook. There are hunts and hunts! Many rich men come out here with guns enough to start a Central American revolution. They engage a safari of 100 or more natives. They take out a dozen or more cooks, camp boys, and personal boys. They bring luxurious tents. They pack a wine cellar and multitudinous cases of food. They engage two, three, or more professional hunters—crack shots. They take along a score of beaters to find the game and drive it in. They live with as much convenience and comfort in the field as they live at home. A short hunt of this character may cost from $5,000 to $25,000.

Before I left Nairobi I told our White Hunter that we sought neither self-deception nor trophies; that we wanted sport. I told him we wanted the privilege of shooting and missing or shooting and hitting. He was not to shoot until we had missed fair. If the animal fell, it belonged to him. We wanted none of it. Nor were we keen on a general butchery; one or two souvenirs of the hunt would be quite enough for us.

He was glad to agree. I find that few of these professional hunters have sympathy for wanton killing. Here, as elsewhere, the "game hog" is unpopular.

After lunch we went out to prepare the dead zebra for lion bait. To keep off the hyenas, the jackals, and the ever-present myriads of vultures, the carcass had to be covered with thorn bushes throughout the day, which were removed at dusk.

Remember, this was a lion hunt! Lions must be baited.

When the dead zebra was fixed just so, we made a 10-mile circle around the plain and saw hundreds of animals within easy shooting range, but we desisted. The spectacle of these beautiful strange animals, in their native habitat, grazing peacefully and unafraid, was rather a satisfactory adventure in itself.

Late that afternoon, at a distance of less than 50 yards, which was nothing on these broad plains, we saw five giant ostriches in single-file parade. There were three black cocks, each with a gorgeous plume of white tail feathers, and two dun-colored females. Off they stalked majestically, not at all in haste, while we sat and watched them.

That night the lions roared all around us. One who has not heard a lion roar on the plains of Africa has not heard the most awe-inspiring sound in all the world! Both of us had just finished reading Colonel J. H. Patterson's "The Man-Eaters of Tsavo." In this book the engineer who constructed the railroad from Mombasa to Nairobi relates his actual experiences with the lions that killed several white men, 28 Indian coolies, and scores of natives. These Tsavo lions actually delayed the construction of this railroad for months, because of the panic they created among the railroad workers....

Of all the books to give one creeps, this best achieves its purpose. I fear we doughty lion hunters rather quaked between our blankets that night, when we remembered that those roars so close outside emanated from beasts whom we were to engage in the morning.

We turned out at 3:30 a.m. to catch the lion on the bait with the first flush of daylight. This meant that we would kill or be killed before sunrise—an inspiring hour!

I carried the gun that delivered the heaviest blow, a .375 express rifle of English make. Therefore I was to have first shot.

...It is a notorious fact that a lion charges when wounded, and he moves with startling speed. His ability to cover the first 80 yards in no time defies the imagination. One must see him do it.... For that distance he is the swiftest animal alive. After that, he tires rapidly.

The unbroken trail led through the high, wet grass. It was still dark. A large black form loomed in front of us. "Sh! What is that?" Up went the rifles. By the slant of the back of the animal silhouetted against the sky, one could tell it was a giant hyena.

Other hyenas and jackals skulked by.

That they were off the bait told us convincingly that a lion must be on it.

By Jove, this *was* sport! This was a thrill!

The morning was cold, *cold*. The East African days are burning hot, and the nights are freezing cold. We wore "woolies" and heavy clothes, but we were cold. We blew on our hands to warm them, the better to grasp the rifles. Another five minutes and we would be there!

Unexpectedly we took the last rise in the land and came in full view of the bait.

"There he is! *Shoot! Shoot!*"

There he was, and no doubt!

Resting flat on the zebra was a full-maned, full-sized male lion. The grass was too high to drop to one knee. I had to shoot from the shoulder.

Masai women, legs sheathed in copper bracelets, stare back at the camera.
The Masai are a dominant tribe of the East African savannas.

He glared at us, but did not move. I put my rifle to my shoulder, said a short prayer to the God-of-things-as-they-ought-to-be, and fired.

The big beast offered me a full side shot, a still target at 60 yards.

I aimed steadily, confidently, for the vital spot, just behind the shoulder. I fired and I missed!

I did not know I had missed. Naturally, I thought I hit him. I was concentrating on another problem. With the first bullet fired, I pumped the magazine to throw out the old cartridge. Out went the old, but the magazine of the gun, which the dealer in Nairobi assured me was in "perfect condition," refused to function.

The cartridge did not jam; the weak spring of the magazine simply refused to throw the next cartridge into the barrel. I could not look up; the task was under my hand! I plunged my thumb into the magazine to stimulate the spring, and took skin off the thumb without result. I found a loose cartridge, snapped it into the barrel, and looked up. I expected to find the lion in front of me, asking, "Am I too late for breakfast?"

While I was struggling with the gun I dimly heard a rattle of musketry. To me it seemed a long way off and far removed. I disassociated it with my dilemma. When I looked up, there was Mr. Lion scurrying over the far hill, with bullets to left of him, bullets to right of him, bullets in back of him. Both Porter and the White Hunter had emptied the magazines of their guns while Mr. Lion buck-jumped through the grass.

Then the two guilty ones turned on me and wrathfully accused *me* of missing the lion! Well, there are times when one can not condescend to argue.

That day we were in a furor of excitement. To kill a lion became an obsession. Lesser animals were suddenly unattractive.

Immediately after breakfast we went out to kill another zebra for bait, and, if possible, to effect the kill in a particular locality, so the bait would be located favorably.

This was no easy task. The zebras refused to come or to be driven where we wanted them. After two hours of stalking them ineffectually, we held a conference. We decided to kill one in the open and then engage native oxen to draw it a couple of miles across the plain, thus leaving a line of scent, and place it exactly where we wanted it. We scattered to get close to a zebra herd a mile away in the open.

Porter and the White Hunter shot simultaneously. The latter dropped his with a bullet through the heart, while Porter turned her zebra over twice with a bullet head-on through the chest.

Then we hailed a Kuku native in a red blanket, who lived in a near-by grass hut. He found the necessary oxen. These were attached to the two zebras and they were dragged to high land, where there were some thorn bushes and small trees.

We planned to build a *boma*. To make the structure seem natural, the near-by landscape must be similar. A boma is a small-sized fort made of thorn bushes, in the form of a complete circle. It is supposed to protect the hunter from the lion. The lion is supposed to fear it as a trap. We could only trust these suppositions were correct.

We planned to sit up all night in the boma, with the bait in front of us, and wait for the lion to come along and settle down to the banquet. Porter was to have first shot, and—well, I could only think thoughts of pity for that lion.

Mentally, I began to select places for the lion's skin on our living-room floor at home.

We wended our way back to the shack for lunch. Along the trail we scared five little foxes out of the bush. They were no larger than house cats. In the afternoon, we refrained from shooting, in order not to frighten off the prospective lion. We took a preparatory nap instead. When the sun set we started for the boma, with a steamer rug each, as protection against the damp and cold.

Once in the boma, we must be as still as death itself. That's an easy task for an hour. But not to speak, not to stir for ten hours—! That night I kept the faith faithfully, but I am through with bomas forever and a day.

Even so, the long night out on the plains with thousands of animals prowling about, the strange and threatening noises, the queer sounds, the smells, the silence, the vastness, the eerie moon—these are to me an unforgettable memory.

Once in the night a circle of little jackals came around and yipped at us. Once a hyena laughed near by. There was something suggestive in his laugh. The lion never came. Porter never killed it! The rug in the living room will have to be an afghan from Peshawar.

Meanwhile, I resolved to get a pair of gazelle horns for the family carving knife and fork. At 200 yards, I was offered a shot at a Thomson's gazelle, a male with very nice, long horns. These little creatures are about the size of a goat, with a black and white stripe down the dun-colored side. The Tommie would only give me his tail to shoot at. He looked back over his left shoulder with a critical eye. My companions waited fretfully while I took his measure.

Then I let him have it with the heavy gun.

I hit him in the hind quarter. The bullet ricocheted and pierced the brain. He died instantly. My reputation as a hunter was restored and on this planet I have shot my last gazelle. Alive, they are beautiful, graceful little beings; dead, they are gory masses.

Each morning we hunted lions without success. Between times we shot several varieties of horned beasts, enough to supply us with fresh meat and a few trophies.

One day as we strolled about the plains we fell in with a monster mother giraffe and her young one. The mother moved off, but the silly youngster stopped to look us over. He halted within 30 yards of us. An hour later we encountered eight giraffes, six grown ones and two youngsters.

What beautiful creatures they are!

The head of the family, a gigantic male, moved forward to inspect us. These animals are royal game in Africa; a hunter is required to have an extra special license to kill them. Therefore, they have been shot over very little, and as a consequence are unafraid. The old male, a wonderful fellow with large, brown spots, and a white head, came as near as 40 yards, and gazed at us quizzically over a tree top.

Whenever we fired a shot on the plains the rumble of the animals' hoofs running for cover (or distance) sounded like thunder.

Africa is a marvelous country....

THREE-WHEELING THROUGH AFRICA

January 1934

JAMES C. WILSON (1900–95)

HEARING THAT HE PLANNED TO RIDE A MOTORCYCLE ACROSS
Africa, those who knew something about the continent might have told James C.
Wilson it couldn't be done. Too few roads, too many dangerous animals, too little
gasoline, and where would he get supplies, not to mention spare parts? But in 1928,
when most of Africa had never even seen a motor vehicle, just the prospect of such
a dashing adventure fired the imagination. It certainly appealed to Wilson, who
with his friend Francis Flood was freighter-bound for India when a chance
conversation with a fellow passenger sparked this wild idea. The intrepid duo dis-
embarked at Lagos, Nigeria, purchased two motorcycles affixed with sidecars,
assembled what spare parts they could find, kicked things into gear, and started off.

What they jocularly called the Flood-Wilson Trans-African Motorcycle
Expedition roared into the crowded, colorful villages of Nigeria. Five months
and 3,800 miles later, what was left of men and machines shuddered to a halt
by the shores of the Red Sea. Theirs had probably been the first motorized trans-
port to pass along the northern shores of Lake Chad, struggling through sand
and grass from one far-flung French fort to another. Even the gasoline and
supplies found at such outposts had to be brought in by camel caravan. As for
spare parts—well, as vividly related here, Wilson and Flood had to improvise.

Jim Wilson's descriptions of the harsh, open landscapes of the Sahel, that
broad zone where the Sahara gives way to sparse grasslands, were penned with a
knowing eye. He had grown up on the Nebraska prairie and had tried his hand
at many things—farming, teaching, travel lecturing, and playing music—before
returning there. (Wilson always picked the banjo, but also played saxophone in
Jazz-Age New York and wrote Iowa State University's school song, "The Bells of
Iowa.") Back in Nebraska he developed new strains of prairie grasses and wild-
flowers while gradually becoming a legend among bikers for his pioneering
African adventure. He lived well into his nineties and died in the same house in
which he was born.

THE TRAIL FROM N'GUIMI TO MAO WAS SO SANDY THAT WE COULD
make no headway at all with our side cars. Therefore we took them off,
draped them across the hump of a dyspeptic-looking camel, let still more air

out of our back tires, and after several disastrous experiments learned to skim over the soft sand on two wheels, after the style of an aquaplane rider.

Flood, who had never ridden a two-wheeled contraption before in his life, took 16 falls the first day. Our bare legs were striped like a zebra's with burns from the smoking cylinder fins.

And then Flood's luggage carrier broke in two. We were 60 miles from N'Guimi and more than 500 miles from the nearest garage—clear back at Kano. However, we had a brass rod, some borax, and a big hatchet in our tool boxes, and there were dead trees in a near-by cuvette. But we had no forge! We made one out of an empty gasoline can and a pair of motorcycle handlebars, and with Flood as the bellows and the big hatchet for an anvil, I stuck that luggage carrier back together.

Next day the cap dropped off Flood's magneto breaker box and a little hard rubber bearing the size of a small pearl—and much more valuable to us—fell out in the sand. The motorcycle wouldn't run without it, and we didn't have an extra or anything to make one out of. We absolutely *had* to have it; but a three-hour search on hands and knees only convinced us that it simply wasn't there. The Sahara had swallowed it up.

But Flood had lost his four upper front teeth, and the replacements were mounted on a quickly detachable partial plate.

"Spit out your teeth, Flood. Let's see that plate.... Hurray!! Hard rubber!!" And I carved a bearing out of it that got us across Africa, but Flood had to run in on the rim to the nearest dentist, in Khartoum—1,500 miles away.

This is the no man's land of Africa, the southern fringe of the desert back of Chad. But wherever there is water there are people—even in no man's land—in a little cluster of grass huts squatting in a cuvette, and 15 or 20 villagers, as lean and sun-dried as the desert itself, anxiously scratching their scanty millet patches and hoping to harvest enough of the coarse grain to keep them alive another season.

There's something gallant about them, these dwellers in a region of eternal want, tenaciously clinging to an existence so rigorous and unadorned that it seems scarcely worth the effort necessary to maintain it.

Sometimes the water is deep in the rock. We stepped off one well rope. It was 154 feet long. No wonder a camel has to be his own windlass when he wants a drink, and no wonder he gets thirsty only once a week or so.

But who dug the wells? The French? Yes, the French have dug a considerable number in the last 30 years. But many of those holes in the

*Plodding through Africa: A chief of the Messeria, a nomadic Sudanese tribe,
stands beside a gaily caparisoned ox, which bears one of his wives.*

ground may well be older than the Bible. I remember one in particular at
which we watered. The four hardwood logs which formed the curb had
been almost sawed in two in dozens of places by the friction of the rope.

A new curb had been laid on top of the old one, and worn out; then
another and another—16 hardwood logs worn out by the sawing of a rope;
and no telling how many times in the remote past history had repeated
itself on successive series of curbs. I should like to know how many skins
of water have been drawn out of that well for thirsty men and camels.

But the most interesting wells are the ones that grow out of the
ground. According to one legend, Perseus, after killing Medusa, flew
across Africa with her head, and the drops of blood which fell on the
sands turned into clusters of writhing snakes.

Look at the twisted limbs of the baobab trees. Who will say that the
legend is false?...

There is a short rainy season, even in the desert, and tiny streams run
in the valleys after a shower. The villagers dam them up, collect the water
as carefully as if it were molten gold, and pour it into the hollow trunks

of the baobab trees. A good-sized tree will keep 500 to 1,000 gallons of water fresh and pure for many months. Dozens of villagers have no other supply than what is held by a grove of these trees. The natives hoard the precious liquid carefully, drawing it up in goatskin bags through a hole in the top of the trunk....

A dry season here means tragedy. And the dry seasons are becoming increasingly frequent, for the grim Sahara is slowly creeping south, turning savannas into sand dunes and mere aridness into desolation. The Lake Chad shore line in places has receded several miles in the last hundred years....

The gallant little villages are losing their fight. There are old baobab trees, but almost no young ones. Wells that were good a century ago are dry holes in the sand today. The millet patches of yesterday may be wind-swept wastes to-morrow. And man can only bow his head sadly, load up his woman and babies and pitiful possessions on a camel, and wearily set out over the path inexorable fate has decreed for him, hunting for a spot a little less grim and hostile, where he may live a few more years before he dies.

A boy guided us to a handful of beehive grass huts huddling together in the sand. It was typical of those little African settlements which dot the central Sudan, so unreal and bizarre to the people on the other side of the world, but so eloquent of homeliness and security to the simple folk who are born, spend their lives, and die here.

Before almost every hut there was a little cooking fire and a woman busy at her pots. Two men were skinning an antelope by the guttering flicker of a twist of grass in a little dish of fat; and squatting on the ground near the light were four little boys intently playing a game with pebbles dropped into holes in the sand. From one of the huts came the soft, wistful notes of a bamboo flute in a melody centuries old. In another a woman was singing her baby to sleep.

Seated on the ground around a bright, crackling fire were 18 or 20 little white-robed figures with scalp locks and pigtails, dutifully droning verses of the Koran from their wooden slates, under the supervision of a watchful old patriarch with a scraggly white tuft on the end of his chin.

We followed our guide though the center of the village to a hut somewhat larger than the others. He went inside, leaving us in the center of a crowd of wondering natives, who stood back in the shadows and whispered furtively to each other about us....

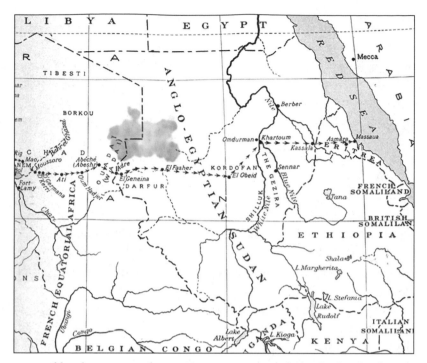

*Although commencing their journey in Lagos, Nigeria, Flood and Wilson found
the sandy grasslands between Lake Chad (just off the map at left)
and the Red Sea (right) to be the toughest going for motorcycles.*

Next morning when we came to tell the chief thank you and good-bye, he went into his hut and came out with a soiled, tattered photograph of half a dozen white men in sun helmets and shorts, standing in front of three tractor-type cars, part of the French Citroen Expedition of 1924-5.

The significance of our reception in the light of the chief's possession of this photograph was not lost on us. He had had previous experience with white men and their "putt-putts." And it was a compliment of the highest order both to M. Haardt and his companions and to the chief and his people that Flood and Wilson, also white men with "putt-putts," had been so graciously treated when they passed that way several years later.

On through the desert, plowing, grinding, pushing, sweating; giving up hope regularly every night, renewing it every morning. A magneto chain gives out. I repair it with a piece of one of the fenders. Our camels catch up with us before the job is done. The sand isn't so bad now, so we attach the side cars again. A spring breaks. We saw off a tail-light bracket and truss it up as best we can. Another petrol tin springs a leak and we solder it out under the broiling sun. We drop over a series of bluffs and breaks into a scorching little valley and find the ground covered with thorns. Sixteen punctures before we notice what's wrong and get stopped. But there's a village near by. We get a tanned antelope hide, cut it into strips, and, after friendly natives have picked out the thorns, install puncture-proof linings in all six casings. No more flat tires!

Almost halfway across Africa, out of water and lost! The last time we were in this fix I tracked a jackal four miles to a stinking little water hole, fished out two carcasses, scraped off the scum, and we made tea. But we haven't seen a jackal for hours. There was supposed to be a village ten miles back, but we missed it. Must be on the wrong trail; that means that we'll miss our camels. Ordinarily we drink over a gallon of water a day—and sweat it out. To-day we've had less than a quart between us.

The long, lonely night is anything but cheerful. We can't sleep, we can't talk, we can't swallow; our tongues are swelled up like prickly pears. It's ghastly to die of thirst!

But who said anything about dying? Ten o'clock in the morning, and here comes an old Mohammedan pilgrim plodding down the trail, driving his donkey ahead of him. He offers his calabash in the name of Allah the Merciful. And all the petty distinctions of race, creed, and color are swept away in a rush of gratitude for this act of human kindness.

Before the pilgrim passes on, our camels appear over the crest of the hill. Allah to be praised—we're on the right trail after all! ...

PART TWO:

Remote Corners of the Russian Empire

AN ISLAND IN THE SEA OF HISTORY: THE HIGHLANDS OF DAGHESTAN

October 1913

GEORGE KENNAN (1845–1924)

ASKED BY HIS FRIEND GILBERT GROSVENOR TO SUBMIT AN ARTICLE for NATIONAL GEOGRAPHIC, an aging George Kennan characteristically chose a Russian subject. The well-traveled journalist might have picked dozens of places, but Russia was where he had made his name, and he remained the top American authority on that country. The subject he chose was not Siberia, the region with which he was most associated, but the wild, storied, and spectacularly beautiful Caucasus Mountains.

Spanning the 800 miles between the Black and Caspian Seas, the Caucasus was a world unto itself. Every valley seemed to have its own tribe, language, and costume. Russia lapped against its northern ramparts; during the 19th century the tsar, seeking to secure his southern flank, had for decades hurled his armies against the great range. "Bow down thy snowy head, O Caucasus!" the poet Pushkin had famously beseeched, but generations of Russian soldiers saw that snowy head still rearing, ominously defiant. For 30 years the legendary Imam Shamil and his Muslim cohorts littered the beech woods of Chechnya with Russian bodies. Although the tsar eventually triumphed, the spell of the Caucasus was such that Circassian dress was fashionable even on the Nevski Prospekt in St. Petersburg.

The Caucasus was the most picturesque and exotic place young George Kennan had ever seen. In September 1870, with a love of rough travel—he had already sledged across Siberia—Kennan arrived in the town of Timour Khan Shoura, in the lee of the mountains. There he met a Georgian nobleman, Prince Djordjadzi, and with him made a two-week horseback journey through little known Daghestan and across the Caucasian range. Few Russians had ever been that way; Kennan was the first American. He was just 25, and though a lifetime of travels would follow, it was this autumn of discovery that he chose to write about 48 years later.

THE CAUCASIAN RANGE MAY BE REGARDED FOR ALL ETHNOLOGICAL purposes as a great mountainous island in the sea of human history, and on that island now live together the surviving Robinson Crusoes of a score of ship-wrecked states and nationalities—the fugitive mutineers of a hundred tribal *Bounties.*

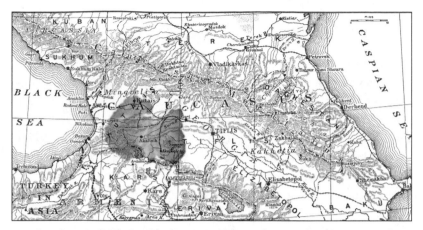

Stretching between the Black and Caspian Seas, the spectacular Caucasus Mountains were long a bulwark between Europe and Asia. Beneath their rugged, snowcapped peaks dozens of distinct ethnic groups—proud, fierce, colorful, and mutually antagonistic—have unhappily coexisted.

Army after army has gone to pieces in the course of the last 4,000 years upon that titanic reef; people after people has been driven up into its wild ravines by successive waves of migration from the south and east; band after band of deserters, fugitives, and mutineers has sought shelter there from the storms, perils, and hardships of war. Almost every nation in Europe, in whole or in part, and at one time or another, has crossed, passed by, or dwelt near this great Caucasian range, and each in turn has contributed its quota to the heterogeneous population of the mountain valleys.

The Aryan tribes, as they migrated westward from central Asia, left a few stragglers among the peaks of this great range; their number was increased by deserters from the Greek and Roman armies of Alexander the Great and Pompey; the Mongols under Tamerlane, as they marched through Daghestan, added a few more. So, too, the Arabs, who overran the country in the eighth century, established military colonies in the mountains, which gradually blended with the pre-existing population. European Crusaders, wandering back from the Holy Land, stopped there to rest and never resumed their homeward journey. Finally, the oppressed and persecuted of all neighboring lands—Jews, Georgians, Persians, Armenians, and Tatars—fled to these rugged, almost inaccessible mountains as to a city of refuge where they might live and worship their gods in peace....

The scene presented by the courtyard of the governor's house when I reached there was, to American eyes, a most novel and striking one.

Prince Djordjadzi, in a muff-shaped hat of Persian lamb's-wool and a green silk *khalat* [robe] confined at the waist with a massive silver belt, stood on the veranda of the governor's house, talking with General Tergukasof and three or four other officers in the brilliant uniform of the Caucasian staff; 25 or 30 mountaineers, in long-skirted maroon coats adorned with rows of ivory cartridge tubes, high cylindrical hats of black curly wool, white stormhoods of felted camel's hair, and tight scarlet leggings bound with golden braid, were already in the saddle, adjusting their silver-mounted rifles, pistols, sabers, and poniards, while they awaited the signal for a start; orderlies were running hither and thither in search of mislaid or forgotten equipment, and the air was filled with the shouting of men, the neighing of impatient horses, and the sharp clank of weapons.

In course of time order was brought out of the prevailing confusion, and at half past two we climbed into our high Tatar saddles and rode away, through the Avarski gate, into the highlands of Daghestan. Our first day's journey ... was not a long one, and after a ride of two or three hours through narrow, wooded ravines we came out, just before sunset, into a shallow, open valley, and caught sight of the village where we were to spend our first night. It was the *aoul*, or mountain settlement, of Joongootai.

The inhabitants had evidently received notice of our coming, and while we were still a quarter of a mile distant a mounted sentinel, who had apparently been watching for our approach, chirruped to his horse and dashed away at a gallop for the village, firing his long silver-banded rifle into the air and brandishing it furiously above his head in order to attract the attention of his fellow-villagers. The signal was promptly obeyed.

In a moment a large party of mountaineers, richly dressed and glittering with silver-mounted weapons and cartridge tubes, came galloping out of the stone gate of the village, lashing their horses with the hinged whips pictured on the monuments of Assyria; shouting, whooping, and yelling in what seemed to be the fierce excitement of battle, and firing at us incessantly as they dashed furiously down upon our escort. It stirred one's pulses to see the splendid impetuosity of the attack; but not knowing what it all meant, I almost instinctively reined in my horse and felt for the butt of my revolver.

On came the charging horsemen, like the Light Brigade at Balaklava, with a tumult of whooping, yelling, and firing that swelled into a great battle crescendo as they drew near. The distance between us narrowed to 50 feet, 30 feet, 10 feet, until the living thunderbolt of men and horses seemed actually to strike us. Then suddenly up went the hand of the leader, back went the trained horses upon their haunches as the sabers of their riders flashed in the air, and the whole attacking force in mid-career halted, slid a yard or two, and stopped within 6 feet of Prince Djordjadzi's saddle-peak.

For an instant the horsemen, with uplifted sabers, faced us in a superb battle tableau; then, with a great cry of *Asalaam alaikoum!* (Peace be with you!) they sheathed their weapons, dismounted from their high Tatar saddles, and advanced on foot to greet Prince Djordjadzi with the clasping fingers and upraised thumbs of Caucasian custom, but without the shaking of hands that is practiced in the West. I have witnessed impressive ceremonial receptions in many lands, but nothing to equal in dramatic effect the Caucasian *jigatofka*—the sham attack of a party of fighting highlanders upon a guest whom they wish to honor.

In 10 minutes or more we were comfortably seated on a rug-covered divan in the house of a mountaineer named Aleskandir Bek, Prince Djordjadzi receiving calls from his friends and acquaintances, while I drank cup after cup of fragrant Russian tea and watched the callers. They were all Lesghians of the clan known as Avars, and in stature, features, and coloring they differed little from men of the Teutonic and Anglo-Saxon stock.

All had the hawk-like intensity of gaze that is characteristic of mountaineers generally, as compared with lowlanders, but in other respects they were west Europeans; and in the dress of Great Britain or Germany they would undoubtedly have been taken for Englishmen, Scotchmen, Bavarians, or Saxons. They would have impressed me, however, in any dress and in any part of the world as outdoor men of strong character and fighting capacity.

In a few moments Aleskandir Bek took a seat by my side, remarked in broken Russian that he had never before seen a foreigner in Daghestan, and asked if he might be permitted to inquire my business. I told him frankly that I was a vagabond American, traveling for the love of it, seeing strange sights and mingling with strange people, in order that I might describe both some day in a book. He laughed pleasantly and said that in Joongootai, at least, I should have something to write about, because he had arranged for that evening, in honor of Prince Djordjadzi, a little Caucasian dancing party, which would give me some idea, perhaps, of Daghestan amusements and social life.

In the course of an hour, before we had finished our last cup of tea, the piercing notes of a Daghestan fife, mingled with the muttering of kettle-drums and tambourines, could be heard in the courtyard, and

A typical chief of the Caucasus a century ago: Black lamb's-wool cap, silver cartridge cases, elaborately decorated weapons, and, above all, a proud and indomitable expression.

we all went out on the broad veranda to see the beginning of a Caucasian night's entertainment. The yard was ablaze with torches and iron cressets filled with flaming firebrands, and was crowded with tall, bearded Lesghians, whose silver-mounted pistols, daggers, and cartridge tubes flashed fitfully in the red torchlight as they moved from place to place.

Near the veranda, in a little group, stood the women, richly dressed in filmy laces and bright-colored Persian silks, with long white veils concealing their hair and hanging down their backs to their red-slippered heels. Overhead was the slender stone minaret of the village mosque, outlined clearly against the dark starry sky, and from its high, circular gallery two white-turbaned *mullahs,* or Mohammedan priests, looked down curiously into the crowded, torch-lighted courtyard.

In a few moments our host cleared an open space in the center of the yard, shouted to the musicians to strike up, and the dancing began. One of the mountaineers stepped into the ring, laid his right hand, palm outward, against his right cheek, extended his left arm at full length, bent down his head, and began to dance rabidly in a narrow circle, keeping step to the throbbing of the kettle-drums and the measured, rhythmical hand-clapping of a hundred spectators.

In a moment he was joined by a bright-eyed, graceful young woman, who floated out to meet him from the little group near the veranda, and from whose outstretched arms hung long, flowing sleeves of pea-green silk to a depth of at least a yard. As she sailed out on tip-toe, with expanded silken wings and downcast, blushing face, she looked—in the estimation of Prince Djordjadzi—"like a terrestrial angel just about to take flight!"

With the appearance of the woman began the exciting part of the dance. The clapping of hands and the roll of the deep-toned kettle-drums almost drowned the shriek of the tormented fife, and now and then both were lost in a crashing fusillade of pistol shots fired into the air by the sympathetic spectators for the purpose of enlivening the proceedings by increasing the noise and enthusiasm. In two or three minutes the young woman glided out of the ring and rejoined her companions; her partner touched his hat and also retired, and a second couple took their places, the clapping of hand and pistol firing going on as before.

Dancing, interspersed with peculiar native games and musical improvisations, which were full of humorous personal hits and excited shouts of laughter, continued until a late hour of the night, when an elaborate Asiatic supper was served on the earthen, rug-covered floor of the stone-walled house. Finally, at 2 o'clock in the morning, we went to bed on the broad divan and fell asleep listening to a serenade sung by the women of the village under our windows with the monotonous refrain of "Hai! Hais! Annan-na-nan-nai! An-nan-nai!" (the Caucasian equivalent of "La! La! La-la-la-la-la! La-la-la!")...

The road—or rather the bridle path—that we followed after leaving Joongootai wound through dark canyons with almost precipitous sides, now descending to the edge of a roaring torrent, then climbing in a series of shelf-like zigzags to a height of a thousand feet, running for a quarter of a mile along the brink of a tremendous precipice, climbing again half a dozen more zigzags, crossing a divide, and finally plunging into a gorge equally dark, gloomy, and precipitous on the other side....

As we gradually approached the main range, the *aouls*, or mountain villages, became more and more daring and picturesque in their locations. Settlements in the valley bottoms grew less and less frequent and finally disappeared altogether, while high overhead every precipice, every terrace, or projecting buttress of rock was crowned with the flat-roofed, closely massed houses of an *aoul.*

Day after day Prince Djordjadzi and I rode from *aoul* to *aoul* through the wild mountain scenery of the eastern Caucasus, sometimes climbing through low-hanging clouds to solitary shepherds' huts on the high mesas, 4,000 feet above the sea; sometimes descending into narrow, gloomy gorges which suggested the canyons of Arizona, and sleeping every night in the flat-roofed stone houses of the fierce, wild but hospitable mountaineers. The state of society in which we found ourselves was as rude and savage in some respects as that which Caesar found among the barbarians of ancient Gaul, and almost every day we had an opportunity to observe customs and methods which were apparently survivals from the early ages of the world's history.

In the houses where we slept, the portholes which served as windows had neither sashes nor glass. Against some of the doors were nailed the bones and shriveled remains of lopped human hands, the ghastly trophies of battle or blood-revenge. Meals were eaten on the floor from a common dish or kettle, out of which every man took his portion with a sharpened pine splinter or a wooden spoon. Fruit was offered to us on huge brass or copper trays bearing Latin inscriptions in old Gothic letters or verses from the Koran in Arabic. Grain was threshed by driving over it a yoke of oxen attached to a wooden toboggan, whose lower surface was studded with sharp-edged fragments of quartz.

Men accused of crimes were tried by the ordeal or cleared themselves by compurgation. Homicide was restrained only by the laws of the vendetta. A murderer who wished to make peace with his blood-seekers let his hair grow long, put on a white shroud, went with uncovered head to the relatives of the man whom he had killed, presented them with an unsheathed dagger, holding it by the point, and took the desperate chance of life or death. Forgiven murderers became members, by adoption, of the clans to which their victims had belonged.

A man who had a quarrel with his neighbor wrapped himself in a burial shroud and went in person to settle it, carrying in his hand money to pay a priest for reading prayers over a grave; and the dead were lamented with keening, borne to the village cemetery on ladders, and buried with Arabic prayers in their hand, to be given to the angel who should awaken them on the morning of the resurrection....

On the 3rd of October we entered the high trough between the snowy range and the main range, spent the night in the Daghestan village of Bezheeta, at an elevation of 8,000 or 9,000 feet, and about the middle of the next forenoon began the ascent of the gigantic ridge which forms the backbone of the eastern Caucasus and which separates Daghestan from the valley of Georgia.

We started up the mountain in zigzags, following as nearly as possible the track of a small but rapid stream which came rushing down from a rudimentary glacier 1,000 feet above. Old, hardened snow soon made its appearance, the noise of the torrent ceased, and we entered a gray canopy of clouds, which hid everything from sight except the *nevé* over which we rode. For an hour or two we climbed steadily upward, enveloped constantly in clouds and hearing nothing but the crunching of snow under our horses' feet.

Suddenly a cold, piercing wind began to blow in our faces. We had reached the summit, 12,000 feet above the sea, and the wind came from the other side of the range. The clouds, however, still hid everything from sight, and the mist, wind, and low temperature made it uncomfortable to stay on the summit long.

Just before we began our descent, however, the gray ocean of vapor suddenly opened beneath us, and there, 12,000 feet below, lay the beautiful semi-tropical valley of Georgia, like a huge colored map framed in clouds. Scores of glittering streams, like shining silver threads, lay stretched across the broad expanse of meadow land which sloped away from the base of the mountains; orchards, vineyards, and olive groves diversified it here and there with patches of darker green, and far away in the distance loomed the purple, snow-clad peaks of Armenia....

At noon we stood 12,000 feet above the sea, on the old, hardened snow which covered the crest of the main range. At 8 o'clock in the evening we were riding through dark olive orchards and vineyards redolent with the odor of ripening grapes, listening to the monotonous croaking of frogs, and breathing the warm fragrant air of a night in June.

In eight hours we had passed from midwinter to midsummer, and the snowy crest of the main range showed faintly, like a dim streak of white, against the dark blue, star-spangled, trans-Caucasian sky. Just before midnight we reached Prince Djordjadzi's estate and dismounting from our tired horses, entered the courtyard gate of his spacious, white-walled mansion, in the far-famed valley of the Alazan.

LIFE IN THE GREAT DESERT OF CENTRAL ASIA
August 1909

THE AFGHAN BORDERLAND: THE PERSIAN FRONTIER
October 1909

ELLSWORTH HUNTINGTON (1876–1947)

THE TIDE OF RUSSIAN EXPANSIONISM THAT ENGULFED THE CAUCASUS and rolled the length of Siberia had by the 1880s washed over Central Asia as well. Those vast deserts, with such shimmering caravan cities as Samarkand and Bokhara, had been the playing fields of the Great Game, where British and Russian officers, disguised as Muslim holy men, camel traders, or Indian fakirs, spied on each other and sometimes left bones bleaching in the sands. Russian conquest had so pacified the Turkomans, once greatly feared as raiders and slavers, that by 1903, in the desert near the Persian and Afghan frontiers, the white canvas tents of the Pumpelly Expedition could be pitched peaceably among the black felt ones of the tribesmen.

Among the expedition members seeking traces of prehistoric villages in the nearby mounds was Ellsworth Huntington. Though holding a recent Harvard master's degree, Huntington, 27, was no stranger to outdoor adventure, having recently won the Royal Geographical Society's Gill Medal for rafting the Euphrates on inflated sheepskins. To him the mounds provided evidence of increasing aridity, and on this first of several journeys into Central Asia, Huntington began formulating his ideas about how civilizations rise and fall on cycles of climatic change. He eventually became the most influential American geographer of his day and over the course of a long career poured forth 28 books and more than 240 articles, 7 of them published in NATIONAL GEOGRAPHIC. *Two selections from his* GEOGRAPHIC *articles follow, one describing a plague of locusts and the other a memorable "invasion" of Afghanistan.*

A WEEK'S RIDE OUT INTO THE SAND NORTH OF MERV AT THE END OF June gave opportunity to see how friendly the Turkomans are and how terrible is their desert. At first our way led through the unkempt fringe of brown stubble and weed-bordered ditches which surrounds every oasis; then came stretches of clayey plain with just a trace of grass; and finally the sand itself, a vast undulating expanse of dunes, indescribably graceful in their smooth crescentic curves, and strangely beautiful in tint and shading during the cool sunrise hours when the long shadows bring out every slightest hollow or ripple.

As the midsummer sun rises higher the landscape flattens and assumes a garish tint of yellowish gray, inexpressibly wearisome. Strange mirages torment the vision, but never are really deceitful—perchance a group of tents beside a pool of sparkling blue water, or a string of camels pacing slowly along above the horizon in the lower portion of the sky with heads to earth and feet to the unsubstantial floor of heaven.

"By Allah!" remarked the guide on the first day of our journey, "I wish I had brought a thicker robe. I had no idea it would be so hot. The sun beats right through this thin thing, and only the grace of Allah keeps me from being burned to a cinder."

During the heat of the day we rested for two or three hours; that is, we lay down on the burning sand in the shade of a bit of cloth or of our horses—thin, patient animals—and wrote up notes, the bane of the explorer's life, or tried to sleep and forget the heat. The end of the noon siesta was always the worst part of the day. We fairly staggered when we rose to mount our horses; and the still, suffocating heat made us clutch at the saddles to keep from swaying and falling as the dispirited creatures plodded heavily on. Soon, however, a little breeze arose regularly, the horses began to step more lightly, the shadows lengthened, and the world grew interesting.

By sunset we had reached a group of tents, a well, some tamarisk bushes, and flocks of bleating sheep, with here and there a camel from whose gaunt leather sides a few handfuls of last winter's coat of hair still clung. Friendly Turkomans took our horses and gave us cool drafts of the acrid sour milk, which all men love in the desert. In the cool of the evening we sat and talked with our hosts while waiting for dinner of curdled milk, coarse wheaten bread, and the flesh of a young lamb pulled to pieces with the fingers. When conversation at length gave place to idle reverie we went to sleep in the open air, regretting the pleasant weariness which made it impossible to remain awake in order to watch the surpassing beauty of the flawless sky and feel the caress of the gentle breeze of the desert.

The purpose of our ride into the desert was the examination of numerous great mounds from 30 to 80 feet high and from 100 to 600 feet in diameter, which are located outside the oasis of Merv. Here in ancient days, when the water supply was greater than it now is, the chief men of the land appear to have lived, raised above the heat of the plain and protected by moats and walls, while around them dwelt the humble peasants whose mud houses have now crumbled into scarcely perceptible heaps covered with countless potsherds. Elsewhere whole villages seem to have been built upon mounds, as they are today in eastern Persia in places of especial danger.

The Turkomans were puzzled when they saw a stranger riding from ruin to ruin, writing, photographing, measuring. "Have you heard what the stranger is doing?" they said to one another, according to the report of the guide. "You know he comes from the west, so he says, from across a lake bigger than the desert. Now these old mounds were built long ago by the Giants whom our ancestors, blessed of Allah, drove far away into the western mountains. There some of the infidels still live. The Americans are infidels. It must be that the Giants are their ancestors, and this man has come here to see where his ancestors lived."

Another matter which puzzled the Turkomans was the fact that I wrote a great deal on horseback. The guide told of their speculations. "It must be," he reported them as saying, "that this is a very religious man. He knows the Koran, or his holy book, whatever it may be, by heart, and as he rides along he writes it down for pleasure."...

One day in April a spirit of unrest appeared among our Turkoman workmen, for a whisper went abroad that this was to be a year of grasshoppers. The rumor was only too true, for before many days the green grass and the fields of tender wheat nearest the mountains were full of round, dark spots no bigger than a dollar, and composed of almost microscopic living creatures.

Day by day the spots grew larger, like the spreading of a plague, at first a foot in diameter, then three feet, and soon ten. Little by little, too, the tiny swarming creatures became visible as individuals—genuine grasshoppers, minute, but appallingly voracious. Here and there a Turkoman could be seen with a spade attempting to cover the plague-spots with earth, but in general the grasshoppers were left unmolested.

The faces of the Turkomans grew graver day by day as the creatures increased in size, and the men stuck to their work of digging more faithfully than before, seeming to feel that they must earn as much as possible to support their families in the hard days to come. There was no

A caravansary on the Persian side of the Afghan frontier, typical of innumerable such establishments once found across Central Asia.

complaint, no cursing; they seemed to look upon the myriad-mouthed horde of grasshoppers as an affliction sent by Allah, and not to be opposed by ordinary human means.

At length there came a day when the grasshoppers, now nearly half an inch in length, began to move more widely, and broad patches of sere brown stubble could be seen where they had devastated parts of the wheat fields.

About the same time a new and most welcome factor entered into the situation; rose starlings, northward bound on their annual migration, appeared upon the scene one morning. A pleasant light came into the faces of the Turkomans as they pointed to the great flocks of rosy-breasted, black-winged birds which circled over the plain in troops like blackbirds in America during the fall of the year. They ate voraciously; and thousands, nay, millions of the pestiferous insects were devoured in a single day.

On the following morning the number of starlings had increased, and the third day the swarms of birds almost darkened the sky when, in their frequent flittings, a flock passed overhead. That day the headman of the village asked us for contributions to a fund for getting rid of the grasshoppers.

"These starlings," said he, "are the children of a sacred spring among the Persian mountains two days' journey to the south of here. Wherever the water is, there the birds gather. Allah, the Merciful, has sent many birds to us, but they are not enough. We must do something to get more of them. There is just one way to do it. If we can get some of the water and bring it here, the birds will follow it. So today I am collecting money. Tomorrow, by the grace of Allah, I will send Verdi, the Mullah, our most holy man, to get the water. In his hand he must carry a good present, for the water is of no use unless it is taken from the spring and blessed by the holy sheikhs who guard it from pollution."

Three days later the headman was radiant. "See," said he, "how thick the birds are," and truly they were circling over the wheat fields in extraordinary numbers. "Last night our messenger reached the spring, and already the birds have begun to come. Today he will stay there; then it will take him two days to get back, bringing the vessel of water. Wait till the fourth day from now, the morning after he arrives, and see the multitude of birds."

On the third morning the headman looked old and weary, and had scarcely a word of greeting. The birds were gone; not a solitary starling was to be seen. In the night, silently, swiftly, as they had come, so they went, flying northward according to their wont, in response to the changing seasons. No thought of migrations came to the Turkomans. One thing alone they knew—the birds had gone, the grasshoppers remained, and the crops were doomed to utter ruin. Perhaps a little of the unripe grain could be saved for fodder, but nothing could be salvaged for food for themselves and their children.

Some one had blundered; perhaps some impious deed had been committed; therefore Allah had refused the further aid of his sacred birds. There was no further talk of a joyful procession to meet the Mullah far from the village and bringing the jar of sacred water home in triumph. The holy man stole into the village dejected and unnoticed, while the villagers thought only of their ruined crops and their families, which would soon be hungry.

The days that followed were like a nightmare. The insects were now full grown, and on a day they all began to move. Northeastward they went toward the desert—slowly, very slowly, but steadily, hopping, hopping, rarely pausing, never turning to one side. A low rattle filled the air like the steady falling of fine sleet, and everywhere there was a faint, sickening odor. It was impossible to walk without stepping on the creatures.

On the morning when the grasshoppers began to move the writer was at work in a round native tent of felt, with the top, perhaps 30 inches in diameter, open to admit light and air. When the grasshoppers reached the tent not one of them turned aside. Straight up the wall they crawled, and straight across the top until they came to the opening. There they paused a few minutes and then jumped blindly.

One after another they landed on the table, which was necessarily placed under the opening for light. Tap, tap, tap, they fell at intervals of a few seconds until it soon became impossible to work. When they righted themselves after falling to the floor, they always turned in the original direction, hopping across the floor, climbed the wall and the inside of the roof of the tent until they reached the opening at the apex, and were able to continue their interrupted journey.

Near our tents flowed a brook about three feet wide, which was used for irrigation. When the grasshoppers reached it they paused a moment, and then, urged by the crowds coming up from behind, jumped into the water and struggled for the other bank. The majority reached it after being carried down a few hundred feet. On the bank they rested in swarms until their wings were dry, and then hopped steadily on.

Many of the weaker insects, however, never got across the stream alive. They were carried down to the point where the brook was distributed over the fields, and there were deposited in great heaps, which soon began to emit a most noisome odor.

The coming of the grasshoppers had a disastrous effect upon our work of excavation. The insects jumped into the diggings in hordes, falling over the perpendicular edges in a steady stream. Crossing the bottom of the excavations in their usual persistent manner, they tried again and again to climb the steep walls, only to grow weary before reaching the top, and so to fall back once more. Thus they piled up to a depth of a foot or two in every excavation.

At first we tried to have them shoveled out, but the accumulation of a single night could scarcely be removed in a day. As most of our work was finished, we merely shoveled earth into the pits to cover the loathsome, dying mass of insects. Once in the bottom of a deep, round well sunk in exploring the ruins, we found a large snake buried in a seething, squirming, ever-deepening mass of living death from which his writhing head alone protruded.

There was one excavation which we determined not to abandon at once. As quickly as possible, which was not till the end of the second day, we procured cheese-cloth and stretched it across the top of the

A Turkoman draws water from a well in the sandy deserts of present-day Turkmenistan, using leather buckets and a wooden bowl for the horse.

excavation. The grasshoppers crossed by legions, their shadows darkening the cloth, and the sound of their hopping was like the patter of heavy rain on a roof....

The Turkoman laborers were clad in baggy white cotton trousers of the common full Turkish type, worn without underclothes. To stand in such garments amid the grasshoppers and shovel them into buckets or bags while the creatures crawled everywhere must have been almost unendurable. Every few minutes the men stopped to remove the clinging insects from inside their clothes. Nevertheless not only did those who were at work keep on faithfully, but scores of others, seeing that the grasshoppers had consumed their sustenance for the year, pleaded piteously for an opportunity to earn something to support their wives and children.

The visitation came to an end at length, and the grasshoppers passed on into the desert. The land was left reaped—consumed, as it were, by fire. There was a strange stillness in the air, and though our tents were pitched in what had been the fruitful grain fields of an oasis, we seemed to be in the midst of the great desert.

In the winter of 1903-04 Huntington, hoping to study "certain geographic and geologic problems," struck out in the company of a young Russian official and headed south. In the ensuing weeks they journeyed along the entire western frontier of Afghanistan, at that time not only a forbidden country, closed to foreigners, but a forbidding one as well, judging from the fierce reputation of its inhabitants. Or so it seemed...

OUR FIRST INTIMATE CONTACT WITH AFGHANISTAN WAS AT THE FORT OF ZULFAGAR, in the northwest corner of the country, where Afghan territory touches Transcaspia on the north and Persia on the west. The Heri Rud River here forms the real boundary between Afghanistan and Persia, although the Afghans lay claim to a considerable area on the west bank. Among the barren Persian hills of white clay capped with a hard corniced layer of dark gravel, our caravan of horses and camels came winding down toward the tamarisk jungle which covers the flood-plain of the Heri Rud. Eastward on the other side of the river, undimmed by the clear December air, we saw a mud fort surrounded by flat-roofed mud houses at the foot of a fine cliff made up of many layers of horizontally bedded sandstone and shale.

At first the village appeared lifeless, but soon it became evident that our approach was noticed, for tiny figures, dwarfed by the deceptive distance, appeared on the higher roofs, and soon a string of white turbans and shining gun barrels could be seen bobbing riverward among the thick, dry tamarisk bushes.

When we emerged from the jungle on our bank of the river a group of soldiers stood opposite us across the broad, muddy stream, while one of their number, a heavy-featured man with well-oiled black hair and a sinister hairlip, was wading waist deep in the cold, swift current with his white nether garments of cotton flung over his shoulder. Coming ashore some distance below us, he clothed himself and forced his way through the bushes, breathing heavily from fear rather than exertion.

"Go away; you can't come here. This is Afghanistan," was his short and peremptory greeting. Our little Turkoman interpreter, Kurban of Serakhs, refused to hear what more he had to say, and sent him unwillingly back to call his chief, with whom alone, according to Oriental ideas, it was fit that foreigners should parley. There was much running to and fro on the other side, with the result that at length a portly man in voluminous white cotton trousers, a huge white turban, and a dark military cloak appeared on the Afghan bank.

"What do you want? What right have you to come here?" he shouted across the broad river in reply to Kurban's flattering inquiry as to his health and happiness.

"Most noble and worthy captain," answered Kurban, with Eastern exaggeration, "my masters are a renowned Russian general, most rich and valiant, and highly in favor with the great Tsar, and a learned American 'Khoja,' who knows all books and can read anything that was ever written. They intend to travel across Afghanistan, and therefore bespeak your hospitality."

"Send them away; send them away. They can't come here," was the captain's quick answer, but, bethinking himself, he added: "Have the most honorable travelers had a comfortable journey? Most gladly would I receive them, but I am a mere captain. If I let them so much as set foot on this side of the river, my king, the great Amir at Kabul, would cut my head off."

Persuasion was useless; the captain would neither permit us to cross nor accept our invitations to come over into Persia and dine with us. He seemed to stand in thorough terror of the Amir's anger.

We might have crossed without permission, but that would probably have necessitated fighting; for during the next two days, as we marched southward, armed soldiers appeared whenever the windings of the road brought us within sight of the river which forms the boundary for some fifty miles.

A few days later we made another attempt to enter Afghanistan, not with the intention of actually going far into the country, but because my Russian companion was extremely eager to learn something as to the defenses of Kafir Kala, a famous fort supposed to be the strongest on the western frontier of Afghanistan. Sending the camels safely into Persian territory, we started for Kafir Kala one glorious December day—the Russian official and his Turkoman soldier, the writer and his Russian servant, and our Turkoman interpreter—five men, well armed and mounted on good horses.

Till noon we rode at a steady jog-trot through an uninhabited desert studded with low, dry bushes. Only twice did travelers appear in the narrow path, and they seemed sadly frightened. We began to think we had lost the road. Then a village came into view across the plain among the tamarisk bushes. Could that treeless group of low, gray walls and flat-roofed mud houses be Kafir Kala? Perhaps those turbaned men running together in the distance were soldiers. Something like gun barrels glistened over their shoulders. Riding nearer we saw that the village was evidently not a fort; but the way in which the villagers gathered in the road to intercept us looked ominous, even though the weapons over their shoulders were only spades for the irrigating. As we turned away from their almost violent questions, a handsomely dressed young chief and two soldiers galloped up with a great show of guns, and we stopped perforce to parley in the middle of the village.

"This is Afghan territory. You are foreigners, and you must go back where you came from," began the chief.

"We understand all that," was the answer, "but we are going to call on the commandant at Kafir Kala. Where's the road?"

"There," pointing in the right direction, "but I won't let you go."

"Thank you. Who is this young man?" we asked, ignoring him and turning to the bystanders.

"Hakim Khan, Hakim Khan, the chief of Kuzzil Islam," came from a dozen voices. We understood now how he had happened to arrive. The old men whom we had met by the river an hour or two before had said that they came from Kuzzil Islam. Evidently they had turned back and given the alarm.

A hot discussion began at once between our men and the Afghans as to whether we should go back or keep on. We cut it short by turning our horses' heads toward the fort. That angered Hakim Khan. He said something sharp and short; the crowd surged forward, and half a dozen hands seized our bridles. Involuntarily we pulled out our pistols, and the crowd fell back in such haste that we could not help laughing to see them stumble over one another. That cleared the air, for the Afghans laughed, too, and we all grew friendly. We flattered the Khan by asking about the many villages which he owned and by expressing wonder at the extent of his travels to Cabul and Kandahar, and at his intimacy with the Amir.

"How much you have seen for so young a man," I said, and added the common Oriental question, "How old are you?"

"Fifteen years," was the absurd answer.

"I am a hundred," I rejoined.

He saw the point, and said hesitatingly: "Well, perhaps I am something over twenty. My age is written in a book, but the book is lost and it's a long time since I've seen it."

In spite of Hakim Khan's protestations, we at length set forward, accompanied by the chief and his two soldiers. When the fort came into sight a mile away we yielded so far as to let him send a man to announce our approach.

"Tell the commandant," we said, "that we have ridden far and are tired. We can talk business better if he has tea ready on our arrival."

The soldier dug his heels into his horse's flanks, the beast jumped, and the rider rolled ignominiously to the ground. His awkward way of mounting and the violent flapping of his legs as he once more got under way confirmed our impression that he was no cavalryman, and that if it came to shooting on horseback he would be more dangerous to his friends than to us. Nevertheless it was an anxious time as we watched him galloping wildly off. At length he reached the castle far away across the plain, and little black dots began to come out on the top of the crumbling old pile to look and disappear. Would we be received with tea and peace, or with soldiers and imprisonment? When finally we reached our destination, Hakim Khan led us up past the ruins of an older fort to the main entrance of the once stately castle, a handsome arch now falling to ruins.

In the doorway stood the commandant, a genuine old martinet, in an ancient British uniform of blue and gilt. His scraggly beard had been dyed some months before, according to the Persian fashion, but now had grown so much that a rim of newly grown gray hair intervened between his dark suntanned face and the bright red fringe of older hair, giving him a strangely simian aspect. An armed soldier stood on either side of the chief, while unarmed men lounged here and there. They might have had guns concealed under their long woolen cloaks, but there was no sign of armament except the two men beside the commandant, and a stack of four old-fashioned rifles to the right of the doorway. Through the door we caught a glimpse of tumble-down buildings surrounding a courtyard in the midst of which a single horse was conspicuously tied. To the left of the arch we gladly noticed an adobe platform spread with rugs, which suggested tea and a peaceful reception.

We were not left long in doubt, for the commandant sourly motioned to us to take places on the rugs with himself and Hakim Khan, while thirty or more soldiers ranged themselves cross-legged or asquat in a circle roundabout, and it became clear that they had no guns. At first one of the two armed soldiers stood respectfully opposite the chief, but soon sat down, while his comrade, who was supposed to be pacing before the gateway, often forgot his unaccustomed duty and stopped to listen. We endeavored to ascertain the Afghan attitude as to a certain disputed piece of territory which we really needed to cross for scientific purposes, but the only result was that an old private in the outside circle often took the words out of his superior's mouth, and the Russian official and the commandant kept contradicting one another in the "katydid" fashion of "It is"…"It isn't."

By the time tea arrived it became evident that the Afghans were much more afraid of us than we of them. Kafir Kala, their boasted stronghold, was plainly defenseless. One can imagine the scene on the arrival of Hakim Khan's expert horsemen. The commandant hears the message in consternation and starts away to put on his faded uniform, but pauses to order tea and to direct that the six rifles be brought out. The four old-fashioned ones are to be stacked by the door; the two modern ones are to be carried by the soldiers whose nondescript garments most resemble uniforms. One of the two well-dressed men is to accompany his chief, the other to play sentinel. While this is being arranged with the advice and consent of the whole garrison, the women go up on the roof to see what they can of the attacking army, and the small boys run to and fro and report progress.

When we bade the Afghans a friendly adieu after an hour's talk and some photography, we were put in charge of an escort, which consisted of a single ragged soldier, who accompanied us around the corner to point out the way back to Persia. Three months later, on our return from Seyistan by another route, we heard the sequel to our raid on Kafir Kala. The representative of the Persian foreign office at Birjand asked if it were true that Russia and Afghanistan were at war. He had heard, so he said, that Russia had sent a party of Cossacks to attack an Afghan fort, and many men had been killed in a bloody fight.

At Turbat the Russian consul, whose guests we were, had received a report that a Russian officer and his companion had been arrested and imprisoned by the Afghans. He at once sent one of his secret agents to Afghanistan to investigate the matter. From this man's report it appears that when news of our visit to Kafir Kala reached the authorities at Herat, the chief town of western Afghanistan, they summoned the commandant to give an account of himself. His inability to arrest us was clearly due to the fact that some higher official had squandered the money intended for the equipment of the fort. Some one, however, must be punished. The commandant was accordingly removed from office, publicly whipped, and sent to the smallest available post. A new man was sent to Kafir Kala, and with him a hundred well-armed cavalry, so it was said.…

WITH AN EXILE IN ARCTIC SIBERIA
December 1924

VLADIMIR ZENZINOV (1880–1953)

EXILE MAY BE CHOSEN, OR IT MAY BE IMPOSED. IN TSARIST RUSSIA it was imposed all too frequently, not only on declared revolutionaries but also on a wide range of ordinary citizens. Anyone—man, woman, doctor, teacher, student, musician—even suspected of liberal sympathies might be arrested and, without benefit of trial, sent to remote Siberia. Not to a labor camp—the Gulag being a later Soviet development—rather, a person "exiled by administrative process" was often sent to some primitive settlement deep in the forest and simply left there for a term of five years. Escape was an option, of course, but vast stretches of wilderness made its success uncertain. Many who attempted escape were forced to become brigands or were murdered by locals. Most exiles simply tried to endure. Books and letters were permitted, but the isolation was psychologically devastating. Some chose the bottle; others suicide. Only a few, here and there, tried to make something of it, losing themselves in ethnographic and natural history studies.

One such was Vladimir Maximovich Zenzinov. Intellectual and idealistic, he grew up in a wealthy Moscow home and studied in Germany, where he fell in with émigré circles and joined the Socialist Revolutionary party. Back in Moscow, he was swept up in the round of arrests that followed the abortive 1905 revolution and exiled to Archangel, where he escaped the day he arrived. Arrested again soon thereafter, he was exiled to Siberia's far Yakutsk district, a dreaded place reserved for repeat offenders. He escaped again, eventually turning up in St. Petersburg, where he resumed "political activities."

Duly apprehended, he was exiled yet once more. In December 1912, at the age of 32, he began the long journey to Russkoe Ustye, a place in extreme northeastern Yakutsk, where the Indigirka River enters the Arctic Ocean—a place, Zenzinov said, "forgotten by God and man." It would be the strangest interlude of his eventful life.

TO CONVEY AN IDEA OF THE REMOTENESS OF THIS PLACE FROM THE rest of the world, I must go into some detail. The distance from Irkutsk, the Siberian metropolis on the Trans-Siberian Railway, to the city of Yakutsk is reckoned at about 2,000 miles. Communication between these points is maintained part of the way in summer by steamship on the Lena, and in winter by horses. The journey requires from 25 to 30 days, and in winter one must travel on horses day and night.

About the same distance must be covered from Yakutsk to Russkoe Ustye, except that communication on this stretch is far more difficult. Travel is possible here only in winter, when all the rivers, marshes, and innumerable lakes of this region freeze. In spring, summer, and autumn this part of the country is entirely cut off from the rest of the world by countless impassable swamps.

I was sent from Yakutsk under the guard of a specially selected Cossack, whose business it was to see that I did not escape again. We started at the beginning of December, 1912. After traveling only 130 miles we exchanged our horses for reindeer. These in turn were exchanged for fresh animals from time to time at various nomad camps.

Our road lay through the encampments of Yakuts, Tungus, and Yukaghirs, for there are no Russian settlements in this region. We reached the Indigirka River about the middle of February, and this was considered rapid progress. Here we were no longer able to use reindeer, and the rest of the trip had to be made by dog-sledge, a distance of more than 60 miles.

Thus the entire distance of 4,000 miles was covered, with the aid of horses, reindeer, and dogs, in about two and a half months....

We traveled north through the still primeval forests (the *taiga*), such as are found only in Siberia. We passed through deep ravines, winding channels, snow-filled beds of rivers, large and small, and crossed tall, rocky, forest-clad mountains. At night we would sometimes stop at a nomad tent or in some unoccupied hut constructed especially for travelers. These latter had always to be put in order before they were fit for human habitation.

We traveled during the coldest part of the year. The mercury never rose above 20° below zero (centigrade), and most of the time it hovered around −50°, and once, at Verkhoyansk, which is supposed to be the coldest spot on earth, I ran into a temperature of −71° C.

But far worse than these frosts and by far more dangerous were the snowstorms, which are considered seasonal in the northern Yakutsk Territory. I know of nothing more terrifying than these blizzards. Only the experience and familiarity of our Yakut and Tungus guides with local conditions brought us through alive.

One of these awful hurricanes of snow overtook us on New Year's Day, and I had to spend the night in the shelter of a wayside hut, buried in snow, roof and all. To the music of this howling Siberian blizzard I read, covered in a fur blanket and by the light of a flickering candle end, de Maupassant's "The Mediterranean Voyage," which made me feel very warm.

Descending from the high altitudes of a spur of the Yablonoi Mountains, we left behind the primeval Siberian taiga and entered the Arctic tundra. The farther north we went the nearer we approached the open sea. The vegetation grew ever more scant. At first there were tall bushes of willow, but gradually they became lower and lower, finally disappearing entirely. All about was a limitless snowy expanse, with nothing on which the eye could rest.

Precisely in such a strip of Arctic tundra is situated the settlement of Russkoe Ustye. Throughout the whole course of the Indigirka River, probably not less than 950 miles in length, Russkoe Ustye is considered the largest settlement. But it consisted of six dwelling houses only. The Russian word *dom* (house) has here become *dym*, which means smoke. And this metamorphosis is perfectly justified, for in this land of polar frost and blizzards, a house without fire, or "smoke," is not considered a house.

The population of this settlement numbered 22 souls. My arrival made it 23. All the colonies on the Indigirka River, scattered along its course in settlements of from two to four cottages each, do not comprise more than 400 persons....

Here the nearest points of "civilization" are Ust-Yansk, a village of about 30 dwellings, not less than 300 miles in an airline to the west, and, in the east, Nizhne Kolmysk, with 25 houses, about the same distance away. None of the inhabitants of Russkoe Ustye had ever gone beyond these two points, nor had any ever been to Yakutsk. Names like St. Petersburg and Moscow sounded to them like fairy tales. It is, therefore, not surprising that the real inhabitants of Russkoe Ustye are not very much above the state of primitive savagery. There is not a single literate person among the settlers along the Indigirka. I was the only civilized person to stray into this peculiar region.

Of postal communication there was, of course, not even a trace. Answers to official correspondence could be obtained from Yakutsk after one and a half years, at the earliest, and this only by special messenger. I was able to receive mail from my home only twice a year, at the beginning and end of the winter. At these seasons we would be visited by traders from the south, who brought merchandise from Yakutsk to exchange for the furs of the local hunters and trappers; but not once did a letter from Moscow reach me earlier than after seven or eight months.

My arrival at Russkoe Ustye was a most extraordinary event. For some time I was visited not only by the natives, but by those of the neighboring settlements as well. They examined me very carefully, in complete silence, just as one scrutinizes some strange animal.

Much of what I had brought with me was seen here for the first time. Almost with a feeling of reverence did they touch my fine Winchester rifle, which I had been permitted to take along after some lengthy "diplomatic negotiations" with the Governor of Yakutsk. The natives themselves are armed mostly with bows and arrows and spears, with which they bravely face the polar bear. Only a few possessed very poor shotguns.

They did not understand the purpose of many articles, such as thermometers, large books, and a photographic camera, which I proceeded to unpack. Especially profound was the impression produced by a very ordinary kerosene lamp. I also managed to bring twenty pounds of oil.

The little boy of a neighbor happened to be present when I unpacked the lamp, and here is how he described the event:

"He took out," said he, breathless with excitement, "a bright shiny teapot and put a plate on top." It was an enameled metal lamp with a china shade.

In the evening word was passed from house to house: "He has lit it! He has lit it!" Then many called expressly to see the lamp, one curious fellow traveling with dogs for more than 50 miles. These people illuminate their houses either by logs in the fireplace or by smoky little night lamps burning blubber. Altogether, I, with my curious baggage, habits, and accomplishments, appeared to them a being out of Mars or the moon, rather than a common mortal.

For 20 rubles a year I rented a house from one of the citizens of Russkoe Ustye and established myself according to my tastes. My interior arrangements, the pictures and the calendar on the wall, dishes, samovar, and books aroused the keenest and most persistent curiosity throughout my stay....

Of course, I had to do everything by myself. With the aid of my Winchester and some nets, I had to obtain my food—reindeer, wild geese, fish. I had to do my own cooking, keep my cottage in repair, and gather firewood and ice (which takes the place of water) for the kitchen.

In a word, mine was precisely the life of Robinson Crusoe, the life of a hunter and fisher, cook, woodchopper, carpenter, and water- (i.e., ice-) carrier, tailor, shoemaker, etc. Therefore, when friends asked me if I was lonely during my exile, I could answer in all sincerity that I had no time to feel lonesome.

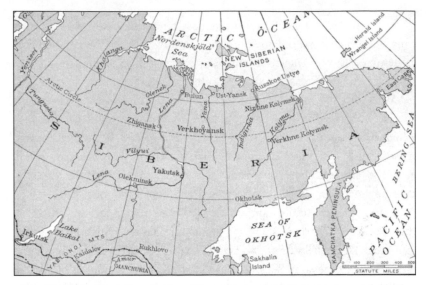

From Irkutsk (bottom left) on the Trans-Siberian Railroad, Vladimir Zenzinov, exiled by the tsar to the dreaded Yakutsk district of Siberia, traveled by horse, reindeer, and dogsled to the forlorn, snowbound huts of Russkoe Ustye (top center), on the shores of the Arctic Ocean.

In appearance, Russkoe Ustye was nothing but a miserable cluster of a few snow-swept wooden huts and barns. In every direction, as far as the eye could see, there was snow, snow, snow. Here and there was a clump of dwarfed shrubbery, buried under the snow in the winter. Amid the monotonous landscape of this white desert one distinguished with great difficulty the cottages, half hidden from sight by the snow piled up against them. The settlement was especially dreary during November and December, when the sun disappeared altogether from the horizon, and the dim twilight called "daylight" lasted only two or three hours. This was the most cheerless season of the year, and the sad howling of the dogs in the darkness seemed almost unbearable to one unaccustomed to it.

The winter nights were at times magnificent. In the black velvet of the sky the stars, which would make their appearance about 3 o'clock in the afternoon and twinkle until 11 o'clock in the morning, blazed like diamonds! Almost every night there was a most brilliant northern illumination, but I got so used to it that I seldom paid any attention to it.

Owing to the nearness of the sea, the cold here registers rarely lower than −50° C. But the winter blizzards are frequent and terrible. They stifle a person, cut off the breath, throw one of his feet with lashing volleys of snow, and make it impossible to see farther than five steps ahead. Woe to the traveler overtaken by such a storm on the road!

When encountering such a catastrophe, only one hope remains: to find shelter, together with the dogs, under the upturned sledge and wait for a change of weather.

In the course of a night these hurricanes are liable to bury one's cottage, roof and all, leveling the snow on the surface so that a person may drive across it without even suspecting that a human dwelling is underneath. My own house was on several occasions snowed under, once on the first of May, and I was forced, molelike, to dig a tunnel in order to get out.

During such a blizzard it is dangerous to go even ten steps from the house, and those who have to do it usually hold on to a rope.... The winter lasts eight long months, from September till May. The summers are warmer than one would expect, the temperature in the sun registering up to 30° C (86° F), but it is very rarely that a summer passes without a snowstorm. A summer "day," during which the sun never disappears below the horizon, lasts almost three months—from April 28 till July 20. The Indigirka thaws generally during the first days of June.

The flora is of the scantiest. In summer the ground thaws to a depth of only two feet; below that it is forever frozen. Throughout this region there are no forests. Not a single native of Russkoe Ustye has ever seen a tree growing; to them a common fir tree is as much a curiosity as a tropical palm tree to a Northern person. The shrubs of the willow extend 10 miles toward the sea and then come to an end (it is about 45 miles from Russkoe Ustye to the Arctic Ocean). There, even grass ceases to grow.

In summer, no matter where one turns, one can see nothing but swamps. In spring and summer the Indigirka brings on its currents from the south large numbers of fallen trees. These are eagerly picked off the banks by the natives, for this driftwood makes it possible for them to withstand the intense winter cold and they likewise build their dwellings of it....

Swamp birds in overwhelming numbers begin to arrive about the end of May—geese, cranes, ducks, gulls, and all kinds of snipes. This influx may be appreciated only by those who have seen it. Screeching, gabbling, and piping shrilly, dense swarms fill the air day and night. The white swans pass in orderly flocks; the geese fly in long chains; ducks glide past in disorderly throngs.

This tempestuous arrival, after the oppressive silence of winter, seems like a triumphant bacchanalia. Between sky and earth strives and quivers an overwhelming wave of life. Every little puddle, every tiny hummock, becomes a whole world pulsating with life. Each bird leaps, jumps, flutters its wings, pipes, and sings, according to whatever talent the Creator has given it.

Each is busy with his own, and, for him, very important and exclusive affairs, paying no attention to his neighbor. When some feathered pirate appears, groups rise into the air as one solid flock, only to return to the same place, which another covey has already managed to occupy. One flock replaces another, and it seems that the migrants feel crowded, even in this boundless vacuum.

It is hard to describe how, after the dreary silence of the winter, this noisy, palpitating stream of life stirs and disturbs the exile. Sleep and food seem bothersome details.

Early in the morning, the gabbling of the geese would drive me from bed, and, getting hold of my rifle, I would start across swamps and snow for the tundra. In the evening I would return, half-dead with fatigue, feet aching, and bones heavy as lead. Even my dreams were full of the cries of birds and the beating of wings....

Geese cast their feathers in summer—in this region, between the 8th and the 20th of July. They molt differently from other birds, losing almost all the feathers from their wings simultaneously. During the molting season, therefore, geese lose the power of flight and become helpless until they grow new feathers.

This fact is well known to the professional native hunters, who try to take advantage of their opportunity. During the molting season the birds collect in huge flocks, millions of them, near the sea and along the shore of the Arctic Ocean. The hunters, knowing where the geese gather, organize hunting parties in boats. These expeditions are frequently fraught with danger. Each man has to travel in a canoe and handle a two-bladed paddle. Only light canoes make it possible to cover long distances, as there is frequent need of carrying the boat from one swamp to another.

I succeeded in obtaining permission to participate in one of these expeditions. The natives were opposed to my going, assuring me that the trip would be too hard and perilous. In their opinion, I was certain to lose my life because of my inexperience....

The expedition really did prove to be full of hardships. We had to make our way down the Indigirka to the Arctic, cross a bay at least 15 miles wide, and finally drag our canoes for a very long time from swamp to swamp. The place where we were to hunt was at least 70 miles north of Russkoe Ustye.

The hunting, as well as the conditions under which we lived, were most

Tungus, nomadic reindeer herders of far northern Siberia, were among the aboriginal tribes, along with Yakuts and Chukchi, who lived near Russkoe Ustye.

arduous. We were in the midst of swamps and even had to sleep in swamps. But I never regretted these hardships, because of the opportunity to take part in an enterprise that even few members of regular polar expeditions have had occasion to witness.

The geese at this place were simply overwhelming in numbers. From afar, the flocks on the water appeared like huge islands. Our hunting party of 15 men bagged not less than 4,500 birds.

A flock of geese is surrounded by the hunters in the canoes, while on the shore the nets are spread like traps, open toward the water. The geese are slowly driven toward the nets and finally chased inside. After the entire flock has entered the nets are drawn tight, and then the killing begins. This is done by grasping the birds below the head, whirling them in the air, and thus breaking the neck, which causes instant death. After a few minutes of this work, a mountain of dead geese begins to pile up alongside the nets.

The entire booty is equally divided among members of this expedition. The geese are buried on the spot in the ground, or, more properly speaking, in the mud, and left to rot for several weeks, until frost sets in. This food is used primarily for the dogs, as it is already well rotted by the time it is dug up. Still, the hunters themselves by no means disdain it; to the native appetite there is nothing very objectionable in food that is tainted.

I, too, was offered my share of the common haul, but refused it, merely stipulating my right to ten live birds. To these I tied letters, prepared beforehand, in several languages, and addressed to my relatives in Moscow. I hoped in this way to be able to send word about myself, when the geese would return to warm regions and would, perhaps, fall into the hands of some hunter. Unfortunately, as I found out afterward, none of my letters ever reached its destination....

That was an act of desperate longing. The blankness, the misery, the loneliness had oppressed even Zenzinov beyond endurance. After little more than a year at Rosskoe Ustye, he tried to escape. Somehow a tribesman got word to authorities, and the attempt fizzled. Zenzinov served the rest of his exile at a village on the lower Lena River, which was not so utterly removed from civilization.

Eventually returning to Moscow, Zenzinov published several small volumes on the ethnography and ornithology of Rosskoe Ustye. Then he was caught up in the turmoil of the Russian Revolution, being swept into power with Kerensky's Social Revolutionary Party, being swept back out with the fall of the same, surfacing here and there to fight the Bolsheviks, and narrowly avoiding execution. Instead he was exiled—yet once more—to China.

This time it was permanent. For the rest of his life he drifted—Paris, Berlin, Prague—contributing pieces to socialist journals before ending his days in New York City, scribbling away at his memoirs.

PART THREE:
The Middle East

PERSIAN CARAVAN SKETCHES
April 1921

HAROLD F. WESTON (1894–1972)

"INTENSITY CONSUMES ME," HAROLD WESTON ONCE WROTE—AND not intensity only but also a peculiarly original style marked every canvas this important modernist artist ever painted. Intensity also distinguished the idealism and organizational ability he displayed while helping Eleanor Roosevelt establish the United Nations Relief and Recovery Administration during World War II, and when laying the foundations for today's National Endowment for the Humanities.

Reared in a progressive Philadelphia home in which Booker T. Washington, William James, and John Dewey were household guests, Harold Weston had tousled hair, a jutting jaw, and thick glasses. He always clutched a cane, for polio had crippled his left leg. That infirmity kept him from joining Harvard classmates in the volunteer Ambulance Corps during World War I, to which young Americans flocked before the U.S. officially entered the conflict. It did not stop him, however, from enlisting with the YMCA, which operated canteens and organized amusements for soldiers overseas. Ending up with the British Army in Mesopotamia, he soon took charge of forward supply bases and ran the YMCA's Baghdad headquarters.

In the summer of 1919, Weston and a friend left Baghdad and journeyed across Persia, then much decayed since its glory days in the 17th century. Despite the British Army's presence, brigands controlled large sections of the country, and the means of travel—camels, mules, or the unsprung hay wagons of the government post—had not changed for hundreds of years. Nor had the tall black hats and white slippers worn by the Persians, nor the sound of camel bells passing in the night, which nearly every traveler at the time remarked. As Weston, 25 years old, sketched and photographed and jotted notes, he may not have known that he was seeing the last of old Persia. Soon Reza Khan would become shah, impose modernization, and build the foundations of modern Iran. Weston's photographs attracted the attention of NATIONAL GEOGRAPHIC. The word pictures he penned for the accompanying article are as vividly intense as his sketches and paintings, bringing this long-vanished world momentarily back to life.

LET ME PRESENT A BRIEF SKETCH OF THE SETTING AS WE WERE waiting to cross the frontier: Tents pure white against the autumn-toned uplands; for, although it was May, the coarse grass, thistles, and wild

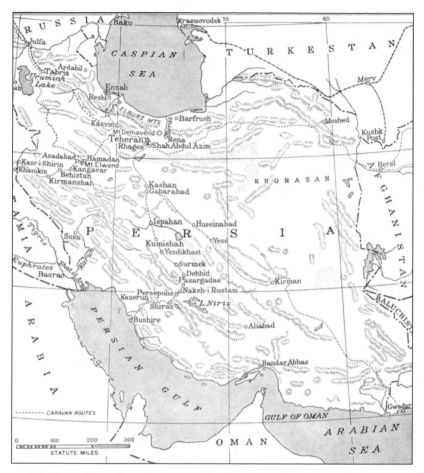

*The high, windswept, desert plateau, seamed with snowcapped mountains, is known today
as Iran but was for centuries called Persia. After the First World War, when
Harold Weston traveled there, large parts of the country were crossed only by caravan trails.*

flowers that carpet these desert hills in the spring had already been
scorched by the sun. Behind, the dark purple ranges that border the
Persian plateau were still spotted with silver streaks of snow.

Black lines were slowly moving—supply carts and cavalry of the British
forces marching up to cross Persia to the Caspian. Squads of khaki-clad
figures on the parade ground near the camp, balanced on the other side by
the dark-brown forms of camels, which were being loaded with bales of
fodder to the accompaniment of an intermittent series of pathetic, enraged,
impassioned roars and raucous gurgles from the protesting beasts.

Half a mile below lay the little mud-built town of Khanikin, half
Arab, half Persian, brilliant in the sun against a dark fringe of date palms.

Along the dusty road between the high-walled gardens there came out of the town a straggling group of donkeys and blue-clad men, returning Persian pilgrims from the sacred cities of Kerbela and Nedjef or caravans of merchandise for the bazaars of Hamadan or Teheran, all with tinkling bells, jangling bells, and clouds of dust.

At last our convoy of Ford cars was ready to leave, and, bumping and chugging, we wound along the white line of the new macadamized road toward the Persian hills.

The journey to Hamadan, some 300 miles, was by stages of twenty miles a day, accomplished in the early morning, before the heat of the day. The cars were driven by unskilled Indian mechanics, which fact added zest to the scenery of successive mountains and rolling valleys. On one day, out of thirteen cars (blessed Fords), one turned turtle, one burned up, one broke its steering gear on a steep pass, and one ran over a Kurd!...

[Having tansferred to a post-wagon] toward noon we arrived at a village of low, mud-built houses, clustering around a miniature mosque, with a sparkling blue-tiled dome. A thermometer would have registered well over a hundred in the shade; so with silent relief cramped legs crawled down from the top of the wagon the moment its creaking and lurching had ceased.

Inside the road-house (*menzil*) we found one large smoky room. A wide platform seat, covered with coarse, ragged rugs and lounging occupants, skirted the edge of the room. The "guests" were effectively indistinguishable from beggars, and our entry had roused most of these habitués from their noonday siesta—or was it a stupor caused by that drug which is the curse of Persia, for there was a smell of opium in the stagnant air.

The innkeeper, identified by a griminess surpassing that of the others and by the fraternal manner of his welcome, had started blowing up the charcoal in the invariable Russian samovar. The smoke curled unconcernedly up to the flat, blackened roof of poplar logs covered with matted branches and earth; it wantonly dissipated.

A pilgrim—one could tell it from his blue hat, shaped like an auk's egg—was chatting in low guttural tones to a group by the doorway, probably telling the latest gossip (*gufti-gu*, the Persians call it) from the bazaars of Bagdad. Several were smoking a *kalian*, water-pipe. Each inhaled deeply a draught or two and the overworked mouthpiece, on the end of a coiling tube, was passed on, while the contented inhaler spat lustily on the earthen floor. Others were sipping tea from diminutive glasses with a loud guzzling noise. A filthy beggar-like chap, who, to judge by the badge on his felt hat, was a Persian gendarme, was drinking from the mouth of a teapot used as the dipper from the kerosene canister in which the daily water supply was kept. I have heard that a Persian's idea of a teapot is that it is a vessel the spout of which is especially adapted to drink from.

Our lunch of tea, unleavened, pebble-baked bread, a thick buttermilk replete with traces of its goatherd origin, raw cucumbers, and a melon, had been placed on the platform beside us. The hot sunlight was streaming through the one doorway and the few green trees outside looked particularly attractive. I said a prayer with each mouthful and sighed, "Well, this is Persia...."

One of the magical charms of Persia is that it continually reveals glorious unexpected contrasts: the cool green of a garden breaking the barren iridescent plain; the sight of a majestic snow peak when you are plodding through dust and sand at 110°F in the shade; brilliantly chiseled bas-reliefs on an abandoned mountain side; the shimmering, opalescent dome of a mosque soaring above a drab city of crumbling mud-built houses.

I had not suspected that the lumbering post-wagon would be the means of first revealing to us the subtle wonders of nights of caravan, moving on the desert Persian plateau as on a silent, limitless sea, under the stars—oh, stars of Persia! nowhere else are there such stars!

The dawn disclosed a huge caravan coming up the long, undulating slope of the plateau out of the night. The vari-toned bells of the camels dinging and donging, first sounded like distant bugle calls or lurking snatches of some forgotten orchestral rhapsody brought to us by the breeze. The high notes blended in a constant ripple of lucid tones, while the plodding "thung, thung" of the low, rich-toned bells of the leader could be heard, fainter but still distinct, even after the last of the caravan had disappeared over the brow of the hill.

Slowly they went by, some 500 camels in all, with Afghan and Baluchi drivers loping along by their beasts or bobbing sleepily high up on a perilous nest among bales of merchandise. One thought of Vansittart's:

> Ding! dong.
> Fugitive throng.
> Out of the dark
> Into the night,

Silent and lonely,
Gone!—the bells only
Tell us a caravan once was in sight.

Suddenly the sun, a pale gold disk, broke the rim of the horizon and outlined the sharp conical pearl-gray peak of Mount Demavend just to the north of it and fully 120 miles away. Then I first fully realized the grandeur, the godliness, of its nineteen thousand feet of height. Half an hour later this vision was lost.

The sun rode high above the nearer barren ranges and the horizon was wrapt in the usual all-enveloping dust and heat haze rising from the desert *lut*, the desolate salt swamps beyond....

While walking out to photograph the turquoise-domed Shah Abbas Mosque, the morning after our arrival [in Isfahan, here called Ispahan], we were startled by the sound of a bugle. A crowd congested the narrow street. Soon a company of white fur-capped Persian police swung into view. In their center marched a tall, gaunt, black-bearded man with hands bound behind his back. It was one of the captured brigands being taken to the great central square to be hanged.

Seven men were hanged the day before, we were told, and nearly two hundred more were to be disposed of that way. They were leaders of the band that for ten years had terrorized the roads and villages around Ispahan. We had passed villages roofless and deserted that they had plundered. Hundreds of innocent peasants are said to have been killed. Countless wealth had been taken from caravans. Some 40,000 *tomans* (about $80,000) in specie, recently seized, had been recovered and the Persian authorities were trying to find out, by the aid of promises and tortures, the hiding place in the mountains where the bulk of the loot had been stored.

Nagar Aliche, the fourteen-year old son of one of the robber chieftains, was among the handful who knew where this treasure lay hidden. His deeds were more the talk of the bazaar than those of any of the older brigands. Popular rumor accredited him with over two hundred human killings by his own hand or rifle. When the Governor of Ispahan threatened to have him blown from the mouth of a cannon unless he told where the booty could be recovered, he is reported to have replied arrogantly: "I kill others every way. Watch them die fast, slow. Myself not yet killed. Like best to be blown from cannon. See quick what comes after."

The quickest way to see what comes next: Being blown to bits at the cannon's mouth was an execution reserved for especially notorious Persian bandits. The tall black hats and white slippers were once as characteristic of Persia as the music of camel bells.

There are other stories of this lad which confirm reports of his fearlessness. When a thousand or so British-trained and officered Persian soldiers had arrived from the south to help the local Bakhtiari [a Persian tribe], and the main gang of bandits had been rounded up, captured, or exterminated, a tiny band of leaders escaped through treachery to their own men. For ten days they were chased among the mountains.

Finally all but the boy, Aliche, and two followers were killed or captured. Four days later the three were cornered behind a garden wall. The two men were anxious to give in. "What's the use?" they said.

The youngster turned, gave them a scornful glance, shot them dead, killed three more of the attacking Bakhtiari with his last three cartridges, and then gave himself up.

When Aliche, led shackled before the Governor, was asked how many men, women, and children he had killed, he haughtily replied: "If I had imagined you were such a fool as to want to know, I would have stopped to count."...

We had letters to the principal chieftains along the route and were provided by them with road-guards to protect us from the attacks of stray bands of robbers. The trip from Ispahan to Shiraz took about three weeks, and every day brought new experiences. Space will allow me to relate only a few typical experiences, while the reader's imagination is given free scope to deck the rest of the way with more vivid incidents yet untold.

It was on the third night of travel, our mules being loaded and ready to leave by sunset. We walked ahead of our caravan, telling our road-guards to follow with the baggage.

We were crossing an uninteresting plain with parallel mountain ranges some five miles away on either side. The route was only distinguishable by dim white streaks, paths trodden by years of caravans. A few hours later the half moon sank. We were alone. Something seemed to have delayed our guards and caravan. We walked slowly on until about 2 a.m. when, all traces of a caravan track giving out, we realized we were lost.

We tried to find our way back and wandered about aimlessly among the strangely quiet hills for a time, until—dull at first, then sharper and sharper—came the pound of horses' feet across the distant plateau. We though we heard our road-guards out searching for us, and I was just about to fire my revolver to attract their attention, when I realized that shots would probably be the answer. I happened to have a pocket flashlight. I signaled with this. The pound of the hoofs stopped as we stumbled across a dried water-course toward them.

Suddenly there was a shout in Persian to halt. It was a chill moment. By the wavering light of my electric torch we could see the supposed guards standing with rifles lowered at us. We feared they were robber Bakhtiari, for they were the wildest-looking gang of ruffians I have ever seen.

We tried to explain who we were and the chieftains to whom we were going; that we were lost, but that our guards would surely be back any minute looking for us. Some of them apparently wanted to strip us and leave without further ceremony. Others seemed to have acquired a curious reverence for my flashlight, which I kept turning on and off, to their terror. They thought it would explode and blow them out into the distant gardens of eternity.

The fears of this group fortunately triumphed and we were set in the right direction, as they hastened off into the silence and safety of the night.

Toward dawn we met our road-guards frantically galloping across the plain, with our poor servant breathlessly running after them. There followed much gesticulation and attempted explanation, mixing in, as we always did, Arabic, Hindustani, or even English words where Persian failed. We borrowed their horses and rode on toward our destination, Kumishah.

We came to cultivated fields, where, even before the sun was up, here and there one could see puffs rising that floated off and vanished like the smoke from a tug down the harbor on a frosty morning. It was the dust from the grain tossed high in the light breeze by the winnowers. We drew nearer.

All at once my horse bounded, as one of our guards lowered his gun and took several shots at the peasants.

"What are you doing?" my companion shouted, horrified, forbidding the guard to reload.

"Must kill one those men. Insulted you," said the road-guard in Persian, and he made a determined effort to fire again.

"What do you mean?" my friend asked, seizing the guard's arm.

"Come to them early this day when you lost. Ask where are *firangi-sahibs* (foreigners). They say, 'Don't know. We thresh grain. What for firangi-sahibs come bother us in Persia?' Insulted you. We fire them. Dark, no kill. Come back. Kill one now."

He was dissuaded with great difficulty....

Three days later, after an exceptionally weary night of caravan, our eyes, accustomed to the unbroken sequence of rolling plateaus, were abruptly presented with a view of Yezdikhast. It is only by realizing this contrast that the picture of Yezdikhast can give one something of the thrill that we felt on coming upon it across the waterless, treeless, almost trackless, uplands of Persia.

Yezdikhast, which means in old Persian "God wills it," is the most strikingly situated town in all Persia. It has been compared to a petrified ship left stranded on one side of a deep river valley.

Approaching it from the plain, one sees only the tops of a few houses and the cracked dome of a single mosque; but on reaching the edge of the ravine, a quarter of a mile broad and fully 200 feet deep, formerly a river-bed and now covered with rich grain fields, one is unexpectedly confronted with the most remarkable picture of a city of the dead—a sheer rock cliff topped by half-ruined mud-and-stone-built houses piled four stories high on its narrow crest, projecting beams of broken wood balconies that thrust their arms against the sky like decaying gibbets, a single drawbridge that spans the deep branch between the town and the former river bank and affords the only possible means of entrance.

All forlorn, it stands baking in the hot sun. One expected to see vultures soaring above it and could not refrain from thinking of the time when a tyrannical shah years ago flung the best of its young men to death in the valley below....

My last night on the Persian Caravan Road will never be forgotten. It was at the caravanserai, then used as a British garrison fort, at the top of the pass at Kamarij. My cot had been placed on the roof. It was a hot night. I had fever and did not sleep.

From the courtyard below came the sound of the *tablas* and *dholkis* (drums) of the Indians. They sang, about thirty of them, an endlessly repeated chorus to an endless verse, taken up by various leaders at various pitches. When they had finally ceased and the moon had set, a dog, five dogs, ten dogs barked furiously in a near-by camp of nomads.

A night caravan passed, with much tinkling of bells and the usual gruff calls of the muleteers. Later, the stillness of the night was abruptly broken. The sentry at the corner tower had challenged and incidentally scared the life out of a Persian who passed too close with, judging by the sounds, three or four donkeys.

A breathless pause, a volley of unintelligible shouts from the Indian, and this lone quivering Persian stole off into the night. But then, his fear overcome, to show his truly Persian bravery, he burst forth into the characteristic long moaning warble of a Persian melody. There was something very sad and yet fascinating about that wailing refrain sung to the grayness of a desert gravel plain at night, with ghostlike mountain ranges, sharp irregular peaks, still catching the faint light of the moon, and with the stars—myriads of stars—overhead.

Contrast again and mystery. Silence and then barren night mothering at her bosom those weird notes of that intriguing Persian rhythm. It will always remain typical of the Persian Road for me, one of its greatest charms, that lonely Caravan Song fading into the night.

CROSSING ASIA MINOR
October 1924

MAJ. ROBERT W. IMBRIE (1883–1924)

GOOD TRAVELERS ARE OFTEN SHARP OBSERVERS; THEY'RE *often good storytellers, too. Robert Whitney Imbrie was both. His droll way of relating his tales borrowed something from Mark Twain and something from* The Adventures of Haji Baba, *that picaresque novel of the foibles and exasperations encountered by travelers in the East. Despite his facetious bent, Imbrie was widely considered, especially after his tragically early death, "an American gentleman—honorable, considerate, and brave."*

Born in Washington and schooled in admiralty law, Imbrie joined a 1911 expedition to the Congo to study chimpanzees, then volunteered for the American Ambulance Corps during World War I, ferrying the wounded from battlefields in France and the Balkans. Many young writers—e.e. cummings, Dashiell Hammett, John Dos Passos, Ernest Hemingway—did likewise, but Imbrie's 1918 book, Behind the Wheel of a War Ambulance, *remains the most vivid and humorous account.*

His talents, apparently, were not merely literary. After serving with the U.S. Army, he surfaced in Petrograd, the Russian Revolution swirling about him. After the United States recalled its ambassador, refusing to recognize the new Soviet state, Imbrie remained behind in a diplomatic netherworld, in charge of whatever American interests also remained in Russia.

In 1922–23 a similar mission brought 40-year-old Major Imbrie to Turkey. Having fought on Germany's side during the war, Turkey had ruptured its diplomatic relations with the U.S. Its defeated empire was dismantled by a harsh peace settlement. Imbrie went to Asia Minor—in most Allied eyes, still enemy territory, where nationalist forces were rallying to overturn that settlement. There 18 months, Imbrie made five journeys across the Turkish heartland. Whatever the nature of his mission, he mentioned not a word of it to readers of his NATIONAL GEOGRAPHIC *account, where he played the jocose storyteller, the modern Haji Baba regaling his audience with tales of travels in the East—a few of which, as follows, can go a long way.*

WE GATHERED OUR DUNNAGE, SADDLES AND PACKS, DROPPED OFF the steamer into a small boat bobbing about below, and went ashore at the little port of Mersina, on the northeastern littoral of the

Mediterranean at the southeastern corner of Asia Minor. It was August, 2 o'clock in the afternoon, and the heat and glare were intense. The heat was of that sticky variety, such as one finds in the Congo jungle; it seems to center one's thoughts on one idea to the exclusion of everything else—the idea of getting out of the place.

It takes a good deal to cause excitement in a country whose chief product for the last three thousand years has been war and whose by-products have been massacre, rapine, and pillage. However, we had been noticed, and presently a fine-faced old gentleman, with that gravity of manner which marks the Turk, came to greet us and invite us to his home. He was the *belederies*, or mayor. Although we were in a sweat, literally speaking, to get away, we knew enough of the Near East to realize that coffee and tobacco must precede any business.

And here let me sound a note of warning to any would-be traveler in Turkey. If your digestion and nerves will not stand almost continual coffee-drinking—the thick, black, syrupy coffee of the Orient—and endless cigarette smoking, venture not into the Near East. No business is ever transacted, no social or official call is complete, no meeting, however casual, is ever terminated without tobacco and coffee.

One must be prepared to drink at least one dozen and perhaps two dozen cups of coffee a day and consume many cigarettes if he is to get along on this trip. Of course, if one can smoke the *nargile*, or Turkish water pipe, so much the better, but if he can he is "a better man than I am." Twice have I essayed to master this quaint instrument, and on both occasions interest was not all I lost. It leaves a feeling as if one had been smitten with what the newspapers describe as "a dull, blunt instrument"...

It was characteristic of Turkey that, though the time of the arrival of our boat was known, the train did not wait, but went on its way a half hour before. The situation in nowise perturbed our host. He had a proverb to meet the occasion—the Turk always has. "To-morrow, *Effendi*," he said, "is also a day," and added that another train would then depart.

We were prepared to concede that tomorrow would, in all probability, be another day, but were prone to skepticism as to the train.

Here another characteristic of the Turk revealed itself—the attribute of courtesy and kindness toward the stranger. I have experienced this kindliness, without exception, from the humblest peasant to the head of the nation throughout some thousands of miles of travel and

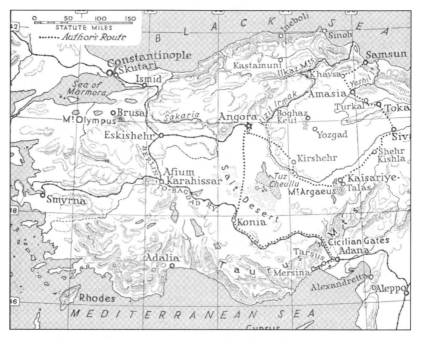

Major Imbrie wound his way across Asia Minor, the bulk of today's Turkey, from Mersina in the southeast to somnolent Angora—today the thriving capital of Ankara—then east and north to the Black Sea coast.

eighteen months' sojourn under the Star and the Crescent. In this instance it manifested itself in the offer by the owner of the only automobile in Mersina of the loan of his car for the journey to Adana ....

We now left the railroad and, with one pack animal for three people, struck out over the plateau for Angora, 150 miles almost due north. Fortunately, we had brought our own saddles, for we would have found it impossible to ride with comfort on the queer contraptions known as Turkish saddles.

On such a journey one goes armed on account of possible encounter with *cheeties* (brigands). Water bottles and colored goggles are essentials, and dread of discomfort must be banished. Neither can one afford to be squeamish as to what is eaten or where one sleeps.

To avoid attracting undue attention, we discarded occidental headgear and adopted the *kalpack*, which has become the distinctive headgear of nationalist Turkey, having supplanted the fez. It has been made familiar to the world, through those shown in the portraits of Mustapha Kemal Pasha, whose collection is said to number fifty. The only redeeming quality of the kalpack is picturesqueness. In a country of searing suns and torrential rains it is wholly impractical. It is a high, flaring, brimless cone, made from the wool of the unborn Bokhara lamb, hugs the forehead, and is heavy and hot. Its color may be gray, jet black, or brown; its cost may be anywhere from the equivalent in American money of $7 to $160. As in Mexico, so in Turkey, a man's position may be judged by the quality of his headgear.

I might remark, in passing, that the Turk never removes his head covering, except, possibly, when he retires at night. At dinner, when calling, at all ceremonies or functions, the kalpack remains seated, so to speak. In saluting, the Turk does not remove his covering; he bends low, touches the hem of his garment, his heart, and his kalpack, the idea being he gives you the earth, his heart, and his head....

Shortly after leaving the lake, skirting some barren hills, we encountered our first caravan of camels. Tied head to tail and led by a diminutive burro, they grunted along. With mincing step and a supercilious sneer on their countenances, they maintained such a superior air of satisfied arrogance as to goad the beholder almost to frenzy. In my experiences, the camel is the meanest animal known to Nature. Every one that I have known has had a disposition that would curdle cream at 40 rods. If Noah had two of these beasts on the Ark, I'll wager he was glad to disembark, and if Job had 3,000 of them, as we are told, he is entitled to all our sympathy.

For several days we rode across the haggard face of the landscape, and at last, late one afternoon, we topped a rise, and there below us lay Angora [Ankara]. We were approaching from the west and the last rays of the setting sun painted the city in a rose glow. Its minarets, its battlements, its walls and towers stood out much as they must have done when the Crusaders rode against them, for the swing of the pendulum through the arch of centuries has brought little change to Angora.

Few cities can boast of more history. There is a record of a battle fought here three hundred years before the birth of Christ. To-day, in the walls of its citadel, themselves seven centuries old, may be seen many blocks, fragments of Roman temples, which were ruins before the construction of these walls was begun.

From a distance Angora is most imposing. Crowning a hill, the old town is crowded within a series of wall-connected towers and the houses sprawl in slipshod fashion down the hill to the swampy plain

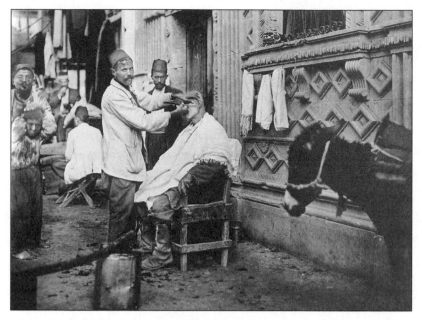

An open-air barbershop in Tarsus, where Alexander the Great walked and St. Paul was born.
The fez, prescribed headgear of male Turks under the Ottoman Empire,
was banned a few years later by Kemal Ataturk, father of modern Turkey.

below. But, as in most of the towns in the Near East, the beauty of distance is lost in the squalor of proximity....

A khan, be it known, is the oriental idea of an inn, and a very poor idea it is. Usually, almost invariably, it takes the form of a mud-wall inclosed courtyard, one side of which is formed by a two-story structure. The lower story is a stable; the upper story is occupied by the more opulent—and more unfortunate—of the khan's guests, for many there are who camp in the open courtyard.

In a khan the guest must bring everything—food, bedding, drink. The management furnishes nothing but shelter—provided the roof doesn't leak—and bugs. These latter are always in stock.

I am now able to recall with amusement my first experience with the khan. I was new to Turkey, new and full of illusions. We were riding in from Ineboli, on the Black Sea coast, heading toward the Ilkaz Mountains. At noon my dragoman said, "To-night, *Bey Effendi*, we shall stop at the finest khan in Anatolia. It is so known throughout Asia Minor."

I was somewhat perturbed. I was in riding clothes, dust-covered and disheveled, with a gun slanted across me. I pictured myself walking into a modern hotel in this condition and the disdain with which I would be regarded by the management. I made up my mind that, provided I should be admitted, I would have dinner in my room and not intrude myself into the public halls.

Toward evening we came to a large log building. We were near the mountains and timber was plentiful. A couple of water buffalo stuck their heads out of a lower window and inspected us with interest. A flock of sheep was just passing into the courtyard. Some fowls were ascending a slanting gangway preparatory to retiring for the night. Out in front an old Turk was engaged in washing his feet.

"Some barn!" I thought.

"This, sir," said my dragoman, with an air of pride, "is it."

"And what my *it* be?" I queried.

"Why, the khan, sir, the best one in Asia Minor!"

And much subsequent travel in Anatolia has confirmed me in indorsing his statement....

At Shehr Kishla, the khanji, a genial old fellow, brought us some delicious melons and, as we bathed in them, he entertained us with stories of cheeties and elaborated on the dangers of the way ahead. It would be better, he said, to remain at his khan, where we would be as secure as under our own vine and fig tree, until our party was augmented by other travelers.

We were always hearing those tales of cheeties, and though on one occasion the party just ahead of us and the party following were wiped out to a man, through five traverses of Asia Minor our outfit never suffered molestation. We felt, therefore, that the old khanji's solicitude for our welfare was born of his desire that we further patronize his khan rather than of real anxiety as to our safety on the road. So we cast off again.

We rode through a land forlorn, between bare hills, and with never a tree in sight. By nightfall we reached a Turkish village, were assigned the guest house, and assured that we "brought joy." It was a fortunate thing in some of these villages that we had brought something besides joy, for the accommodations were not elaborate. However, friendly hospitality makes up for much....

The Sivas of to-day, a town of 65,000, is wholly Turkish and Kurdish, and therefore picturesque. Its streets swarm with the life of the East. There is an endless amount of going and coming, though no man seems to know what it is all about. The curb market is very active. Formerly the place was noted for its silver work, but now this art, like so many of the arts of Asia Minor, has lapsed. Even to-day, however, one may occasionally find exquisitely wrought chains, to be had for the value of the silver in them, the modern dandy preferring the imported machine-made chain as being more swank.

The bazaars are interesting. Squatting cross-legged on a divan, sipping Turkish coffee, and smoking a Samsun cigarette while examining the unusual wares is not the least interesting of pastimes. One is never urged to buy; there is no loud-voiced extolling of articles, such as one encounters in the bazaars of Istamboul (Constantinople). The goods are there; you can see them. If you wish to buy, the price is thus and so. If you do not care to buy, so it has been decreed by Allah. Say no further, for is not tomorrow also a day, and is not man but a road over which the events of life, both good and bad, pass?...

One July day in 1924 Major Imbrie, now a vice consul in Tehran, went out to photograph the crowds gathering at a fountain reputed to have healing powers. Intrigue was roiling the Persian capital, and American and British oil interests were playing a high-stakes game for valuable oil concessions. Meanwhile, at the fountain, a mob—already incited to flashpoint by other purported insults—exploded on Imbrie, and he was savagely murdered. Or that was the official version. Doubts still linger. Was his murder related to the oil intrigues? American and Persian relations were so damaged by the incident that Britain won the concessions. Major Imbrie won only an early grave in Arlington.

INTO BURNING HADHRAMAUT
October 1932

DANIEL VAN DER MEULEN (1894–1989)

FOR CENTURIES BUT A NAME ON THE MAP OF SOUTHERN ARABIA, the Hadhramaut was little known other than having once been part of the ancient frankincense trail. Access was so difficult, and its inhabitants were so warlike and xenophobic that by the early 20th century the number of Western explorers who had traveled it could be counted on one's fingers. In 1929, Royal Air Force planes from the nearby British base at Aden flew over, obtaining the first bird's-eye look at the spectacular canyons hidden beneath the rocky tableland, where mud-built skyscraper cities beaded a string of oases.

Their homeland was hidden, but the Hadhramis themselves were not. Thousands worked abroad, particularly in the Dutch East Indies (now Indonesia), where they had such an economic impact that the Dutch government decided to learn more about their mysterious birthplace. The task fell to diplomat Daniel Van Der Meulen, a strong, principled Dutch Calvinist in his late 30s with the intensity of an Old Testament prophet. Having cut his teeth in Sumatra, where bloody resistance to Dutch rule smoldered, Van Der Meulen could handle the clans of the Hadhramaut and their interminable civil war.

In 1931, accompanied by German geographer Hermann Von Wissmann, Van Der Meulen set out from Mukalla, chief port of South Arabia, and made his way north across the stony plateau to where the wadis, or valleys, of Hadhramaut opened in dramatic chasms. As they proceeded down the maze of canyons and traversed the spectacular 400-mile-long Wadi Hadhramaut, they met wariness and hostility but were generally treated hospitably. As Van Der Meulen related in NATIONAL GEOGRAPHIC, they were the first Western explorers to see many places, although automobiles—brought in piecemeal on camels' backs, then reassembled—had beaten them there. Episodes recounted here include their arrival at the brink of the Hadhramaut; a visit to Tarim, one of the dreamlike cities shimmering in the valley; and journeys made to a sacred pilgrimage site and a legendary cave called the "Mouth of Hell."

WE PROCEEDED FARTHER TOWARD WADI DU'AN, THE GREAT tributary of the Wadi Hadhramaut, a marvel of overpowering beauty. After the days of exhausting travel through the dull, endless spaces of the plateau, with no sign of life but an occasional lizard, we now stood on the threshold of our "promised land." Our eyes, tormented as they had been by the glitter of the sun reflected on stones, were now caressed by the restful shades of green in the depths of the wadi.

Perpendicularly the *jol* [plateau] broke off; 100 to 150 feet below lay the wadi bed, like a wide, jubilant river of green. In its middle wound the gleaming white ribbon of the sand bed of the flood waters, along which the stream flows after the rare rains, searching for a course through the wadi. Palms grew halfway up the rocky banks of the wadi. On these steep declivities the towns are built, so as not to waste a single square foot of the valley soil that can be irrigated.

These houses, rectangular and built entirely of adobe, are often five or more stories high. Under a noonday sun the towns are scarcely distinguishable, since they are the same color as the gray-brown slopes against which they are built. No one goes out of doors at this time of overpowering heat, so that no living creature was to be seen. No sound rose to us. It was like looking down upon a petrified, forgotten city, sleeping the long sleep that awaits the Day of Resurrection....

So it came to pass that we left Hureda on a burning hot afternoon, in an unexpectedly modern conveyance, for the desert portal of Hadhramaut Valley. The motorcar, packed to fullest capacity, was soon swallowed up by the dry and burning wilderness. The hot wind cut face and hands like the keen, frosty wind of northern winters. The curtain of air over the desert quivered and distorted the contours of the rock walls of the ever-widening wadi. Where Wadi Amd opens into Wadi Kasr, the banks draw so far back that we had almost the feeling of sailing in a boat on a vast ocean of sand.

Certain crags, which appeared only now and again through the mist of heat and dust, served as landmarks by which our driver gauged his direction. Long, thin columns of sand rose in front of us, mounting to the sky, their summits frayed by the wind. With great velocity more and more of these yellow-brown columns raced over the plain. Soon we ourselves were caught in one. The burning wind whistled from all directions and we could scarcely see each other. We covered our faces with towels and bent forward, silent, holding our breath.

As the shroud of dust became more transparent, heads would appear with a sigh out of the enveloping cloths, and Bin Marta would

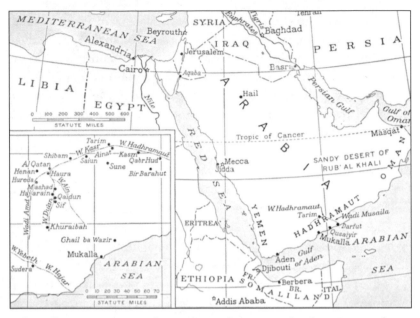

The Hadhramaut region in southern Arabia was for centuries so hostile to Western explorers that little was known about it. The inset (left) shows its chief towns and the winding course of the Wadi Hadhramaut.

start his engine again. At another time we had to get out and push: then again we had to cling to the sides of the car to avoid being bumped out, as almost impassable stretches of road had to be taken at high speed to avoid stalling in the soft sand.

Suddenly there loomed out of the cloud of sand a high, unreal, light-gray fortress. Far out in a wilderness of sand rise the Dijar Al Buqrie, three well-built, lofty forts in which an obstinate warrior has for years entrenched himself against encircling enemies.

We longed for a short respite from the sand storm, and for a drink of hot, bitter coffee; so Bin Marta honked his horn loudly in the deep stillness. Immediately sentinels thrust black heads above the parapet, to look down upon us in mute astonishment. We shouted that we wanted to call on their commander. They called back that we must drive around to the other side, as the gate on this side lay in the line of possible enemy fire and could not be opened.

While our visit in the Dijar Al Buqrie was short, it was full of interest. As I stood opposite the commander in the great council hall, my eyes wandered round the walls where the soldiers on entering had hung their rifles and cartridge belts on long wooden pegs. He guessed my thoughts and said, "War is a manly job!" I looked at him and denied it shortly. "Why not?" he asked. "Because of war," I replied, "you are imprisoned in your own proud citadel, the last palm tree in your gardens has perished long ago and the desert has encroached upon your very threshold." The soldiers listened with interest to our interchange of thoughts on war and kindred subjects; but we could not tarry here, at the very portal of Hadhramaut....

"*Tarim wa la teroom ghaira!*" That is to say: "After Tarim you desire nothing more." That is a well-known play on the name of the most easterly and most remarkable of the three towns and one that is essentially different from the other two. After Hirsch's brief visit in 1893, no other Western explorer had been here, though in 1929 some scouting planes of the British Royal Air Force from Aden had circled low above it. But when inquisitive Bedouins fired on these "wonder birds," with the object of getting a closer view of them, they rose again to higher levels and Tarim was not disturbed. Shortly afterward, Lieut. Col. the Hon. T. M. Boscawen, accompanied by a Hadhramaut Arab, went so far as Tarim via the Du'an and Hadhramaut wadies.

Forty years ago Hirsch was besieged by a fanatical crowd in the house of his host; the sayid's party, which was powerful, demanded his surrender to them. It would have gone ill with him had his host not stepped in on his behalf and promised that he should leave the town immediately. Times have changed since then! Abu Bakr Bin Sheik al-Kaf, the most influential sayid of Tarim, threw his palatial dwelling open to us. He offered us not only a hospitality that made us marvel, but also arranged for our further travels and made them possible, through his great influence over the Bedouins of the region.

Tarim is called the town of religion and science; this honorable title it owes to its past glory, much of which has passed away. The saying that it has 360 mosques was probably true at one time, but it is no longer so, though their number is still impressive. One afternoon Von Wissmann and I climbed what is said to be the loftiest minaret in Hadhramaut. It is 175 feet high and made entirely of adobe, whitewashed on the outside. Unfortunately the usual rounded form has been replaced by the modern square, and the simple decorations of stripes have been marred by windows cut in the tower.

The mud stairs become narrower, so that finally, toward the top, only very slim people can worm themselves through the corkscrew tunnel. By

"A petrified, forgotten city…" A glimpse into Arabia's mysterious Hadhramaut, where brooding mudmade towns, built by feuding clans for defense, cling to the walls of majestic canyons. Because of the intense heat, they often appeared deserted during daylight hours.

keeping close together we could just stand under the dome, which is encircled and supported by pillars of mud. The top swayed gently in the hot, dry wind. We did not notice this at first, but when we did our imagination exaggerated the motion and we were seized by the thought that we were standing there, 175 feet above the ground, on a shaky pinnacle of baked mud! Silently, hurriedly, we made the necessary measurements and took photographs. Then, with a feeling of relief, we crept down the brown, narrow stairway. Yet we could not but admire these Arab architects who, though unable to calculate tension and strain, have learned by experience how to create lofty structures of clay....

Although we were in a town which is supposed to satisfy all earthly desires, we wished eagerly to investigate the two mysteries of Hadhramaut, i.e., that national shrine of pilgrimage, the tomb of the Prophet Hud, and Bir Barahut, the Mouth of Hell....

Toward evening on the second day we approached the ravine of Nabi (Prophet) Hud. In the desolate, silent valley we saw, sharply outlined against the almost black slopes of rock, the white buildings of the cult. Somewhat lower lay the town, Qabr Hud, inhabited for only three days in the year, when a general armistice makes it possible to come to this sanctuary from the farthest corners of the land. From this thinly populated, barren wilderness of a country about 3,000 souls congregate in this remote valley to pray for inner peace and greater happiness.

My companion and I had far outdistanced our caravan and were alone when we set foot on this holy ground of Hadhramaut. Everything was motionless. At first we saw no living thing, but later caught sight of a group of pilgrims, bowed in prayer, among the pillars of the *naqa* mosque. Fortunately, absorbed in their devotions, they did not notice us and we were able to approach this shrine of pre-Islamic times.

Where we had expected to find primitive and neglected buildings, encircled by a half-collapsed village of hovels, we saw instead graceful, gleaming white, substantial mausoleums, mosques, and pavilions for purification; and, deeper in the valley, a town of large, well-kept, imposing houses of three or more stories. Deep devotion and love have been shown in the building and maintenance of this sacred place.

We, the first pilgrims from the West, stood sunk in admiration, and gazed down upon that which, being the highest in man, seeks expression everywhere, even here, at the extreme edge of a barely habitable land. Here gather together Bedouins and town dwellers during the few days in the year when all strife and vendettas cease. Here man stands with his need and sorrow and with an indestructible hope, on the borders of a better land.

Hud was a prophet, sent by Allah to the Addites, the aboriginal inhabitants of Hadhramaut. As a preacher of repentance, he called the people to conversion and threatened them with Allah's terrible punishment if they did not obey. His words resounded in the wilderness. He was persecuted and is said to have fallen into the hands of his enemies on this spot; but Allah intervened and cleft open a rock, which received him. His faithful *naqa*, or racing camel, on whose milk he lived, died at his tomb and was turned into stone.

The naqa mosque was later built against the petrified camel and over the split rock a repentant posterity erected the domed tomb of Hud. The body of the prophet, more than 13 feet long, projects far out beyond the cupola and is marked by a whitewashed stone railing. Inside the dome we saw the split rock, whose sides were polished smooth by tens of thousands of hands, passed prayerfully over it, and by countless lips which in ecstasy had kissed the holy stone.

By Qabr Hud, Wadi Barahut opens into the main wadi. At the end of this wild, rocky valley is situated the place of terror, mentioned by all writers on Hadhramaut, even the earliest. It is the spot which Allah came to hate most and which therefore he ordained as the abode of the souls of Unbelievers. The stories which had been handed down about it made Western geographers think that there must exist here an active volcano; if so, it would be the only one on the whole Arabian peninsula and would be important from a scientific point of view. No wonder, then, that our Christian predecessors in Hadhramaut had always tried—though in vain—to reach Bir Barahut as well as Qabr Hud. Now that we were in Qabr Hud, it was inevitable that we should try also to reach Bir Barahut and if possible to descend into its terrifying depths.

Following a day full of emotions came a night in which alternating hope and doubt, endured amid suffocating heat, rendered restful sleep impossible. We camped together on the flat roof of a house belonging to the al-Kaf family. Black crags towered threateningly above us and radiated the heat that they had absorbed during the day. Even the roof was hot and remained so all night; to lie still and wait to see if sleep would come was the heavy test laid on our will-power.

Not only we Westerners but also the Bedouins were concerned over what might happen on the morrow. Some of the more venturesome Arabs had made up their minds to accompany us, but others hesitated and were leaving it to their dreams or other omens to decide for them.

Before dawn we were on our way with a small group of men and with a camel laden with water-bags. As guides we had Manahil, Bedouins who roam in small groups with their flocks through this, the remotest of the still inhabited part of Hadhramaut—the southern border of the great Empty Quarter, the Rub' al Khali. We had with us electric torches, a kerosene lamp to test the air inside the cave, a rope, and compasses. The Bedouins had also armed themselves against the expected onslaught of snakes and other fearsome monsters!

After two or three hours on the march, during which the longing for the unknown drove us to even greater speed, we came to a place where high up above us, in the steep crags, the black mouth of Bir Barahut became visible. Here the wadi had become much wider, the almost perpendicular bluffs were more rugged and cleft than anywhere else in Hadhramaut, and dark caves yawned between the masses of rock; yet all this seemed hardly enough to account for the antipathy which Wadi Barahut arouses among the Arabs.

We all clambered up the cliffside as fast as possible to gain a closer view of the mysterious cave. No suffocating fumes, or flames, or explosions, or rumblings were to be noticed. Inside the high, wide entrance gigantic boulders lay scattered, and farther back was a black fissure through which we soon clambered. We had to creep through a low but wide cleft to get inside this mysterious world, and then an opaque blackness cut us off from the outer sunlight. The absolute stillness and the almost tangible darkness assailed us; the rays from our electric torches could not penetrate to the bottom of the abyss, along the edge of which we had to proceed. Even the boldest was affected by the atmosphere of this underworld and each one recalled the stories of what would happen to the explorer that disturbed the peace of these hidden depths.

Courage failed some of the company, who turned back while they could still feel their way out; no one ventured to reproach them. Von Wissmann, with tape and compass, made measurements and sketches of our route in the cave. The passage we followed had many side corridors, each of which we examined to their ends. It was as hot in these blind corridors as it is in the stokehole of a steamer in the Red Sea!

Sometimes these side passages were very steep and occasionally it was necessary to enter them by crawling through small openings. Once most of the company shrank back from a descent that seemed to lead to a bottomless pit. Only Von Wissmann and one of the Arabs ventured in. Standing on the loose rubble, they let themselves slide down the steep incline and disappeared into the darkness. At first we could hear the falling of pebbles and then all was silent.

We extinguished our torches to save the batteries and stood waiting in pitch blackness for what seemed like hours. Finally we saw the flicker of a light gradually approaching, and with a feeling of relief we helped our friends through the narrow opening back to our side.

After two hours of hard work we shuffled and groped our way back to the entrance. The layer of fine powder on the floor of the cave deadened all sound. The temperature improved and we were guided by compass and sketch-map. Finally a faint glimmer became visible and we knew that the exploration of Bir Barahut, which was neither the "mouth of hell" nor a volcanic crater, had been brought to a successful conclusion.

At the entrance we found our waiting escort in deep slumber. They stared at us in dumb amazement when we wakened them. We looked more like chimney sweeps than spirits from the underworld! When at the end of half an hour we had not returned, they took for granted that we had met with the punishment we deserved for our reckless dare-deviltry!...

Returning from the Hadhramaut to the coast, the explorers skirted so many battles between the feuding clans that Van Der Meulen, shortly afterwards, helped broker a lasting peace in the region. With Von Wissmann, he then helped compile the first accurate maps of the area. These pioneering efforts led, in 1947, to his receiving the Patrons Medal from the Royal Geographical Society for his contributions to the geography, archaeology, and ethnography of southern Arabia.

Today the Hadhramaut is part of the Republic of Yemen, and has become a tourist destination of sorts, although admittedly not one of the everyday kind. Its strange name? It might derive from an Arabic phrase meaning "to welcome death." It is the birthplace of Osama bin Laden's father.

AN UNBELIEVER JOINS THE HADJ
June 1934

OWEN TWEEDY (1888–1960)

THERE IS NO ARRIVAL WITHOUT A JOURNEY. EACH YEAR FOR WELL over a thousand years, pilgrims have arrived at the Holy City of Mecca. Once they made significant journeys—some by camel, some under sail, some by foot; some thousands of miles long or many years in the making—for this was the ultimate pilgrimage, the hajj (or hadj), one of the five pillars of Islam.

In 1930 an Anglo-Irish writer named Owen Tweedy made the rare decision to join the hajj pilgrimage. He traveled from northeastern Africa to Jeddah, the Red Sea port of Mecca. An unbeliever himself, he was respectful of Islamic tradition and in the long run stepped aside, never actually seeing the Holy City. In the article he wrote for NATIONAL GEOGRAPHIC, though, one still glimpses the age-old patterns of pilgrimage.

Son of a Dublin physician, the Arabic-speaking Tweedy had graduated from Cambridge and served in World War I before turning to diplomacy in Cairo. He became so enamored, however, of the Islamic world that he resigned in order to travel through North Africa and the Middle East, writing about his experiences. He became well acquainted with Arab leaders and fellow Westerners who considered themselves devotees of Arab culture. His host in Jeddah (unnamed in this article) was Harry St. John Philby, self-styled as the greatest Arabian explorer of his day and the father of Kim Philby, the notorious 20th-century spy.

Once it was the journey, so long and so difficult, that heightened the rapture of arrival. By 1960, however, when Tweedy made his last salaam and stepped off life's stage, the camel caravans, the pilgrim ships, the medieval trappings of the hajj he described were fast disappearing. Most pilgrims were arriving in the Holy Cities by bus over paved highways, a development that soon, because of a tenfold increase in numbers, began causing an annual Mother of All Traffic Jams. Then came the jumbo jets, hundreds landing each day at Jeddah airport—the pilgrim's conveyance of choice today.

AN INFALLIBLE METHOD TO INSURE ORIGINAL AND UNORTHODOX travel is to imagine the world a plate and oneself a tiny globule of

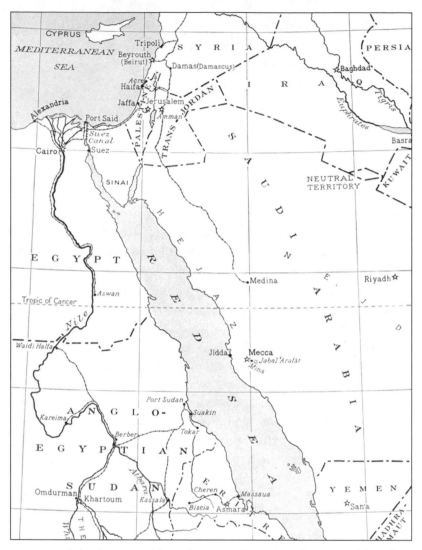

For centuries before the coming of the jumbo jet, untold myriads of pilgrims crossed the Red Sea by ship to the Arabian port of Jeddah, where they mounted camels that carried them up the final 46 winding miles to the Holy City of Mecca.

mercury on it. Then let the plate tilt itself, and the oddest and the jolliest things do happen!

I had just arrived in Khartoum and my host, a prosperous Arab cultivator on the vast cotton fields of the Gezira, was entertaining me in his mud and wattle adobe, which at first sight, with its tall, pointed, straw-thatched roof, reminded me of a mammoth candle-extinguisher of my Victorian youth. He was keenly interested in my travels. "And where are you going next?" he asked. I had no fixed plans and told him so; then he tilted the plate and I, the tiny globule of mercury, was off.

"Why not join the pilgrims?" he said. "You are on the Pilgrimage Road, the Darb el-Hadj, across Africa and over the Red Sea to the Holy Cities. Join them. They are travelers like you—good travelers; and from them you will learn much."

"But I am an Unbeliever."

He smiled. "Maybe," he said; "so of course you will not reach their goal. But you can share their spirit of the road."...

My road lay to Kassala, on the Sudan border, east of Khartoum, and from there I purposed to work through the mountains of Eritrea, which lead up to the highlands of Ethiopia, and thence down to the old Arab seaport of Massaua, on the Red Sea. There I would take boat for Jidda [or Jeddah], in Arabia, by way of Suakin. It was a fine plan if it worked....

Eritrean time-tables are printed with a wise proviso—"subject to the exigencies of service." What the exigencies were on that particular Sunday I do not know. Anyhow, the "express" would not run, and it was only after a long and agitated conversation with the Italian station master that I was at length given permission to travel down to Massaua on a goods, or fourth-class train. I shared the van with an elderly Turk from Aden and a charming Arab, who with his young son was making his way to Mecca, having been four years on the road from the western Sudan. He had started with a wife, but she had died when the boy was born; so when he and the baby reached Asmara he had delayed a season, working in the fields, until the child was old enough to face the sea.

He was delighted to talk Arabic. When I spoke of his Nile, his face lighted up, and while the aged Turk snored in a corner on a heap of faggots, he talked and talked. His father and his grandfather had been to the Holy Cities, and, when their time came to die, had gone to Paradise. Now he and his son would become Hadji (pilgrims) in their turn, and after them the generations unborn. Islam does inspire enormous conviction.

I met my Arab companion next day on the boat, which was to take us both to Jidda; but he had no eyes for me. He was in the peak-hold, engrossed in conversation with the medley of other pilgrim deck passengers, while I was well astern in the first class. For me, too, the boat had fresh and equally intriguing interests.

I clambered down the companionway into the gloomy saloon and there I had the surprise of my life. The paneling of the walls was studded with carved medallions—the Rose of England, the Thistle of Scotland, and, dearest of all to me, the Shamrock of my own country. Over the clock were the Arms of the City of Dublin. Like myself, my boat was an exile from the West and, what was more, an old friend. Before she had drifted into Red Sea coasting trade she had plied as the *Lady Hudson Kinahan* between Dublin and Liverpool and had been the favorite boat of my brother and me on our way back to school in England....

The wind had died down and we had a lovely crossing. Early next afternoon my fellow pilgrims and I were all on deck straining our eyes into the east for a first view of the promised land. From the captain's bridge I looked down on to the foredeck, which was full of the tense bustle of an imminent arrival.

The pilgrim arriving in Jidda has much to think about. Once the coast is sighted, he enters the Sacred Zone and his ceremonial initiation as a full-blown Hadji has to be performed. The men were already bareheaded and shoeless. Suddenly from the masthead crow's nest there was a loud shout: "*El Belad!* The City!"

With a sort of gasp all hastened to the ship's side and stood in excited silence gazing deep into the horizon. Slowly they turned and joined their womenfolk and children squatting on top of the main hatch.

Then as slowly, with ceremony and reverence, they took off their ordinary clothes and put on the prescribed dress of pilgrimage, the *ihram*. It consists of two lengths of white calico or toweling, purposely seamless to avoid any possible contamination from the touch of an "unbeliever" tailor. One length they wore knotted round the waist, the other over the head and shoulders like a shawl.

Once dressed, life became normal again, and pandemonium ruled while fathers collected the family luggage and agitated mothers tidied and polished their jolly pot-bellied babies.

Two hours later we were anchored safely inside the reefs. Across two miles of glasslike sea Jidda shimmered at us, a vivid contrast of white walls and black shadows against the pale pink of the gently rising desert behind. Leaving the bridge, I went down among the pilgrims to find my friend of the Massaua goods van. But easier said than done. In the ihram all the men looked exactly alike—tall, ghostly figures in the terrific sunlight—and in the end it was he who spotted me. He came running up with the boy pattering at his heels. His face was almost beautiful with excitement.

"Soon we shall be ashore," he said, "and I shall seek out my cousin, who arrived two years ago and has stayed here. He will see after us, and tomorrow or the next day we shall be on the way to Mecca." For ten minutes he talked plans and how he had told the boy of everything—the prayers at the Kaaba, the prayers and sermon at 'Arafat, the stoning of the Devils at Mina, the whole routine of the pageant of the pilgrimage— and while he talked the *sambuks*, large, wide-bottomed, single-sailed barges, were slanting through the reefs to take us ashore.

Then the fun began, the disembarkation. First, over went the luggage, slung over anyhow, and next, panting with excitement, the pilgrim families. Once in the sambuks, each family was taken over by a licensed guide, who would be responsible for its lodging in one of the pilgrim hotels ashore and would later arrange for its transport by camel to Mecca. The Hadj, one of the oldest ceremonies in the world, has a ritual of organization dating from centuries back. Once the pilgrim reaches Jidda, there are conventions which he must follow as strictly as rules of dress.

The last I saw of my Arab friend was when his guide, rather roughly, I thought, stowed him and the child at the bottom of their sambuk between two enormous sacks of cotton. But he still smiled. His day was being indeed "blessed."

An hour later I was ashore. My host's house stood by the walls, for Jidda is a walled town, and from his living room I looked out west over the sea and south into the cruel, broken desert stretching blankly into a misty horizon. My bedroom was as large as a golf green. It had six windows, unglazed but beautifully latticed with *mushrabeyeh* tracery. With the sun dropping into the west, the cool stone floor was patterned with entrancing shadows. In the days before the war, it had been part of a Turkish pasha's harem.

And so to a European tea and then a long walk through the town, past numerous hotels clustered with pilgrims' baggage awaiting distri- bution among its owners, out along the northern wall past the Consular Quarter, past the odd and extremely dangerous-looking leaning minaret of one of Jidda's principal mosques, and so out through the Medina Gate and into the open desert.

The sun was low and our shadows ran long ahead of us as we walked into the east. Flocks of goats were being shepherded back into the town for a night's safety, and we met a few Arabs swinging past on their way home, with the long, slow strides of men of the desert.

Guides at Jeddah, who met the pilgrim ships and showed the hajjis the sights of the port, primary gateway to the Holy City of Mecca.

There was absolute silence, but it was somehow no ordinary silence. It was far too tense. The reason was that the day was the eve of Ramadan. All the good folk of Jidda were waiting for word that the young moon had been seen which would inaugurate their annual month of fasting. During this month no morsel of food and no drop of drink might pass the True Believer's lips between sunrise and sunset.

That night we dined in the Consular Quarter—a happy gathering of the local diplomats. They could not have been kinder to me, the stranger. Just as we were sitting down to table, there came to us through the stillness of the night the roar of the Ramadan salvo of guns fired from the harbor fort. The sickle moon of the month had been seen by some keen Arab eye a thousand miles away, in the desert of Nejd....

We broke up in the early hours of the morning, and through narrow, overhung streets my host and I made our way to the market.

There the appearance of Ramadan's sickle moon had turned night and day. The shops, tiny arched recesses in the walls, were all open and glaring with roaring petrol lamps; meals were being busily prepared in the cafés against dawn and the morrow's strict fast; Arabs chaffered with Arabs and every purchase was an argument and every argument a commotion; agile money-changers poured the new Saudi dollar like streams from hand to hand and invited me to exchange my Egyptian notes.

Strings of camels and donkeys, preparing for the trek to Mecca, barged their way heavily through the teeming crowds, and everywhere was the scent of the East, which I love—a scent that cannot and should not be analyzed—part human, part earthy, part spice and musk, and wholly intoxicating....

Camel-feeding, like everything else connected with the Hadj, is a ritual. Five animals, always the same five, barrack around a large, circular, woven mat on which the grain is heaped. Their heads point inward and their tails where the figures would be on the dial of a clock. They seemed to me to eat with the exaggerated delicacy of Victorian matrons, never bumping each other's noses and each giving way to the other with deference.

When we arrived they were just finishing their meal and were about to be equipped for the road.... I returned to the hostel, opposite which was a convenient coffeehouse, where I drank four tiny glasses of Mecca coffee—bitter, aromatic stuff, but very quenching for the thirst. Back came the guide with his twenty camels, roped head and tail in four groups, and all were fitted with canopies, over each of which had been drawn strips of grass matting to protect the pilgrims from the heat of the noonday sun.

Once assembled, they were untied and barracked in a long line ready for loading. First, in went the baggage, all heaped at the tail end of the canopy, after which the guide portioned out the waiting pilgrims among the animals. One by one the huge beasts were urged to their feet. First, up went the rump; then, with a terrific heave, each camel struggled from its knees.

The loading of the human freight was a revelation to me. The hostel keeper produced a flimsy ladder, which was leaned up against the animal's neck. Then, with many birdlike screams, up scrambled father and mother and perhaps a baby or two, while the camel-man pulled the camel's indignant head as far away from the ladder as possible, so as to remove from the beast all temptation to bite the climbers.

Once inside the canopy, the pilgrims behaved exactly like dogs settling into their baskets for the night, twisting and turning among their baggage to make comfortable beds for the long journey ahead. Finally they looked for all the world like so many Roman emperors and empresses reclining after a particularly large meal.

It was nearly an hour before all were safely aboard, but at last the cavalcade had been retied into teams, head to tail. Off it lurched in a long sagging string, which had meantime been reinforced by sundry other stray pilgrims riding camels, under umbrellas, in solitary state.

The assembly point was the main street of Jidda—a long, straight thoroughfare, arcaded on both sides, rather like the Rue de Rivoli. There we waited for more guides with more parties to join us, until we were perhaps sixty camels strong. Then off again, out into the east, and at the Mecca Gate, a fine piece of battlemented architecture set in the walls, the pilgrims bade farewell to Jidda, which they would not see for at least another two months....

The road from Jidda to Mecca is a sand track, worn to a thin powder by passage of countless plodding camels. When I was there they had the place almost to themselves, save for a few very decrepit motor busses, which, for a fantastic fee, took the richer pilgrims to Mecca with quite as many bumps and alarms as they would have experienced had they been on camel-back. The guides were loud in protest and abuse of the motors, which flung choking clouds of dust all over the pilgrims.

"Away, thou son of a dog! By Allah! What an invention of the Devil! May your bones break and be burnt cinders by the sun!"

But in another few years the poor cameleers may have still more cause to protest, for the road along which I was walking will probably be the route of the proposed Jidda-Mecca railway. But neither I nor my fellow pilgrims were thinking of such anachronisms in the future....

After three miles, the heat and the welcome appearance of the last coffeehouse along the road told me that I would be wise to halt. Its Bedouin proprietor was thrilled to have a European customer, a phenomenon which he assured me had never occurred in his business career before. At once I began to ply him with questions about the Hadj. But he answered without interest, and I quickly realized that what he wanted to talk about was England. Soon I found myself trying to explain to him the size of London in terms of Jidda, and telling him of railways and airplanes, of horse races and cinemas. His last words when I rose to trudge back to Jidda were eloquent of changed times in the East.

"I wish," I had said, "that I, the Unbeliever, could go on the Hadj and see Mecca and enjoy all the great festival."

He shrugged his shoulders.

"As for me," he answered, "I have seen enough of Mecca. After what you have told me, the place which I shall next visit will be London."

OLD AND NEW IN PERSIA
September 1939

MARY IRENE CURZON, BARONESS RAVENSDALE (1896–1966)

THE LURE OF FORBIDDEN PLACES HAS ALWAYS TEMPTED adventurous travelers. In 1853, the legendary Sir Richard Francis Burton, disguised as a pilgrim, had visited Mecca, forbidden to non-Muslims, merely to slake his curiosity. Yet the equally intrepid Sir Alexander Burnes, who in mufti had visited hostile caravan cities in Central Asia, thought better of risking his life to glimpse the tomb of Imam Riza in Mashhad, revered by Shiite pilgrims in Iran. He called it a case of "judgment conquering curiosity"—a rare admission from an empire-builder, a tribe that rarely balked at trespassing.

Mary Irene Curzon, Baroness Ravensdale, was daughter of one of the greatest of empire-builders. Her father, George Nathaniel Curzon, a viceroy of India and British foreign secretary, had as a young man made a long horseback journey over the length and breadth of Iran—then Persia—and his resulting book, Persia and the Persian Question, was the most comprehensive work then published on that country in English. Yet when he visited Mashhad, he contented himself with merely glimpsing from afar the sacred mosque and its complex of buildings, concluding it would be foolish for a foreigner to risk a closer look. Not just personal safety but national embarrassment were at stake.

In 1935, Baroness Ravensdale, then 39, followed in her father's footsteps and traveled extensively over Iran, not by horseback but by automobile, for the reforming Shah Reza Khan had improved transportation and communications. He was also imposing modernization on the country, emancipating women and wresting education and the legal system from the control of the mullahs—in short, undermining the influence of religion on national life. That meant opening some of the holiest mosques to foreign visitors.

The baroness was known for her wit, beauty, and independence. Would her curiosity conquer her judgment? Her father may not have seen the glories of Mashhad, but she might, as related in this excerpt from the account she published in NATIONAL GEOGRAPHIC.

SINCE MESHED [MASHHAD] IS THE MOST SACRED CITY OF PERSIA, I desired to go there, if only to look on the exterior of the dome of Imam Riza's tomb, and peep from afar at the polychrome exterior of the Gawhar Shad Mosque, unsurpassed anywhere else in the country. Black-browed Afghans, wild Baluchis, Indian traders, Caucasian devotees, Turks, Tartars, and Mongols make a bewildering kaleidoscope as they pour in Meshed. On the approach to the city from the mountain heights, piles of small pebbles by the roadside testify to the first glimpse the pilgrims have had of the "Mecca."

Originally I had not the faintest hope of entering the sacred shrine; up to the time of this visit only a limited few Infidels, disguised, had succeeded at the risk of their lives. Everywhere, however, the Shah is slowly breaking down fanaticism, and in all cities one now can visit the mosques with a guide. Qum and Meshed are the sacred Shia strongholds and were the last to succumb.

The power of the mullahs is slowly being broken. Many so-called mullahs had no right to bear the name, or to wear the green turban as descendants of the Prophet, and so batten on the masses. His Majesty now demands a stiff and honorable examination of all wishing to become or remain mullahs.

Some weeks before I reached Meshed an unpleasant episode had complicated the situation as regards Imam Riza's shrine. A certain mullah had gravely inflamed the pilgrims by attacking all forms of modernization, such as the abandonment of the chuddar [chador, or woman's veiled head-covering], the drinking of wine, and the wearing of European clothes.

Pilgrims were requested to leave the mosque precincts. Misunderstanding the situation, and imagining the sacred precincts were a sanctuary against all trouble, they remained and got involved in a wildly inflammable group which raided the shops in the Bast [the sanctuary and the buildings and bazaars inside its gated fence], breaking them up and tearing the European clothes off the shopkeepers. The Governor rushed in Baluchi troops with machine guns, and many were killed. The true figures will never be known, as lorries were hurried down to bury all dead, and it is better to ask no questions.

This was all the more reason, one would think, for my not being allowed to enter the shrine when I got to Meshed; but two of my friends from the British Legation in Tehran had been conducted through it under the protection of the Governor before my arrival and this raised my hopes considerably....

Soon after my arrival the Governor graciously sent for me with my friends about 8:30 a.m. My companions sat completely mute, while for twenty minutes I discussed with His Excellency in French the possibilities of a police escort for the four men of our party who were leaving for

*For generations Western travelers saw little more of the shrine of Imam Riza—
the "Mecca" of the Shiites at Mashhad, Iran—than its outer gates.
To penetrate further was to risk death as a trespassing unbeliever.*

Afghanistan at dawn next day. He explained to me the dangers of the road were very great, since a notorious bandit who had held up and robbed several Britishers had not yet been caught. After an endless argument on this subject, we discovered the bandit was on another road.

How was I to get to the prime question haunting my mind? Luckily, the acting British consul chimed in, remarking, "Lady Ravensdale and her friends are all earnest pilgrims." Even then the Governor shied from the subject and continued about the police escort, but before my departure he surprisingly came back to it and said he would arrange for us to go through the shrine that afternoon. My woman companion and I must go disguised in the black chuddar, but he could not attempt to disguise six-foot Englishmen as Turkish pilgrims.

Since time is often of little importance to the Iranian, the supposition was that the expedition would take place in the late afternoon. My companion and I were to rehearse the wearing of our chuddars at 2 p.m. with two charming Iranian ladies who were to lend us two of theirs and accompany us through the shrine as guides. On entering the consulate for this rehearsal, I found the shrine official waiting to conduct us to the mosque immediately. I quickly sent for the Englishmen, while we went through such hasty efforts at keeping the chuddars on our heads as time would permit.

We four ladies went in my car to the entrance of the shrine, while the men were to follow in a cab. That wait outside the Bast was nerve-racking. A policeman kept asking our two Persian ladies why we were hovering about. I expected discovery and a row any moment, for spies and devotees were always hanging around the outer fringe of the mosque and pushing away any foreigners with cameras or impertinent peering eyes. I thought we should never get to the other side of the heavy chains that hang across the Bast gateways. At last our men appeared with the head official, and we moved nervously through the Bast into the great tiled courtyard.

I had unbuttoned my shoes, ready to shed them quickly. I feared my chuddar would slip, and I was in an agony lest I should lose my little Iranian lady. She was tiny, and the crowds were terrific, swaying and surging in every direction. These two admirable ladies propelled us through the great gold doorway which guards the shrine of Imam Riza, and we deposited our shoes with hundreds of others in a lobby entirely used for that purpose.

By that time we had missed the men of our party, and we four women were alone in this swaying, struggling mass of pilgrims, all surging toward the innermost shrine. It was about the most terrifying experience of my life.

Picture a succession of chambers decorated in cut glass like the glittering facets of millions of diamonds. These rooms were packed with a shrieking mob of devout worshippers kissing the exquisite silver doors leading toward the shrine, murmuring verses of the Koran, kneeling in scores, and bumping their heads on the lovely alabaster floors in a frenzy of devotion. All this took place long before we got to the Imam's tomb. When we arrived there, we slowly made a procession around the sarcophagus.

That innermost chamber, of glorious cut glass, with floral designs in gold, was a seething mass of excited zealots, struggling and fighting to get near the great silver cage in which the coffin lies, handing their children over the heads of the crowd to kiss the bars or tie on a tiny piece of cloth. Though I suppose that no devout pilgrims ever look up at the unbelievable tiles in the different domes and adjacent chambers, I meant to see as much as my frightened eyes could take in.

Having completed this alarming progress around the shrine minus any protection, we emerged into a neighboring chamber. Shrine officials by that time had discovered our direction and hustled us into another room where the males of our party were waiting to commence with us the walk around the Imam's tomb. Since we had got through safely once, the temptation was too great not to repeat the experience and have yet another glimpse of the chamber.

This time we had several shrine officials and a chanter, who murmured verses of the Koran, in our peregrination around the tomb. I noticed some superb jewels, swords, diamond aigrettes, and scabbards hung over the Imam's tomb, offerings from previous rulers in Persia. The supposed burial place of Harun-al-Rashid [author of *Arabian Nights*] in the same area has faded into insignificance by the side of the Eighth Imam. Forever indelibly stamped on my mind will be the agonized look of about eight mullahs, kneeling by the wall, reading their Korans. They saw our little group filing through; their looks were not of murder or hatred, but of pain, as if we had done some injury to their innermost souls that could not be repaired. They had the appearance of cowed and beaten men. One of our Englishmen, knowing Persian, heard many times muttered, "Foreigners," "Infidels."

We were permitted to gaze all too briefly on the beautiful polychrome façade of the Gawhar Shad Mosque, built in 1418 by the wife of Shah Rukh. In a private room looking full onto the burnished gold dome of the Imam's shrine, we were shown Korans from the Treasury that made the spirit weak for sheer beauty and delicacy of design.

As we left the mosque, the hour of evening prayer was approaching, and the great drums and gongs were thundering out the invitation to prayer. The pilgrims were kneeling in thousands or performing their ablutions in the sacred fountains. A sinking sun caught the great gold doorways in a fiery glow as we hurried out. The thrill was over! Today visitors may readily pass through those splendid courts and chambers, but they will never know what others experienced in the days when Meshed was still an unapproachable stronghold of the Shia faith...

The indelible image is that of the mullahs, whose look is not one of hatred but of pain. Once again the empire-builders, who jealously guarded the threshold of their own private clubs, had felt entitled to intrude upon others' sacred precincts. Baroness Ravensdale would go on to serve as president of the World Congress of Faith and be one of the first four women admitted to the House of Lords. The mullahs, who had retreated to the mosques in face of the Shah's purported reforms, would eventually emerge not cowed and beaten men but victorious ones, in the Iranian Revolution of 1979.

BACK TO AFGHANISTAN
October 1946

MAYNARD OWEN WILLIAMS (1888–1963)

IT WASN'T UNTIL AFTER THE FIRST WORLD WAR THAT AFGHANISTAN, long closed to foreigners, cracked open its fortress gates and peered out at the modern world. The ruling emir must have liked something in what he saw, for if that gate did not swing wide at least it opened enough to allow in a few intrepid Westerners.

As in so many places, the first to cross the threshold for NATIONAL GEOGRAPHIC *was Maynard Owen Williams, chief of the magazine's foreign editorial staff and the cheerful, friendly man who once visited the tomb of Tutankhamen. In 1931, less than a decade after the first American diplomat set foot in Kabul, Williams traversed the country as a member of the Citroen-Haardt Trans-Asiatic Expedition, which will appear again later in this volume. Enchanted with the starkly beautiful landscapes and surprisingly friendly people of Afghanistan, he hoped that some day he might be able to return. Ten years later, in 1941, while another war raged in far-off Europe, he obtained the necessary permits from Afghan authorities.*

He was not allowed to see much nor to go far. All foreigners, it seems, were restricted within a six-mile radius around Kabul. Yet Williams was given special treatment and was permitted to visit one of his favorite spots, Bamian, site of the great Buddhist statues carved into the cliffs (and now, sadly, destroyed). There, as he relates below, he nearly fell off the top of one of the colossal heads. Beyond that, he had ample opportunity to watch a country "making haste slowly," a place with the occasional cinema but also one where camels still outplodded motor vehicles and where people's habits, to Western eyes at least, could still be ... well, a bit quirky. Herewith some whimsical snapshots of the Afghanistan Maynard Williams found in that autumn of 1941.

IN [KABUL'S STREETS] THE CHIEF SYMBOLS OF PROGRESS ARE stiff-jointed traffic cops, directing the uncertain movements of donkeys, camels, and *tongas* (two-wheeled carts) with the fanatic precision of recruits.

Afghanistan, like many another land, has a gasoline shortage. Having partly divorced itself from the slow pace of camels, this land now looks to trucks and buses, some of which don't move at all.

Afghanistan, land of the Hindu Kush and the Khyber Pass, was long a buffer state between British India and tsarist Russia. Suspicious of foreign influence, it has alternately opened and shut its gates to the outside world.

Outside the Customhouse and in the caravansaries they stand, awaiting fuel. No wonder the camels sniff and burble as they pass! Even the Prime Minister rides a horse, and woe betide the minor official who indulges in a joy ride!

Gay trucks, decked out in red, blue, and gold, bear highly imaginative paintings of Italian lakes and waving palms. Neat in cream paint and chromium, new buses are ready for their close-packed travelers. In the display windows of the Motor Monopoly there are neat little Balillas, shiny Fords, streamlined Buicks, and sturdy Chevrolet trucks. But they stand on idle display while haughty camels plod past, making haste slowly and casting contemptuous glances on these modern beasts of burden which cannot go "eight days without a drink."...

Across wide roadways barelegged workers, scooping up water from roadside streams, tossed it into jeweled arcs which, falling, turned the dust to mud. Bending low under bulging brown goatskins, other street sprinklers swished wide swaths amid the scattering feet. White-

The gaze, frank and appraising, of an Afghan coppersmith
fingering prayer beads in a Kabul bazaar in 1941.

shrouded women, fleeing the flush of street sprinkling, lifted modestly wrinkled skirts, revealing neat two-tone slippers.

Sitting surrounded by bright-red apples, yellow melons, and festoons of lady-finger grapes, turbaned fruit sellers with well-trimmed Moslem beards looked with amiable eyes on this dust-laying operation, which would save them much polishing. Near many a soft-carpeted shop, pet birds in quilted cages greeted the sunshine with cheery songs.

As I tramped along half-familiar roads, men beat down autumn-colored leaves and stuffed them into sacks as winter fodder. Little girls in red watched their pet sheep gorge themselves at the foot of the bare-limbed poplars whose white skeletons rose starkly into the unbelievable blue.

Amid such simple pastoral scenes I came to the tomb of a man in whose veins flowed the blood of Timur and Genghis Khan; the man who bridged the gap between Mongol and Mogul; who ushered in the age of Shah Jahan. To the recovery of his opium-drugged son,

Humayun, Baber [or Babur, founder of the Mogul dynasty in India and a king of Afghanistan] pledged his own life, and back from the capture of Delhi and the Kohinoor diamond his body was brought to the valley he loved.

Close to his grave is a large, clear swimming pool, gold-flecked by autumn leaves. Below it is a shady-verandaed café and a tennis court. Kabul's most modern place of sport centers about the tomb of Baber, King of Kabul. His philosophy was "Enjoy life freely, O Baber, for none enjoys it twice." He loved practical jokes, a good drink, and a good fight. But he never forgot this peaceful valley.

With the bugles of an army band echoing from the mountainside and the wives of the foreign diplomats sunning their brown backs beside the swimming pool, Baber's final resting place is pleasant. Probably it is as congenial as was his first place of interment at Agra, although there the loveliest of all tombs, the Taj Mahal, was soon to push its wide arches, bubble dome, and tall minarets into the Indian sky.

Camels file past the garden where Baber lies; farmers sit behind small piles of produce; wrinkled grandsires circle the first steps of sturdy babes with their protecting arms; and talk centers about the smoking samovar.

Hardy villagers, calf-deep in the ice-fringed water, laugh and joke as they sweep the air with dripping laundry and spread it in snowy patches along the river bank....

North of Kabul we crossed a wide, fertile plain, famous for its grapes and mulberries, almonds and peaches, and turned into the narrow valley of the Ghorband, where the road clings to a ledge between steep mountain and swift river. Following the peach-and-apricot valley where isolated farmhouses stand between the tall poplar windbreaks, we came to Chehar Deh. While I lunched on hard-browned chicken in a clean-swept teahouse, my driver piled big hunks of dried mud into the trunk of his car. These earthen cylinders were an Afghan substitute for [a] tin can. Each of the mud gobs had been formed about big clusters of delicious grapes. Months later the Afghan splits the mud container like a coconut shell, revealing luscious fruit still well preserved.

The valley beyond the wide-open Shibar Pass would appeal to any sportsman, for the clear, swift streams teem with trout, and full-breasted partridges and pheasants range the rocky hills.

Bamian's great Buddhas, one 175 feet high, the other 116, still face with sightless eyes across a rich valley dotted with fortresslike farmhouses, as they have since vandals worked their destruction centuries ago. At the giant Buddha's feet, old Central Asian bazaars and caravansaries, dating back to the Silk Route's opulent days, had been destroyed. New shops lined the roadway. A fine new school was being built. Across the valley a new hotel occupied the site of the resthouse where we stayed in 1931. But from the wide arch above the old Buddha's low brow, the matchless view of the snowy Koh-i-Baba range is still framed in ancient tempera paintings. In one a rich but relatively insignificant patron bows in homage to smiling Buddhas. The time-worn frescoes hang like a polychrome aureole about the giant Buddha's head.

When I climbed down from the Buddha's head—higher than Niagara Falls—my legs still shook from an experience which might have sowed superstition at Bamian, where there are already vague wonderings why those who have worked on the great statue are now dead. Archeologist Joseph Hackin and his wife were lost at sea. Their assistant, Jean Carl, committed suicide out of grief at the news. Paris and Boston are robbed of Alexandre Iacovleff's varied talents, including faithful copies of Buddhist tempera paintings, reproduced in their own medium.

Everyone knows the momentary dizziness which comes when he rises quickly after sitting on his calves. My tripod was a pocket affair, and for some time I squatted low, seeking, better than before, to picture these delicate-toned paintings of the long ago. These operations took me far out on the statue's forehead, and when I straightened up, the Bamian valley and the Koh-i-Baba range went out of focus into a dizzy blur. Luckily there was ample space amid the bird droppings on Buddha's rough pate, but my guide seemed to wonder why I sat down so suddenly and gripped my little camera with so trembling a hand. The curse of Tutankhamen's tomb would be less dramatic than a dive past the towering limbs of the massive Buddha of Bamian....

At Ghazni I again experienced, as I had in Kabul, the independence of a tonga driver. Whether he was hungry, or his horse was, or whether some atavistic sense of liberty hit him in mid-route, I can't say, but he stopped his two-wheeled cart, said the ride was over, and could he have his fare?

Smilingly I paid, grateful that it was not a cold night.

Here in Ghazni, saddled with a motor that wouldn't mote and a driver who wouldn't drive, progress seemed an illusory thing. Luckily, I could walk. And I did, homeward through the bazaar....

PART FOUR

Along china's
Turbulent frontiers

THE LAND OF THE YELLOW LAMA
April 1925

EXPERIENCES OF A LONE GEOGRAPHER
September 1925

JOSEPH F. ROCK (1884–1962)

JOSEPH ROCK MUST HAVE LEARNED A THING OR TWO FROM THE *Tibetan devil dancers, for no one else has cast quite the spell over* NATIONAL GEOGRAPHIC *readers as he. In the three quarters of a century since the last of his ten articles was published, Rock's legend continues to flourish. His tales of lamas, bandits, and warlords on the Chinese frontier typify the golden age of adventure at the magazine.*

This botanical explorer was a complex and contradictory man. Short, stocky, and bespectacled, Rock had courtly manners and old-world charm, yet he could be touchy, temperamental, and so obstinate that one exasperated editor called him the "most cantankerous of human beings." He was aloof, having no close friends, yet also profoundly lonely. He chose to live in China and be borne about like a potentate by his caravan, yet he fastidiously insulated himself from all things Chinese. On the march, he scrubbed off defilements in an Abercrombie and Fitch folding bathtub, sprinkled fumigating powder around his bed, demanded European-style meals, and listened to German operas on a portable phonograph in his tent at night.

Rock's bent for self-dramatization made him a spellbinding storyteller. He captivated listeners, speaking with an accent betraying just a hint of his Viennese birth. Moreover, he was undeniably brilliant. As a schoolboy he taught himself Chinese and Arabic, and as a young drifter in Hawaii he learned the local flora so thoroughly that he came to be regarded as the father of Hawaiian botany. A position with the U.S. Department of Agriculture as a plant hunter eventually took him to southwest China, where for most of the 1920s and '30s he roamed the steep gorges and unmapped mountains of Yunnan and Sichuan Provinces, rich in rare and unusual plants—and in rare and unusual peoples, too.

The plants he collected for the USDA and Harvard University, but his stories and photographs of people made wonderful material for the GEOGRAPHIC. *Ethnically Tibetan, these picturesque populations may have owed nominal allegiance to Peking,*

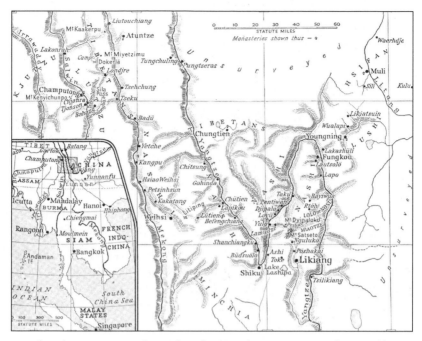

Through mountainous southwest China flow some of Asia's greatest rivers: the Irrawaddy, the Salween, the Mekong, and the Yangtze. Departing his headquarters near Likiang in 1924, Joseph Rock crossed this steep, broken country before arriving in the Kingdom of Muli (upper right).

but they lived in a remote and medieval world of their own—as Rock soon discovered. In January 1924, he gathered his caravan and, after a freezing 11-day journey over high mountains and through leopard-haunted woods, arrived in the little Kingdom of Muli, nestled in gold-veined hills and ruled by a lama-king who was absolute monarch over 6,000 square miles.

AT DAWN WE BROKE CAMP ON THE RIVER, NOW ONLY A BUBBLING brook, and climbed the western hillside. We had gone about two miles when we met a lama, dressed in deep-red woolen cloaks, and riding on a horse whose saddle blankets were made of leopard skins and Tibetan rugs.

He dismounted, took off his turban, bowed deeply, and humbly presented the king's card, then made a little speech in Tibetan, which my cook, whom I had asked to ride with me to Muli instead of staying with the caravan, interpreted as kind greetings and an invitation to be the king's guest.

The lama led the way up and around the hillside, past prayer pyramids of carved rock bearing the ever-present sacred formula, *Om Mani Padme Hum* (Oh, the Jewel in the Lotus, Amen).

Turning a sharp curve around a spur, we were confronted with the walls of Muli and the main gate to this lama stronghold. A row of courtly priests stood waiting and bowed at my approach.

I was conducted along the wall to a new house with a terrace, outside of Muli proper, and when I was comfortably settled, I was asked when I wished to see the king, who was anxious to meet the stranger.

I requested the lama to convey my greetings to His Majesty and say that I would call as soon as my caravan had arrived, after I had changed my riding clothes for those suitable to wear in the presence of royalty so illustrious as the King of Muli....

My caravan finally arrived. I donned my best and sallied forth to meet the king. The prime minister, or lord treasurer, and the king's secretary, who spoke Chinese excellently, accompanied me to the palace—a large stone structure on the lower edge of Muli, built 60 years ago. I took with me my Siamese boy, the Tibetan cook, and two Nashi servants, all dressed in their best and carrying as presents for the king a gun and 250 rounds of ammunition.

We were escorted to the palace square, which is surrounded by a temple, from which issued the discordant sounds of trumpets, conch shells, drums, and gongs, besides weird bass grumblings of officiating monks. The gateway to the palace was imposing. At either side of it two large bundles of whips were displayed to impress the villagers. Immediately within the gate is the king's stable, ill-smelling and dark, leading into a small, oblong courtyard graced by a stunted tree, supposed to lend cheer to the somber place.

We ascended a broad, steep stairway in utter darkness. The steps were close and narrow and the railing was so low to the ground as to be useless. I had to feel my way. Two flights up and we stood before a greasy curtain, black from the marks of buttered fingers. A Hsifan servant drew it aside and we passed through an antechamber, then a large, bright room, and we were in the presence of the king.

On my approach he rose, bowed, and beckoned me to a chair next to a small table loaded with Muli delicacies. He occupied a chair, facing me. I had great difficulty in distinguishing my host's features, as he sat with his back to the light coming from an open bay window, while he watched every muscle of my face.

The king stood 6 feet 2 inches, in high embroidered Tibetan boots of velvet. He was 36 years old, of powerful frame; his head was large, with high cheekbones and low forehead. His muscles were weak, as he neither exercises nor works. His manner was dignified and kind, his laugh gentle, his gestures graceful.

He wore a red, togalike garment, which left one arm bare. Below the tunic was a gold and silver brocaded vest and on his left wrist a rosary....

At the king's right was a group of lamas in most deferential attitudes, with bowed heads and folded hands, awaiting his slightest suggestion. Next to the lamas stood my servants, much bolder than the king's prime minister.

I spoke first, saying that I had heard much of the splendors of Muli and of the king's beneficence, and that I had long wished to meet him. He replied that Muli was a very poor place, and that he felt honored by my visit, coming, as I had, from so distant a country as America, whence no other man had ever come to Muli.

I doubt whether until that time he had known of the discovery of America. He did not have the slightest idea of the existence of an ocean, and thought all land to be contiguous, for he asked if he could ride horseback from Muli to Washington, and if the latter was near Germany.

During a lull in the conversation, he whispered to his prime minister, but kept an eye on me. The embarrassed official translated, with folded hands and forward-bent body, a most astonishing question: "Have the white people stopped fighting and are they again at peace?" The next question was whether a king or a president ruled great China. Then, the king suddenly held forth his hand, asked me to feel his pulse and tell him how long he was to live! From this he jumped to field glasses, asking if I had a pair with me which would enable him to see through mountains.

He then whispered some orders to a lama, who, with great reverence and hands folded in prayer, said "Lhaso, Lhaso," a term of humble acquiescence, and, walking backward, retired.

I glanced around the audience chamber. It was a room of considerable size, well decorated with frescoes in rather garish colors, depicting scenes from the life of Buddha and lesser gods. The pillars supporting the ceiling were red and adorned with a sort of gold appliqué work.

Odd as it may seem, in all this Lamaistic splendor there was a Western touch, for on the crimson-painted posts were clothes-hooks with white porcelain knobs, such as one would expect to find on trees in a cheap Berman beer garden. Suspended from the rafters and from the walls were old-fashioned kerosene cellar lamps, with rusty rings for

*The seldom seen Living Buddha of Muli emerged from seclusion
for the benefit of Rock's camera. So sacred he was worshipped even by the king,
this 18-year-old incarnation of divinity wore a hat of solid gold.*

protection from the chimneys. That they were meant for decoration was obvious, as no kerosene ever reaches this king's domain.

No matches or candles could be had here, and the black, greasy necks of all the lamas, including the king and Living Buddha, showed that soap was not in demand.

The prime minister soon returned with a stereopticon and some faded photographs. The king evidently thought this a splendid opportunity to satisfy his curiosity. The pictures were handed me one by one, and I had to explain what they represented, from the captions in English on the cardboard. The first was the dining room of the White House, in Washington; the others ranged from Windsor Castle to Norwegian fjords, and wound up with a jolly pre-war crowd in a German beer garden.

I interpreted, as best I could, these representations of our Western life, to all of which the king nodded silently, not much the wiser, I should judge.

After the lecture, the king urged me to partake of Muli delicacies. There was gray-colored buttered tea in a porcelain cup set in exquisite silver filigree with a coral-studded silver cover. On a golden plate was what I thought to be, forgetting where I was, Turkish delight, but it proved to be ancient mottled yak cheese, interspersed with hair. There were cakes like pretzels, heavy as rocks.

It was an embarrassing situation, but, in order not to offend His Majesty, I took a sip of tea, which was like liquid salted mud. I then requested the privilege of taking photographs in Muli, and, if he would permit, some of His Majesty himself; whereupon he smiled in acquiescence. The hour was set for the next morning after prayers....

Hardly had I arrived at my rustic house when there appeared nine stalwart Hsifan men, accompanied by the prime minister, bringing gifts from the king. There were eggs in plenty; a large bag of the whitest rice, two bags of beans for the horses and one of flour; one wormy ham; dried mutton; lumps of gritty salt, more of that doubtful yak cheese, and butter wrapped in birch bark. All the gift-bearers stood as I distributed silver coins. Three cakes of scented soap were presented to the prime minister.

As the king's porters left, a hungry mob of beggars gathered outside our gate. The dried legs of mutton and yak cheese were literally *walking* all over the terrace of our house, being propelled by squirming maggots the size of a man's thumb. I was informed that these were the choicest delicacies from the king's larder. As none of my party wanted the lively food, we gave it to the beggars, who fought for it like tigers.

All afternoon there droned forth from the sword temple, near the palace, the mournful sound of trumpets, gongs, and conch shells, occasionally accompanied by brass cymbals and the beating of a drum. In the evening, the king's soldiers played the bugles and drums in military fashion; a shot was fired at 8 p.m. and a bugler sounded taps.

When I had opportunity to decipher the king's calling card I learned that though his name is, briefly, Chote Chaba, his full appellation is "Hsiang tz'u Ch'eng cha Pa, by appointment self-existent Buddha, Min Chi Hutuktu, or Living Buddha, possessor of the first grade of the Order of the Striped Tiger; former leader of the Buddhist Church in the office of the occupation commissioner, actual investigation officer in matters relating to the affairs of the barbarous tribes; honorary major general of the army, and hereditary civil governor of Muli. Honorific: Opening of Mercy."...

The next afternoon I took dinner with the king. The meal was served in the reception room, on separate tables, before the window, while lamas, including the king's brother, held prayer service in his bedroom.

A steaming iron pot inlaid with silver contained a great variety of meats vertically arranged in slices, below which were vegetables of every kind. Rice and several other dishes were served, besides buttered tea gray as mud and of the consistency of soup.

Dessert consisted of a bowl of solid cream. Neither spoons, forks, nor chopsticks were placed beside the bowl. Not knowing Muli table manners, I waited for the king to make the first move. He raised the bowl to his mouth and took one smacking lick. I followed suit. It was the best dish served that day, but, as my tongue was not so agile nor of the proper length, I had to leave a good deal in my bowl.

The lama's secretary, who acted as interpreter, sat humbly on the floor and was not offered any delicacies. He had only buttered tea served in a wooden bowl, while ours were of gold.

After informing me that there would be a great procession of lamas in front of my house later in the evening, the king arose and remarked that the next day he would go out to pray among the hills, but I was to see him late that evening to say farewell.

I had just arrived at my house at sunset when, from the north gate of the Muli wall, stalked forth the religious procession—some 40 lamas preceded by three boys in armor, wearing helmets and carrying long spears. The first group was followed by four minor lamas with two 12-foot telescopic metal trumpets. The two priests in front held up the instruments to the mouths of the two other lamas, whose cheeks worked like bellows and produced bass notes meant to frighten lurking devils.

Other lamas followed with cymbals, while a fourth section carried trays with red images made of *tsamba* (barley flour) and yak butter, pitchers, and brass vessels. The remaining lamas carried large circular drums, which they struck with curved sticks. Over their red garments they wore yellow cloaks, and on their heads yellow-crested woolen helmets shaped like those of the ancient Greeks.

Just below the rampart of my house a mound of dry oak brush had been erected, and thither marched the lama throng. The last person in line was the Ghiku, a sort of abbot of the monastery. He was more elaborately dressed and carried, or rather dragged, in his hand a long, quadrangular metal staff.

The brushwood pile was now lighted and the images representing devils were thrown into the fire, amid terrific noise and exploding bombs.

The ceremony over, and the devils driven into the flames, the procession made its way back to the monastery and night fell over Muli.

Our last day in Muli was a glorious one, during which I took photographs of the town's prayer wheels. One long row of cylindrical yak-hide wheels stood on the south side of the palace and were let into its wall.

They contained miles of paper, tightly wound and covered with prayers of "Om Mani Padme Hum." All monks when passing give each wheel a turn—a most convenient way of saying millions of prayers....

At 5 o'clock that afternoon I called upon the king to thank him for his kindness and hospitality. He graciously received me and seemed loath to have me go, saying he hoped I would come again. I was about to leave, when the lord high treasurer entered with a large tray loaded with gifts. Of these I prize most a golden bowl, two Buddhas, and a leopard skin.

His Majesty accompanied me this time not only to the door, but to the stairway, on which had gathered many curious slaves, who flew headlong in fear down the steps at the king's approach.

At the palace gate were assembled the church dignitaries, who escorted me to the big gate of Muli, lined up, and bowed me out.

We left Muli before sunrise, but took one last ride through the gates of this lama stronghold past the palace. We were met by the lama officials, among them the magistrate and judge, as well as our friend the military chief. They bowed, and we passed out through the south gate into the Muli Valley.

We were soon overtaken by the king's secretary, mounted and accompanied by a Hsifan servant. Despite his poverty, he presented me with two large brass ladles as souvenirs. Then he rode with us as far as Sili, on the other side of the Muli Valley. There he emptied a bag full of mandarins and walnuts, a parting gift from the Muli king.

We proceeded through the wilderness. The mountains were sharply outlined against the sky. In the north was one vast sea of ranges, pink and yellow, with black slopes indicating fir forest interspersed with brown meadows.

Higher and higher we ascended through silent forests. The deep valleys were lined on both sides with snow-capped crags. Little Muli lay on the steep hillside, beautiful in the morning sun, an oak forest surrounding it like a somber garland.

A peculiar loneliness stole into my heart as I rode through the firs draped with long, yellowish lichens. I thought of the kindly, primitive friends whom I had just left, living secluded from the world, buried among the mountains, untouched by and ignorant of Western life.

I climbed a ridge and lingered to take a last look at the tiny capital, where I had been received with such extraordinary courtesy and hospitality by its lama sovereign....

Chote Chaba was executed by the Chinese in 1934, which saddened Rock but did not surprise him. Violence, civil war, and rebellion stormed across China during the 1920s and '30s. Competing warlords fought each other viciously, and their discharged and unpaid soldiers often became bandit hordes. Rock doggedly pursued his explorations, but his movements were everywhere hampered. Local officials, legally responsible for protecting Westerners, scrambled to provide enough guards to accompany his sumptuous caravans, but sometimes even that seemed not enough. In 1925 Rock, nerves clearly on edge, detailed his tribulations in sheaves of handwritten letters to the GEOGRAPHIC'S *editors, pulled together and published as "Experiences of a Lone Geographer" in the September 1925 issue.*

Much of a most unpleasant nature has happened to me in recent months. I was delayed about one month in Yunnanfu on account of my Nashi assistants, who were held up by brigands between Talifu and the capital. Between Yunnanfu and Tungchwan, in east Yunnan, we met brigands twice and had some real scares. A number of the people who followed in my train for the sake of protection lost some of their belongings and two loiterers were captured.

From Tungchwan to Chaotung is five days' journey north and just two days out of Tungchwan I had the most terrible experience of my life. I had been informed that there were about 1,000 brigands between the two places, and that the road was practically closed. The magistrate of Tungchwan assured me, however, that all the brigands were in the Chaotung district. He said he would send 20 soldiers with me, and that I had nothing to fear in his district, at any rate.

I was informed by various other parties that if I once reached the Chaotung district I was safe, and that all the brigands were in the mountains near Yichehsun, two or three stages from Tungchwan. I saw the mandarin several times, and he finally admitted he had only 60 soldiers in the town, and that the rest, 120 of them, were fighting brigands near Lutien, not far from Chaotung. He agreed to give me 40 soldiers and again protested that there were no robbers in his district....

With much misgiving I left Tungchwan. The first day passed without incident, but the second had much in store for us. After lunch under an old walnut tree, I made my way over the mountains with my 12 Nashi men, 26 mules, 40 soldiers, and all the followers who took advantage of the protection afforded by my guard. We had not gone very far when my head muleteer reported that robbers were behind the caravan. I waited for the mules to catch up with us, and as they came in sight I rode on, but not for long, as my boys yelled in Chinese, "Robbers are coming," and at that moment the bandits began to shoot.

My soldiers behaved admirably, climbing to the ridge and opening fire on the brigands, but we soon found that we were considerably outnumbered. We pushed on as best we could over a pine-covered slope, down a deep ravine and up the other side, along a terribly rocky trail, the soldiers covering our retreat under the fire of the brigands.

The shooting continued all afternoon, but, thanks to the bad marksmanship of the brigands, we lost only one soldier killed.

When we finally reached the small plain of Yichehsun, on the edge of which is the hamlet of Panpiengai, I thought we were safe. But the brigands followed us. They looted the little place, capturing three soldiers and their guns.

We eventually reached the village of Yichehsun, where we had to stop for the night. Just as I arrived and passed through the dilapidated old gate (but no wall) there also came up 35 soldiers from Chaotung.... As I was talking with their officer, one of the Tungchwan soldiers came running into the village to tell me that a band of 200 robbers was only a mile and a half away. The Chaotung soldiers went to help the Tungchwan soldiers, but soon all returned with the robbers at their heels.

I was quartered in the center of the village in a miserable old temple full of coffins. The brigands came to within a half mile of the hamlet, where stood a large temple, and of this they took possession.

Darkness came on. At midnight the officers of the soldiers came in and announced that the brigands were outside and that the town could not be held against the impending attack. I never spent such a night in all my life.

I opened my trunks and distributed $600 in silver among my men, wrapped up some extra warm underwear, a towel, condensed milk and some chocolate, besides ammunition for my two .45-caliber revolvers.

Fully clad, I sat waiting for the turn of events. Every minute we expected the firing to commence. The soldiers said that they could protect me, but not my boxes, and that the safest move would be to retreat and try to find a hiding place if the brigands rushed the temple.

The natives of the village began burying their few valuables and great excitement ruled. It was a terrible wait and the longest of nights. Outside the hamlet heads of brigands that had been captured some days

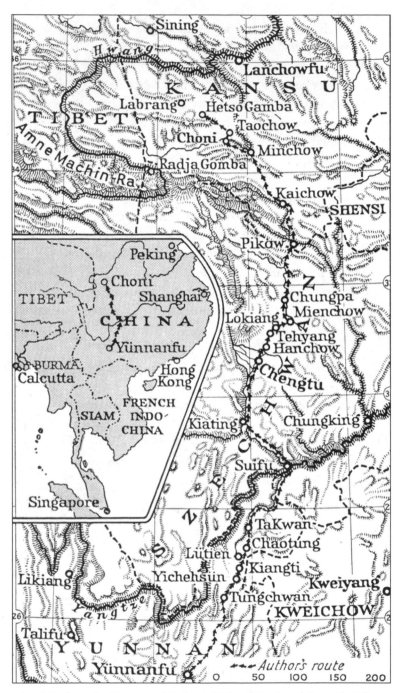

Joseph Rock country: Yunnan and Szechwan [Sichuan] Provinces, between the Yellow [Hwang Ho] and Yangtze Rivers. The route of Rock's beleaguered 1925 caravan north to the Amne Machin Mountains is traced across a turbulent, bandit-infested region.

before were hanging from poles. I was informed that several hundred bandits were surrounding the village and that capture was inevitable. At 4 a.m. our besiegers were still outside but no shot had been fired. At dawn there was not a bandit to be seen! They had vanished.

The people of Yichehsun begged me not to leave, saying that if I departed with the soldiers the robbers would come and burn the village the next night. I replied that I could not remain indefinitely, and that my presence was only an incentive for an attack. We had come to the conclusion that the people of Yichehsun intended to turn me and my caravan over to the brigands as a sort of peace offering on condition that the latter would leave the village alone.

As day broke the order to proceed was given.

The people said, "Oh, the bandits went ahead to a terrible mountain pass called Yakoutang and there they will intercept you!" This I had feared myself, but, save for a rear attack by a band of robbers on that day's march, we reached Chaotung without further molestation....

I camped in an ancient temple outside the city walls. It was a lonely place, my only neighbors being the occupants of a few graves just beyond the temple walls. It was bitterly cold and I had to pitch my tent in the one long room in the temple proper among the idols; the roof was defective and the snow came through. It was, indeed, a miserable place. Charcoal was impossible to get, as the people from the outlying villages did not come in, owing to the heavy snow.

A few days before my arrival a burial had taken place near my temple, and there was a new grave just beyond the wall. One moonlight night wolves came to the temple door and howled for hours. I was afraid that they might jump over the low walls and attack us, but they contented themselves with digging up the newly buried man and devouring him. All we found the next morning were a few blue rags and the open coffin.

I was glad to resume my journey.

I had a peculiar military escort from Chaotung on. My soldiers were former bandits, whose chief, a famous brigand, had accepted employment with the Yunnan Government and undertook to escort parties through territory infested by robbers who were formerly members of his gang. Anyone accompanied by his men could rest assured that no one would attack him.

Often I was told: "To-day there are robbers on the road." Sometimes it was a band of as many as 80 bandits well armed, but my escort would say,

"We will go ahead and arrange things with the robbers and then we will escort you through their district and you will have nothing to fear."

Thus I reached the Ta Kwan River, a tributary of the Yangtze, above Suifu. Here I chartered a boat, which brought us safely to Suifu. From there I went to Kiating and by river to Chengtu, the capital of Szechwan.

In Chengtu I was delayed by fighting to the north and also on account of illness. Governor Yang of Chengtu took the city of Mienchow five days north of the capital and drove out an independent general with 10,000 troops. The latter and his soldiers looted the city before they left, and the incoming soldiers of Governor Yang looted what remained. They even attacked the mission, and a missionary family—a Mr. Willistan and his wife and boy—was captured by bandits only 40 li (16 miles) from Mienchow. Traveling was very unsafe, as the defeated soldiers scattered into bands and turned highway robbers.

I left Chengtu with an escort of 140 regular soldiers and some cavalry. As we neared Mienchow the guard was increased to 190 soldiers, who marched with loaded rifles and fixed bayonets. Often, when I looked back from a hill, my train was over half a mile long, with a caravan of 26 mules, my helpers, 17 muleteers, and the soldiers. We were quite a formidable party.

Many people joined my train for protection. However, in spite of my strong escort, we had to take a narrow and tortuous trail over mountains little frequented by travelers, as the main road to Mienchow was closed by a small army of brigands. Even the military did not dare take the shorter main road.

My escort was changed from town to town, and, as some of the places, like Hanchow, Tehyang, and Lokiang, were "on the fence," so to speak, my soldiers from one community were not permitted to enter the next, for fear that they might fight and loot. Each group from the preceding town had to turn back at the city gates. Soldiers of the city at which we were arriving usually waited for me outside the gates and escorted me in.

We passed many dead soldiers on the road. Sometimes only the trunk was left, the head, hands, and feet having been chopped off. We also met many half-dead stragglers, who sooner or later joined their dead companions stark on the road....

You will hear again from me when I shall have emerged from the Ngolok country. If you do not hear from me, well, then, it may be that

Wrapped in silk robes like a mandarin, Joseph Rock poses with his picturesque bandit escort high in the Konka Ling Mountains of Sichuan. He was perhaps the first Westerner ever to set foot in this outlaw stronghold.

I shall have found a final resting place in that land. This is my last word to you until November or December, when I hope to turn up again either at Taochow or Sining. My plan is next year to explore the Richthofen Range and then come out through Chinese Turkestan.

Once more, au revoir, not good-bye....

Not good-bye at all, for Rock emerged safely from the Ngolok country and for years to come continued captivating readers with tales of Tibetan masked dancers, yak butter festivals, unexplored mountain ranges, bandit strongholds, and other adventures in China's far southwest. His stories influenced the poet Ezra Pound and may have inspired James Hilton to create Shangri-La, the fictional lamasery of his novel, Lost Horizons.

China was the closest thing to home the solitary Rock ever found. After the Communists evicted him in 1949, however, he was never able to return. Cast once more adrift, he washed back up in Hawaii, where he ended his days nearly penniless, living off the generosity of others.

BY COOLIE AND CARAVAN ACROSS CENTRAL ASIA

October 1927

WILLIAM J. MORDEN (1886–1958)

WHEN WILLIAM J. MORDEN TOOK TO THE FIELD, IT WAS NOT adventure he was seeking. Too much adventure hampered the progress of an expedition, a sure sign of careless planning. Yet even as careful an explorer as Bill Morden might on occasion find himself enmeshed in adventures against which he could not have adequately prepared.

Morden, son of a wealthy Chicago industrialist, had initially followed a well-trodden path, first to Yale and then into the family business of railroad equipment manufacturing. But when that began to pall, he turned to natural history explorations. In 1921 he led his first expedition, to the Yukon in search of bighorn sheep. The following year he sailed to Asia and Africa, collecting specimens of rare animals. By early 1926, at the age of 40, he had finished planning the first of four major expeditions for the American Museum of Natural History in New York, where he soon became an honorary fellow and field associate in mammology.

The Morden-Clark Asiatic Expedition took to the field in March 1926, intending to collect such rare species as the Marco Polo sheep (Ovis poli) and the ibex, which inhabit the highlands between Kashmir and what was then called Chinese Turkestan (now Xinjiang). That goal meant winding 8,000 miles through some of the most magnificent landscapes in the world. It also meant crossing dangerously sensitive political frontiers. Morden and his colleague, James L. Clark, were among the first Americans ever to enter the Russian Pamirs (now Tajikistan). They planned, after traversing Western China's Tien Shan Mountains, to pass through Outer Mongolia on their way to Peking. That entailed some risk, for the Chinese and Mongolians were on the verge of war. Morden and Clark felt sure their Russian visas would help, for Outer Mongolia relied on the Russians for protection against the Chinese. Little did they know, as they strapped down their load of valuable specimens and prepared to take their caravan over the frontier, that the situation had drastically deteriorated.

WE LEFT KUCHENGTZE OCTOBER 23, ON A PERFECT, SUNSHINY DAY, and looked forward to good weather for at least another month. That night, however, a *buran*, the violent wind of Turkestan, struck us, and for over two hours we struggled to keep our tent and kit from being scattered about the country. Next morning the ground was covered with snow, and from then on, for the remainder of the journey, we had constant snow and cold weather.

The guide decided that our best route from Kuchengtze would be diagonally northeast into Mongolia, bringing us to the main caravan road south of Ulyasutai. Saiga antelope were believed to range not far from the trail at one point and we were hopeful of finding them.

Owing to the scarcity of water, there is little summer travel along this route, though, as the ground was covered with snow, we were able to camp wherever a sparse growth of bush furnished fuel, melted snow being our water supply. One camel carried two water casks, but these were unused much of the time.

The country was barren, having no growth except dry bunches of grass, with here and there small areas of low, thorny bushes. Ranges of hills showed dimly in the distance, and after several days' marching we came to a more broken country, where rocky ridges ran from northwest to southeast. These were the foothills of the Mongolian Altai, the great range which spreads diagonally across western Mongolia from the high mountainous country of southern Siberia.

We met few people, as this part of our route crossed a desert where even wandering Mongols do not come.

After two weeks of steady traveling, our guide said that we were in the neighborhood of the first Mongol outpost. He suggested a detour around it, as the Mongols might rob our caravan of its grain. We rejected this advice, however, as we wished to present credentials at the post and obtain a new guide, a local man who knew the country in more detail.

We did not, of course, anticipate any trouble with the Mongols, as there had been none with the Russians in the Pamir, nor with the Chinese in Turkestan. Our Russian credentials, we thought, would be of service, particularly as we knew Soviet influence was strong in Mongolia.

On the evening of November 6 we noticed dark objects to the right. We first thought they were wolves, but as they advanced in the growing darkness we saw they were horsemen. They halted the caravan and rode up and down the line of camels, fingering loads and looking carefully at everything. At their shouts, soldiers came from different directions, and we suddenly realized that we were surrounded. The horsemen wore peaked helmets similar to those of Russian soldiers in the Pamir, so we knew we had found the outpost.

It seemed best to make ourselves known; so, turning our pocket flash lights on our faces, we told the interpreter to tell the soldiers that we were white men wishing to go to the post. These Mongols had never seen electric flash lights, and the sudden light, without fire, amazed them. They encircled Clark and me and hustled us downhill where dark objects in the gloom indicated the post. We were hurried into a yurt, where eight or ten men squatted about a fire. They looked up with scowls, and we could see at once that they were suspicious and unfriendly.

Through the interpreter, we asked for the commanding officer, but received no response. Then one of the soldiers inquired if we had Mongol passports. We were forced to admit that we had none, although we at once produced our American passports, Russian letters and permits for their inspection. These they examined upside down and backward, finally contemptuously throwing them aside.

They looked at us fixedly, whispered together, looked at us again, and finally one by one left the yurt. As we could hear our camels coming in and could get no information from the Mongols, we decided that the interview was ended for the evening, and that the best thing to do would be to make camp and await the pleasure of the officer the next day.

We arose and started to leave the yurt, our man Mohammed, being nearest the door, going first. As he stepped forward, a Mongol struck him in the face and knocked him down. Before we could get the meaning of this, the Mongol raised a shout which brought soldiers rushing into the yurt, two carrying ropes.

Clark and I were set upon by several men. Our struggles, though ineffectual, seemed to infuriate them, and both of us went on the ground. As I lay, I saw one Mongol take a kettle of boiling water from the fire to pour on my face. I shut my eyes, turned my head sideways, and fortunately the water did not strike me.

They tied our wrists as tightly as two men, seated on the ground with feet braced against our crossed wrists, could jerk the ropes. Then they poured hot water on the ropes, so that in drying they would shrink and tighten even more. Our men were also set upon and bound in like manner, being badly beaten in the process.

After we were helpless they rolled us on our backs and carefully went through our clothing, taking everything from our pockets. We asked

In quest of the rare and elusive Marco Polo sheep (Ovis poli), the expedition crossed the roof of the world, floundering through the high passes of the Karakorums and Pamirs, where Russia, China, and British India met.

the interpreter what they intended doing and were told that he had heard a Mongol say that we were to be shot, although he was uncertain whether it would be immediately or the next day.

Strangely enough, instead of being frightened by the prospect, as the ropes grew tighter our sincere hope was that they would make it short and quick, without dragging out a process which promised to be exceedingly unpleasant. There was but one thing to do: take what might come as quietly as possible, without giving our captors the satisfaction of seeing us weaken.

We talked of various things, among others whether the outside world would ever learn exactly what had happened to us. As nearly as we could decide, the actual facts would never be determined. The Mongols would probably not admit having seen us, or, if they did so, would claim that we had attacked them, and that they had been forced to kill us in self-defense.

As our hands became cold we tried to warm them over the little dung fire, but at each attempt we were struck in the face and knocked back to the ground.

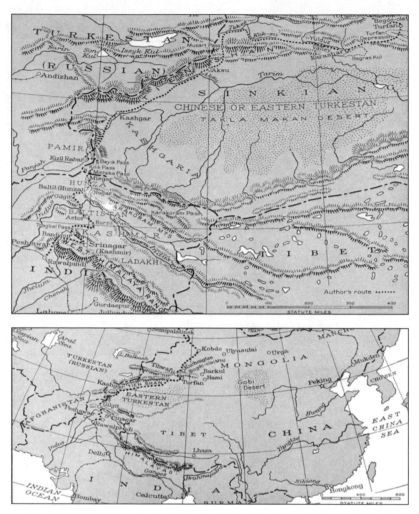

Departing Kashmir in 1926, the Morden-Clark Expedition traversed thousands of miles of mountain and desert, collecting animals for the American Museum of Natural History, before arriving at the Mongolian border—where things went drastically wrong.

How long we remained in the yurt it was impossible to know; probably between one and two hours. Then we were ordered outside. As we left the yurt we could see a squad of soldiers with rifles silhouetted against the stars. Clark and I said good-bye to each other, because, so far as we could see, it was a firing squad which awaited us. We were led a short distance to the right, apparently being marched to a selected spot to be shot.

We were directed, however, into a small caravan tent which we had not seen before. There we were again thrown to the ground. Seated back to back against a tent pole, ropes were passed about our bodies and arms and we were securely tied to the pole, our wrists still bound in front of us. Then the crowd left us, after placing an armed soldier on guard. We thought we were there for the night. This brought up an even more unpleasant prospect, for were we kept several hours in that position, with the circulation in our hands absolutely stopped, by morning they might be frozen. As we were hundreds of miles from any medical attention, this might mean the loss of our hands or death, even though we were later released.

The pain became excruciating. As we had been without food since early morning, we were weak and hoped we might faint. It was probably well that we did not, for there would have been greater likelihood of our hands freezing, as the temperature was well below zero.

Mongols were continually entering and leaving the tent. One of them, we believe, really saved our lives. He was an older man, not a soldier, who could speak a certain amount of Chinese, as could our servant Mohammed. They were thus able to converse with the interpreter, who had proven himself of little use, particularly when thoroughly frightened.

I caught enough of the conversation to realize that Mohammed was telling the Mongol about us, particularly emphasizing the fact that we were friends of the Russians. In the yurt we had told the Mongols that we were Americans, but that had meant nothing to them; apparently they had never heard of America. They did, however, know Russians, and we afterward thought that our being represented as their friends probably prevented them from shooting us as spies.

How long we remained in the tent with our wrists tied we never knew; probably from one to two hours. Now and then a soldier came in and felt our hands. Though this meant nothing to us at the time, the Mongols probably knew how long they could apply torture by this method before doing permanent injury. That it was intended solely as torture we now know, for Dr. Andrews [Roy Chapman Andrews] had since told me that he has seen it being done in the Mongol jails at Urga.

After another long wait, they again felt our hands and, apparently finding that the limit of endurance had been reached, unbound them. That gave us our first slight hope that, even though we might be eventually shot, we were not to be tortured to death. They gave us heavier coats, some salty tea, which is the usual beverage of the Mongol, and later some hard bread. They even brought a few of our own cigarettes, which had been taken from our pockets, put them into our mouths, and lighted them for us. Then they tightened the ropes which bound us to the pole, posted an armed guard in the tent, and left us for the night. Toward morning, probably through sheer exhaustion, we got a little sleep.

Sometime after daybreak they violently awakened us and ordered our man Mohammed outside. He had hardly left the tent when two shots barked out. It seemed that surely the end had come, and one of us remarked, "There goes poor Mohammed; I wonder who's next."

We had guessed wrongly, however. Two hours later he was led back and we learned that they had taken him out to open various boxes, so that they could see the contents. The shots had been fired by a soldier who was experimenting with my automatic pistol. Our arms and ammunition, of course, had been taken from us immediately on arrival at the post.

Late that afternoon a young officer arrived and had us brought before him. He looked over our papers and questioned us. We hoped that he might tell us something, but we were taken back to the tent still wondering, and once more tied to the pole to spend another uncomfortable night.

On the second morning, after 36 hours of incarceration, we were released and ordered to make camp by the post. Then the officer went through our kit thoroughly, confiscating field glasses, compasses, and instruments.

The following day he sent us under guard to another post 30 miles away, where we were again tried by two officers. We asked to be sent under guard to Ulyasutai, as this was on our route, but permission was quickly refused. Then we requested to be allowed to return to Turkestan. This was also refused.

We were curtly told that we must go under guard to Kobdo, the head of the district. This meant a journey of 250 miles across the Altai Mountains on a trail that, as we later learned, is not used by caravans in winter.

The journey took 12 days and was exceedingly difficult and unpleasant throughout. During one march of 20 miles we crossed four 9,000-foot passes, working steadily from 11 in the morning until 5 the following morning, and 20 of our 30 camels were down in the snow at one time.

It grew very cold during the later part of the journey. We were forced to discard the tent, as there was almost no fuel of any kind and sleeping bags became so full of frost that they could not be used. There were yurts at intervals along the way, and we slept with the Mongols. This arrangement was unpleasant, but much warmer than the open air or our tent.

At last we reached the small town and military post of Kobdo, where a garrison of 300 soldiers is maintained. We had hoped for release, but were still under suspicion. Four hours were spent trying to convince two young Mongols of the police that we were not spies. Each time that we informed them who and what we were they roughly told us that we lied, that we were spies and dangerous characters.

Finally another Mongol entered the yurt where our examination was being conducted. This man, a Buriat from southern Siberia, could read a certain amount of Russian, and, seeing our Russian letters, sent hurriedly for the governor general, the head of the district.

Unlike the other Mongols we had met, he had slightly more brains than a child. Also he was able to use them. He asked a few searching questions, seemed satisfied at our answers, and ordered us taken to the house of a Russian whom we had met on our way to Kobdo. He gave us his entire time during our stay in Kobdo, and through his help we reached the Russian consul.

This official induced the Mongols to return our confiscated arms and instruments, and did everything in his power to persuade them to allow us to continue to Ulyasutai and Urga. But permission was absolutely refused.

We decided, therefore, to take the most practicable route to Peking, which was by wagon and sleigh to a branch of the Trans-Siberian Railroad at Biisk, in Siberia, thence by rail to Manchuria and Peking. The Russian consul gave us visas and permits and arranged for the return of our men and camels to Turkestan.

Before reaching the railway, we encountered exceedingly cold weather, our registering thermometer sticking several times at 44°F below zero. Peking was reached on New Year's Day, nine months after leaving Kashmir. We had traveled 7,900 miles across Asia, from the Indian Ocean to the Yellow Sea.

That unsought adventure didn't stop Bill Morden. Three years later he led another American Museum of Natural History expedition into Soviet Central Asia and far eastern Siberia, searching for saiga antelopes and Siberian tigers. Eventually he became a director of New York's famed Explorers Club and spent the rest of his life leading expeditions, most of them to Africa.

THE DESERT ROAD TO TURKESTAN
June 1929

OWEN LATTIMORE (1900–89)

ONE DAY IN 1925, AT KWEIHWATING, WHERE THE PEKING (NOW Beijing) railway reached tentatively into the desert just beyond the Great Wall, a young agent for an export-import firm observed the encounter between two worlds. There, stepping gingerly among sidings packed with freight trains, was a camel caravan, unloading cotton and wool from distant Central Asia into waiting boxcars. As he watched this, Owen Lattimore realized that steam from the locomotives was not the only thing dissipating around him. The last tendrils of romance still clinging to the Silk Road were vanishing, too. He was witnessing the end of an era—and, characteristically, he wanted to experience it before it was gone for good.

Born in Washington, D.C., and educated in England, Lattimore grew up in China. His father, a teacher there, tried to shield his talented children from their Chinese neighbors, fearing that otherwise they might "go native." While brother Richmond became a famous translator of Homer and sister Eleanor a noted children's writer, Owen went about as native as he could, turning an innate gift for languages into a fluency in Mandarin. Moreover, because his job took him into remote regions of the country, he learned to live and travel as the Chinese did, too.

Owen had a scholarly bent, but to understand the immemorial ways of the caravans he became a caravaneer himself. Such an opportunity was quickly closing: Brigandage and civil war were overrunning the age-old routes. But he had added incentive. In March 1926 he was married, and the only honeymoon fit for such a young and adventurous couple was a journey across the remotest regions of Central Asia. His new bride would travel through Siberia and meet him on the borders of Chinese Turkestan (Sinkiang), while he made the dangerous crossing of Mongolia with the last of the camel caravans.

Owen Lattimore, 26 years old, short, bantam, and plucky, followed a path no Western explorer had yet traversed, mostly because he refused to play that role. Instead, he plunged in among the Chinese and became one with them, ate their food and slept among their bugs during a year of such political instability that large, well-prepared expeditions refused to budge.

Two great routes lead from China into central Asia: one from central China up through the provinces of Shensi and Kansu to the edge of the western Gobi Desert, and then across into Chinese Turkestan without touching Mongolia; the other from northern China up into northern Mongolia, and then westward to Chinese Turkestan.

I could not follow the first route, because of banditry, civil war, and anti-foreign feeling. Nor could I follow the second, because in recent years the tribes of Outer Mongolia, largely under Russian influence, have succeeded in breaking away from China, and will not allow caravans to traverse their country.

Thus I was led to the new and unknown route, the Desert Road to Turkestan. Opened up by trading caravans, to avoid the hostilities of both China and Outer Mongolia, it runs through Inner Mongolia, which is nominally under Chinese sovereignty. It traverses the most barren country in all Mongolia, and partly for that reason has remained virtually unknown....

After arranging for camels to meet me about 120 miles out in Mongolia, I left Kweihwating secretly in a closed cart. My caravan consisted of nine hired camels. I was accompanied only by the owner of the camels, a thorough rascal, and "Moses," a Chinese servant, who had been with me for years, and with my father before me. Moses was a sturdy fellow, so honest, reliable, and resourceful that I doubt whether I could ever have got through without him.

In traveling we attached ourselves to large trading caravans. I came to live among these caravan men exactly like one of them. My tent was the same, my food the same, my routine the same, and before we had finished the journey my clothing more than half the same. Among them I passed as I suppose few, if any, other white men ever have, observing and mastering their peculiar customs and traditions and learning their life.

We traveled a great deal at night and turned the camels out to graze during the day, when we could keep an eye on them to prevent their straying. Beginning late in the afternoon and ending about midnight, our average march was seven or eight hours—a stage of 20 miles, which was very long, slow, and tiring, because a loaded camel, carrying 350 pounds, never goes faster than two and a half miles an hour. When we halted, the loads were parked in the squares at the sides of the tent, and the camels were made to kneel in front of it until dawn. Then they were turned loose in charge of a couple of men.

We made tea at dawn, using a very coarse grade of brick tea, the kind most common throughout Tibet, Mongolia, and many parts of Siberia and Turkestan. In Mongolia this tea is as good as currency. Prices of cattle and wool are often quoted in terms of tea bricks, and for small purchases pieces can be broken off the large compressed blocks and weighed.

Our one regular meal, taken about noon each day, consisted mainly of half-cooked dough. We would moisten white flour and roll and thump it into dough, then either tear it up in little blobs, or cut it into a rough kind of spaghetti and cook it with bread-sauce.

This bread-sauce is what the Chinese call a *pao-peitung-hsi*, a precious thing. It is the mainstay of caravan life. The basis of it is bread, which has been first fermented and then moistened. When it is covered with a rich, cheeselike mildew, it is put out in the sun and dried. Then it is mixed with bean-sauce, beans, bean-curd, ginger, red and green peppers, and anything else that will make it more pungent, and cooked with lots of mutton fat and minced mutton, and about half its weight in salt. When it has reached the consistency of a thick paste, it may be packed in a wide-mouthed wicker jar and carried along on a journey. In spite of the salt, a green and blue scum sometimes gathers on it in hot weather; but this can be stirred in again and the mixture is as good as ever....

In a big caldron hung over a fire of camel dung or the twigs of desert shrubs we would fry some sauce. To this we would add cold water. When the water boiled briskly, we threw in the spaghetti, or blobs of dough, and left it for not more than two or three minutes. As soon as the dough was partly cooked, we ladled it out of the caldron into our eating bowls, put a little more sauce on the top, and shoveled it down with chopsticks....

We drank enormous quantities of tea, because the water was so bad. Running water was an extreme rarity, and usually our supply came from shallow wells, heavily tainted with salt, soda, and I suppose a number of mineral salts. The worst we had was in tamarisk regions. The tamarisk is a desert shrub which sends its roots down to a great depth for moisture. In such regions surface water is turned yellow by the rotting roots and becomes thick—almost sticky—and incredibly nasty....

At the beginning of the journey we passed a number of Mongol lamaseries, or monasteries, but later we entered the true desert, which was almost uninhabited. Not only were Mongol camps infrequent, but the people were shy, if not hostile. We were traveling in a year of great turbulence and disorder. The civil wars in China, the increase of banditry along the border and in Mongolia itself, and the troubles in Outer Mongolia had sent vague, terrifying rumors flying through the desert, and no man knew who might be an enemy or a friend.

At intervals we met caravans and exchanged news of regions where bandits or raiders from Outer Mongolia had last been seen. I sent letters back by several of these caravans, each time offering payment, which was always refused with grave courtesy.

"It is the business of the Gobi," the caravan master would say. "Who would not do as much?"

With all these men, "the business of the Gobi" was a phrase covering everything that can happen to a caravan in the desert—friendship and enmity, good fortune and calamity. Every letter I sent was safely delivered, but that was because the men had recognized me and admitted me into their own fellowship....

Most of the caravans we met carried wool, cotton, raisins, pelts, and hides from Chinese Turkestan; but some of them carried queerer freight. We encountered a series that were conveying corpses.

Chinese traders out in Turkestan abhor the idea of being buried in such a strange, faraway country, and they belong to guilds which look after them in case of their death on the frontier. Bodies are buried in temporary graves until most of the flesh has fallen away. Then the guild has them dug up, put in traveling coffins, and loaded on camels, four corpses to the camel load. They are carried across the desert, delivered to another office of the guild at the end of the route, and eventually distributed, each to its ancestral burial ground.

Not long after one of these corpse caravans had passed our camp, one of our men fell ill of a violent stomach ache, and at the same moment somebody saw beside the trail an empty coffin, which we had not noticed when we camped in the dark. A panic ensued. Every man of our band cleared out as fast as he could, pulling his camels after him. All they did for the sick man was to leave a camel hobbled beside him, where he lay rolling on the ground.

The coffin found by the way had been left by the corpse carriers. Evidently it had been battered to pieces, and the men had taken out the body and stuffed it into another coffin along with another corpse. Our men thought the ghost of one of the corpses had resented the crowding and had jumped out and, being very lonely and terrified in the desert, had seized upon our unfortunate fellow traveler for a new place of abode.

A honeymoon to remember: Traveling with a Chinese camel caravan, Owen Lattimore crossed Mongolia from Kweihwating near Peking to Urumchi, where he met his bride, who had arrived there by rail and sled from Siberia. Together they journeyed by horseback and cart to India.

The man's pains, they believed, were the result of a struggle between the stray ghost and his own spirit.

If the man died, the ghost might come after some one else. The only refuge was in flight. If the sick man got better, he could mount the camel and ride after his fellows. If he did not turn up, they would send back from the next camp to see what had happened; it would be a pity to waste the camel, anyhow.

The wretched fellow, helpless with his own pain and terror and the hypnotic effect of being deserted by the others, would probably have curled up and died of pure fright, but, luckily for him, I had gone back that day with one of the men to fill the water casks at a well not far behind. When we set out to catch up with the caravans, we saw the sick man rolling about in agony on the ground, with a bored-looking camel standing close by.

He was groaning and crying, "Alas! my mother! Alas, my old mother, I shall not see you again, I shall die here! Alas, Old Man God, can this yet be suffered? Alas, alas! my mother, this is waiting for death!" After questioning him a bit, I calmed him somewhat, and discovered that his ailment was nothing but a stomach ache, caused by a chill. I sent the man who was with me to tell the caravan to stop until I could get some powerful foreign medicine out of a box. Meantime I unrolled the man, so to speak, and began to rub his stomach. It was not a promising looking stomach on the outside, but after a hearty rubbing it began to feel better on the inside.

Eventually the frightened traders were persuaded to halt, and I gave the sick man some medicine; but they were uneasy. I tried to calm them, and to persuade them that the man had not really been invaded by a ghost. I even invented some symptoms to describe how he would have behaved if he had been ghost-possessed.

Not long after this, as we approached the borders of Chinese Turkestan, we fell in with a border patrol, and without warning I found myself in jail.

The province of Chinese Turkestan is kept very tightly closed to strangers, and nowhere more tightly than on the borders nearest to China. A foreigner who enters from India gets a better reception than one who comes from China, because officials know that they can rely upon the friendliness of the Government of India, whereas they are far from trusting the officials in the provinces of China proper.

The limited group who, under the old Governor, control Chinese Turkestan are in perpetual fear that some general in China will force a civil war on them, invade the province, and take it over; and they are well aware that in recent years their soundest defense has been the wide deserts protecting them in the direction of China and Mongolia. Consequently, every traveler coming from these politically dangerous regions is detained at the frontier until his papers have been minutely examined and verified, and his case has been referred, if necessary, to the Governor.

I had the awkward luck to arrive at a small post off the regular line of travel. The two officers in charge were ignoramuses, only one of whom could read even a little. This man wanted to have me kept in close confinement. First he accused me of being a Japanese spy; and when I laughed him out of that idea, he insisted that I might be one of the Russian officers in the employ of General Feng Yu-hsiang, looking for a way to invade Chinese Turkestan. At that time it was very much in the cards that such an invasion might be attempted.

I should undoubtedly have been in for a bad time, had the men once convinced themselves that they had really caught a "hostile" Russian; but

Owen Lattimore, pipe in mouth, stands beside Moses, the longtime family friend whose wiles saved the author from many pitfalls when together they plunged into the world of the camel caravans.

luckily I had had some experience with the type with which I was dealing, and above all I had the faithful Moses. In fact, it was Moses who brilliantly established us on an almost favorable footing.

I had thought it best at first to explain myself in a simple, straight-forward way. Moses thought otherwise. "Don't you know," he said, "that the first rule of travel is, 'Never tell the truth'? Tell them what's good for them."

He understood the situation rightly; for an attempt on our part to lay too much stress on our innocence might, according to our captors' tortuous way of thinking, simply have proved we were guilty of something. The thing to do was to impress them with our importance, the sound old Asiatic rule being that no one who is important enough is guilty of anything.

Moses was ready with a yarn that I was the nephew of an American ambassador, and after the tale had been repeated a few times I was rapidly promoted to be the nephew of an American prince, who was of the blood of the American emperor.

After that, I was always addressed as the Young Prince and accorded much better treatment than I should otherwise have received. I was also permitted to retain my arms and to go about during the day under guard. I was even given leave to take my rifle and go out shooting antelope—probably because I kept the whole garrison in meat. At night, however, Moses and the camel men and I were shut up in a tiny, unheated, tumble-down hut.

My capture was reported to the town of Barkul, 80 miles away across a snow-covered mountain range, and from Barkul the report was relayed to Urumchi (Tihwafu), the capital of Chinese Turkestan. I was not permitted to send messages myself, probably for fear I might discredit my captors; but through a friendly caravan man I managed to smuggle a letter off to two English missionaries whom I knew to be at Urumchi, and to a Chinese friend in the province, an important official. Through their mediation with the Governor, word came back in about a fortnight that I was to be released....

It was the beginning of December and a winter of record cold and deep snow which amazed even the old hands among the caravan men. My camels were worn out after three months of travel, and although they had been resting for the fortnight while I was incarcerated, they had not had enough to eat during that time. Worst of all, the big trading caravans had all gone by; so we had to find our way alone, with little chance of help if we got into trouble. Soon after we started, we began to find all along the road prostrate camels that had been abandoned by the caravan before us. Trodden places in the snow marked numerous points where caravans had been overtaken by blizzards.

Many of the abandoned camels were still alive. When a camel gets to a certain stage of weakness, he can no longer get up and walk; but he has such an incredible vitality that even then he may live for many days, in spite of bitter cold and violent weather. Caravan men will not kill these camels for fear of bad luck. Even the wolves will not put them out of their misery. A wolf will pull down a standing camel, or one that runs from him; but when the camel just lies and watches him, he simply waits until his quarry dies.

Some of the camels we saw were plated with ice on one side, evidence of the bitter weather they had lived through. They were unable to move their bodies, but as we approached they would turn their heads to watch us, and as we passed they would look to the front again to watch us going on into the snow....

Four months and 1,600 miles after leaving Kweihwating, Lattimore's caravan arrived at Kuchengtze, Xinjiang. For him, though, it was not an end; rather a new beginning, for soon he met his bride and together they spent their honeymoon roaming the mountains and deserts of Central Asia.

Owen Lattimore became a noted expert on China and Mongolia, with honors ranging from the gold medal of the Royal Geographical Society to the Mongolian Order of the Golden Nail. During World War II President Franklin Roosevelt appointed him Advisor to Chiang Kai-shek, leader of the Chinese Nationalist government; and when the Japanese surrendered in 1945, Lattimore's Solution in Asia was one of only two books on President Harry Truman's desk. So it might seem strange that Senator Joseph McCarthy charged him with being the "top Soviet espionage agent in the United States." He was exonerated, of course, but not until after a feisty, turbulent, five-year battle to clear his name.

FROM THE MEDITERRANEAN TO THE YELLOW SEA BY MOTOR
November 1932

MAYNARD OWEN WILLIAMS (1888–1963)

LOOKING BACK OVER HIS LONG CAREER, MAYNARD OWEN WILLIAMS, chief of the NATIONAL GEOGRAPHIC'S *foreign editorial staff, always returned to the ten months he spent traversing Asia with the storied Citroen-Haardt Expedition. As constant reminders he had his Legion d'Honneur ribbon, awarded for his being the only American on this French undertaking, and his hands, which ever after bore the scars of Gobi frostbite. He had his memories, too, and considered the journey the greatest adventure of his life.*

The Citroen-Haardt Trans-Asiatic Expedition, bankrolled by French auto magnate Andre Citroen and led by Georges-Marie Haardt, was the third in a series of motorized transcontinental treks. The first two rolled the length and breadth of Africa. Like them, the third—promoted as the first overland crossing of Asia since Marco Polo—depended on a fleet of Citroen-designed trucks and half-tracked vehicles to convey archaeologists, scientists, film crews, mechanics, and Williams, the official expedition photographer, across Asia.

Departing Beirut in April 1931, the convoy crossed Syria, Iraq, Iran, and Afghanistan, up to the mountain ramparts of the Karakorum, which the vehicles could not cross. The men proceeded by pony and yak to Xinjiang Province in far western China. There they met the expedition's second wing, which had driven Citroen vehicles west from Peiping (as Peking was then called), leaving supply caches along the way for a return journey. The united expedition was to turn and make a triumphal procession together back to the Imperial City.

Unfortunately, the fires of rebellion were sweeping Xinjiang and a renegade general, Ma Chung Ying, was on the rampage. As this excerpt opens, the Citroen-Haardt convoy was assembling in Urumchi, the provincial capital. Forced to flee, they embarked on an exhausting 2,300-mile eastward journey down the "Great Road," from one walled Chinese town to another, facing the Gobi winter winds and Ma Chung Ying, somewhere ahead.

Haardt led in his command car, called the "Golden Scarab." Riding shotgun in the "Silver Crescent" was 43-year-old Maynard Williams, who, despite the hazards ahead, was ever his imperturbably sunny self, seeing smiling faces everywhere and having the time of his life.

Georges Le Fèvre, Expedition historian, regarded our delay in Urumchi as a heaven-sent blessing. An ardent seeker for facts, he kept busy day and night and his voluminous notes increased by many pages a day. During our stay he and I had a delightful discussion with a Mongol princess. She wore riding boots, a tight blue skirt, and a simple white blouse, lightly touched with coral embroidery. Her hair was slightly disheveled by her dashing ride on a tough-mouthed pony. Attractive, intelligent, objective, this oriental woman spoke French without accent and Anglo-American English seasoned with slang. Dancing with her had seemed strange. Talking with her seemed utterly natural.

"Why do occidentals and orientals dislike one another?" we asked, our actual relationship belying our thesis. Hitherto we had looked at Asiatic peoples through occidental eyes. We now looked at ourselves through theirs. Here, in Sinkiang [Xinjiang], the Governor held all the tricks. Our world was far away, robbed of influence by censorship and desert.

"Why call conservatism dislike?" she replied. "Do you always welcome strangers to your clubs and homes? The oriental has his psychological Great Wall, whose protection is beginning to seem less sure. The man behind it doesn't want to be loved or even appreciated. He wants to be undisturbed.

"People seek to protect not only property, but modes of life. Perhaps your way of life is right for you, but it threatens ours.

"You are in a hurry, and hence barbaric. You are entranced by mechanical toys, which you haven't mastered. You like frankness; but until real understanding exists, even formal politeness helps. You dominate world ideals, which differ from ours.

"You are men of auto, railway, radio. You find this a backward land, without roads, speed, a free press, a balanced budget, sanitation, or familiar forms of justice. Hence you pity the Chinese. But they live in the Celestial Kingdom, the center of all the world that counts. Your progress is chaotic, at least in its impact on orientals, because its spiritual values are not realized. We Mongols are emancipated. 'A good horse and a wide plain under God's heaven,' that's our desire. And we realize it...."

From Urumchi to Peiping is 2,300 miles. Two of our caravans had been pillaged. The rebel Ma Chung Ying stood astride the Great Road waiting for us, with tons of our supplies already in his hands. Sand dune and river, desert and rocky defile lay across our path. The cold of the Mongolian plateau was often in our thoughts.

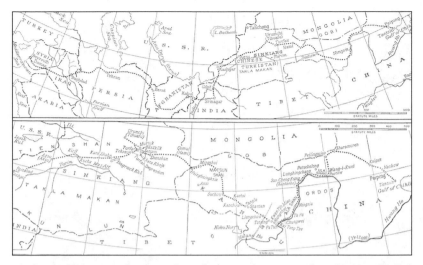

Last leg of an epic journey, the 2,000-mile run from Urumchi to Peiping, down the string of walled towns marking China's Mongolian frontier, proved exhausting for the Citroen-Haardt Expedition, embarked on the first motorized crossing of Asia from the Mediterranean to the Yellow Sea.

Fur coats and boots were made. Our wind-proof "Shackleton" trousers were lined with sheepskins or fur. Blankets were made for our motors and felt inner curtains added to protect ourselves. Urumchi is accustomed to cold and the necessary materials were at hand and cheap.

Penaud invented a heater, shaped like a speaking trumpet, which was bolted to our exhaust manifold. Its funnel collected air from the fan and conducted it into the car. With an excess of faith and scant ideas of a Mongolian winter, he added a metal stopper to "keep us from roasting in our furs." That proved unconscious irony....

At Kara Khoja we were overtaken by the main party, and the drive to Peiping was on....

The tents were seldom pitched. Valises and even washbasins were ignored for days at a time. Not only actual cold, but the threat of greater, always hung over us. Seldom were we free from fatigue. We might resign ourselves to subordinating scientific and artistic work to the onward march of the motors and have great admiration for the mechanics, toiling with bare hands in the dead of the winter night; but the cars, lacking light oil and anti-freeze because political delays had not been foreseen, demanded unceasing care. Men and cars were both tired out and mutually dependent.

Once started on one section of our journey, there was no real rest until it was completed. Night after night we felt our way ahead over atrocious trails, with a theoretical rest for men and motors from 2 to 5 in the

A cold bookseller huddled by his open-air stall around New Years Day, 1932,
when the Citroen-Haardt Expedition passed through Liangchow,
the earthquake-ravaged town about halfway between Urumchi and Peiping.

morning. The driver slumped forward over his wheel. His seat-mate, who could doze during the day, watched the temperature dials for water and oil. Whenever a radiator got cold or a bearing stiff, a motor woke with a roar. A hundred fantastic landscapes tossed up by our ranging headlights are now mingled in what some of us feel was reality and others a bad dream....

At Hsinghsinghsia, a hundred miles or so from Qomul, a supply of gasoline had been buried months before. But with two-score military motors operating in Sinkiang, at a time of war and requisition, it seemed better, before leaving the main route, to keep our actual gas reserve high. Native carts had carried ahead 300 gallons, together with two cases of food, a spare motor-block, and Whymper tent, and left it in a village called "Ever Flowing Water" because of its never-failing source.

My notes covering this period were recorded by a pen which had to be thawed out after every few words by placing it in my mouth. But the memory would have lasted in any case. Some one waked me from my doze beside Gauthier, driver of the "Silver Crescent."

"Eh *bien*, it seems that there are two or three dirty rooms, one occupied by fifteen frozen corpses, and an open shed."

"Better sleep with fifteen to-night than be one of sixteen to-morrow," I thought, for during several nights my breath had been freezing to the edge of my sleeping sack. So when I discovered a room with a raised platform in it, I made my bed. Behind was another room, which I thought better not to investigate....

After a thirty-hour run without sleep, we passed through a flood of refugees fleeing from Ma Chung Ying and arrived at the gates of Suchow. A sumptuous tea made things look brighter. Our home was a new but drafty building constructed as a semisocial, semireligious club of Shensi and Chihli merchants.

The Commandant, who had just acquired a new 14-year-old wife, sent word that if we'd send over a case of motor oil, negotiations for our departure would proceed more smoothly. Delay was no tragedy for me, for the city is unusually interesting, and among the hundreds of youngsters who followed me about there were many whose smiles were worthy of record. Behind my camera curious children trailed along as behind the piper of Hamelin. With a stand camera, you are at the mercy of the mob. Offend them and you might as well go home. Inspire their good will and they'll warm your heart.

There is a mid-city temple in whose courtyard open-air restaurants, barbers, and medicine men ply their trade. Back against the main shrine, a story-teller, younger than most, was spinning such an endless tale as the Chinese love, with—first time I ever saw this—his prompt-book before him. On the stage, so placed that the temple gods can see, a theater was in action, with gongs and rattles agallop.

Meanwhile the rebels under General Ma Chung Ying were near—and coming nearer. A night attempt to use our wireless brought a colonel down on us. Bu Li and Gao, our interpreters and confidential agents, were instructed to lose $29 to him at mah jongg, and the flurry passed.

The following morning permission to leave came—unexpectedly. After a delay of several hours, the city gates at last slowly swung open and our cars filed out. Twenty-four hours later Ma Chung Ying's troops entered Suchow. By then we were at Kaotai, with a bandit's head—one sample from 27 fresh ones—dangling by a cord beside the city gate. We picked up 60 tins of gas, which a German missionary had kindly stored in the Sunday-school room, and pushed on....

The trip from Kanchow to Liangchow was one of those unexpected experiences which pounce upon the explorer and test his mettle and metal. Perhaps the mechanics trusted the latter a bit too far. But if they did they paid the price.

With Ma Chung Ying just behind and the promise of plenty of spare parts in Liangchow, at the end of only 200 miles of supposedly decent road, we set out after lunch on December 26. Just at dark we passed the twilight-magnified walls of Tanglo and at 2 a.m. stopped beyond Shantan. A broken distributor disk kept some of the mechanics busy all the cold night, and one mechanical difficulty after another hounded their second day.

Sunset brought us to a miserable village, wrecked by earthquakes and said to be bandit headquarters. In the steep, rocky passage beyond, perfect for ambush, a tractor band gave way. By 10 the motor caravan again moved on. By 3 in the morning we entered another "bandit village," with a score or so armed men still abroad in the silent streets. A dazzlingly pretty Chinese girl, with bright dress, gold bracelet and earrings, picked out by our lights against this drab, ruined region, did more than the armed men in sheepskins to give an illusion of evil to this sordid street of tumble-down shacks....

The score of parallel ruts beside the line of the Great Wall, here merely a succession of bulky towers, gave little evidence of recent use. Ages of traffic had worn them so deep that even a high-wheeled cart must continue in the track in which it starts. But there was dust at the bottom of all. A massive memorial stone, its top writhing with carved dragons, cut the sky, and I turned aside long enough to let one of the old watchtowers of the Great Wall impress itself upon me....

Even we were tired. Fifty-two hours at a stretch was enough. But for the last car it was sixty-four. It had broken a tractor band only 600 yards from the Mission, and a driver had dropped beside his car from sheer fatigue. As usual, Haardt stuck by his admiring mechanics till the finish....

A cold ride down a rough trail between miles of grave mounds brought me to the somber-walled city of Liangchow for the last day of 1931. Earthquakes, whose center was farther east, had swept the region years before, but isolated idols still rose above the wreckage. Homeless gods, some with their heads broken off, or the straw-and-mud stumps of once regal arms sticking out into the cold haze.

The city within the walls had also been touched with destruction, against which new life was making brave but slow progress. On the main street red-and-gold posters were being pasted on the wooden posts. This was a special act of political piety, dutifully paid to the newly accepted official calendar, for the people still hold to "China New Years" in February as their popular festival.

If the Chinese indulged in holiday resolutions, opium-smoking was certainly not under the ban. Great greasy gobs of the drug were displayed for sale and pipe-bowls, lamps, and all the complex paraphernalia of that most exacting of vices lined the street....

From Lianghcow we must turn north and the "Da Han," or "Great Cold," was due. We were halfway from Urumchi to Peiping, but the harder portions lay ahead.

On January 5, 1932, the "Silver Crescent," the "Heavy Cinema," and the "Frigate" truck left in the direction of Ningsia to blaze a trail toward the Yellow River, along the line of the Great Wall. At half past 2 in the morning we stopped at a dirty little inn at Tatsing, where sixty 10-gallon tins of gas had been safely stored.

We found Kwan Yin Miao, the Temple of the Goddess of Mercy, outside the Great Wall instead of inside, as shown on the map, and rolled slowly on through bitter wind, over an awful trail, until—just before sundown—Piat broke a fork in his gear box. By night we went on over one long succession of crevasses, rocks, and side slips. The sigh of relief at arriving in the seemingly deserted village of Hungshui soon died away in sound sleep, with the thermometer at 8 degrees below zero, Fahrenheit.

When strangers arrive in a Chinese village at night, prudence suggests quiet, for requisitions are common. Hungshui, which had seemed deserted until we had paid our bill, suddenly blossomed into life, and a considerable crowd came outside the walls to see what manner of men and machines we were....

Just before dark the "Silver Crescent" headed for Chungwei, making excellent time along a sandy route to catch up with the two other cars of our light party. Our companions, fearing detention, had not entered the walled town, but had left a guide to conduct us to a house beyond, where we were all to partake of Chinese noodles, the kitchen car being with the main group.

While the mother mixed the paste, two youngsters played on the bed platform, at the end of which a wrinkled granny, lying on one side in the yellow glow of the opium lamp, went through the minute details connected with smoking the drug, her beady eyes watching the smoky gob on its long needle or peering down at the blunt pipe into which she forced the drug with fingers as bony and dark as those of a mummy.

After the noodles we rolled on until 2:30 and started again at 4. From here on we entered another world. The route was relatively good. The people were well dressed and clean. Not a beggar did we see. The wide plain beside the Yellow River had a rich look about it, even in winter, and skirted men riding bicycles gave us a sense of arriving somewhere. We stopped at a tomb of a general of 250 years ago and, although the stone lions seemed to turn up their noses at it, found the deeply sculptured memorial arch surprisingly fine. At Ta Pa tiny eavesdropping temple bells were murmuring in the evening breeze, and narrow temples with steep curving roofs were delightfully framed in city gates or reflected on the night-dark ice of small pools....

North of Ningsia, at midnight, the "Silver Crescent" crashed through thick ice [of the Yellow River] and my camera suddenly went afloat in icy water between my porous leather boots. The headlights were well under water, and still lighted, before I could turn off the current and join my companions on shore by way of a scramble over the roof.

Hundreds of films and color plates, expressly stored as high as possible, were still unharmed, but we were settling fast. Every man was busy at his own tasks, but Pecqueur immediately helped me bridge the watery gap and drag to safety the heavy trunk of photographic records.

Flashlights threw the chaotic scene into wild relief. Remillier, mounted on the radiator, wielded a piston-like crowbar against the thick ice, the car wallowed lower and lower, finally submerging the entire hood, and after more than an hour of feverish struggle in bitter cold, three other tractors dragged our car, like some submarine monster, spewing out water, to the opposite bank. Thirteen hours' delay....

San Cheng Kung is built like an ancient city of refuge. Within its fortified walls, defended by men and boys with flintlock blunderbusses, a Christian community lives with its cattle and sheep. When bandits threaten, men of all faiths are welcomed within the protecting walls....

On Sunday, January 24, we set out with a following wind. Each car moved slowly ahead in an opaque dust cloud. Dust filled our nostrils and mouths. With cold-cracked fingers we scooped out gobs of grit from between our lower teeth and lips. Dust crept through our cylinders as if no air filters were there. Pistons developed unusual wear and oil fouled the spark plugs. While a trifling repair was being made, the water froze about the cylinders. A camel or horse would have seemed very efficient....

At Lunghingchang clean, alert officers came to inspect our passports and invite us into one of the two walled towns. Walled towns were a nightmare to us. From several we had escaped only after long negotiations and exchange of presents which amounted to levies. We skirted the walls and gaily continued our ride toward the east, with railhead at

Paotow only a day or two away. At Patsebolong armed and uniformed men, whose exact status no one knew, pointed their guns at us and then jumped upon our running boards, asking for information, which we gave without halting. Hundreds of unarmed but uniformed men were in sight, but we passed through the town without trouble.

Farther along, just before nightfall, the "Silver Crescent" came to a narrow bridge to which the approach was difficult. The two Citroen trucks had passed some minutes before. The "Golden Scarab" was well ahead. Audouin-Dubreuil and Commandant Pecqueur were in the back seat, closed in by curtains with small windows. Gauthier was busy guiding car and trailer. From my seat beside him I looked into the barrel of a gun held by one of the handsomest young Chinese I ever saw. At three or four miles an hour, it took a long time to roll past that swinging rifle barrel.

When we were a few feet past the Chinese, who were ambushed behind chest-high mud walls, four or five yards away on each side of us, a salvo of shots rang out. Eleven bullets took effect on the "Silver Crescent" and its trailer. All of them had been fired from slightly or wholly behind.

Deploying behind a diagonal bank, we brought our arms into action. "Fire high or at a wall," ordered Audouin-Dubreuil.

Balourdet handled his arm like the soldier he was. "The idea was to make them know I had a machine gun, but not waste ammunition." His plan was masterly. Four rapid shots. Then a wave of silence. Four more shots. Silence. Four more shots. He had fired twelve cartridges in all when a flag went up over the Chinese headquarters. Men from both sides advanced for a conference, from which Point, bare-headed and laughing, returned.

"This is a terrible country. They had the nerve to call it a 'slight misunderstanding.'"...

At high noon, on February 12, 1932, the Citroen-Haardt Trans-Asiatic Expedition swung into the grounds of the French Legation in Peiping, was welcomed by the elite of many nations, and came into well-earned glory. In 314$^{1}/_{2}$ days Georges-Marie Haardt and Louis Audouin-Dubreuil, partners in the first motor conquest of the Sahara and the first motor crossing of Africa, had blazed a 7,370-mile trail across Asia, the first overland exploration from the Mediterranean to the Yellow Sea since the days of Marco Polo....

EXPLORATIONS IN THE GOBI DESERT
June 1933

ROY CHAPMAN ANDREWS (1884–1960)

JUT-JAWED, COMMANDING, SQUINTING BENEATH THE WIND-WHIPPED campaign hat, pistol belt cinched around his waist, Roy Chapman Andrews in the Gobi desert looked the very image of a soldier as much as an explorer. Yet in the 1920s and '30s no one outside of Charles Lindbergh and Richard E. Byrd so filled the role of explorer in the public eye. Little wonder that Andrews is widely assumed to be the model for Indiana Jones.

Andrews had always wanted to be an explorer. Even after graduating from college, the Wisconsin native was willing to scrub floors if necessary to join the staff of the American Museum of Natural History in New York. Instead he became the museum's—and the world's—leading authority on whales before turning to Asia, exploring little-known corners of Korea and Indochina.

But it was the great series of expeditions to Mongolia and the Gobi, undertaken when he was between 38 and 46 years old, which captured the popular imagination. There were five expeditions in all—1922, 1923, 1925, 1928, and 1930—and there was a reason for their quasi-military look, for Andrews boasted that they represented something new in exploration, large enterprises in which an army of specialists, from cartographers to paleontologists, fanned out across the sands and gravelly plains, mapping geological strata or discovering fragments of extinct animals. Most importantly, Andrews' all-out assault relied on a fleet of Dodge automobiles, which were resupplied at intervals by huge camel caravans and which carried the scientists from one far-flung outcrop to another.

Dust storms nearly buried the camps. Civil wars in China and brigands in Mongolia occasionally meant the cancellation of a season's work. Nevertheless, the Central Asiatic Expeditions, as Andrews called them, made spectacular finds, especially the trove of dinosaur eggs that did so much to stimulate widespread interest in paleontology generally and dinosaurs in particular.

In the following extracts from his NATIONAL GEOGRAPHIC article, one can clearly hear his clipped and peremptory tone.

THE CENTRAL ASIATIC EXPEDITIONS WENT TO MONGOLIA WITH a very definite purpose. After all, knowing exactly what you want to do is the first requisite of any expedition.

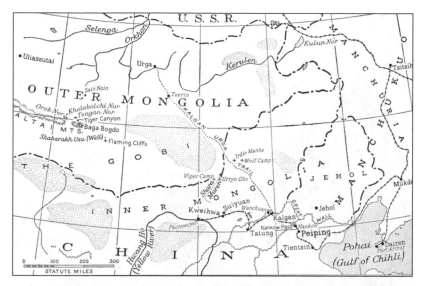

Thousands of square miles of desert Mongolia were the setting for Roy Chapman Andrews's famous Central Asiatic Expeditions, five of which in the 1920s fanned out to explore the sandy, dramatic outcrops between Kalgan and Urga (today's Ulan Bator).

The main problems of the Expedition were to discover the geological history of Central Asia; to find whether or not it had been the nursery of many of the dominant groups of animals, including the human race; and to reconstruct its past climate, vegetation, and general physical conditions, particularly in relation to the evolution of man....

Early in March 1922, the camels left Kalgan for the first expedition. The caravan leader was instructed to travel straight up the Kalgan-Urga trail and await us at Tuerin, a monastery at the northern edge of the Gobi, 500 miles away, as the crow flies.

It was bitter cold when they started. Snow still lay on the desert and spring blizzards raged. Brigands were reported along the trail. Nevertheless, old Merin, the Mongol leader, swung himself to the back of his camel with a happy smile as he waved farewell. He was going into the desert, where he had been born. Blizzards and brigands were part of his daily life.

Shortly after leaving Kalgan, he learned that 500 bandits were only a few miles ahead. He abandoned the main caravan road and struck across the plains, going from well to well. During the day he kept the camels close-herded in deep valleys and traveled only at night. He played hide-and-seek with the brigands and arrived at the rendezvous safely and on time.

Brigands must be considered in every expedition to the interiors of Mongolia or China. They swarm like devouring locusts, even up to the walls

Old meets new in the Gobi desert as Mongols try on radio headphones.
They were particularly fascinated by time signals broadcast from the Philippines,
used by the Expedition to check its chronometers.

of the cities. Usually they are soldier-deserters from unpaid or defeated armies. The thinly settled region at the edge of the Mongolian plateau is their favorite hunting ground, because most of the major caravan routes across Central Asia converge in China at Kalgan and at Kweihwa on the railroad.

At the time of our fourth expedition, in 1928, bandits occupied this entire region. There were about 10,000 of them, and every camel, cart, or car that left Kalgan was certain to be robbed before it had gone 50 miles. The merchants were being ruined and the brigands were starving because they had no one to rob. As usual in China, the matter was settled by the chamber of commerce. Several of the bandit chiefs came into Kalgan and $5 a camel was paid to them as a tax for crossing the brigand area. In one week 13,000 camels left Kalgan under this arrangement.

We had to accept the same conditions. But I had one advantage, for the chief bandit proved to be an old friend. Over many cups of tea I argued that I ought to get cut rates. He finally agreed, and I paid only $2.50 for each of my camels. For the motors he wanted the usual fee of $100 a car. I balked at this and hinted at a machine gun, as well as 30 men with rifles. We didn't have a machine gun, but the word went out, and we were not attacked that year....

Before the first season in Mongolia was ended, it was evident that we had discovered one of the richest and most important fossil fields in all the world. The dinosaur eggs alone made it famous, but they were by no means the most important of the thousands of specimens we brought from the Gobi. We were surprised at the universal popular interest that the dinosaur eggs aroused.

The discovery was important because no one knew that dinosaurs laid eggs. We supposed that they did, for most reptiles lay eggs, and dinosaurs are reptiles. Still, in all the hundreds of deposits of dinosaur bones in various parts of the world, not a single trace of eggshell had been known.

Shackelford, our photographer, discovered the place in 1922, and at that time found the skull of a small dinosaur representing a type unknown to us. We spent only a few hours in the deposit, and Granger picked up some bits of dinosaur egg-shell which we did not then recognize. It was not until we returned the following year that the real discovery was made....

The Flaming Cliffs, where we found this deposit, represented a favorite dinosaur breeding place. Probably the sand was just the right consistency to allow the proper amount of heat and air to pass through to the eggs after they had been covered and left to hatch. During several millions of years countless thousands of dinosaurs laid their eggs in this one spot. Probably most of them hatched, but many did not, and the 70 or 80 eggs we found represent an infinitesimal part of those still buried in the rocks.

The most perfect nest of all was a chance discovery. Norman Lovell, one of our motor experts, was interested in getting young birds for pets. One day he saw an eagle's nest just under the edge of the great pene-plain which sweeps down from the Altai Mountains and breaks off at the basin.

After several unsuccessful attempts to climb the face of the cliff, he gave it up and approached the nest from above. Crawling on his hands and knees to the very edge, he lay flat on his stomach, trying to peer into the nest, when he scratched his hand on something sharp. It was the knifelike edge of a broken dinosaur egg-shell! Several eggs were partly exposed and evidently there were others buried in the rock.

To remove the eggs was a delicate and dangerous operation. A high wind blew, and while at work Walter Granger had to lie at full length to avoid being swept over the brink. He took out a section of sandstone weighing several hundred pounds and sent it to the Museum.

Although the exposed surfaces of the eggs are weathered and broken, the lower halves are intact and make a superb exhibit. In the block there are 18 eggs standing on end in an irregular double circle. Doubtless the nest originally contained more, for there was evidence that others had broken out as the edge of the cliff crumbled away....

The Gobi is so dry and cold that there are very few reptiles. Pit vipers, the only poisonous snake of the Gobi, caused us some annoyance at times. Once our tents were pitched on a lofty promontory, which projected far out into the basin of the dry river, Shara Muren. Near them was an *obo*, or religious monument, and shortly after our arrival two lamas came to call. They were delegates from a temple four miles away and asked us to be particularly careful not to shoot or kill any birds or animals on the bluff.

It was a very sacred spot and the spirits would be angry if we took life in the vicinity. Of course, I agreed to respect their wishes and gave orders to this effect at once. But we had promised more than we could fulfill, as events proved. Within the first two hours of prospecting for fossils three pit vipers were discovered close to the tents. A few days later the temperature suddenly dropped in the late afternoon and the camp had a lively night, for the tents were invaded by an army of vipers which sought warmth and shelter.

Norman Lovell was lying in bed when he saw a wriggling form across the triangular patch of moonlight in his tent door. He was about to get up to kill the snake when he decided to have a look before he put his bare feet upon the ground.

Reaching for his electric flash lamp, he discovered a viper coiled about each of the legs of his camp cot. A collector's pickax was within reach and with it Lovell disposed of the two snakes which had hoped to share his bed. Then he began a still hunt for the viper that had first crossed the patch of moonlight in the door and which he knew was somewhere in the tent. He was hardly out of bed when a serpent crawled from under a gasoline box near the head of his cot.

Lovell was having a rather lively evening of it, but he was not alone. Morris killed five vipers in his tent, and Wang, a Chinese chauffeur, found a huge snake coiled up in his shoe. Having killed it, he picked up his soft cap which was lying on the ground and a viper fell out of that. Dr. Loucks actually put his hand on one which was lying on a pile of shotgun cases.

We named the place "Viper Camp" because 47 snakes were killed in the tents. Fortunately, the cold had made them sluggish and they did not strike quickly. My police dog was the only one of our party to be bitten. He was struck in the leg by a very small snake and, as George Olsen treated the wound at once, he did not die. The poor animal was very ill and suffered great pain, but recovered in 36 hours.

This snake business got on our nerves. The Chinese and Mongols deserted their tents and slept in the cars and on camel boxes. The rest of us never moved after dark without a flashlight in one hand and a pickax in the other. When I walked out of the tent one evening. I stepped upon something soft and round. My yell brought the whole camp out, only to find that the snake was a coil of rope!

We had to break our promise to the lamas and kill the vipers, but our Mongols remained firm. It was amusing to see one of them shooing a snake out of his tent with a piece of cloth to a place where the Chinese could kill it....

I have often been asked what is the most important specimen the Expedition has discovered in all its work. The answer is easy, but it will disappoint the layman. The majority will expect me to say, "The dinosaur eggs." Far from it.

Scientifically, the most important things are seven tiny skulls, no larger than those of rats. They belonged to the most ancient known mammals, which lived at the end of the Age of Reptiles.

One of the letters which I had brought for Granger was from the late Dr. W. D. Matthew. Matthew was one of the least excitable men I know, but he was really stirred when he wrote that letter. He said that a tiny skull in a nodule of sandstone discovered on the second Expedition and labeled by Granger "an unidentified reptile" was, in reality, one of the oldest known mammals. It had been found in the Cretaceous formation which yielded the *Protoceratops* and dinosaur eggs.

In his letter Dr. Matthew wrote: "Do your utmost to get some other skulls." Granger and I discussed it for half an hour; then he said, "Well, I guess that's an order. I'd better get busy."

He walked out to the base of the Flaming Cliffs and an hour later was back with another mammal skull!... Such things do not sound possible, I will admit, but they do happen, and frequently at that.

We had to leave for the West the next day, but when we returned, in August, Granger and Olsen, Buckshot and Liu did some intensive searching. It was close and trying work, for the skulls were in little nodules of sandstone that had broken out as the cliffs weathered away.

There are literally millions of such concretions on the basin floor, so it was simply a matter of examining as many as possible during the day. When one has inspected a thousand or more with no result, and in the scorching sun, the job loses interest and becomes decidedly discouraging. Nevertheless Granger and his assistants stuck to it and in a week they had a total of seven skulls. It was possibly the most valuable seven days of work in the whole history of paleontology....

We left the Flaming Cliffs for the last time with much regret. This single spot had given us more than we had dared to hope from the entire Gobi. When the Expedition took the field in 1922, Mongolia was virtually an unknown country from the standpoint of natural science. We had been told that it was barren paleontologically and geologically as well as physically.

Yet the first dinosaur eggs known to man, a hundred skulls and skeletons of unknown dinosaurs, the oldest-known mammals, and the primitive human culture of the Dune Dwellers all had come from a few square miles in this lovely basin.

Is it surprising that a wave of sadness swept over me as I looked for the last time at the Flaming Cliffs, gorgeous in the morning sunshine of that brilliant August day? I knew that I never would see them again. "Never" is a long time, but the active years of an explorer's life are short, and new fields are calling for those that remain to me.

Roy Chapman Andrews' active years, however, were essentially over. After 1930 the Chinese government—accusing him of stealing fossils, of spying, of oil prospecting, and even of opium smuggling—refused to grant him further permits. Pushing 50, Andrews soon capped off his 35-year career with the American Museum of Natural History by serving as its director from 1935–42. With a broad grin and a commanding air, he enthralled audiences and dominated innumerable black-tie fundraisers, still finding time to write a series of popular books, including This Business of Exploring *and his autobiography,* Under a Lucky Star.

PART FIVE

The Himalayan Realm

TIGER-HUNTING IN INDIA
November 1924

GEN. WILLIAM MITCHELL (1879-1936)

OF ALL THE SPLENDID TRAPPINGS OF THE RAJ, FEW THINGS EXCEEDED the extravagance of the traditional shikar, or tiger hunt. The spreading pavilions, the exquisite carpets, the caparisoned elephants, the turbaned gunbearers, the hundreds if not thousands of villagers impressed as beaters, the sumptuous banquets— it was all quite dazzling, and anyone who could, whether prince, duke, viceroy, general, or millionaire, enjoyed the prestige of attending one.

Then there was the thrill of the hunt itself. In the years just after the First World War an estimated 40,000 to 100,000 tigers still roamed India, and authorities were quick to marshal statistics proving that old or lame tigers killed hundreds of humans and thousands of cattle each year (Shere Khan in Kipling's Jungle Book was a lame cattle killer). Thus the shikar was justified on the grounds that it helped control dangerous man-eaters.

Pageantry, excitement, the chase—it was just the kind of thing William "Billy" Mitchell loved. A career soldier, Mitchell had emerged from the war as the youngest general in the U.S. Army. Impetuous and arrogant, he advocated radical ideas about the use of airpower—ideas that a hidebound military hierarchy routinely spurned, though he would be proved right in the end.

In 1923 the short, ramrod-straight officer married Elizabeth Trumbull Miller, a Grosse Pointe, Michigan, debutante who shared his taste for adventure and the sporting life. What's more, she was his equal as an equestrian and just as fine a shot. He was 43, she 32, when they departed on an eight-month honeymoon that doubled as an inspection tour of U.S. military facilities in the Far East. They visited Hawaii, China, Korea, Japan, Burma, and had an audience with the King of Siam. But it was the prospect of tiger-hunting in India that stirred Mitchell's blood and set his pulse racing.

Eventually the couple arrived in the princely state of Surguja, 6,000 square miles of jungle-clad hills with a population of half a million, all ruled by a welcoming maharajah who was the keenest tiger hunter in India.

SEVERAL MILES BEFORE WE REACHED AMBIKAPUR, THE CAPITAL OF Surguja, we could plainly see the Maharaja's palace, with the little houses of his subjects clustered around it....

We left our road cars and accompanied the [prime minister] to a little garden, where carpets had been spread on the lawn and comfortable chairs awaited us. After partaking of cooling drinks and being presented with flowers, we were taken to the state automobile, a large limousine embellished with the royal arms and yellow pennant of the Maharaja, to make our entry into the capital.

An escort of lancers was in attendance, and as we entered the city, school children were drawn up on each side of the road waving small flags, with their teachers among them, also with flags. Beyond them was a guard of honor of infantry in brilliant Indian uniforms, and then we passed the line of picturesque temples and the palace to the guest house, where the Maharaja received us and bade us welcome. Garlands were placed around our necks and bouquets of flowers presented.

Outside the guest house porte-cochère stood Gurkhas of the household guard, who had come from the Maharani's home country, Nepal. Domestic animals of all kinds passed the doors—asses, horses, elephants, bullocks, and camels. To the left of the entrance, in a long, narrow edifice, the falconers kept their trained pedigree falcons, with all their accouterments. These falcons had been trained in and brought from Nepal. Unfortunately, we had no time to do any hunting with them. The sport is greatly appreciated by the princes of India, and is done according to strict forms and methods and is richer in lore than our own fox-hunting.

Next to the falconers' quarters were the Maharaja's chamars, busy working over many panther and tiger skins that had fallen to his rifle...

The Maharaja said that he had ordered more than 30 buffaloes tied out as tiger bait, and he explained the system of reporting a kill and the method of keeping track of the tigers in each jungle. The organization was perfect and very much like a military system of outposts. I found the precision and discipline among his people to be remarkable....

At 8 o'clock the following morning a kill was reported about three miles away, and off we went in an automobile. Arriving at the jungle in which the tiger was located, we mounted elephants and started for the *machans* [platforms in trees, of questionable safety since tigers sometimes leapt up and pulled hunters down from them]. These were the fastest-moving elephants that I have ever seen, going through the forest at a gait of about 5½ miles an hour. They were picturesquely decorated with painted caste-marks on their foreheads, the carmine of the goddess

Kali predominating. The Maharaja had all sizes of elephants, from large tuskers to small females, and all were trained to hunt tigers.

Upon reaching our machans we found our rifles, drinking water, and sandwiches had preceded us. The Maharaja gave his final instructions and off went the head *shikari* [hunter].

About 600 beaters were employed, this being the slack season, after the harvest had been reaped and before plowing had commenced. Fifty or 60 men acted as stops. They deployed on either side of us and climbed trees, after having strung their turbans and body cloths through the bushes to scare the tiger toward the machan.

The object in beating is to inclose the tiger in a wide-flung circle of men and then gradually to drive him into an ever-narrowing funnel of stops to the waiting guns. This is a very much harder thing to do than it sounds. If the tiger is driven too rapidly, he becomes surly and charges the beaters. If he is driven in a direction that is not his natural avenue of advance or retreat, or if he is disturbed too soon after or while eating, the same thing results. Each tiger is studied and his individual habits are well known, particularly the older ones.

We ascended to the machan, a large one, constructed of four uprights, pole floors, leafy roof to keep off the hot sun, and comfortable seats...

The beat began. The large number of beaters covered a great extent of ground. They were kept in alignment by the shikaris, who rode from side to side on their elephants. These head beaters were provided with guns and blank ammunition, used to keep the tiger moving. The shikaris are also provided with ball ammunition, in case the tigers attack the beaters.

The present tiger was a very canny animal—a great cattle-killer, who had carried off innumerable cows and buffaloes. The natives were very anxious to have him destroyed, as their herds were never safe while he was in the vicinity. Six times before he had been inclosed in beats, but his cunning was so great that he had escaped on each occasion. The natives were beginning to suspect that he had a charmed life.

On came the beat with no sound from the tiger. An hour passed and the individual shouts of the men could be heard as they advanced, and soon we could see them on our left. The elephants came up from that side and reported that the tiger had been in the beat and had vanished, but had not broken out. The beaters to our right were still a little distance off, as their alignment had not been properly kept.

Everyone appeared to me to have come up, so I unloaded the rifles. Just as

"Every great man is a tiger hunter..." Striking an imperious pose, Elizabeth Mitchell stands over the tigress she has just shot, while ranged about her is the traditional panoply of shikaris, gunbearers, beaters, skinners, and elephants.

I did so the Maharaja told me to load, and as the words left his mouth the great tiger rushed the narrow strip between us and the stops. He stuck to the densest jungle and was very hard to see. All the men jumped for the trees. I slipped a cartridge into Mrs. Mitchell's .405 Winchester and tried a snapshot, but it hit a tree immediately beside him and he was through a beat for the seventh time.

There was nothing more that could be done, so we returned to the palace, hoping for better luck next time....

Mrs. Mitchell had become quite ill and was unable to accompany me for several days. She had not yet killed a tiger, and as our time was growing short she began to worry a little. Just as she began to improve, news came that a large tiger had made a kill about 16 miles off.

We drove 10 miles of this distance in our motor car; then Mrs. Mitchell was carried the remaining 6 miles in a palanquin improvised from one of the native beds. Everything was in readiness when we reached our machan, which was near the banks of a broad, dry river bottom.

The beat started with great vigor and the country reverberated with shouts. Several shots of blank cartridges from various directions indicated to us that more than one tiger was in the beat. Soon a number of beautiful peacocks passed us, some on the ground and some on the wing. Their necks and heads were iridescent in the sunlight and the tails of the cocks appeared like jewels of many colors. No wonder the Great Mogul made up his famous thrones of jeweled peacocks.

Presently we heard a clapping from the stops on our right and a low growl from a tiger. The stops have to know just how much noise to make on the approach of the beast, for if they overdo it the tiger may charge them direct.

Soon we caught sight of a beautiful tigress. She was neither unduly alarmed nor irritated. Again she went toward the stops and was gently turned back from them. She waited for a moment in the stream bed in our front, then came walking rapidly over the hill directly toward us. As she arrived within 40 yards, she sensed some trouble and was just drawing up her muscles for a leap when Mrs. Mitchell sent a .405 bullet right through her heart. The great cat leaped toward us and crossed the stream at the foot of the machan, falling back dead, as we gave her two more bullets, which were really unnecessary.

Ten minutes elapsed and we heard a great roar from the male tiger and strenuous efforts on the part of the beaters to turn him back. He was furious. He came to the second watercourse in front of us, but would come in our direction no farther. He sat down on his haunches and looked around, concealed from our sight, though several of the stops in the trees could see him.

The beaters reached the ridge about 75 yards from him and were warned by the stops to take to the trees and to wait for the elephants, who came through the beaters with their trunks held high, as they caught the scent of the tiger. An ordinary elephant under these conditions would have made a hasty retreat, but these were trained for the work. All of them were now in plain view of our machan. The beaters from the trees put up united shouts, while the elephants crushed down heavy underbrush and waved branches in the air in an attempt to drive the tiger on.

"Stripes" had been perfectly still during these proceedings, but suddenly like a flash of orange light, accompanied by a great roar, I saw him rush straight for two elephants, which he reached in the twinkling of an eye. They trumpeted and dexterously avoided him, as he charged by them. Fortunately, the beaters were in the trees. He had escaped. But to us it was even more interesting to see this happening than to have killed him. The male tigers often cover a female's retreat in this fashion.

We started back, the dead tiger being carried on a palanquin much like Mrs. Mitchell's. The natives covered the animal with leaves and the scarlet flowers of the "flame of the forest"; for although their greatest enemy, they pay the utmost respect to the tiger, dead or alive....

The day following Mrs. Mitchell's successful shot we returned to the capital, where we learned that the huge tiger which had escaped us the first day and who had gotten through seven beats had killed a large buffalo out of a herd and had walked off with him into the woods, carrying him by the nape of the neck, as a cat carries a newborn kitten. We had no time to waste. Mrs. Mitchell did not even change her silk dress for her hunting togs.

Mrs. Mitchell and I occupied the machan, while the Maharaja placed his motor car on the road, in a clearing about 200 yards behind us, so that if the tiger escaped us, either wounded or unhurt, he would have a good shot at the beast. The beat came on in splendid fashion. We could tell that perfect alignment was being kept, as the men profited by their former experience, when the tiger immediately took advantage of the fact that one side of the beat had gotten ahead of the other. Great numbers of peacocks and red jungle fowl passed the machan. Several jackals slunk by.

Without any warning, we heard a commotion among the stops to our left, followed by a roar that resounded through the forest, and we knew that the tiger was close by. Again quiet, and then he was turned back by the stops to our right. He remained still for a few minutes. I had no doubt then that he knew exactly where all the elements of the hunt were ...

Quick as lightening, he dashed for the stops immediately on our right, where one of the principal shikaris had been placed. With great shouts, clapping of hands, pounding of trees with hollow bamboos, he was barely turned. Not slacking his pace for an instant, he came straight for us, using every bit of cover there was to conceal his approach.... We awaited our opportunity and both Mrs. Mitchell and I fired at the same instant. He fell stone-dead, in his full stride, without uttering a sound or making any motion whatsoever. One bullet had hit him exactly in the center of the forehead and death was instantaneous.

He was a beautiful creature, about 14 years old, 10 feet 4 inches between pegs. He must have been fully 4 feet or more high at the withers. His paws, one blow of which could fell the largest buffalo, were as big around as the largest soup plate, while the leg muscles and tendons stood out like whipcords. He was the biggest tiger that I have ever seen....

The time had arrived for us to say farewell, and to mark it the Maharaja had arranged to hold a durbar. This function may last for only a short while or extend over several days. It consists of holding court, receiving distinguished guests, providing entertainment for them, and turning out all the state forces and equipment in their best costumes and accouterments. In this case the durbar was held in the evening. Promptly at the appointed time the prime minister, in his court attire, came to our house to conduct us to the palace. We had dressed accordingly—Mrs. Mitchell in evening dress, while I had donned my uniform and full decorations. We entered the state automobile, and escorted by lancers of the guard, proceeded toward the palace, first down the line of brilliantly lighted temples, glistening and beautiful in their many colors of the evening light, then to the left, along the offices on one side and the royal stables, with many horses, on the other, across a small square in front of the palace, on one side of which lions and tigers roared in their cages at the discharge of the saluting cannon.

The palace itself, a structure about a block square and of fine proportions, is colored brightly with tiles, paint, and mortar. Along the top is a crenelated wall with gold decorations. Over the gateway was the Maharaja's flag, of triangular shape, made of gold leaf on a baser metal.

We left the automobile at the outer gate and were met by the heir apparent, a fine young man of about 15 years, and his little brother, clad in their long brightly colored, gala robes, with splendidly bejeweled turbans, and surrounded by functionaries of the court. The band and escort of honor were drawn up on each side of the approach. Everyone and everything looked so beautiful, so bright, and so friendly that we hated the realization that we were to leave on the following morning.

The young rajah led us across a broad courtyard, around which were the dwellings of the various people of the palace. It was like a Spanish patio, brightly tinted, well lighted, and cool. On the other side of this we entered another courtyard in the inner palace, where a second guard of honor was drawn up. Across it and to our left stood the Maharaja, on the front steps of his reception hall and throne room.

I had formed a great affection for him during the time that we had hunted together. There he had always worn the hunting costume of jodpurs, or tight breeches, and the ordinary European coat, but now he was dressed in his resplendent court robes, with the great ancestral jewels around his neck and on his chest. These consisted of diamonds, emeralds, and other large gems. His turban, ornamented with white egret plumes, held a very large diamond in the center, a large spray of pearls pendent over his right forehead, and many other jewels.

The figures of these athletic, high-caste Rajputs are tall, slender, erect, and stately. He received us with the easy grace characteristic of him, while all around stood members of the family and his principal officers. He conducted us into the throne room and across it to a raised dais, where three gilded chairs had been placed. Ranged around our seats were the prime minister, the chiefs of the various departments, and the Maharaja's aged uncle.

After we were seated the Maharaja took garlands from a table and placed them around our necks, then sprinkled attar of roses on our shoulders and handkerchiefs, and bade us welcome to the durbar. The prime minister now arose and declared the durbar opened. The Maharaja thereupon stood and read, in excellent English, a most eulogistic account of our visit in Surguja, the different episodes of our hunting, and the pleasure they had had in receiving Americans in their midst for the first time.

He traced with remarkable accuracy little incidents that had happened, how these had been handled, and what the jungle people and beaters had thought about them. Our hosts were particularly impressed with Mrs. Mitchell's ability with the rifle and her coolness in front of the charging tigers. Tiger-hunting with them is the one great supersport. In addition, it is taken very seriously and its methods and forms are as carefully observed as religious ceremonies. A great tiger-hunter is a great man, and every great man must be a tiger-hunter....

Whether a great man or not, Billy Mitchell is regarded today as the father of the U.S. Air Force—yet he was a prophet without honor in his own lifetime. Shortly after his return from India, he accused the military of incompetence and was court-martialed in retaliation. He died before the events of World War II proved he was right all along, and in 1945 a chagrined nation awarded him a posthumous Medal of Honor. His ultimate fate was to be portrayed by Gary Cooper in Hollywood's The Trial of Billy Mitchell.

The tiger's fate, of course, has been far worse. Throughout the 20th century its numbers plummeted. The Maharajah of Surguja himself held the notorious record of having personally killed 1,157 tigers. In 1972, the first government survey of remaining populations could account for barely 1,800 animals. Subsequent conservation efforts have hardly stemmed the decline. As Jim Corbett, perhaps the most thoughtful of the old-time tiger hunters, wrote decades ago, "The tiger is a large-hearted gentleman with boundless courage and when he is exterminated—as exterminated he will be unless public opinion rallies to his support— India will be the poorer for having lost the finest of her fauna."

ACROSS TIBET FROM INDIA TO CHINA
August 1946

LT. COL. ILIA TOLSTOY (1903–1970)

REMOTE, CLOUD-WREATHED LHASA, CAPITAL OF TIBET, WAS ONCE THE MOST mysterious city in the world, unseen by Westerners unless glimpsed from beneath a disguise, for strangers caught trespassing on this forbidden territory were always turned away. In 1904, however, a British column marched up from India and bullied its way into the sacred city. From that point on, Britain controlled access to Tibet and protected its quasi-autonomy, despite the protests of distant Peking, which claimed suzerainty but was too embroiled in civil wars to do much about it.

Then came World War II and the Japanese conquest of East Asia. Not completely overwhelmed, China fought back from her western provinces, supplied from India via the Burma Road, until the Japanese severed that artery. Supply planes were then flown from India "over the hump," across the soaring Himalayan spurs, but too many of them crashed. A new land route was desperately needed. So in the summer of 1942, with the approval of President Franklin D. Roosevelt, the American Office of Strategic Services (forerunner of the CIA) planned a secret mission to survey one—across Tibet.

That task fell to an unlikely pair. At 39, Maj. Ilia Tolstoy cut a trim, impressive figure. A grandson of the novelist, he had fought in the White Russian cavalry during the Russian Civil War. Escaping to the U.S., he then participated in farranging expeditions for the American Museum of Natural History. He knew how to travel in remote places, as did Capt. Brooke Dolan, 33, who had led several natural history expeditions into the Tibetan borderlands. A wealthy young Philadelphian, his stints at Princeton and Harvard had done little to tame him. He "hated civilization," and with his wild ways he needed to be kept far from it. These two officers comprised the first American diplomatic mission to visit Lhasa. They felt their chances of surveying a road were slim, since they depended on permission from the ruler of Tibet, the 14th Dalai Lama—then only seven years old.

TWENTY-FIVE MILES OUT OF LHASA WE WERE MET BY AN ESCORT sent out from the court of the Dalai Lama to greet us. It was headed by a powerfully built, fine-looking young monk, Kusho Yonton Singhi, who was to become our guide and inseparable adviser during our stay in the city of mystery.

He presented us with a warm letter of welcome and greetings from the joint Foreign Ministers of Tibet, and with the usual scarfs. Knowing our animals were tired, the Ministers had sent two fresh ponies for Brooke and me. It was a pleasure to ride the excellent Mongolian pacer, the kind that in Tibet only wealthy men can afford. By Tibetan custom horsemen walk down steep hills, but from the moment Kusho joined us, we were not obliged to dismount. One of Kusho's outriders would halt at the top of each steep place, give his horse in charge of someone else, and lead our mounts carefully down the trail. We began to feel as if we were precious china dolls.

At noon we rode up to several gaily decorated Tibetan tents, where we had tea with our guide. The next day we woke up early and rode off briskly with an unmistakable feeling of excitement. Our first goal was near.

Entering the valley of Lhasa, we rode along the Kyi, which flows through the city. We crossed its tributary on Tibet's only modern steel bridge. On a concrete foundation, the bridge was built several years ago by Tsarong without the help of foreign engineers. The feat was remarkable in that all the pieces of steel had to be brought from India over the Himalayas by coolies, and the girders were too heavy for pack animals to carry.

Somewhere within the last four miles of Lhasa we knew a delegation waited to receive us, and one of our men rode ahead to herald our approach. The greeters, thus notified, rode out to meet us a couple of hundred yards from the place where they had been stationed. When about 100 feet apart, our parties dismounted and greeted each other.

Greetings were in strict Western fashion. After the introductions our entire cavalcade rode on to a small roadside park where several decorated Tibetan tents had been set up for the occasion. We were welcomed at the gate by the officers representing the court of the Dalai Lama.

Escorted into the central tent, we were given the seats of honor behind a little table laden with the usual dried fruits, candies, etc. Our hosts, in order of rank and position, sat down to our right and left, on hassocks of diminishing heights. The farther away from us, the lower the seats became, until, as the line passed out the entrance of the tent, overflow guests were sitting on the open ground on flat cushions. There were tables only a few inches high in front of all guests.

Buttered tea was poured from large, silver-ornamented copper teapots, and the ceremonial rice was served. In front of each person was placed a Chinese rice bowl with the rice patted in a high mound. We took a few grains of this rice with our fingers, threw some of it over our shoulders for the appeasement of spirits, and swallowed the few remaining grains. The rice bowls were then taken away, and the representatives of the court gave us letters of welcome and scarfs on behalf of the court.

This part of the ceremony over, we rode through the little wooded parks that surrounded Lhasa. To our right a large part of Lhasa's population was congregated on small grass mounds. On the left was lined up a detachment of the honor guard of the famous Tibetan Trapchi regiment, which serves as the bodyguard to the Dalai Lama. We were surprised and our horses startled by a sudden outburst of stirring military music from a brass band, the only band of occidental instruments in Tibet. Presumably the instruments had been taken from a Chinese army in 1911. The magnificent flag of Tibet stood out in its brilliant colors, showing the sun and two Lions of Tibet facing each other, holding the Wheel of Life under the Precious Gems.

Dismounting, we reviewed the detachment of soldiers, smart-looking in their practical native uniforms, and shook hands with their commanding officer. We then proceeded to the attractive Tibetan house of our host, Mr. Ludlow [a British diplomat], just outside the West Gate of Lhasa, from where we could see the walls of the Potala [the magnificent palace] topped by the Dalai Lama's personal quarters. In accordance with Tibetan custom, we were not to call upon any officials until after His Holiness, the Dalai Lama, had granted us an audience. A few days after our arrival we were informed by the Tibetan Foreign Office that the audience would be at 9:20 on the morning of December 20. That date was selected as the most auspicious for the Dalai Lama, a highly important factor in all of his undertakings.

Early that day we rode out toward the Potala in a sizable cavalcade with all our men, the monk guide and his assistants dressed up in their finery. The Potala is situated on a hill, and the Dalai Lama's throne room is on the very top. Usually visitors must make a long and tedious climb up the broad steps of the palace. We, however, were extended a great courtesy, being allowed to ride along a narrow path up the mountain to the back of the palace, where we left our horses. Then we were escorted through the courtyards and long labyrinths of the Potala building to a small, unpretentious waiting room.

Here we were joined by the representatives of the Foreign Office, a few other dignitaries, and a charming young Tibetan official named Changnopa, whom everybody called Ringang. Ringang had studied at Rugby and spoke beautiful English. After tea had been served, we rehearsed the procedure for greeting the Dalai Lama, the Tibetans explaining to us

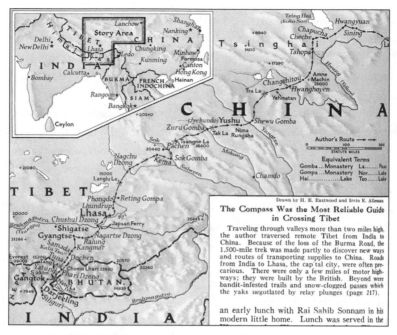

Drawn by H. E. Eastwood and Irvin E. Alleman

The Compass Was the Most Reliable Guide in Crossing Tibet

Traveling through valleys more than two miles high, the author traversed remote Tibet from India to China. Because of the loss of the Burma Road, the 1,500-mile trek was made partly to discover new ways and routes of transporting supplies to China. Roads from India to Lhasa, the capital city, were often precarious. There were only a few miles of motor highways; they were built by the British. Beyond were bandit-infested trails and snow-clogged passes which the yaks negotiated by relay plunges (page 217).

an early lunch with Rai Sahib Sonnam in his modern little home. Lunch was served in the

During World War II, after the Japanese had blocked the Burma Road, Col. Ilia Tolstoy and Capt. Brooke Dolan crossed forbidden Tibet on horseback, scouting a new supply route to China.

some of the fine points of etiquette. A monk entered soon and announced that we were to proceed to the throne room.

Escorted by a stately procession of monks, we ascended to the roof of the Potala, above which rose the single room used for receptions. On both sides in front of the entrance were seated in rows of high monk dignitaries, and in the background were crowds of lesser monks and some laymen and pilgrims who were to be given a blessing by the Dalai Lama after our reception.

We stood in line for a few moments until the heavy curtain was drawn from the entrance, then walked into the richly decorated throne room. Rows of monks and lay officials were standing along the walls, but the central portion of the room remained open. Directly in front of us stood the Dalai Lama's throne, a square, flat-topped seat about four feet high and four feet wide, with a straight back.

His Holiness was seated cross-legged, a high-peaked yellow hat on his head. We were immediately impressed by his young but stern face and not at all frail constitution. His cheeks were healthily pink. A few feet away to his right, on a similar but lower throne, sat the dignified Regent of Tibet. Until the Dalai Lama becomes of age at eighteen, the

Regent assumes his duties and is the highest authority in Tibet, ecclesiastical or civil. Still farther away to the Regent's right was seated the Dalai Lama's father, a layman, dressed in rich robes and hat. Ruddy and youthful in appearance, and wearing a neat little down-turned mustache, he presented a contrast to the ecclesiastical dignitaries.

As we stepped inside the threshold of the throne room, we saluted. Our hats were kept on throughout the entire ceremony. We then walked up to the throne of the Dalai Lama and, standing before him, saluted again. A monk came up and laid a presentation scarf across my outstretched hands, then placed a bread-and-butter offering upon the scarf. Bowing, I presented the offering to the Dalai Lama, who took it into his hands and passed it over to a monk on his right. This procedure was repeated as a monk placed in turn upon the scarf I held an image of Buddha, a religious book, and a chorten. These objects I passed on to the Dalai Lama.

Meanwhile, Captain Dolan, standing to my right, had been holding the casket containing President Roosevelt's letter to the Dalai Lama. He now passed it to me, placing it on the scarf. In the same manner I presented the casket to the Dalai Lama. So far as we could learn, this was the first time in history that direct communication had been made by a President of the United States with the Dalai Lama of Tibet. I then laid the scarf across the throne in front of His Holiness, saluted, and proceeded to the throne of the Regent at my left. Captain Dolan stepped up to the throne of the Dalai Lama, a scarf over his hands, and presented to His Holiness a photograph of President Roosevelt. He then saluted and joined me in front of the Regent's throne. At this point our servants presented the gift of President Roosevelt, a gold chronographic watch, to the major-domo standing away from the throne. This functionary accepted it in behalf of the Dalai Lama, together with the personal gift Captain Dolan and I had brought, a silver ship.

Saluting the Regent, I bestowed upon him gifts similar to those presented to the Dalai Lama: an image of Buddha, a religious book, a chorten, and objects of silver. After placing the presentation scarf across the Regent's hands, I passed on to the throne of the Dalai Lama's father. Brooke also saluted the Regent, presented him with a scarf, and joined me at the left. The father of the Dalai Lama was saluted in turn and honored with scarfs by us both. No gifts were presented to the father on this occasion, but were given at a later date.

The presentation of gifts and scarfs accomplished, we returned to the right-hand side of the room, where we sat on a long, low cushion placed

The 14th Dalai Lama was all of seven years old when he received Tolstoy and Dolan, the first U.S. diplomatic mission ever to arrive in Tibet. Ultimately His Holiness would spend most of his life in exile—and receive the Nobel Peace Prize.

near the center. A low table was set in front of us. From the far corner of the room came a monk bearing a pot of tea. He stopped before the Dalai Lama, joining another monk kneeling in front of the throne, who reached into his robe and pulled out a silver cup into which a little tea was poured. This monk then tasted the tea to insure its being satisfactory. We were then served tea and rice. Although we were offered three cups of tea, we drank only two, leaving the third untasted as custom dictates. We ate a bit of the rice and threw a few grains over our shoulders.

While we were thus occupied, our retinue of servants proceeded to the Dalai Lama's throne and presented scarfs which a monk, standing by the side of His Holiness, accepted on his lord's behalf. The Dalai Lama then blessed them by touching their heads with a holy wand. They paid the same respects to the Regent and the Dalai Lama's father.

The servants were followed by a chain of monks and other people specially admitted to the throne room. These also presented scarfs and bowed before the throne to receive the blessing of His Holiness. When the procession to the throne had ceased, the Dalai Lama addressed us through an interpreter, inquiring about the health of the President of the United States. I stood up to answer his query, then again sat down....

Upon the close of the official reception in the throne room, we returned to the waiting room of the Potala, presently to be ushered into the private chamber of the Dalai Lama. He was sitting on a small, low couch, with a table before him holding religious objects. Beside His Holiness sat the Regent on a similar couch. We were seated on chairs directly in front of them. Ringang accompanied us. He acted as interpreter in the ensuing conversation, which continued in an informal vein for about a half hour. The private audience was then ended, and we left the Potala....

Deke Lingka, headquarters of the British Mission, in which we lived, was next to the famous Holy Walk which stretches for seven miles around the Potala grounds. Along that walk we could see pilgrims from all Tibet circumambulating the Potala, some by prostrating themselves along the walk, getting up and stepping the length of their bodies, then prostrating themselves again. Thus they measured their way around the Potala like inchworms. At the end of the month, when the New Year's ceremonies were almost over, permission was granted us by the Tibetan Government to proceed to China...

That was the first such permission granted in 22 years, Tolstoy reported. He did not mention secret negotiations with Tibetan authorities—or his suggestion that Tibet take part in any peace conference. This unauthorized offer caused subsequent diplomatic embarrassment, but it gained Tolstoy permission to continue his journey. After many weeks of riding north across the wild, starkly beautiful Tibetan plateau, scouting a passable supply route, the two men arrived in China.

Because of diplomatic disagreements, that route was never opened after all, and pilots kept flying the hump to supply the Chinese. Nevertheless, the two officers, each of whom received a Legion of Merit, had brought back the best intelligence to date on Tibet, and their notes, photographs, and maps long proved valuable.

In 1950 China invaded Tibet, and the Dalai Lama fled to India. Brooke Dolan apparently shot himself in 1945. Ilia Tolstoy founded Florida's Marineland, of all things, but never ceased lobbying for Tibetan causes. The months he spent there in 1942–43 were, in the words of one historian, the "high point of his life, literally and figuratively."

CAUGHT IN THE ASSAM-TIBET EARTHQUAKE

March 1952

FRANK KINGDON-WARD (1885-1958)

In 1924, after clambering around in Tibet's Tsangpo River Gorge with Frank Kingdon-Ward, Lord Cawdor remarked: "It drives me clean daft to walk behind him ... If ever I travel again, I'll make damned sure it's not with a botanist. They are always stopping to gape at weeds."

Gaping at weeds was Kingdon-Ward's livelihood. Born Francis Kingdon Ward (he added the hyphen) in Victorian England, he grew up enthralled by stories of jungle exploration, and by his mid-20s he was collecting seeds and plants at the "the edge of the world" where China, India, Burma (now Myanmar), and Tibet meet. It was a botanical paradise, and from 1909 to 1957 Kingdon-Ward roved its peaks and valleys, identifying hundreds of species—rhododendrons, lilies, irises, gentians, and the Himalayan blue poppy—and introducing them into Western cultivation.

He considered himself an explorer first. He mapped uncharted territory, produced a steady stream of adventure-filled books and articles, and was more proud of his Royal Geographical Society medals than of his many horticultural honors. He frequently found himself lost and once survived by sucking nectar from flowers. He fell from innumerable cliffs, miraculously saved by providentially placed bushes or limbs. He routinely scrambled over dizzying gorges in Asia, despite his fear of heights. He just had a genius for survival.

That genius was called upon in the late summer of 1950, when he pitched his camp near Rima, a Tibetan village near the juncture with Burma and India. Though 65 years old, he was still tough and sinewy enough to have made the grueling march up from Sadiya in India's Assam Province. Accompanied by his wife, Jean, he had followed the Lohit River through the steep, forest-clad Mishmi Hills, trekking up trails so precipitous that just reaching Rima was a challenge. The trip back would be infinitely worse: On August 15 their camp was struck by one of the strongest earthquakes on record.

DARKNESS HAD FALLEN OVER THE UPPER LUHIT [LOHIT] VALLEY IN rugged far-eastern Tibet. Our simple evening meal was finished; my wife was already in bed.

Near by our two servants were sleeping peacefully in their tent. I was seated near the entrance to ours writing in my diary by the light of a hurricane lamp. I glanced at my watch; it was 8 o'clock.

Suddenly a most extraordinary rumbling noise broke out, and the earth began to shudder violently. Shattering the dead silence of the night in that remote mountain retreat, the ominous rumble swelled to a deafening roar. It was as though the keystone had fallen out of the universe and the arch of the sky were collapsing.

Alarmed, bewildered, but also curious, I sprang up and thrust my head between the tent flaps. The night was black, for there was no moon, but I remember seeing a dark ridge silhouetted against a planet-powdered ribbon of sky become fuzzy for a moment. The whole bristling edge of forest was shaking violently.

My wife leaped out of bed shouting "Earthquake!" I seized the lantern, and together we rushed outside, only to be thrown immediately to the ground. The lantern went out.

A dozen yards away our boys were crawling out of their tent. We yelled to them to join us, and, although they had not heard our shouts, a minute later they crawled across to where we lay.

All four of us held hands and lay flat, waiting for the end.

My first feeling of bewilderment had given place to stark terror. These solid mountains were in the grip of a force that was shaking them as a terrier shakes a rat. Yet, frightened as we were by the din and violent earth tremors, we spoke quite calmly to each other.

The earthquake roared on. Something was pounding the ground beneath us with the force of a giant sledge hammer. Our once-solid ground felt like no more than a thin covering stretched across the valley floor and attached by its edges to the mountains. It seemed that the very foundations of the world were breaking up under the violent blows, that the crust on which we lay would crumple like an ice floe in a rough sea and hurl us into a bottomless pit.

Besides the roaring of the earthquake itself there was another more familiar sound—the crash of rock avalanches pouring into the valley on every side. The mountains themselves seemed to be falling into the gorge as cliffs broke in half and boulders poured down a hundred scuppers with a clatter and a rumble. Not far from our camp the mountain rose steeply for hundreds of feet to a higher terrace. Surely the slope would give way and we should be crushed to death or buried alive.

But presently the battering ceased, and the noise died away except for an occasional avalanche. Then without warning came four or five sharp explosions in quick succession, seemingly high up in the dark sky. They sounded like ack-ack shells bursting. It was the cease-fire; everything became quiet, and the madness was over for a while. The initial shock had lasted only four or five minutes. It had seemed an eternity.

Returning to our tent, I noticed that my traveling clock was on the table and ticking, the altimeter still registered exactly 5,000 feet, and the thermometer showed 73°F. Nothing inside the tent was disturbed except a glass of water that had been upset. Luckily the steep slope near our camp had not slipped badly; at any rate, no boulders or slides reached us. Apparently we could not have selected a safer site.

Not until weeks later did we learn the magnitude of the earthquake. Over thousands of square miles it created utter havoc. All communications were disrupted. Avalanches buried whole villages and flung rock dams across rivers. When the dams burst, devastating floods raced down valleys, sweeping everything in their path. Fortunately, in this sparsely settled region the loss of human life, though in the hundreds, was surprisingly small for such an upheaval. Stock died by the thousands.

Seismologists, whose instruments all over the world had been jarred, calculated that the epicenter of this frightful cataclysm in August 1950 had been along the border between Assam and Tibet, very close to our campsite, on the outskirts of the Tibetan village of Rima....

There was not much sleep for anyone that night. I dozed fitfully for a few hours, my wife not at all. Violent tremors succeeded one another at intervals; stars dimmed and went out as a vast curtain of dust veiled the sky.

A song like that of a blackbird roused me at dawn. Then came the raucous cry of a small boy scaring birds away from the crops in a near-by field. When presently a procession of women and girls filed out of the village on their way to work in the fields, it was apparent that the world was not yet completely topsy-turvy.

I dressed and went out. This very morning we had planned to be on our way up the Lat Te River, a swift torrent tumbling down from the Burma frontier into the Luhit. But overnight the Lat Te had changed from a blue-green crystal stream to a raging flood of liquid mud.

Rising some four feet, the rock-filled river had smashed several small water mills along its bank. Invisible boulders rumbled as they ground against one another on the bottom.

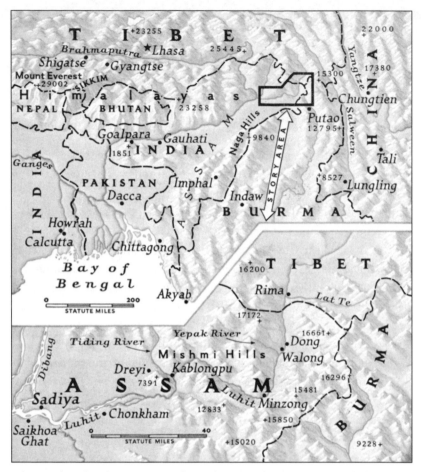

The rugged, earthquake-prone region where India, Burma (now Myanmar), and China meet
is where botanist Frank Kingdon-Ward spent a lifetime hunting unusual plants. He and his
wife were camped at Rima in Tibet when one of the strongest quakes of the century struck.

The Luhit had also risen, carrying a forest of pine logs which had
already begun to jam. The previous night we had watched the water in
Rima's main irrigation channel, whence we drew our own supply, dwin-
dle until it ceased to flow. For the next three weeks, until we found a
spring, drinking water was a serious problem.

In Rima itself every house had lost its roof, every outhouse had collapsed.
Its little monastery, with prayer flags bravely fluttering, lay on its side. Cattle
and pigs had been killed by falling beams, but there was no loss of human life.

Cracks had opened in the fields, terrace banks had slipped, and here and
there whole blocks of land had sunk several feet. Worse, the rope bridge
across the Luhit River, connecting Rima with the only trail to Sadiya, had

been swept downstream after breaking. The most startling changes were, of course, in the mountain landscape. Steep and craggy, with only thin pine forest for cover on the exposed face, almost every hillside had been torn open. Strips of green pasture half a mile long had peeled off, leaving dead-white scars. Nor was this damage confined to the outer ranges. A later view revealed that the mountains up to 15,000 feet, and right back to the main divide, had been ripped to pieces and scraped clean, and that millions of tons of rock had been hurled into the narrow valleys....

The day was sultry. The wind rose about midday, lifting a curtain of dust which rose until the ragged outlines of the mountains became like shadows, and the red sun looked like a copper gong. I could almost believe it clanged as its rim struck the western range. The raging river swept by in a coffee-colored flood, hundreds of tree trunks bouncing on the waves.

Night came again, an uneasy night marked by more severe tremors, each preceded by a noise like distant gunfire, or perhaps thunder, since it seemed to come from the sky. So it continued night after night and day after day, the earth trembling as if frightened at the havoc it had wrought.

As the ground shook, avalanches of rocks rolled and rumbled down the mountainsides, and the dust cloud thickened and swelled till every leaf of every plant was caked with the finest gray powder. We tasted and breathed dust; it filled eyes, nose, and ears. When rain fell it was a shower of mud.

To our other worries was added the uneasy feeling of being trapped. Early efforts to get a rope bridge across the river failed, and after three days the attempt was abandoned. We should have to wait till the river fell.

I turned over in my mind other routes out of the Luhit Valley, but could not hide from myself the fact that every alternative to the way we had come was long, difficult, and certainly dangerous. We could not cross the high passes, or even reach them, nor could we go down the Luhit to Sadiya on the Rima side of the river. To attempt to go farther up the valley, were that possible, was to get uncomfortably close to the Communists, who were taking over Tibet. In fact, any escape from our predicament was out of the question until we could cross the river.

We took careful stock of our position and prospects. It was impossible to reach the alpine meadows from Rima now. On short rations we had food for only about two months, nor could we buy more locally. We heard a rumor that a political officer, who, because of the Communist menace, had lately come up to the frontier with an armed escort, had been killed by the earthquake. An Assam Rifles patrol working on our side of the river up toward the Burma frontier was, however, reported safe by hunters who reached Rima exhausted. When at last we made contact with the patrol leader by messenger, we were able to send them some food.

So the sticky, hot days passed in slow procession. On the last day of August, more than a fortnight after the earthquake, the indomitable lost patrol marched into our camp, having overcome almost incredible difficulties. Their clothes were torn, their boots worn out. They had no food, and we handed over more than half of our rations to them. We ourselves were now reduced to a mere 10 or 12 days' supply of flour and rice; for weeks we had lived on little else. Something had to be done quickly.

At our urging the local people tried again to establish the rope bridge across the Luhit, and by September 2 they at last got a line across. By the 5th a newly plaited bamboo rope was in position, and we decided to leave on the 7th. But first we sent off an urgent message south to Walong, an Indian outpost in Assam near the border of Tibet, asking for rations and for the patrol and ourselves.

Porters for our journey arrived early on the morning of the 7th, as promised by Rima's headman, and the whole party set out for Walong. We crossed the river by the rope bridge safely. Each passenger was suspended by leather thongs from a half cylinder of hard wood which slid easily over the bamboo.

Earthquake damage beyond the river, though conspicuous, did not seriously impede us; in places cultivated ground was so badly fissured as to be virtually plowed up. By evening we had reached a large village, and here we met a party of Assam Rifles who had been sent up from Walong to help us back to comparative safety. They brought a few days' food for all, much to our relief, for we had enough left for only two days, even on reduced rations. On the way the party had bridged torrents which, since the earthquake, had become ungovernable....

On the following day we crossed a tributary of the Luhit at a place where we had camped for a month on the way up, half a year previously. We hardly recognized the place. For two days after the earthquake the river, dammed by an avalanche, had ceased to flow. When the dam broke, a flood swept down the narrow valley, ripped out its thick lining of forest, and plastered boulders to a depth of several feet with gray mud whose fetid smell fouled the air.

Now the water had fallen and the mud hardened; thus we had no great difficulty in crossing.

The only means of crossing the raging Lohit River—one of many challenges in escaping the earthquake-ravaged area: A plaited-bamboo rope down which people slid, hitched to a leather sling and using a wooden slider to protect the hands.

From this point on the going grew steadily worse. Drinking water was scarce, and we had to make long stages to reach it. The goat track we were following climbed to dizzy heights above the river and crossed hair-raising traverses where the whole mountainside had slipped.

To the peril of falling over the edge of the precipice on one side was added the danger from falling stones on the other. Our fear of this danger was heightened by the rock falls we watched across the river. At one spot opposite our camp, where the cliffs rose almost sheer from the river for 2,000 feet, a fall occurred regularly every half-hour.

I have never watched a more terrifying sight. Immediately after the sharp crack of the rocks breaking loose came a crashing, grinding roar as they poured into the narrow chute, gaining speed. Then, toward the bottom, huge boulders leaped out to meet the river, spinning in the air as if fired from a gun, while the dust hung in clouds like smoke.

On the night of September 10 we camped near a hot spring after an exhausting day's march of eight and a half hours. Each morning we had started at daylight in order to get over some of the most dangerous places before sun and wind combined to start the boulders slipping and sliding. We were now only about a mile from Walong, but it was a mile of dangerous screes. More than ever was it necessary to start early. We got up at 4 o'clock, packed hurriedly, and before 5 o'clock were on our way.

Thus, on September 11 the whole party, now numbering (with riflemen, porters, and our own group) about 60 people, marched into Walong amidst the congratulations and handshakes of the garrison....

On October 16 we set out for Sadiya, hoping to reach the plains in 12 days. Little did we realize what was in store for us. The 10 days' journey across the Mishmi Hills is divided into three rugged sections of one four-day and two three-day marches. At the end of each section there is a small military outpost where we changed porters and could, if necessary, halt for a day's rest. The first day's march, which included crossing the unleashed Yepak, was not as difficult as we expected, though when we halted that evening at the foot of a tremendous precipice I guessed we were in for trouble on the morrow.

On our journey into Tibet we had walked around this cliff, but now eight feet of swift, ragged water battered at its foot. Up the face of the cliff now climbed a narrow timber gallery suspended by loops of wire from iron pitons driven into the cracks. It sloped upward at an angle of some 30°, curling around the smooth buttress and disappearing from sight around a corner. There was just room enough to inch along between the rock wall and a loose handrail, which was meant to give moral but no other form of support. After we had turned the corner, the gallery ended abruptly, and we found ourselves on the brink of the cliff hundreds of feet above the white-capped river, with a dangerous traverse of several hundred yards across a smooth, steep slope.

This was bad enough, but what made it infinitely worse was the ever-present threat of a rock bombardment from above, or even of the whole track sliding into the river as a fresh stratum peeled off. The slope began a thousand feet or more above our heads. All such slopes were dangerously unstable and still very active, though it was nine weeks since the earthquake. We had the uncomfortable feeling that the next avalanche might start at any moment.

It was impossible to run across crumbling faces of this sort; there was no path, nothing but a series of toe steps slanting upward or downward, often nearly obliterated, with nothing to hold on to. We leaned our weight against bamboo staffs, as on a snow traverse, keeping as upright as possible to press nearly vertically on the loose material. It was a matter of balance, and balance alone. Luckily my wife's nerves are not affected by height. The porters, carrying nearly their full 60-pound loads, crossed the most frightful slopes as steady as guardsmen.

Late that afternoon we had to negotiate another hazardous traverse even worse than the first one. At one point stones were whizzing down, and we crouched against the rock as they sang over our heads. Their velocity may be gauged by the fact that we passed a pine tree in whose trunk several sharp-edged rocks hurled from the cliff above were deeply buried. So began our baptism of fire on this leg of the trip....

And so it continued, rock slide after rock slide, the mountainsides flayed open, the rivers in spate, for the next several weeks. Finally, on November 4, after nearly three months of effort, they arrived on the plains of Assam. The massive quake, registering 8.7 on the Richter scale, the strongest in half a century, had killed 1,000 people and destroyed 2,000 houses in a thinly populated area.

It wasn't long before Kingdon-Ward was back at it. In 1955, when he was 70, he was climbing 10,000-foot mountains in Burma; the following year he was sprinting to escape a roaring forest fire. But in 1958, when he suffered his fatal stroke, he was not dangling from some crag on the edge of the world.

He was sitting over a pint in a London pub.

TRIUMPH ON EVEREST

July 1954

SIR JOHN HUNT (1910–98)
SIR EDMUND HILLARY (1919–)

A SOLDIER, A BEEKEEPER, AND A YAK HERDER—AN UNLIKELY TRIO to achieve the crowning glory of high adventure. Yet Hunt, Hillary, and Tenzing stand roped together in history for accomplishing the last great feat of exploration to rely more on heart, leg, and stamina than on technology: the conquest of Mount Everest.

For years the mountain had seemed indomitable. It was virtually inaccessible, guarded by two closed countries, Nepal and Tibet. And it was practically insurmountable, its untrodden snows demanding better climbing gear and techniques. By 1952, however, a number of attempts had been made, all defeated by bad weather and worse luck. That was the year Col. John Hunt, stationed in Germany, received a telegram from the Joint Himalayan Commission of the Royal Geographical Society and the Alpine Club, asking if he would lead yet another British expedition to the slopes of Everest.

John Hunt, 42, a born leader, decorated war hero, and seasoned mountaineer, planned a military-style assault on the peak. He molded a team of 14 of the best climbers he could find. Among them was Edmund Hillary, 33, a rangy New Zealand beekeeper, and Tenzing Norgay [here spelled Norkey], 38, the Sirdar, or foreman, of the Sherpa porters and the man who probably knew Everest better than anyone, having worked with climbing parties since the late 1930s. This was his sixth expedition to Chomolungma, "Goddess Mother of the World," which he had first dreamed of climbing as a boy, herding yaks above his native village.

On May 29, 1953, Hillary and Tenzing crested the peak, first men to stand on the top of the world. The story has been told and retold, but rarely with such succinctness and drama as in the July 1954 NATIONAL GEOGRAPHIC. Spreading over 64 pages, "Triumph on Everest" was composed of two parts: "Siege and Assault" by Sir John Hunt and "The Conquest of the Summit" by Sir Edmund Hillary, their names burnished with newly minted knighthoods.

From "Siege and Assault" by Sir John Hunt:

A LONG STORY, AND NOT MERELY MINE. IT INVOLVES THE FATE AND fortunes of many gallant mountaineers, and it really begins, I think, not in London nor at Everest's base, but in the far-off, cloud-capped Tibetan city of Lhasa. Here, one winter morning, in the Inner Enclosure of the Jewel Park, the Dalai Lama of Tibet handed the British political agent a precious document. It was only an unsigned strip of paper, but on it Sir Charles Bell could read: "To the west of the Five Treasuries of Great Snow Mount in the jurisdiction of White Glass Fort near Inner Rock Valley monastery is the district called 'The Southern Country where Birds are Kept.'"

This note, and the official passport which followed it, signified the first permission—long denied—ever granted Europeans to climb earth's highest peak. The "Five Treasuries" were the five summits of Kanchenjunga; "White Glass Fort" was the hill town of Shekar Dzong; the monastery lay in Rongbuk Valley; and "The Southern Country where Birds are Kept" held the massive eminence called Chomolungma, "Goddess Mother of the World": Mount Everest.

That was December 9, 1920. In the 32 years that followed, seven major expeditions sallied forth to conquer Everest, well equipped, led and manned by mountaineers of superlative caliber, and in most instances supported by small armies of porters. Each party pressed the attack to the utmost limits of human endurance, threw all its resources, skills, hopes, and even lives into the attempt—and fell back defeated.

Until May 1953, Everest, towering 29,002 [actually 29,035] feet astride the border of Nepal and Tibet, stood inviolate. Seven British climbers, one Sherpa, and a Swiss had struggled up its slopes of ice and rock to within 1,000 feet of the summit. Of this valiant band, two— George Leigh-Mallory and Andrew Irvine—had in 1924 vanished forever into the mists along the Northeast Ridge, ascending no man knows how high before they died.

What manner of mountain is this which for so many years so easily shrugged off all assaults and claimed the lives of at least 16 men?

Other peaks demand more actual climbing. Alaska's Mount McKinley, for example, measures 19,000 feet from its lowland base, while Everest rises only about 12,000 above the 17,000-foot Tibetan plateau. Himalayan winds are fierce, but the Scottish Highlands, battered by the North Atlantic's hurricanes, endure gales as terrible. Everest's crags and crevasses test any man's ability, but half a dozen Alpine peaks offer technical problems of greater severity. Everest can chill a man to the marrow with summer temperatures down to −40°F at night; yet on the Greenland icecap and elsewhere explorers have lived through cold worse by 30 or 40 degrees.

What makes Everest murderous is the fact that its cold, its wind, and its climbing difficulties converge upon the mountaineer at altitudes which have already robbed him of resistance.... Yet for even the best acclimatized mountaineer, and men differ sharply in their ability to acclimatize, Everest offers only slow deterioration. Above 25,000 feet the climber's heavy legs seem riveted to the ground, his pulse races, his vision blurs, his ice ax sags in his hand like a crowbar. To scoop up snow in a pan for melting looms as a monumental undertaking. In the words of a Himalayan veteran, Frank Smythe: "On Everest it is an effort to cook, an effort to talk, an effort to think, almost too much of an effort to live."

If, nevertheless, there were an "open season" upon Everest the year round, some expedition hardier or luckier than the rest would long since have stumbled to the top.

The mountain's subtlest defense is the prohibition it places upon climbing it at all except during a few unpredictable days in late spring, between the lulling northwest wind's gales and the arrival of the snow-laden monsoon, and for a brief spell in the autumn.

In winter the peak's flanks may lie invitingly bare of snow, but the wind which has scoured them clean is too brutal for mortal men to face. In summer the great snows deposited by the monsoon, lying high above the evaporation line, rarely pack down into dependable slopes; to flounder across such powdery drifts is to invite at the least exhaustion, at worst a fatal slip or the detonation of a suffocating avalanche.

Why, then, do men pit their frail resources against a citadel so well protected? Mallory had his classic answer: "Because it is there." But there is another reason, rooted fast in the sheer, stubborn tenacity of man. Capt. Geoffrey Bruce, of the 6th Gurkha Rifles, stopped in his tracks at 27,235 feet by a technical fault in his oxygen apparatus, was rescued in a critical condition by his companion, George Finch. He paused to shout up at the summit before he turned back: "Just you wait, old thing, you'll be for it soon!"

As for those of us who set forth against Everest in 1953, I think we shared a sense both of high adventure and of fellowship with all those who had done battle with this mountain before and who had passed on to us, with open hands, the heritage of their experience. It was not only glory we sought, unless it be the common glory of man's triumph over Nature—and over his own limitations. Mallory, again, spoke the final word on the conquest of mountains: "Have we vanquished an enemy? None but ourselves."...

Our plan, in its main outlines, was clear. The northern approaches to Everest via Tibet, used by all previous British attempts at the summit, were now closed to us by the Iron Curtain of the East. Nepal, however, ending its long ban on European entry, had in 1949 opened up to us the little-known southern aspect of the mountain.

This side had never been considered promising. It condemns the intruder to climbing up the long Khumbu Glacier, surmounting its fantastic 2,000-foot, crevasse-riven icefall, traversing the abrupt ice slopes of Lhotse to Everest's South Col, and only then—still 3,200 feet below the summit—beginning the final assault. Mallory, having gazed upon this frozen cataract from the north in 1921, described it as "one of the most awful and utterly forbidding scenes ever observed by man" and called it quite unclimbable.

But Shipton and his men had hacked their way to the top of the ice-fall in 1951. The Swiss team had penetrated it again in 1952, emerged in that strange freak of Nature, the hidden valley called the Western Cwm, cut a route to the South Col, and very nearly achieved the summit itself. We were convinced that, in mountaineer's jargon, the Nepalese approach "would go."...

Our route cut squarely across the Himalayan watershed, plunging us into deep valleys, carrying us over foaming torrents and swift-flowing rivers and up the far hillsides. This was big country, warm and welcoming. Along the track we passed Nepalese girls ajingle with earrings, glass bangles, and necklaces of crimson beads. Their wide-grinning men were close-cropped and scantily attired. On the ridges we trod a carpet of mauve primulas, and in the forests the heavy-scented white magnolia blossoms lay like fallen snow.

Flickering in and out above the gnarled, full-flowered rhododendrons darted gay sunbirds, flycatchers, scarlet minivets, green-backed and red-headed titmice. Up on the steep slopes, laboriously terraced, hayricks planted in the branches of trees drew our astonished glances.

These were enchanted days, bright with the promise of adventure and free from the exasperation of the winter's paperwork. We ate heartily and with what Everester Bill Tilman used to call "dogged greed." For on the topmost heights far ahead of us, we could each anticipate a rapid loss of weight.

As we strolled along, I was able at my leisure to become better acquainted with our Sherpas—and especially with their renowned leader, Tenzing Norkey. Lighthearted, simple in manner, but with an evident authority,

Tenzing impressed me at once. Few men had seen more of the world's highest mountains. Ours was the sixth Everest expedition he had joined; the first had been in 1935 when he served as a 21-year-old porter. His great exploit of reaching the Southeast Ridge in 1953 with Lambert had, we feared, undermined his health, and he himself had written me that he could probably serve only as far as the icefall. Yet now, to my delight, he seemed not only fit but frisky....

Fifteen days out of Katmandu we climbed the last ridge overlooking the village of Namche Bazar. There ahead of us, overwhelming the horizon, loomed suddenly the solid mass of Everest, its peak swept almost bare of snow. Mallory, seeing it for the first time from the north, had called it a "prodigious white fang excrescent from the jaw of the world." Wind-whipped, the fang was now black. But it was no less awesome.

From Namche Bazar we climbed with ever-increasing exhilaration to the monastery of Thyangboche—surely the most magnificent grandstand ever provided for mountain scenery. Here, on a grassy 13,500-foot alp where yaks grazed, we pitched camp. We had much to do; yet again and again we looked up from our tasks, transfixed by the majesty, the sheer icy splendor of the peaks that rose around us: the Everest group; Ama Dablam, whose cruel summit makes the Matterhorn look tame; the twin spires of Kangtega and Thamserku, delicately fluted; Kwangde's long and lofty barrier...

Over the next few weeks Hunt hacked a series of camps into the slopes at ever higher altitudes. It was rough work, the men crossing crevasses, dodging avalanches, and bending beneath blizzards, but by late May the lead climbers had pitched their tents on the South Col. Hunt himself could go no higher. The first assault team, composed of Charles Evans and Tom Bourdillon, started from the South Col, reached the South Peak, but did not have enough oxygen to make a bid for the summit. The second team, Hillary and Tenzing, prepared to go. From "The Conquest of the Summit" by Sir Edmund Hillary:

NIGHT ON THE SOUTH COL. THE WIND SCREECHES ACROSS THE RIDGE AND sets the canvas cracking like a rifle range; an awful noise. I'm braced between Tenzing and the tent wall, no room to stretch out. Whenever my head falls back against the roof it's as if I'd run my brain into a pneumatic drill.

The other side of Tenzing are Alf Gregory and George Lowe, hunched up in their sleeping bags, twisting, heaving around, trying to find some position less cold and miserable. We're using the oxygen sleeping sets, one liter per minute. Makes it easier to doze. But up here you dribble a good bit in your sleep, and when your bottle gives out you wake up suddenly, as if somebody had turned on the light, and your rubber face mask is all clammy and frigid.

I keep looking at my watch, wondering if it's stopped. The hour hand finally creeps around to 4, and I strike a match. The thermometer on the tent wall reads: -13°F. It is still pitch dark. I nudge Tenzing, mutter something about breakfast, and retreat callously to my bag. Pretty soon the primus [camp stove] has warmed the tent a few degrees—just enough to make it seem safe to sit up and eat. Scruffy, cramped, somewhat depressed, we gulp down cups of sugary hot water flavored with lemon crystals, munch some biscuits, and argue about which one of us has spent the worst night.

Greg claims the honor, contending that sleeping between Lowe and Tenzing is like being caught in the jaws of a vise. But Lowe scores heavily when he points to a small heap of snow on his sleeping bag, blown through a pinhole in his side of the tent. Scraping it off, he grins at us and says: "Well, at least you're having a good holiday. I hope you're feeling better for it."

Nobody bothers to answer. We sprawl about for five hours, waiting for the wind to die down. It doesn't.

At 9 I bundle up and stumble over to John Hunt's tent, which he's sharing with Bourdillon and Evans. John agrees we must postpone the attempt. He decides, too, that everyone but Greg, Lowe, Tenzing, Ang Nyima, Pemba, and I should go down; no point in depleting the slim reserves of food we've hauled up here.

An hour or so later they are packed and ready. Hunt, gray and drawn but with his blue eyes frostier than ever, grips my arm. Above the howling wind he says: "Most important thing—is for you chaps—to come back safely. Remember that. But get up if you can."

We watch them slog across the col, up the ridge, and down the slopes toward the traverse: four tired figures dwindling against the monstrous icy face of Lhotse. Then we turn back to our own chores....

The climbers succeed in establishing a new camp even farther up the mountain. There, once their companions turn back down, Hillary and Tenzing remain alone.

Four a.m. We poke our heads out of the tent door. The wind is mercifully still. Far off, the valleys of Nepal still sleep in darkness, but the

VIEW FROM SOUTH
Assault Phase

EVEREST'S 29,002 feet attained
by Hillary and Tenzing, 11:30 a.m.,
May 29, 1953.

SOUTH PEAK, 28,700 feet. Reached
by Evans and Bourdillon, May 26, then
man's highest climb.

CAMP IX, 27,900 feet. Lowe, Gregory, and
Ang Nyima left Hillary and Tenzing here,
pitching tent on eve of final assault.

27,350 feet. Hunt and Da
Namgyal carried supplies
here from Camp VIII for
victorious summit team.

Lhotse
27,890 feet

CAMP VIII,
25,800 feet.

SOUTH FACE, drops 8,000 feet
from summit to Western Cwm.

Geneva Spur

Lhotse Face

The Traverse

Western
Cwm

Nuptse Ridge

11

Tibetans Know Everest's Sky-piercing Eminence as Chomolungma, "Goddess Mother of the World"

Youngest of the world's great ranges, the 1,500-mile Himalayan barrier curves east and west in a protective arc that, through history, has blocked Mongolians and Tibetans from the lush Hindu lands. Two Sanskrit words—*hima* and *alaya*—give this vast uplift an apt name: "The Abode of Snow." From its glaciers stem three of India's holiest rivers: the Ganges, the Indus, the Brahmaputra.

Mallory, gazing over into the Western Cwm on his reconnaissance in 1921, named it after highland glens he had explored in his youth. Cwm, a Welsh term pronounced "coom," is an enclosed valley, usually on a mountain's flank. Col, another oft-used climber's word, means a depression or pass on a mountain chain.

Mount Everest
29,002 feet

Mount McKinley
20,300 feet

Pikes Peak
14,110 feet

Mount Washington
6,288 feet

PIK-Tso
Tingri Dzong
Shekar Dzong

T I B E T

26289

Rongbuk

Cho Oyu
26867

Mt. Everest
29002

Tsomo
Tretung

Makalu
27790

Katmandu

Chola

Thyangboche

Kanchenjunga
28166

Patan
Bhadgaon
Bhimphedi
Risingo

Solu
Namche Bazar

Dudh Kosi

SIKKIM

N E P A L

Gangtok

450 porters carried expedition's
15 tons of supplies 175 miles from
Katmandu to Thyangboche, the
first base camp.

STATUTE MILES
© National Geographic Map

Darjeeling
INDIA

Empire State
Building
1,472 feet high.

Golden Gate Bridge,
746 feet high,
6,450 feet long.

Highest point on the planet, Mount Everest, or Chomolungma, "Goddess Mother of the World," remained unconquered until 1953, when a team of British and Sherpa climbers approached the summit via the South Col, the swale between Lhotse and the South Peak.

summits of Makalu and Ama Dablam have caught the sun; and Tenzing, pointing past me, picks out the monastery at Thyangboche, 14,400 feet below us, where even now the lamas are offering special prayers for our safe return.

While Tenzing melts water for our tea, I haul the oxygen sets inside, knock the ice off the valves, and test them. My feet had been a bit damp the night before and, in order to let them dry out and warm up, with less risk of frostbite, I had pulled my boots off and used them to prop the toe of my sleeping bag off the cold ground. Now the boots are frozen as stiff as medieval armor.

I cook them over the primus. It takes me a good hour to thaw them, and the smell of leather and rubberized fabric toasting in the little tent is gruesome; but finally the boots are soft enough to wiggle into, and we can set out. Tenzing breaks trail through the powdery snow until my feet have warmed up; then I take over the lead....

We push on. About 400 feet from the South Peak we are brought to a stop: which route? Bourdillon and Evans took the ridge to the left; then, on their way back, came down the broad face. But I think the ridge looks jolly dangerous, with all that loose snow masking the rocks. We decide on the face.

You can't zigzag up a steep slope like this or you'll undercut it and find yourself aboard an avalanche with a one-way ticket to the bottom. So we go straight up. At least, we go up five steps, walking on eggs, and then the whole crust for 10 feet around breaks up and we slide down again three steps. We don't so much climb the face as swim up it.

Halfway, I turn to Tenzing and say: "What do you think of it?"

"I don't like it at all."

"Shall we go on?"

He shrugs. "Just as you wish."

I make a quick decision. In ordinary mountaineering terms, the risk isn't justifiable. I know that. But this is Everest, and on Everest you sometimes have to take the long odds, because the goal is worth it. Or so I try to convince myself. We go on, and we get a break. A few yards higher up we run into some snow that's packed harder. Chipping steps, we make our way quite rapidly up to the crest. At 9 a.m. we are standing on the South Peak.

To size it up, we scoop out a seat for ourselves just below the South Peak, remove our masks, and study the summit above. The true crown is out of sight, somewhere up above the ridge that turns its blade right in our faces now. It looks a fair cow, all right, as we'd say in New Zealand. Cornices on the right, overhanging a little drop of 10,000 feet to the Kangshung Glacier on Everest's eastern flank; on the left, steep snow sloping to the lip of the big rock wall that looms over the Western Cwm.

We don't need to talk much. It's obvious that our only route lies between the cornices and the cliffs on the left; the joker is the state of the snow. If it's firm, we have a chance. If it's loose and dry, we've come a long way for very little. I lead off, cutting a 40-foot line of steps, resting, and taking a few turns of the rope around my ax as Tenzing comes up to join me. Then he belays me as I carve another flight. We move along steadily, giving the rickety cornices a fairly wide berth and taking an occasional gander over the rock face on our left. About 7,500 feet below I can just make out the tents of Camp IV, and I flap my arms up and down like an Abominable Scarecrow, with no particular hope that anyone will see me.

Tenzing has begun to drag a little on the rope by now, and his breathing seems more rapid. As we halt on one tiny ledge, I ask:

"How does it go, Tenzing?"

"All right."

I know, however, that like most Sherpas Tenzing has only a vague notion of the way his oxygen set works. He may be getting groggy and not even realize it. So I check his exhaust tube and find the valves almost completely blocked with ice; he's probably been getting no real benefit from his oxygen for some minutes.

I examine my own tube; to my surprise, ice has begun to form here, too, though not enough yet to interrupt my air flow. Obviously, this is something I'll have to keep an eye on for both of us. Fortunately, my habit of doing mental mathematics on our oxygen supply as I plug along, plus the fact that I'm leading the rope, will keep me fairly alert.

We resume the climb, and I cut another line of steps for perhaps half an hour. Then we find ourselves staring at an obstacle we've dreaded ever since we spotted it on the aerial photos and through our binoculars from Thyangboche: a ghastly great rock about 40 feet high, plunked down right across the ridge. No route on it worth talking about. And no way around it except—

Except where the snow cornice on the right, pulling away a little from the rock, has left a thin gap, a kind of chimney. We look at it with rather mixed emotions. I'm not one of those blokes who says to himself, "I'll get up, come hell or high water." Mountains mean a lot to me, but not that much. I just say to Tenzing:

"Well, we'll give it a good go."

He takes a belay, and I jam my way into the crack. With my back to the cornice, I face the rock and grope for handholds along it, kicking my crampons into the snow behind me and jacking myself upwards. I use everything I have—knees, elbows, shoulders, even the oxygen set on my back—trying to get a purchase and exert some critical leverage.

My tactics depend on one little consideration: that the cornice doesn't peel off. Of course, Tenzing has me belayed on a bit of rock, which provides a certain moral support. But if the snow gives way, and I find myself dangling over the Kangshung Glacier, it isn't going to matter enormously whether Tenzing can hold me for five minutes or fifty.

Foot by foot I hump and wriggle and pull myself up the chimney. The crack is only a rope's length long, but it's a good half hour before I can reach over the ledge at the top and drag myself onto it. I lie there, panting like a gaffed fish, surprised somehow that I've scraped together enough energy to make it. Then I give Tenzing a taut rope and signal him to come along. For the first time the conviction seeps through me that we are really going to go all the way. I check the oxygen sets again. The flow rates seem all right. Turning to Tenzing, I say: "How do you feel?"

He just grins and waves his hand upward toward the ridge. I lead off once more, cutting steps. My ax work is still pretty rhythmical and relaxed; I've been chipping away for well over an hour, but, so far, I've avoided the kind of tension that can turn up a sore arm.

One flight of steps, then another, and another. We follow the ridge as it curves around to the right, wondering where the top can possibly be, or if it exists at all. I cut around the back of one crag, only to have a higher one stare me in the face. It seems endless.

Tiring, I try to save time on one stretch by skipping the step cutting and relying on my crampons. After a few yards I go back to my ax; the angle is still too steep, too dangerous. The zest we have known at the top of the rock step is draining away. Dully, grimly, I hack a route around still another knob. Suddenly I realize that the ridge ahead doesn't slope up, but down. I look quickly to my right. There, just above me, is a softly rounded, snow-covered little bump about as big as a haystack.

The summit.

One last question concerns me: is the top itself just a large, delicately poised cornice? If it is, someone else can have the honor of stepping on it.

I cut my way cautiously up the next few feet, probing ahead with my pick. The snow is solid, firmly packed. We stagger up the final stretch. We are there. Nothing above us, a world below.

I feel no great elation at first, just relief and a sense of wonder. Then I turn to Tenzing and shake his hand. Even through the snow glasses, the ice-encrusted mask, the knitted helmet, I can see that happy, flashing smile. He throws his arms around my shoulders, and we thump each other, and there is very little we can say or need to say.

My watch shows 11:30. Two hours and a half it has taken us from the South Peak; five hours from our tent. It seems a bit longer. I turn off my oxygen and remove my mask. In the thin air of 29,000 feet my breathing becomes slightly more rapid, but not too uncomfortable. I fish out the camera I have kept warm inside my shirt; it will be necessary to take shots down every ridge if we're to prove conclusively that we've been up here.

Moving down the cone a few feet, I snap a picture of Tenzing holding up his ice ax with its flag standing out stiffly in the wind—the flags of the United Nations, Great Britain, Nepal, India. It would be nice to have Tenzing take my portrait, too, in some heroic pose, but unfortunately he doesn't number among his many virtues a knowledge of photography, and the top of Everest strikes me as a poor place on which to conduct classes.

We look about for any signs that Mallory and Irvine may have been here before us; there are none. I take care, however, to photograph the route which they and the other great climbers followed up from North Col and along the rugged Northeast Ridge. Then I point the camera hopefully at unclimbed Makalu, at the fantastic hulk of Kanchenjunga on the far horizon, at Cho Oyu in the northwest, at the ranges of Nepal receding into the distance, wave on glittering wave.

Scooping a small hole in the snow, Tenzing buries a few offerings to the gods that many Buddhists believe inhabit these heights: a small blue pencil given him by his daughter, a bar of chocolate, some biscuits, a cluster of lollypops. I place near these gifts a little crucifix that John Hunt has received from a friend and passed over to me on the South Col.

It's time to go down now. I replace my oxygen mask, suck the air in gratefully, and move off without a backward glance. Reaction has set in; we both are tired....

Forty steps more. Twenty. Five... We are down and can slant over to the relative safety of the Southeast Ridge. We look at each other, and with a kind of sigh shrug off the weight of fear that has sat on our shoulders all this long day. The worst is over; we are nearly down.

Picking up the reverse cylinders left by Charles and Tom, we trek down to our dismal little campsite; already the wind has ripped the tent half away. It is 2 p.m. Tenzing heats up some more lemonade on the

A typical tableau on the slopes of Everest: A Sherpa (top) anchors the rope supporting his partner, a British climber crossing a crevasse. Just such a team, composed of Tenzing Norgay and New Zealander Edmund Hillary, finally reached the summit.

paraffin stove, while I change our oxygen sets onto the last bottles and cut the flow rates down to two liters a minute. We sip our drinks, looking rather dazedly down at the South Col where a couple of dots that may be Lowe and Noyce move out now from the camp.

On our feet again, we load up our air mattresses and sleeping bags and stumble off, numb with exhaustion, to the top of the couloir. Here we get a rude surprise: the wind has wiped out all the steps we cut the day before, leaving only a smooth, frozen slope beneath us. With a grunt of disgust, I start chipping a new flight, 200 feet down the gully, pausing only when a particularly vicious gust tries to tear me loose from the mountain and forces me to dig my ax in fast and hang onto it, shielding my face from the pelting snow.

Once at the couloir's foot, it's only a long, rough tramp down to the South Col. Before we get there, a lone figure stumps up to meet us—George Lowe, carrying hot soup and emergency oxygen. I grin weakly at old George and say: "Well, we knocked the blighter off!"...

That's not exactly what he said. What he really uttered was, "Well, we knocked the bastard off." GEOGRAPHIC *editors could be a pusillanimous lot.*

When news of the achievement flashed around the globe, a troubled world had new heroes to enshrine. Accolades and honors piled up, and newly crowned Queen Elizabeth II promptly knighted both Hunt and Hillary. (Tenzing was not a British subject.) Modesty became all of them. Sir John believed that, since men feel small in the presence of mountains, "to feel you've conquered them is a presumption."

Though multitudes prostrated themselves before Tenzing as before a reincarnation of divinity, he remained unchanged. Sir Edmund went on to set further milestones in exploration, including the first motorized trek to the South Pole. But he devoted his energies to improving the lot of Sherpas as well, saying that "the building of schools and medical clinics ... has given me more satisfaction than a footprint on a mountain." As for fame, "as long as you didn't believe all that rubbish about yourself, you wouldn't come to much harm."

PART SIX

The far east

THE RECENT EARTHQUAKE WAVE
ON THE COAST OF JAPAN
September 1896

ELIZA SCIDMORE (1856–1928)

A HUGE WALL OF WATER REARS OVER TINY FISHING BOATS AND FRAMES a distant Mount Fuji—that picture, from an 1830s woodblock print popularly called the "Great Wave," became the best-known image of Japan in late-19th-century Europe and America. In that era, Japan was emerging from feudalism, opening her gates to the outside world, and a great wave of Western travelers was quickly captivated by this singular island nation.

Among them was Eliza Ruhamah Scidmore, a sharp-eyed, skeptical young American writer with a vivid prose style, an ironic outlook, and the ability to live out of a steamer trunk for months and still look fashionable. Author of wonderful travel books, Miss Scidmore was an early member of the National Geographic Society, and for a brief flurry of years in the 1890s was its foreign secretary, an associate editor of its magazine, and the first woman to serve on its board. She was not naturally effusive, but upon first arriving in Japan she was enchanted. Everywhere she looked, from temples to teahouses, Japan was "a dream of paradise," its people interesting and graceful, its customs worthy of emulation. She spent the rest of her life explaining the Japanese to Americans, and helped bring Japanese cherry trees, with their annual bloom of tremulous blossoms, to Washington, D.C.

It was almost too perfect, too theatrical, and she waited, she wrote, for the "bell to ring and the curtain to drop." That came soon enough. Japan is perched in an earthquake zone, and the Japanese word for "great wave" or "storm wave" is tsunami. Too often in the past—1293, 1703, 1854—tsunamis had cascaded onto the island nation, killing thousands at a time. The tsunami of 1896, the largest one ever recorded on these coasts, still looms large in the country's collective memory. Originating in an offshore earthquake deep in the Japan Trench, it slammed without warning onto the northeast shores of Honshu (or Hondo), the main Japanese island. Eliza Scidmore's riveting account of this tragedy has a distressingly familiar ring to anyone who has read the graphic accounts of the catastrophic December 2004 Indian Ocean tsunami.

ON THE EVENING OF JUNE 15, 1896, THE NORTHEAST OF HONDO, the main island of Japan, was struck by a great earthquake wave (tsunami) which was more destructive of life and property than any earthquake convulsion of this century in that empire. The whole coastline of the San-Riku, the three provinces of Rikuzen, Rikuchu, and Rikuoku, from the island of Kinkwazan ... northward for 175 miles, was laid waste by a great wave moving from the east and south, that varied in recorded height from 10 to 50 feet. A few survivors, who saw it advancing in the darkness, report its height as 80 to 100 feet. With a difference of but thirty minutes in time between the southern and northern points, it struck the San-Riku coast and in a trice obliterated towns and villages, killed 26,975 people put of the original population, and grievously wounded the 5,390 survivors. It washed away and wrecked 9,313 houses, stranded some 300 larger craft—steamers, schooners, and junks—and crushed or carried away 10,000 fishing boats, destroying property to the value of six million yen. Thousands of acres of arable land were turned to wastes, projecting rocks offshore were broken, overturned, or moved hundreds of yards, shallows and bars were formed, and in some localities the entire shoreline was changed.

They were all seafaring communities along this coast strip and the fisheries were the chief industry. The shipment of sea products to the great ports was the main connection with the outer world. A high mountain range bars communication with the trunk railway line of the island, and this picturesque, fiord-cut coast is so remote and so isolated that only two foreigners had been seen in the region in ten years, with the exception of the French mission priest, Father Raspail, who lost his life in the flood.

With telegraph offices, instruments, and operators carried away, word came slowly to Tokyo, and with 50 to 100 miles of mountain roads between the nearest railway station and the seacoast, aid was long in reaching the wretched survivors. When adequate idea of the calamity reached the capital and the cities, men-of-war, soldiers, sappers, surgeons, and nurses were quickly dispatched, and public sympathy found expressions in contributions through the different newspapers, amounting to more than 250,000 yen, for the relief of the injured. The Japanese journalists and photographers were quickly on their way, and the vernacular press soon fed the public full of horrors, yet the first to reach the scene of the disaster was an American missionary, the Rev. Rothesay Miller, who made the usual three day's trip over the mountains in less than a day and a half on his American bicycle.

There were old traditions of such earthquake waves on this coast, one of two centuries ago doing some damage, and a tsunami of forty years ago and a lesser one of 1892 flooding the streets of Kamaishi and driving people to upper floors and the roofs of their houses. The barometer gave no warning, no indication of any unusual conditions on June 15, and the occurrence of thirteen light earthquake shocks during the day excited no comment. Rain had fallen in the morning and afternoon, and with a temperature of 80 to 90 degrees the damp atmosphere was very oppressive. The villagers on that remote coast adhered to the old calendar in observing their local fetes and holidays, and on that fifth day of the fifth moon had been celebrating the Girl's Festival.

Rain had driven them indoors with the darkness, and nearly all were in their houses at eight o'clock, when, with a rumbling as of heavy cannonading out at sea, a roar, and the crash and crackling of timbers, they were suddenly engulfed in the swirling waters. Only a few survivors on all that length of coast saw the advancing wave, one of them telling that the water first receded some 600 yards from ghastly white sands and then the Wave stood like a black wall 80 feet in height, with phosphorescent lights gleaming along its crest. Others, hearing a distant roar, saw a dark shadow seaward and ran to high ground, crying *"Tsunami! Tsunami!"* Some who ran to the upper stories of their houses for safety were drowned, crushed, or imprisoned there, only a few breaking through the roofs or escaping after the water subsided.

Shallow water and outlying islands broke the force of the wave in some places, and in long, narrow inlets or fiords the giant roller was broken into two, three, and even six waves, that crashed upon the shore in succession. Ships and junks were carried one and two miles inland, left on hilltops, treetops, and in the midst of fields uninjured or mixed up with ruins of houses, the rest engulfed or swept seaward. Where the wave entered a fiord or bay it bore everything along to the head of the ravine or valley and left the mass of debris in a heap at the end. Where the coast was low and faced the open ocean the wave washed in and, retreating, carried everything back with it. Many survivors, swept away by the waters, were cast ashore on outlying islands, or seized bits of wreckage and kept afloat. On the open coast the wave came and withdrew within five minutes, while in long inlets the waters boiled and surged for nearly a half hour before subsiding.

The best swimmers were helpless in the first swirl of water, and nearly all the bodies recovered were frightfully battered and mutilated, rolled over and driven against rocks, struck by and crushed between timbers. The force of the wave cut down groves of the large pine trees to short stumps, snapped thick granite posts of temple gates and carried the stone cross-beams 300 yards away. Many people were lost through running back to save others or to save their valuables.

One loyal schoolmaster carried the emperor's portrait to a place of safety before seeking out his own family. A half-demented soldier, retired since the late war and continually brooding on a possible attack by the enemy, became convinced that the first cannonading sound was from a hostile fleet and, seizing his sword, ran down to the beach to meet the foe. One village officer, mistaking the sound of crashing timbers for crackling flames, ran to high ground to see where the fire was, and thus saved his life. Another village officer, living on the edge of a hill, heard the crash and slid his screens open to look upon foaming waters nearly level with his veranda. In a moment the waters disappeared, leaving a black, empty level where the populous village had been a few minutes before. Four women clung to one man, seeking to escape to high ground, and their combined weight resisting the force of the receding wave, they were all saved.

The only survivors of another village were eight men who had been playing the game of "go" in a hillside temple. Eight children floated away and, left on high ground, were believed to be the only survivors of one village, until one hundred people were found who had been borne across and stranded on the opposite shores of their bay. One hundred and fifty people were found cast away on one island offshore. From two large villages on one bay only thirty young men survived, hardy, muscular young fishermen and powerful swimmers, yet in other places the strongest perished, and the aged and infirm, cripples, and tiny children were miraculously preserved.

The wave flooded the cells of Okachi prison and the jailers broke the bolts and let the 195 convicts free. Only two convicts attempted to escape, the others waiting in good order until marched to the high ground by their keepers. The good Pere Raspail had just reached Kamaishi from his all-day walk of 50 miles over the mountains ... when his assistant called to him from the street. The priest came to the veranda, but in an instant the water was upon him. He was seen later, swimming, but evidently was struck by timbers or swept out to sea, as his body has not been recovered.

Japanese men-of-war cruised for a week off Kamaishi, recovering bodies daily. The Japanese system of census enumeration is so complete and minute that the name of every person who lost his life was soon known, and the official Gazette was able to state that out of a population of 6,529 at Kamaishi 4,985 were lost and 500 injured, while 953 dwellings and 867 warehouses and other structures were destroyed or carried away, and 176 ships carried inland or swept out and lost.

The survivors were so stunned with the appalling disaster that few could do anything for themselves or others. With houses, nets, and fishing-boats carried away and the fish retreating to further and deeper waters, starvation faced them... The great heat continuing while so many bodies were strewn along shore and imprisoned in ruins, the atmosphere fast became poisonous.

The north-coast people are opposed to cremation and insisted on earth burial, which delayed the disposal of the dead and augmented the danger of pestilence. Disinfectants were sent in quantity, and the work of recovery and burial was so pressing that soldiers were put to it after all available coolies had been impressed. The Red Cross Society, with its hospitals and nurses, had difficulty in caring for all the wounded, the greater number of whom, besides requiring surgical aid, were suffering from pneumonia and internal inflammations consequent upon their long exposure in wet clothing without shelter and from the brine, fish oil, and sand breathed in and swallowed while in the first tumult of waters. Besides the generous relief fund subscribed by the people, the government has made large assignments from its available funds and sent stores of provisions, clothing, tools, etc., to the 60,000 homeless, ruined, bereaved, and starving people of the San-Riku coast.

The wave was plainly felt two hours later on the shores of the island of Yesso, 200 miles north of the center of disturbance on the San-Riku coast, the water advancing 80 feet beyond high-tide mark on the beach at Hakodate. Eight hours later there was a great disturbance of the waters on the shores of the Bonin islands, more than 700 miles southward, the water rising three or four feet and retreating violently. Six hours later, on the shores of Kaui, the most northern of the Hawaiian islands, distant by 3,390 miles, the waters receded violently and washed on shore in a wave some inches above the normal height......

HERE IN MANCHURIA
February 1933

LILIAN GROSVENOR COVILLE (1907–85)

A RUSSIAN CITY ON CHINESE SOIL AND RULED BY THE JAPANESE ARMY,
Harbin was unique. Built in the 30 years since 1896, when the Tsar wrested
Manchuria—a region of forests, Siberian tigers, and bitterly cold winters—away
from a prostrate China, Harbin by 1932 was a thriving commercial and indus-
trial center with enough onion-domed roofs that it was called the "oriental St.
Petersburg." It clanged with the energy of a railroad town, for the trans-Siberian
railroad was the reason the Tsar had picked this former fishing village as the
center of his Manchurian concession. Yet the Russians were now eclipsed by the
Japanese, who had just invaded Manchuria and annexed it as Manchukuo, a
new province in their expanding empire. With its mixture of Russian émigrés,
Japanese soldiers and officials, Chinese soldiers and merchants, a large and var-
iegated foreign colony, beggars who may once have been generals—and facing the
threats of civil war in China and a devastating flood—Harbin was a place where
several historical fault lines were converging.

That's when Lilian Grosvenor Coville, 25, arrived with her husband, who
had just been transferred to Harbin from a diplomatic post in Tokyo. Lilian grew
up in the shadow of the National Geographic Society: Her father was Gilbert H.
Grosvenor, editor of the magazine, and her grandfather was Alexander Graham
Bell, second president of the Society. She possessed a sharp pen and eventually
contributed articles to The New Yorker *and* Foreign Service Journal *as well as*
NATIONAL GEOGRAPHIC. *Here she captures something of the never-failing*
interest that comes from living abroad in dangerous or exciting places, the sense
of being caught up in unfolding events yet insulated from their impact by the
transparent sheath of diplomatic immunity.

I LIVE IN HARBIN. WE HAVE RESIDED IN THE FAR EAST SEVERAL YEARS
now, and we moved to this North Manchurian city in May 1932.
Nowhere has the drama moved so swiftly as in the few months we have
been here. Each day's news is so unpredictable that surprises have almost
ceased to surprise.

These are the chief events of one twenty-four hours: Yesterday
bandits tried to kidnap two English friends of ours, the manager and

assistant manager of a British bank, while they were playing golf. Both were clubbed with their golf sticks and one was shot in the arm.

Earlier in the day the small daughter of a former representative of an American automobile manufacturer was kidnapped on the street a block from our house. She is now being held by bandits for a sum of money the family does not possess.

Late last night the main southbound and northbound passenger trains were wrecked by bandits a short distance from Harbin. Among the passengers was an American youth who had been a guest at our house the previous evening. He was robbed of everything but his life and a shirt.

Is it any wonder that we feel insecure, that we feel the chaos of China is closing in about us?...

Looking down Kitaiskaya, the main street of Harbin, from one of the many balconies of the "Moderne" Hotel, Harbin appears a rather shabby continental town. The buildings are strongly built of stone or concrete, with tall double windows and doors ready for the below-zero weather, when the ground is frozen solid four feet deep for months, and Siberian winds blow. The signs above the stores are in Russian and the letters look as if they were turned backward, until one has spent an evening learning the fairly simple Russian alphabet.

Dilapidated carriages are passing along the main street, and an occasional ricksha or rattly jitney loiters by, looking for fares....

A troop of soldiers comes swinging down the street, or an armored car makes its rounds. Occasionally there is a glimpse of the dainty kimono of a Japanese lady. Probably she has come to Harbin recently, for the Japanese population has nearly doubled the past year; and, like most other Japanese women, she undoubtedly loathes the place.

This street is most interesting in the evening, when all the beaux and belles of town are parading, some casting sidelong glances at each other and some walking arm and arm, their heads close together. There are, too, the beautiful Russian girls of Harbin, against whom wives are so repeatedly warned.

When we first came here someone told me that all the girls in Harbin can be divided into two classes—attractive ones, who are cabaret girls, and unattractive ones, who are dentists! There are many women dentists and uncountable numbers of girls who work in cabarets, either as hostesses or entertainers. Among them are excellent ballet dancers, many trained in Moscow and smuggled out of Russia to Harbin. Here they will give a delightful performance for a dollar or two in American money and provide their own costumes. Each one has her own exciting and pitiful tale.

There is another class of Russian girls, daughters of fine old families, well educated, speaking fluent English and French. All Russians are good conversationalists, amusing to talk with, and nearly all the girls are pretty. Many of this class marry foreign business men and live happily ever after.

What of the men that correspond to all these girls? I don't know—I have never been able to find out. I think that they are not a very provident lot. Anyway, there is not much for them to do in Harbin, now that the railway is open only to Soviets. Many enterprising ones drift away. Some stay and are supported by their dentist wives, or they just exist. It is amazing how they can exist and enjoy themselves on nothing at all....

It was a thrilling time last February when the Japanese soldiers marched in through New Town and the Chinese scuttled out. The occupation was orderly and well controlled, and the poor Russians who ran the jitneys and street cars were astonished when uniformed Japanese soldiers paid their fares like everyone else.

Despite their good conduct, however, the newcomers have much to overcome in the attitude of both Russians and Chinese. Instead of putting an immediate end to banditry, as they had hoped, the condition was only aggravated. The supplanting of the previous government has meant many soldiers thrown out of work, and in Manchuria, as in any other part of China, brigandage is the primary unemployment relief measure. We are repeatedly treated to the sound of firing across the river and the incessant buzzing of planes practicing overhead. At times they are on their way to bomb some unfortunate town that happens to be harboring brigands.

Consequently, life in Harbin is full of excitement and suspense. One always feels that something is going to happen, and it generally does. The miniature forts of sandbags—there is one on our street corner, left over from the February occupation by the Japanese, the ever-present soldiers, the camouflaged tank filled with Japanese soldiers, which makes its silent rounds at night, and the fact that our apartment house is protected by three private guards, on duty day and night, add to the interest of life.

The discussion of the latest bandit raid is a daily subject of conversation. When we picnic across the river a mile from Harbin, guns are always carried and stacked on nearby chairs, and two privately employed sentries stand watch....

My friends always write me, "Well, don't get killed in a war over there," or, "Don't get carried off by the bandits," but no one has ever thought to warn me, "Don't get drowned in a flood." I never thought much about a flood overtaking Harbin, primarily, I suppose, because Harbin has never had a serious inundation before, and because the Sungari has always seemed a small and placid river.

The spring had been unusually rainy and reports reached us of the rising of the river above Harbin. Soon we noticed it gradually coming higher on the banks, creeping up to the tiny houses of poor Russians and Chinese across the river. A wharf crowded with people gave way one Sunday and a number were drowned. The water covered the garden of the bungalow where we were going to picnic, with the guns and the guards. The chickens were drowned, but the ducks were happy. Islands began to disappear and other islands were formed where previously there was only land. People moved up to their roofs if they had no other place to go, and some started to take off their cows and pigs in old Chinese barges; but still the water came higher, and it was said there was a foot of water in Chinese town.

Conversation veered from bandits to the flood, and how much damage it had done. Soon it became apparent that the rains and floods had done more harm than all the military operations and banditry in Manchuria the past year. Half of all the crops of North Manchuria were destroyed.

On the morning of Sunday, August 7, we looked out of our dining room windows and saw two camps of Chinese huddled on the sidewalk. This was the first information we had that the wall protecting Chinese town, Fuchiatien, had broken and the water was pouring in.

New Town, where we live, has always seemed like any little European town, with its cobbled streets and rows of shade trees along the sidewalks, and its substantial foreign buildings. Even its population is white. Had we not been in a place where incredible things are always happening, I suppose we would have been as startled as any one in a similar town of Europe.

Before the day was out we were surrounded by thousands of homeless Chinese. They squatted in our streets with their few miserable bundles and their half-naked children; with their sick women and their old men and their pigs. They came up in hordes from the Chinese quarter.

Perched in the stern, dark-haired Lilian Coville ventures out onto the flooded streets of Harbin. In 1932 the Manchurian city was not only drowned by a rampaging river but also harried by bandits, overrun with refugees, and invaded by Japanese troops.

There was a continual stream of wagons, carriages, rickshas, street cars, and people toiling up hill. A usual carriage load drawn by one staggering horse consisted of all the clothes and bedding a family could pile into it, and on top the women, with their bound feet, the children, and a few men hanging to the steps. Overflowing street cars bearing the Chinese Red Cross emblem, the red swastika, ran back and forth, collecting no fares.

As the refugees arrived they were herded by the police to the bluff which stretches for several miles, overlooking Chinese town. And there they swarmed and watched the water rising about their homes 10, 15, and in some places 20 feet, until the river flowed in freely. What little they had was lost, and because of this the position of the foreigners was considered precarious. The private guard of our house was tripled and groups of soldiers were everywhere among the refugees.

That first night most of them had no covering at all, at best a few rags slung over a pole or an old straw mat against a garden fence; but many unfortunates lay exhausted by the side of the road, wherever they happened to fall. All night long, and for many nights to come, the donkeys brayed like foghorns, and when they stopped the roosters and geese took up the chorus.

The next day everyone was working to improvise better shelters. Old patched bean sacks, tattered quilts, and straw mats were utilized, and some of them had even found a few boards for flooring; but the hogs and sheep still wallowed in the mire close to the sick.

Several acres of high ground were devoted to giant, ever-growing piles of sacked beans which had been saved from the flooded city. They were guarded by Japanese and Chinese soldiers with ever-ready rifles, and the newest straw mats protected the beans from the elements. If I had any doubt that Manchuria produces six million tons of soy beans a year, it was removed by the exhibition.

Food stalls had been opened by enterprising young Chinese and the smell of garlic was strong in the air. Everything was out to dry between the intermittent thunder showers; slippers salvaged from a shoe store, hundreds of furs, grain, woolen material; there were even a few bedraggled birds from a pet store. Still the most cherished possession of each family was a sack of flour—a precaution against the famine sure to come. That flour represented blood money, for many of the destitute bought it with the two or three dollars gold they received when they sold their small daughters.

On this, the second day of the inundation, the Japanese military authorities took command of the situation, which was now serious, for the danger of a devastating cholera epidemic had been added to the other complications. The disease had gradually worked its way up to North Manchuria, and by the first of August a death or two had been reported in Harbin. Not by the Chinese authorities, however; for even when the death rate mounted from 25 to 50 daily, they maintained officially that there was not a single case of cholera in Harbin.

We went many times through the refugee camps those first days, before the stench became unendurable, and we saw no sign of disorder. They were for the most part quiet, and many of the women sat impassively smoking long pipes. But one day our chauffeur stopped the car and pointed out a head hanging on a tree. A group of Chinese was looking at it and then reading the sign, which said that the man had been a robber of refugees, and that he had been executed by order of the Chinese chief of police as a warning to all who would take advantage of the refugee encampment. It was an incongruous and ghastly sight, seeing the head, with its black hair, dangling from a limb of the tree, in full view of automobiles and street cars passing back and forth....

We ventured to Fuchiatien two days after the water came in. There was not a sign of the wall. First we went by ricksha. The coolies waded in water over their waists, and people grinned at us from windows. Then we bargained for a boat and were rowed for two hours through the deserted streets. An occasional dog or cat chased the vermin off a thatched roof and a stray family lived on a raft. Rounding a corner, we came upon a 300-ton barge loading from a third-floor window. A drowned city, and yet we carried a revolver for protection.

After Fuchiatien the poor-Russian settlement on the other side of Pristan succumbed, and the destitute Russians also fled, weeping and wailing, to our district. Volunteers were called and all the young men were eager to help stem the tide. We saw them feverishly tossing sandbags into the water in an attempt to defend the railroad, but no one had sat down with a map to find the strategic points, and their efforts were futile.

Then Pristan itself was threatened. Everyone talked at once and no one knew exactly what to do about it. The shop-keepers rushed to barricade their doors with sandbags and hastily made masonry work. The sewers burst with the pressure of water backed up from the river. Sewage was thrown into the streets....

Hundreds of boats appeared from nowhere and the destitute Russians and Chinese who were living on their roofs across the river rowed over every morning and made a nice little bit of pocket money before evening ferrying people around town.

There were the oddest boats on our river. Anything, as long as it would float, would do. Two old doors nailed together and a couple of poles, or a few boards slung together with empty Standard Oil tins tied underneath, were equal to almost any emergency. Children were in seventh heaven, bobbing about in the family washtub. One man had equipped his raft with a stool about ten inches high and was paddling along quite comfortably. New, unpainted rowboats appeared every day, their cracks stopped with lead. One foreigner had his two private rowboats tethered to his front door, and they floated over the heads of the drowned asters and zinnias.

There were established boat landings, where the shouts of competing boatmen resembled the cries of the gondoliers on the Grand Canal. Every boatman called "*Lodka! Lodka!*" every three seconds, and I think I shall never be able to forget that *lodka* is the Russian word for boat.

Still there was a serious aspect. Everyone knew that cholera spreads chiefly because of impure water, and those who live in Pristan rely for water on their individual wells, which of course were flooded. Chinese drinking-water vendors waded through the streets with two overflowing buckets of water slung from a pole across their shoulders, the lower half of the pails swinging in the muddy water....

The power house was inundated and for two nights the whole of Pristan was plunged into complete darkness. That was the most nerve-racking time of all, for who could tell what 150,000 homeless, wretched people would do under cover of darkness? Then, too, we learned that an important bandit stronghold upriver had been flooded and that thousands of lawless men were congregating outside of Harbin. Japanese soldiers were everywhere helping the Chinese soldier guard.

For several nights there was street shooting a few doors from our house. The first two times I naively thought it was a series of punctures, but I can tell the difference now....

Harbin was cut off from the rest of the world by rail. It was all in vain to be a great railway junction and the metropolis of North Manchuria. The eastern line to Vladivostok had been closed for months because of truculent bandits; the flood paralyzed the southern and western lines.

After two weeks travelers began to struggle in over the southern route, bringing tales of walking across tottering bridges in the dead of night. Then a train got off for Siberia and Europe, and we all sent letters by the Senator's son, who had been cooling his heels in Harbin for half a month....

What will happen this winter no one can tell. Water has been pumped out of Pristan and the streets are white with the disinfectant the Japanese have spread to forestall a typhus epidemic; but the Chinese town is still uninhabitable. The river freezes at the end of October.

The Japanese and the Chinese Eastern Railway have built barracks for forty thousand, but there are tens of thousands more who will have nothing but a few rags to shield them from the 40-below-zero weather. They may become bandits. Already it is not safe to be on the streets, for bandits consider even the most wretched white worth at least one hundred dollars in potential ransom money.

Nearly every man carries a gun these days—and a permit to use it.

AMONG THE BIG KNOT LOIS OF HAINAN
September 1938

LEONARD CLARK (1907–57)

OF THE COUNTLESS EXPLORERS WHOSE GRAVES LIE THOUSANDS *of miles from their homes, some were victims of murder, accident, wild beasts, starvation, or drowning, but most fell to disease. Exploration of the tropics in particular was hampered not merely by distance or inaccessibility, crocodiles or poisoned arrows, but by invisible curtains of deadly microbes and clouds of malaria-bearing mosquitoes. Malaria, according to some experts, has killed perhaps half the people who have ever lived.*

By the early 20th century even solitary explorers did not venture into the tropics without a medicine chest, containing bandages, antiseptics, instruments, and purgatives; vials, perhaps, of cocaine (a local anesthetic) or laudanum (tincture of opium for pain relief); that all-purpose remedy, brandy; and plentiful quinine, either in solution or tablet form. At the time, quinine, quaffed regularly as a prophylactic, and the mosquito net were the only practical defenses against malaria.

Leonard Clark carried a chest like this when in 1937 he arrived on Hainan, the large island in the South China Sea overlooking the route from Hong Kong to Hanoi. Once described as "not one of those pith-helmeted Park Avenue explorers," Clark was a soldier of fortune—and a bit of a rogue. As Colonel Clark, he apparently spent World War II behind Japanese lines in China, directing an O.S.S. intelligence network. In the Peruvian Amazon, he claimed to have found five of the fabled Seven Cities of Cibola, and his subsequent book was jammed with tales of slave traders, cannibals, anacondas, jaguars, and those poisoned arrows. He served Chinese warlords, led an expedition to the Tibetan source of the Yellow River, killed two Europeans in a drunken brawl in Canton, and finally died at age 49 while on a diamond mining expedition in Venezuela.

When he arrived in Hainan, he was 30 years old. The island had hardly been explored. Tribes in the remote mountains had a reputation for ferocity and headhunting, but in the summer of 1937, with war clouds looming, Clark discovered that the tribesmen were not the danger: Disease was. One might cock a skeptical eyebrow at some of Clark's subsequent adventures, but this one reflects an experience shared by many explorers who, deep in the field, had also played doctor and apothecary, diagnosing symptoms, dispensing medicines, and dodging disease themselves.

ON JUNE 26, 1937, AT BLAZING NOON IN THE CHINA SEA, Nicol Smith and I first sighted the cloud-mottled sandbars of Hainan. I did not realize that nearly two months were to pass before our expedition—or rather its remnants—were to emerge from the interior of Hainan, and I was to see again that lonely but bewitching shore of ivory, jade, and moving brown sails.

Because of shallow water the steamer dropped anchor about two miles off the flat north coast and opposite the port of Hoihow. Our boxes and bags were quickly passed by Chinese Customs officers and placed aboard a junk, one of a fleet that had come out to take off several hundred Cantonese troops.

Hot winds from the unseen and mysterious mountains far over the rolling plains to the south filled the creaking brown mat sails overhead. In an hour, with flying salt-spray in our faces, we approached long sandspits. Junks sailed all around us and gave the impression that they were scudding over dry land! Long lines of fishermen, carrying nets on bamboo poles, were wading far from shore, and looked like grotesque sea monsters as the late sun cast giant shadows beyond them.

At Hoihow, a compact Chinese town of several thousand inhabitants, we were met by the Reverend John F. Steiner, American Presbyterian missionary, and taken in rickshas through teeming streets. Many rickshas were needed for all our equipment and supplies, which totaled over a ton.

Hoihow, we found, was desperately fighting a cholera epidemic. We were told that over a hundred patients a day were dying. In many parts of the city could be seen flying the jagged black-and-white cholera "dragon-flags," swaying symbolically from bamboo poles.

That night an officer of the Governor notified us that our expedition could not immediately advance into the interior. The cholera dead were so numerous that the Government had established martial law. This measure prevented the people from fleeing en masse into the surrounding countryside and so spreading the epidemic.

All bodies were buried at night. Above the street hung huge banners with painted pictures instructing the people how to avoid getting cholera—by not buying cut fruit and by killing flies. At night for weeks we slept but slightly, for the hammering with wooden mallets in the coffin shops thumped like a monstrous and diseased heart.

At last, one night at dinner, Mr. Steiner bent forward, listening.

"There is no more wood left to build coffins," he said quietly.

That night, for the first time, we slept soundly.

But in the meantime obstacles other than cholera arose to guard Hainan's secrets from us. Because of the war on the mainland at Shanghai and elsewhere, special passports were required, and more than three weeks—sweltering weeks—crept by before we were finally able to start.

Hurriedly we gathered our supplies, equipment, and the personnel we had recruited among the north Hainanese, and at 6 o'clock one morning, heralded by the daily lightning bursts across the plains of the southern horizon, we took two automobiles to the Chinese city of Nodoa, some sixty miles to the southwest. It lay very close to our destination—the looming mountains of the wild Loi country.

In Nodoa, the Reverend P. C. Melrose, one of the few white men who have been into the interior, warned us against malignant malaria. No white person living on Hainan, he said, escaped it, but since the bubonic plague was rampant in Nodoa, and since Governmental problems on the mainland might cause our long-awaited passports to be revoked any moment, we felt we could delay no longer for the height of the malarial season to pass.

Early in the morning of July 20, 1937, our boxes and bags were loaded into a Ford which we were told had once belonged to Wallace Beery, the actor, and we took the narrow military road through paddy fields and jungle to Nam Fong, a Chinese-Loi market town a few miles beyond. There we camped in the school compound and Chiah Jee Hong, our tall and genial cook, prepared a simple meal over a charcoal stove; he hardly realized as he did so that misfortune had already singled him out as a victim.

That afternoon the schoolhouse bustled with last-minute preparations for the march on the morrow, as the restless carriers arranged their loads laughingly, and the entire trading village of 160 families surrounded our portable phonograph. The records that delighted them most were those of Lawrence Tibbett [a popular opera singer]! All this gayety stood out in sharp contrast to the silence and slavish work to follow in the weeks ahead.

At 5:30 the next morning we started on our eventful trek deep into the interior of Hainan and out to Kachek near the east coast. Extra pairs of new rope-sandals hung from the packs; apparently the carriers expected rough going.

Occasionally we passed groups of six to fifteen Loi men on their way to Nam Fong's market. Tall, lean, and bronzed, they were dressed in short aprons, fore and aft, and carried at their backs big knives in "Loi baskets." There also contained water pipes, bows and arrows, and food.

Although strategically located between China's port cities and Indochina (today's Vietnam), Hainan, an island about the same size as Taiwan, was virtually unknown in the 1930s. The dotted line traces Leonard Clark's passage across its wild, mountainous interior.

Their long black or brown hair had been combed forward and knotted over the forehead, standing about four inches straight out. This characteristic "Big Knot," from which the Hainan aborigines take their name, has now lost its significance. Various tribes, as I later learned, do up this peculiar knot in various positions on the head. The Ba-Sa-Dung, for instance—whose territory we were traversing—do up the knot on the back of the head. The ones we passed in the trail, with the big knot over the forehead, were Ha tribesmen from the far south. They were carrying herbs, dried monkeys on bamboo frames, snake skins, and antlers, all of which are used in making Chinese medicines.

Distant mountains—half clothed in lianabound jungle—rose in the south. And from them came a high, hot wind that bent down the tall *lalang*, or coarse grass, around us, roaring through it with a mournful sound like waves on a distant cliff-coast. Occasionally flocks of green parrots were flushed, turning and screeching in protest overhead, and the chattering of busy monkeys came down to us from the trees.

We camped that night on a jungle ridge about twenty miles due west of Hung Mo, "The Mountains of the Red Mist." Often we had discussed this fascinating name, and its possible origin, with foreigners and Chinese on the coast. But no one had seemed able to shed light on the matter.

White bursts of lightning now flashed around the ridge; the daily shower had arrived. The rain drove hard against the taut and swaying tarpaulins overhead, giving the impression that some unseen hand was tearing cloth in little jerks.

Nicol was reclining on his army cot beneath a mosquito net, thankfully bathing his swollen feet by extending them into the stream of water that drained steadily off the canvas.

Presently the rain and lightning seemed to be subsiding. It was nearly sunset. Tree cicadas overhead—sounding like piercing automobile horns—had already started their evening jungle symphony, which was almost deafening. I was resting on my cot, eyes closed, but not yet asleep.

Then, suddenly, "Look, Leonard!" Nicol exclaimed.

Wondering if one of the restless water buffalo nearby had invaded camp, I rolled over quickly and opened my eyes. Nicol had raised his mosquito net and was standing beyond the tarpaulins in the rain—now reduced to a drizzle—apparently regardless of the buzzing mosquitoes out for their night of feasting.

I saw almost immediately that the entire sky over the ridge had magically become an intense ox-blood red. The shiny translucent jungle surrounding camp reflected this red mist, so that it seemed that the very air I breathed was something tangible, tinted red! On all sides—toward the unseen setting sun westward, toward the north, the south, and the east—the sky's original clouded marble gray had become uniformly, intensely, red.

The whole effect was uncanny, and at the time it seemed almost supernatural. With loud exclamations the coolies appeared from under the tarpaulin. They were afraid.

Wong, the interpreter, who had once been an estate manager in Malaya, approached and, bowing, said apologetically, "Sir." He hesitated. "Sir, this is a warning from the Loi devils who are watching us from the tops of Hung Mo..."

"That is superstition," I said, "and superstition is not believed in by educated men like yourself."

"We Chinese know that these Loi devils are very powerful," he answered gravely. "When a Loi curses a Chinese, that man dies!"

In about twenty minutes darkness overtook the strange, prodigious red mist. Nicol and I talked late that night, speculating on the unknown country before us. But the men were very quiet, content to squat under their tarpaulin and smoke on thick green bamboo water pipes cut from a nearby thicket. Their premonition of trouble was soon to prove only too well founded.

I wakened at dawn to find the coolies moving about in the dark, breaking camp. Nicol and I had scarcely dressed when Wong brought two of them up to me, saying, "These coolies are sick with malaria, Master." Both men complained of having chills and fever during the night. Lightening their loads by distributing them among the other porters, we started again, following the ever-dwindling trail into Pak-Sa (sometimes called Bek-Twa, or Nga-Sa).

By late afternoon, two miles from Pak-Sa, we were overtaken by a lightly laden, fast-moving caravan. It belonged to the Chinese Magistrate who represented the Government in its dealings with the Lois. Seeing that Nicol and I were weary, he and his companion, who had attended school in America, dismounted from their tiny Hainanese ponies, and graciously insisted that we ride. Their armed escort helped our lagging porters into Pak-Sa.

Before retiring to my mosquito-netting-enclosed cot I gave each of our men ten grains of quinine in the hope of preventing a further outbreak of malaria.

Next morning, as the sun began to light the village, the entire population woke to be on hand to give us further advice concerning the major intricacies of shaving with a cup of cold water.

The two sick coolies could not continue farther and it was arranged that two Lois take their places.

As we started on, through jungle and tall grass, one of the carriers nearly stepped on a bamboo snake, which is a beautiful green and gold but feared as much by Hainan natives as the deadly king cobra. The coolies' snake-consciousness increased, as sandals are little protection.

There were many rivers to cross that day. The trail led us through several rather large villages of twenty to forty huts, the women of which were tattooed in strange block-like designs on face, hands, arms, and

The Big Knot Lois were named for the lock of hair draped over men's foreheads.
Not to be outdone, the women wore enormous brass earrings that often weighed five pounds,
so they were usually looped up and worn like a hat.

legs; the men were adorned with big knots on the back of the head, wore G-strings—brief breechclouts—and sported baskets with weapons....

Next day Chiah Jee Hong, the cook—no longer happy—came to me and said in pidgin English that he was very sick and must return to Pak-Sa. I sent him back in care of two Lois, for he could barely walk.

We stayed here three days, bartering and making motion-pictures of the Lois. By the third night, six men were down with malaria, one with an abscessed ear, and another with a badly infected shoulder where his pole had rubbed off the skin. These men would have to return, immediately!

Only five healthy coolies now remained, and Wong. We began to realize why Hainan had not been thoroughly explored.

Next morning, July 26, Nicol could not rise from his cot. Though he had taken only boiled water and had eaten only from our canned supplies, he began vomiting; his nausea continued all day. That night I sent a Loi runner back to Pak-Sa for the Magistrate's pony. When a soldier arrived next morning with it, I put Nicol aboard and sent him, with all the weak and sick coolies, back to Pak-Sa.

Nicol and I decided that I should take the five remaining coolies, and Wong, and go on alone in an attempt to make the penetration of central Hainan. I selected only absolutely essential articles: food, medicines (40 pounds), instruments such as cameras, films, aneroid barometers, thermometers, trade articles, and the like. I myself had suffered an aching back which was a symptom of malignant malaria; I took twenty grains of quinine that afternoon.

On July 27, 1937, at dusky dawn, my tiny expedition continued on its course.

At a large village built on tall poles in a valley, I stayed two days getting motion pictures and other photographs. On the afternoon of the second day, Wong was told by Foo Kwi Heick, who said he was headman of 76 villages, that I could not take more pictures. The people were angry, he said, and believed that they would die if anything happened to our likeness. I had been unwise in showing them finished photographs.

Wong, who once in his versatile life had been employed as a chemist in a British Malay hospital, handed out medicines to the needy people, and endeavored to cure Chief Foo Kwi Heick's persistent ringworm. In some villages we had to show the people that the medicine would not harm them by swallowing some of it ourselves!...

I gave away 5,000 quinine pills (20,000 grains) and was gratified to see many a fever broken up. Our forty pounds of medicine, which Wong gave out, helped various other ailments.

Lois are apt in the use of herbs, but even herbs have their limitations. Wong told me that during our trek we saved probably seven or eight lives, merely through having medicines.

One child's arm had practically rotted away from an infection. How this child lived—hardly more than a skeleton—I will never know. Without instruments, except a carving knife sharpened on a piece of leather, the deft Wong put his ex-hospital knowledge into practice and cut away a great deal of flesh from the arm—with nothing of any kind to ease the pain of the silent child. Then he applied some of his Chinese medicine and a bandage. He said the child had a chance to live, but I doubt it....

Five weeks after he began, having visited numerous villages, Clark emerged at Kachek on the east coast of Hainan. Only one of the original carriers remained with him.

PART SEVEN

The Malay Archipelago

BY MOTOR THROUGH SUMATRA

January 1920

MELVIN A. HALL (1890–1962)

"I AM A PART OF ALL THAT I HAVE MET," SANG TENNYSON'S ULYSSES, that world-wanderer, in a poem that ranked among Melvin Hall's favorites. Soldier, aviator, sometime spy, occasional diplomat, and friend of kings and presidents, Colonel Hall had met with much in the course of a most picturesque life. Detached, wry, and amusing, he was of that dauntless breed who never settled long in one place, instead hitching his wagon, as he put it, "to a restless star."

Melvin Hall was born in Vermont (Rudyard Kipling was the next-door neighbor), the only child of parents as merry as they were rich. His father had purchased one of the first automobiles ever sold in the United States, and as early as 1902 the trio was careening down roads all over Europe, leaving terrified horses and overturned hay wagons in their wake. This series of madcap adventures culminated a few years later when Melvin's father motored through Poland, using vodka for fuel and relaxing by drawing an occasional drink from the carburetor.

In 1911, after graduating from Princeton, young Hall became one of the first people ever to take an automobile around the world for pleasure. With his parents along, he began the trip by driving a Packard touring car through Europe and the Balkans before arriving in India for the splendid Coronation Durbar of King George V. His father departed to attend to business, but Melvin and his mother motored on, through Ceylon, the rubber plantations of Malaya, and across the rice paddies of Java before making a "side trip" to Sumatra.

Sumatra, larger than California, had seen a handful of cars in its lowland tobacco plantations, but no automobile had penetrated its rolling, jungle-clad interior, where tigers and orangutans might still be found. Accompanied by a Malay-speaking interpreter named Joseph, the Halls made their way inland and headed for the volcano-girt highlands, home to the Bataks, once known for ritual cannibalism. Since the lonely wagon roads they followed had been soaked by 17 days of rain, the stage was set for another automotive misadventure.

EARLY THE NEXT MORNING WE CONTINUED OUR CLIMB OVER THE PASS. The semi-tropical vegetation which had succeeded the coarse grass of the denuded plains gave way in turn to magnificent virgin forests, unbroken except for the narrow, winding path of the road.

The enormous straight-trunked trees, ensnared by giant creepers, vines, and huge air plants, made so thick a canopy overhead that only a dim twilight filtered in, and that failed to reach the ground through the dense, impenetrable tangle of vegetation.

Little brooks of clear water rushed steeply down the mountainside, hurrying along to the sluggish yellow rivers of the plains their tiny contributions for the extension of Sumatra's coast. Butterflies flitted in the blue-black shadows; jungle fowl, their brilliance all subdued in the obscure half light, vanished silently from the edges of the road as we approached, and other little creeping and fugitive things sought the security of the unbetraying jungle.

Insects with voices out of all proportion to their probable size screamed shrilly from the branches, and the occasional whistle of a bird or the dull boom of a falling tree echoed through the silent, dark recesses of the wood....

The swaying of branches overhead as we zigzagged up the pass did not mean wind in the quiet forest; it meant monkeys, and their antics were an unfailing amusement, whether we kept on or stopped to watch them. Some waited in silence until we drew near, then plunged back into the forest with a crash of branches which inevitably produced on us the shock they seemed to have designed. Some tore furiously along beside us through the trees in a desperate attempt to cross in front of the car before we could catch up to them.

When they did cross, far overhead, in a stream of small gray bodies flying through the air between the treetops, they as furiously raced along on the other side and crossed back again. Others clung to swaying branches and bounded up and down in a frenzy of excitement, shrieking gibes in sharp crescendo as we passed.

Often in the midst of their agitation they suddenly lost all interest and forthwith paid no more attention to us; or sat in silence with wizened, whiskered faces peering solemnly down from the trees. As in Ceylon, it would have been disastrous to leave the motor unguarded anywhere in a Sumatra forest, for everything that prying fingers could unscrew or remove would soon be reposing merrily in the treetops....

As we neared the summit of the pass, a narrow break in the forest revealed a superb view through the trees, over the blue ravine and densely timbered mountainside, to the wide coastal plain shimmering

Kebon Djahe, a Batak kampong, or village, in Sumatra where thatched gables and cupolas are crowned by carved wooden buffalos and mounted horsemen. From a courtyard tomb, the upright body of the last chief gazed out upon his former village.

in the heat-haze below; then the foliage again closed in until we reached the height-of-land and looked out on the other side.

A dull, treeless expanse, scarcely lower than the top of the pass, stretched out before us in limitless brown waves, a desolate tangle of grass broken only by detached volcanic heights. Two active volcanoes, the northernmost of the range, towered threateningly above the others—Sibajak guarding the entrance through which crept the highland road; Sinaboeng rising from the plateau in majestic isolation, its smoke-crowned peak and deep purple sides outlined against the heavy white clouds that hung behind it.

The first strong impression of loneliness and monotonous solitude that the highlands gave was little changed by the few scattered compounds and occasional patches of cultivation later revealed as we progressed....

The sun had gone down unobserved in the clouds and the early twilight had fallen before we left Kebon Djahe [a native *kampong*, or village, in the highlands that Hall and his mother were visiting]. Vague misgivings of the road from there to Sariboe Dolok in the dark had begun to assail my mind, when the car, which had been rocking and skidding over the rain-soaked trail, suddenly plunged deeper into the mud, stopped short, and began to sink.

There was a little hole in the center of the track, no bigger than a man's hand, which on the way up had scarcely been noticeable, but in passing over it in returning, the whole road seemed to open up and engulf us. A furious effort to clear the chasm, whatever it might be, only succeeded in hastening our doom. When we stopped settling the car was so deep that a list to the right brought the top, which was up, to the level of the road surface, while between the top and the ground on the other side there was barely enough space left to crawl through.

Any further sinking of the car might have permanently imprisoned us, so we hastily crept out on our stomachs through the sticky clay-mud and viewed the catastrophe. It was not encouraging. A careful survey of the car showed it to be hopelessly buried, beyond any possibility of my disinterring it unaided.

The chainfalls, in the equipment box on the rear, were completely out of sight some four feet underground; but even had I dug them out there was nothing to which to attach them, and in any case the car was too thoroughly in the grip of the mud to have yielded to single-handed efforts.

With difficulty I discovered the cause of the accident. A bamboo culvert far under the road, which had rotted peacefully and undisturbed since it had been laid, had finally collapsed from our weight, after being weakened by our first passage over it.

To extricate the car was a task for a first-class train-wrecking crew, and I felt little confidence of being able to raise half a dozen helpers in that country, especially as I had left Joseph in Sariboe Dolok and would be unable to explain our predicament to any natives I might meet

Kebon Djahe seemed the one light on the situation; but night was falling rapidly, and as my speedometer cable had broken in the morning and there were no noticeable landmarks, I had only a dim idea how far away the compound might be.

For my mother to be left alone at night in the wilds of a country until recently addicted to cannibalism, while I set out on an indeterminate search for help, was an unpleasant prospect; but as Kebon Djahe might have been eight or ten miles away—a nasty walk in the mud and the dark—that seemed the only solution.

For over an hour I walked, or rather waded, down the road in the utter stillness of the desolate highlands. Then a few barely audible shouts drifted up from across the plain, and I struggled through the grass in their direction to a tiny paddy field on the top of a low hill.

Through the dusk I could see a little bamboo lookout, such as is erected in every grain field, and, squatting on its platform, two blue-clad figures, who stopped their shouting as I approached. But to my weak efforts in Malay they merely stared in silence and continued to jerk on the strings which, tied with fluttering bits of cloth, intersected the field to frighten away feathered marauders.

From the hill, however, I discovered in the twilight two solitary little white houses about a mile away and struck off to investigate. Soon a tiny light sprang out of the darkness, and when I arrived in its cheery glow I found the Dutch Controleur just returning from inspecting a jail which was in course of construction, and I accosted him with my tale of disaster and appeal for help.

"Certainly," he promptly said, as if foreign motorists mired in the interior of Sumatra came to him every day with requests to be dug out. "I will lend you my prisoners."

Although his jail was not yet built, he had a fine collection—thirty-eight Bataks and Achinese in whom respect for Dutch control had not been sufficiently evident. This was my wrecking crew, and joined by a Dutch planter, who was recuperating in the higher altitude of the Batak lands from an assault made on him by two coolies, we marched as if on a night attack back to the buried motor, with two armed native soldiers as a guard.

I had been absent several hours before the lanterns picked out ahead of us the dark outline of the sunken car blocking the road. As we approached I saw the figure of my mother apparently seated in the clay mire of the roadside, with a dozen motionless forms standing in a shadowy row on the bank behind her. She struggled stiffly to her feet, revealing one of the mud-soaked seat cushions that she had succeeded in dragging from the car, and the silent row melted back into the darkness.

"Who are your friends?" I asked, after ascertaining that she had suffered nothing more than an unpleasant wait.

"I don't know," she replied, "but I'm very glad to have you back. I've felt rather 'shivery'; first watching them appear out of the dark, one or two at a time; then hearing them talk in low voices. I didn't know whether they were planning to eat me or simply discussing why I chose this particular place to sit in. But for the last half hour they haven't made a sound, and that was the worst of all!"

"These are not bad people around here," said Mr. von der Weide, the Dutch planter, "but they are not always to be trusted. I do not think it well to be alone in the highlands at night."

Armed with native spades, shaped somewhat like a wide-bladed adze, and a small forest of strong cut poles which we had fortunately discovered piled by the roadside, the crew attacked the motor.

The prisoners were strong and willing; my training in the recovery of automobiles from strange places had been varied and thorough, and, aided by the untiring efforts of Mr. von der Weide, we soon had a wide excavation made around the car, supporting it meanwhile with shores to prevent further sinking.

Then with the poles as huge levers we pried up each end of the machine a little at a time, filling the chasm underneath with a cob-house of other poles cut into various lengths, until the car, resting on a wooden pier, rose to the road level and was dragged to comparatively firm ground. I scraped off the worst of the clinging mud from those parts that were completely choked with it, and coaxed the motor into starting.

There seemed to be no damage except for twisted mudguards, and we ran back to Kebon Djahe accompanied by Mr. von der Weide, who insisted on our spending the night there—we did not require much urging—while our army was marched ceremoniously back to jail....

[On another occasion] dark, ominous clouds bore down upon us as we splashed over the soft level stretches, skidded down short, slippery descents, and labored on the upgrades among the holes and crevasses of deep washouts.

In one place the road was evidently being lowered, and for several hundred yards more than half of it had been cut away, leaving a shelf on one side too narrow to drive on, and on the other a six-foot trench which was simply a morass of mud and water. As the shelf was quite impossible, I chose the trench, started up it with a rush, and promptly stuck fast.

No efforts could move the car in either direction. The sticky clay formed solid disks about the flying wheels, completely hiding tire-chains and rope under its smooth yellow coating.

After an hour of unavailing labor, Joseph and I abandoned the effort to extricate the machine, and as darkness was rapidly falling we held a hurried consultation to determine what should be done. It was finally decided to desert the car and attempt to flounder through the mud to the nearest native village. It was a desperate decision, but the only alternative was a night in the car.

Detaching one of the side lamps, whose rays would enable us to avoid the deepest pools of water, the three of us began the sliding, splashing tramp.

About a mile beyond where the car was entombed we came to a cut, and at its edge the dull rays of another lantern showed half a dozen natives putting away some tools in a little shed. Joseph and I immediately scrambled over to question them. Only one spoke Malay; the others were part of his gang of road laborers—an evil-looking lot.

I was surprised at finding human beings there, and, feeling consequent misgivings over the security of our abandoned car and luggage, I asked the man in charge if he or one of his men would, for a suitable consideration, spend the night in an automobile about a mile down the road, to guard it from being molested during my absence. To my astonishment he promptly refused, and, asking the question in turn of his men, met with immediate negatives.

I could not account for their unwillingness. The cushions of the tonneau would surely afford as comfortable quarters as any they were accustomed to; it could not be the storm of which men of the highlands were afraid; and the reward I had offered, though small enough, was probably equivalent to about a week's income.

Then it occurred to me that they were afraid of the automobile itself, and I hastened to assure them that it was not only dry and comfortable, but quite safe; that I had locked it up, and that it could not move until I myself released it.

"Oh, it is not that," said the spokesman, with an air of having slept in automobiles most of his life.

"Well, what is it then?" I was both curious and a trifle annoyed.

"Tigers."

"Tigers?"

"Yes, indeed," said Joseph nervously, translating. "He say plenty of tigers here come down sure and eat him up!"

"But not in the automobile," I objected.

"Oh, no; tiger first take him out."

I readily persuaded the men to help carry our luggage to the village, five miles as he estimated it, but nothing would induce any of those natives to spend the night within reach of the great prowling beasts....

Hall, of course, eventually freed his automobile. He and his mother continued their "quaint and original motoring" through Singapore, Hong Kong, the Philippines, Japan, and across the United States, where they found the worst roads of all.

THE ISLAND Of NIAS,
AT THE EDGE Of THE WORLD
August 1931

MABEL COOK COLE

KNOWN CENTURIES AGO TO ARAB SAILORS AS THE "ISLAND OF GOLD," Nias was like no place else in the Malay Archipelago, those thousands of islands comprising today's Indonesia, Malaysia, and the Philippines. Lying off the west coast of Sumatra, Nias developed its own unique civilization. Even the Dutch, long established elsewhere in the neighborhood, did not probe its forbidding coast until the mid-19th century, and then were washed back off for a time, not only by native resistance but also because their initial settlements were destroyed by one of the offshore earthquakes and resulting tsunamis that periodically ravage the island.

Eventually the Dutch returned to stay, and by about 1910 they were gradually halting such age-old Niasan customs as headhunting and human sacrifice. Shortly thereafter, in the 1920s, a topee-clad American couple and their interpreter arrived. Dr. Fay-Cooper Cole was an anthropologist with Chicago's Field Museum and a leading authority on the ethnography of the various Malay peoples. Mabel Cook Cole was his wife and assistant.

The Coles, who had traveled extensively throughout the Malay Archipelago, were among the first anthropologists to set foot on Nias. Their visit began unpromisingly enough, in the island's hot, malarial lowlands. Then it suddenly became a journey into enchantment as one by one, marvelous miniature cities opened glimpses onto this singular culture—"another world," as Mrs. Cole described it, still lingering into the 20th century.

ON A MAP OF THE WORLD, THE ISLAND OF NIAS IS A MERE DOT OFF the west coast of Sumatra. On a chart of the Dutch East Indies, it is nearly an inch long. In reality it is about 80 miles in length—miles which seemed to stretch out longer and longer as we made our way up hills and down valleys from one end of the island to the other.

This bit of land is quite apart from the rest of the world. Neither wireless nor cable connects it with civilization, and only when the occasional boat calls does it have brief contact with other lands. Yet here flourished an ancient civilization, reports of which lured us 15,000 miles across the seas....

We left Padang, Sumatra, on a supply steamer which stops at the north end of Nias on its monthly trip to Achin and at the south end on its return. After two nights and a day, we landed at Goenoeng Sitoli, a pretty little village with a palm-fringed beach, and as we stood watching our vessel steam away, we realized that our last connection with the outside world was broken.

The Dutch Resident was away, investigating the case of a man who had lost his head a few days before, but the other official, the Controleur, was most friendly and anxious to do all in his power to assist us. His face fell, however, when we told him that we wanted to go to the other end of the island. "It is quite impossible," he said, "especially for a lady." And he eyed me with pity for having such an idea.

"How about the motor boat?" hopefully questioned my husband, for we had been assured by officials in Sumatra that we could make the trip in it.

"I believe there was a boat here at one time," replied the Controleur, "but there has been none in the ten months since I came."

"Could we get a native craft to take us down?"

"That is impossible. The natives are no seamen, and in places the coast is very dangerous. There is no way," he continued, "except on horseback, and that is a five-day trip and most difficult."

Feeling the barometer of our spirits rise with this possibility, my husband hastened to say, "We will go by horseback, then." He asked for carriers and for four horses, as we had with us two native boys, one acting as interpreter.

The officer looked dubious. He never had come into such close contact with the undaunted strenuousness of America, but he arose to the occasion and promised to do his best.

"The natives are very poor," he warned us, "and there are only a few horses on the island."

Three days later three horses were ready for us—all that could be obtained from near and far.

The trail led gradually up to a hogback. We rode above little valleys covered by a wild growth of underbrush, which was dotted here and there with mighty monarchs of the forest, relics of the virgin timber, their straight trunks shooting up as if they would raise their great heads for a breath and a glimpse of the sea....

Finally we came to villages with great stone seats in front of the houses, resting places for the spirits of the ancestors, for the ancestral cult is very strong; and we passed through the deserted villages where

Ringed with cliffs and difficult of access, the island of Nias, off the west coast of Sumatra, developed its own peculiar civilization. It is frequently shaken by earthquakes and pounded by tsunamis.

the stones still stood before houses that were in ruins. The inhabitants, turned Christian, had left these evidences of heathen worship and built new towns at some distance.

Lolowua, which we reached the second evening, seemed to have so much of interest that we decided to stay over for a few days. The chief was an old man, but a lively one. He came to us wearing a wonderful upstanding mustache of gold, a high headdress with golden ornaments, and an enormous earring.

When he danced with the other men, leaping high in the air and performing strange antics with the greatest agility, we could well believe the reports that he had had his fun at taking heads. In fact, when we went to his house to return his visit, we saw a small boy slip out secretly, conveying something which looked very much like a human skull, and we suspected that the old man did not care to take us into all his confidences. He fondly stroked a worn and weathered old wooden figure which stood in front of his house and told us that it was his grandfather.

When we returned the visits of our neighbors, we found in each house small carved wooden figures, and leading from these, through the windows to the stone seats outside, were long chains of bamboo. These, they told us, were "ladders" on which the spirits could, from time to time, ascend from the stones to the images and become a part of the family life....

On our way once more we rode over a sun-baked trail, so hard and smooth that our horses slipped and slid. Long stretches we walked, up steep, stony grades and down to bridgeless rivers, where we dragged our tired feet through the water only to find that it, too, was warm. The air was hot and humid. We have ridden on horseback many miles in the Tropics, but never under a sun so hot as that which shone on Nias....

In the afternoon of the second day from Lolowua, we came to a very long, rickety old bridge, quite impassable for horses. As crocodiles infested the river, fording was out of the question, and we had to send our horses back. Then, aware of our fate should the supports give way, we gingerly crossed the swaying bridge and continued on foot. Within an hour we entered a different world, the land of our dreams.

Ascending a long flight of broad stone steps, past stone crocodiles guarding the entrance, we entered a wonderful city, whose straight, broad street was paved with flat stones. This was once a city of 2,000 inhabitants, whose houses, erected in two long rows, faced this paved court.

In front of the houses were stone slabs, polished like glass and wonderfully carved, beneath which the people had placed the skulls of their ancestors. Tall pillars of stone form backs to the "seats," and, resting on these places of honor, the souls of the ancestors take part in the festivities of the mortals.

Halfway down the court was the leaping stone, 10 feet high. Here the young men keep in trim for battle by running, jumping onto a rock, and springing over the pile of masonry. Nearby was a huge chair protected by an umbrella, both cut from solid stone. This is the seat of justice, whence the chief passes sentence of death. Its ornate appearance gave little evidence of its austere use....

During the cool of the day and in the evening, they all gathered in the courtyard, where the ancestral spirits were supposed to share the smooth, broad seats with the bare brown forms of mortals.

Under the light of the moon the natives laughed and talked and sang—sang of the new moon, the hand of their first ancestor, in which man was created; sang of its various phases, the growth and development of that man; and sang of the full moon shining above, where even then we could see the reclining figure of their forefather....

We left this city seated in homemade rocking chairs bound to bamboo poles. Two men at each end bore us over the rough stone path; but it was not wide enough for two to walk abreast, so one side of us was always much lower than the other. The carriers were always changing, and we experienced the sensations of bumping the bumps— a continuous performance for three hours.

Though we knew it to be quite beneath our dignity, we insisted on walking at times, hoping to regain our equilibrium; but the sun was intolerable and we were always glad to resume our bumpy ride. The coolies puffed and perspired, as they bore us up and down over the steep and slippery paths, but they were cheerful and shouted encouragement to each other, which helped us momentarily to forget our discomfort.

Finally we were carried through coconut groves, straight up a long flight of stone steps, into a second marvelous city. Here we rested in the home of the chief.

There was no front door, and in order to enter we walked under the house, through rows of pillars, until, about midway, ladderlike steps led through a hole in the floor up into a fine, large room. The floor and sides, as well as the raised platform across the entire front, were of highly polished boards, while the walls were hung with suits of metal armor, fine krises [daggers with ridged serpentine blades] bearing amulets encased in tigers' teeth, spears, shields, and many of the small ancestral figures.

While we sat admiring these things, there appeared in the doorway the most spectacular figure I have ever seen. Nitoo, the high chief of this district, stood before us in all his glory—an elaborate headdress with high golden ornaments, enormous golden earrings and heavy necklace,

A Nias priestess with golden headdress, bracelets, and girdle was an important figure
in the ancestor cult that pervaded the marvelous paved cities of what Arab traders called
"the island of gold."

bright-red coat with yellow bands, a yellow clout [cloth] falling skirtlike to his knees in front, and a kris with sheath of gold. He was splendid.

With all the ease and grace of a monarch, he greeted us, and, walking ahead, he escorted us to his own village, Bawomataluo.

Dignity demanded that we ride, and we frantically grasped the arms of our chairs while the panting coolies bore us over the stone path, up 900 feet to the top of a hill, to the most wonderful city of all. The hardships, the heat, and the weariness from our journey were forgotten and we were enraptured with the picture. The houses, finer than any we had seen, faced a paved court in two long rows, while the home of the chief, at the end, dominated the whole.

The high polish of the massive ancestral stones glistened in the sunlight, giving a fantastic setting for groups of fully armed warriors who awaited us. Clad in metal armor and medieval helmets of iron, copper, and gold, they formed in solemn procession and escorted us about their city, pointing out the house of the chief, especially fine ancestral seats, and other points of interest.

In the broad, flat stones of the pavement they showed us where the art of advertising had sprung into being. A necklace cut in the stone denoted the home of the goldsmith; a kris was carved before the house of the worker in iron; a severed hand and a knife in the stone foretold the punishment for theft, while a circle showed the official size of a rice measure, and four depressions of a pig's hoofs fixed the size of a full-grown hog.

Bawomataluo, this city fortress on the hill, is the center of a primitive empire; and, winding out from it in every direction, leading to coconut groves and rice fields and on to other cities, are stone walks, and here and there a stone seat on which the ancestral spirits and weary mortals may rest. Here the chief rules, passing on questions of life and death, according to the customs of his ancestors....

Our home during our stay was in the council room of the house of a former chief. Walking through a long row of great pillars, we ascended steep steps and entered a large room the floor of which was of rich brown boards polished like glass. On the broad platform across the front we unpacked our belongings and proceeded to survey the beautiful room, for it was not one to be taken in at a glance.

On the walls realistic scenes were splendidly carved. There was a boatload of people fishing, the line extending to a fish swimming beneath; there were monkeys, birds, and crocodiles; there were necklaces, betel-nut mortars, and earrings; and there was an armchair protected by an umbrella, all finely cut in the polished hardwood.

Along the sides of the room were massive wooden seats, while at the far end was an enormous fireplace, our temporary kitchen, with swimming fish carved beneath. Artistic steps on either side led to a little room above.

Hidden doors were opened to show us tiny rooms, sleeping berths, in various places; and the more we saw the more we wondered that such a house could be designed and constructed by primitive people. With stupendous labor these heavy boards, from three to five feet in width, and the huge pillars had been brought in native craft from the Batoe Islands, which by steamer are 12 hours distant, while each heavy stone had required from 500 to 600 men to bring it from the quarry.

The rafters were hung with hundreds, perhaps thousands, of pig jaws, remains of festivals held by chiefs of generations past, for each candidate must give a certain number of feasts, at each of which many pigs are slaughtered.

The people are divided into chiefs, magicians, nobles, commoners, and slaves. There is a sharp distinction between them, but it is not impossible to pass from one grade to another. Even a slave might become a chief.

Many slaves are held, mostly by the nobles; some of them are prisoners of war, but the majority are debtors, who may go free if they pay their obligations. Often a rich and notable man gives a great many feasts to make himself popular, and he may be given a high-sounding title, such as, "Base of the Earth," "Higher Than the Comb of the Rooster," "Real Fire," all of which may some day aid in his becoming a ruler.

At the death of a chief, his eldest son usually succeeds if he is normal. If he is not, the dying ruler is supposed to designate his successor with his last breath. At times people not directly related may be named or may lay claim to having been chosen.

As a rule, each village has one chief, but Bawomataluo had two, one whose power was confined to the city on the hill, and Nitoo, who held supreme sway over the city and all the surrounding villages....

One day we were escorted through a door which opened by our fireplace and were surprised to find ourselves in another large room almost as fine as the one we occupied. Seated on the platform, we looked on while two royal sons, with an air of reverence and mystery, unfastened several heavy locks on a chest. Raising the cover, they removed two smaller chests, each fastened with more locks. Opening these, they took out, one by one, the state jewels—a coat of mail covered with sheets of solid gold, a kris with a golden sheath, umbrellas heavy with golden bands, enormous earrings, necklaces, and other ornaments of gold.

It was a wonderful display. These pieces, which are of great value, may be worn only by a high chief on festive occasions. The making of each had been accompanied by the sacrifice of a slave or a head secured by warriors sent for that purpose to the interior or to a hostile village....

One night we strolled to the end of the long court and stood for some time leaning against the stone crocodiles while we watched a glorious sunset and the changing light on the placid sea in the distance. When we returned we found awaiting us, on the stone seats before the house of Nitoo, 80 brown-skinned men clad only in clouts and bark headbands and carrying wooden shields and lances with copper bands.

Forming a circle around us, they danced and sang. The brown forms of the dancers glistened. Again and again they leaped high in the air and stamped with their feet, broke into a shouting, clanging mock battle, then fell back into the regular circle and marked time. It was a weird performance, another world.

Later, when we stood on the deck of the steamer that was headed toward civilization, we looked up to the hills, toward that spot where we knew a fortress village stood, hidden by the palms; and we forgot the heat, the moisture, and the malaria that had marred our first picture of Nias. We saw, in our mind's eye, only that strange city on the hill, and we breathed a prayer that it might long survive.

Bawomataluo, Mrs. Cole might be pleased to learn, survived as long as might be expected given the waves of tourists and surfers that have since discovered Nias. It was damaged but not devastated by the colossal earthquake (8.7 on the Richter scale) that staggered the island on March 28, 2005.

KEEPING HOUSE IN BORNEO

September 1945

VIRGINIA HAMILTON

GENERATIONS AGO, FEW PLACES CALLED TO MIND MORE READILY the Old World tropical forest than did Borneo, the world's third largest island sweltering beneath the Equator at the heart of the Malay Archipelago. Its luxuriant vegetation, its myriads of creatures, its deadly diseases, and the fearsome reputation of the Dyaks, its headhunting inhabitants, all combined to send a shudder through the average Westerner. Yet tales of Borneo had undeniable appeal, and for years NATIONAL GEOGRAPHIC'S editors had been seeking someone with a thorough knowledge of the island, especially that part administered by the Dutch East Indies, to write an article about it for them. Then one day a self-styled housewife wrote in, pointing out minor errors on a recent map of Southeast Asia, and the editors realized that she might fit the bill.

Mrs. Gerrit Middelberg, it turned out, had lived with her Dutch husband, an oilman, for ten years in Borneo before the Second World War and Japanese invasion made her flee to California. In the tradition of amateur contributions to the GEOGRAPHIC, she was encouraged to try her hand at a manuscript, especially because the war, and Borneo's strategic oil wells, was then putting the island in the headlines. The result, the editors were relieved to note, was "charming" and "original," and it was published as "Keeping House in Borneo" in the September 1945 issue. Because her husband had remained on the island, perhaps engaged in behind-the-lines activities, she signed the article with her maiden name, Virginia Hamilton.

In her account she touched on all the elements of the classic Bornean travel narrative: lurid tales of the Dyaks, river voyages into the deep interior, and the experience of the all-encompassing forest. It was all told, moreover, from the perspective of a long-term resident and not from that of a passing traveler or explorer. In the following excerpts, readers who cherish small comforts might nestle deeper into their armchairs, for this was a place where everyday domestic challenges were, well, of a different order of magnitude.

WHEN DARKNESS FALLS, THE COCKROACH COMES OUT OF HIDING or flies in the window, bent on a night of destruction. He eats almost anything from soap to silk. I spent ten years with a native slipper not far from me after nightfall. Never did I become accustomed to the pop of these two-inch-long brown insects as I swatted my way from room to room, armed with the supple sole.

Beds and their nettings are of first importance when moving into a new house. Everything is done with a thought to keeping cool; and hard beds are, no doubt, cooler. There are planks where springs should be, under thin kapok mattresses. If the netting is not up at nightfall, mosquitoes sting unmercifully, and one is subject to the invasion of other insects and even snakes. In the newest homes, however, a metal screen enclosure around the beds makes a cool, sure protection. During the day a burning punk keeps the dangerous malaria carrier at a distance.

The netting and a clean water supply are perhaps of the greatest importance in maintaining a happy, healthy Indies home. Rain water collected from tin or shingle roofs into cement containers or oil drums serves for drinking, cooking, and generally for bathing. This water must be boiled for 20 minutes, filtered through porous stone, and boiled again before it is safe to drink.

The few later types of city homes are built on the ground. The greater number of older houses may lack in beauty, but, built high off the ground on stilts, they are immensely more practical protection against reptiles and bugs, and the breeze sweeping beneath keeps them cooler and far less damp.

In the long building, separated from the main house by a roofed walk, there are kitchen, storerooms, servants' quarters, and, at the farthest end, the bathroom. Because of the few dry spells, river water is piped to kitchen and bath. There is never hot running water I had no real bath in Borneo, as a bathtub is a luxury rarely found in even the best hotels in Java.... With the aid of a coffee can to pour water over me as I stood on the cement floor, I found the Indies method of bathing refreshing and practical.

Temperature varied little day and night. Terrific humidity made whiskers grow on shoes and powdery mildew collect on books; mattresses had to be aired every day in the sun. All year long one was in a constant state of perspiration, for the climate seemed to change only from the rainy to the rainier season....

A group of road coolies called me to the door one morning. They shouted with excitement, flourishing their knives. There was a huge python in the high grass across the road. Yes, I had a chicken and would give them the long rope they wanted. Soon the fowl was tethered securely about a hundred yards from my front door. Next day several gunny sacks sewed together were towed onto our lawn, to lay there undulating as a 23-foot python coiled inside. The coolies had caught him while he slept after eating the chicken. Their proud grins faded when I asked who was going to kill the reptile.

The python remained in the sacking alive and uncomfortable for two days on our lawn until a Chinese realized he could make good money selling the meat. I told him I would pay him gratefully to take the awful thing away if I could have its skin later. I have five other skins now, smaller ones, all caught near our house.

A black snake coiled and uncoiled on the curtain rod in my bedroom one night for two hours while my servants were out and my husband was away. Fortunately, the reptile was as worried as I. Neither of us dared take our eyes off the other till the houseboy came home and quickly made an end of him.

Atmah was somewhat disgusted with me for acting as I did. Didn't I know the snake had come only to warn me that we would be moving soon? Indeed, he was right, for we moved within a week. It almost seemed that there was something to this native superstition. Five times we moved within two weeks of finding a snake in the house. I must add that usually I was grateful for the change after living in such close proximity to the reptiles.

When I put my hand down on the stair railing right on top of a deadly *ijzerslang* ("iron snake"), it jumped farther than I could, and fortunately in the opposite direction. These very small reptiles look like pieces of wire and are hardest of all snakes to see.

Four-inch centipedes were at home in the dampness under potted plants, making gardening not always pleasant. Wooly spiders and black scorpions sometimes found their way indoors. But when I found five young cobras in three days sunning themselves on the doorsill and realized that the parents must be near by, I nearly moved out....

There are no tigers on Borneo. Elephants, a source of much destruction but little danger on Sumatra, are found only in the north. A few wild oxen may become vicious, but only if molested; and occasionally a "man of the jungle," the orangutan, will resent a disturbance near his home.

In the forest near one of our homes a real jungle story took place. One of our coolies was stolen away by a huge female orangutan. The man was found three days later unhurt, but the fright of his experience had permanently unhinged his mind.

Rivers were highways leading into the heart of Borneo when the forest seemed omnipresent and inexhaustible. Today the gold bugs, the orchids, the splendid moths, the orangutans, the majestic trees, are going if not already gone as deforestation continues apace.

Occasionally thieving monkeys robbed our kitchen, one side of which was usually built with a large window of wire netting for ventilation. Tables, cupboards, and even the baby's crib were set in kerosene cans of moth balls as protection from ants. There were no double walls for rats to live in.

Inch-long termites invaded our house at times in such numbers that a room would be clouded with their swarming. Thousands of them crawled into crevices in the walls, leaving behind a layer of glistening wings like a fall of miniature autumn leaves.

Coolies working on oil wells catch large numbers of termites. They cook them on the hot pipes of the engine and make a feast of them.

Always there were a few insects which followed the lights. But in the wet season many nights were made uncomfortable wherever a light burned. Screens in windows added just that last touch of heat which made a room unbearable. But when thousands of bugs were flying, screens afforded the only protection. Then the evening noises of the jungle entered our home in the metallic buzz-saw din made by cicadas and giant katydids.

Usually green or brown, the cicada was sometimes striped in gay colors. They can grow to three inches long, and they fling their hollow bodies on silver wings to crash against anything in their path. Their bumping and buzzing, my dodging and swatting sent me early to bed in the rainy season, for netting and darkness were the only protection from the invasion of our house.

There in the darkness I would lie awake listening to the hum of mosquitoes, counting the loud *talk-kay* of the big lizard in the trees, for when his call is repeated seven times it brings good luck. I would hear the fluttering of hens when a great prehistoric-looking lizard attacked the hen house and would wish for drier weather and the cessation of so many night activities.

There are other flying things which come with the night, bringing fairyland on their wings. I don't know the names of the many moths. I only know that I could sit for hours near a white wall with a low light shining on it, watching silver and gold lace on tiny white-satin wings, lime and brick-red shades on five-inch wings with trailing spiraled ends. These dainty things are lovelier than jewels themselves. Their glistening and iridescence, their soft mat qualities hold more beautiful combinations of color and intricacy of pattern than a designer of fine silks or jewelry could dream.

The goldbug came to my house, too. He was a small beetle which, when he sparkled on the floor, looked at first like a gold earring lying there. He had what resembled a little Greek letter in dull gold on his back. For all the years since he was chloroformed and wrapped in cotton he has continued to sparkle when taken out.

I felt that I must have a collection of these lovely gems, to me the most beautiful things in Borneo. But it was the only collection I made. My husband was always bringing home a *wah-wah*, friendly gray gibbon, or a fawn, lost from its mother. Once a diminutive mouse deer, shiest of them all, wandered into my dining room. I fed them all and set them free...

Kees, a red-haired baby orangutan, had special permission to live in the village, for these apes are protected by the Government and are rarely allowed in captivity. He had the friendliness and mischief of a two-year-old boy. Hans was a deer who bullied the dogs with his antlers. Pete, a solemn, stiff-legged marabou, visited tea tables in the gardens.

Ever-present sparrows twittered in the leaves and hornbills squawked in the distance. Suddenly, on walks through the jungle, we would come upon a cleared space where the ground was trampled to a hard floor. This was the dancing place of the argus pheasant....

Just before the durian season began, the jungles held a particular smell, forecasting the time of ripening for the strange tree fruit. Soon an intangible odor permeated villages and jungle alike, and the market was full of durians for sale. The large, hard, prickly-skinned durian is very popular with the Indonesians. Europeans who cannot learn to eat it are sorely tried during the short season of the ripe fruit. I started eating durians in self-protection, as one eats onions when everyone else does. At first this was no real triumph, for after I had managed to get close enough to one—fingers pinching nose—the soft, creamy sections of the fruit seemed quite unpleasant to my taste. Perseverance brings great satisfaction, however. To eat a durian is to learn to like it, even though the nearest thing to it in consistency and flavor would be a mixture of melting maple mousse and garlic.

Indies fruit is of many sizes, colors, and shapes peculiar to the foreign eye. The *sawo* resembles a common potato, but has a luscious malty flavor. Pale applelike *jamboes*, the fleshy stalks of the cashew fruit, are known only in America for the curved nuts which grow on the ends. There were so many different, tangy flavors that our buffet could always hold a colorful basketful.

Surpassing the fruits in exotic color and diversity—indeed, vying in beauty with the moths—are the orchids. The path to my house was lined with potted ground orchids. The wire netting of our chicken coop hung with some 18 varieties. Besides the big lavender ones there were sprays of inch-high white pigeons, lifelike scorpions, tiny yellow-and-brown bees, and many others, in shape and color resembling insects and butterflies....

For a last glimpse of Borneo let me take you up the wide, winding Mahakam River to a land and a people little changed over the ages.

Leaving Balikpapan at midnight, we had breakfast at the Sangasangadalem oil field. From there on, our 65-foot boat made about twelve miles an hour for three days. Samarinda was the last European settlement. Past Tenggarong, home of the Sultan, native villages were scarce. We were alone in a green world of pure primitive living, on a highway of shining brown water where there were no straight stretches or long-distance views.

Except for an occasional crashing fall of a heavy dead branch, the jungle was almost silent. Numberless shades of green composed the jungle, while the type of foliage gave variety and quality to colors. There were the deep, dull shades of the wild-rubber leaves; the gray-green needlelike tassels of the *tjimara* (beefwood); the low plumes of the banana tree; and the feathery fronds of the giant fern. Waringin, a fig, and other spreading shade trees tried to force space for their thick branches.

The impertinent trunk of the coconut palm, with its tousled head, seemed trying to show the great *kajoe radja*, king of trees, how to push its heavy trunk and sparsely covered branches to the sky.

Only at the highest point, which each tree seems struggling to reach, does the blue sky begin to show.

Dead trees, still upright because there is no place to fall, make streaks of tan or startling beige. Half-dead trees with yellowing or red-brown leaves add an autumn touch. Young growth brings vividness, while occasional flashes of red, delicate lavender, and small cascades of white pigeon orchids lend excitement.

There was much we could not see, many blossoms blending their small loveliness with the dense vegetation. Each plant and tree seemed vying with the others to reach light and air, while all appeared bound together with lianas and parasitic plants.

The year round, twilight is a matter of minutes only, but it is the grandest time of the day. A fresh, cool breath comes from the darkening skies, where the clouds turn for a moment into wondrous hues, haze to a pink glow.

For a short while here in the lonely jungle I could almost imagine I was living inside an opal. It was then that the colors of the foliage acquired new and still more varied shades, for the slanting rays of the sun touched spots which never felt the sun at another time. One could believe that the lower trees were giving thanks for this momentary glimpse of the wonders they would perhaps someday reach in their struggle to grow tall.

Our voices were stilled in awe at the beauty surrounding us. The boat's engine, chugging so long, was finally stopped for the night; and the splash of the anchor put a period to the last sentence of its chatter. To our ears came no civilized sounds.

As the night stretched black curtains across the sky and huge solitary bats appeared, a crescendo of sound filled the jungle. Millions of insects began their buzzing, monkeys called, and other animals howled. Later the creatures would concentrate on hunting, and the jungle's voices would be modulated.

On our boat, anchored in the middle of the river, we could see the trees along the banks fill with twinkling fireflies' lights, and only a whisper of sound told us the jungle was awake through the night....

PART EIGHT

Alaskan Adventures

NARRATIVE OF THE
ST. ELIAS EXPEDITION OF 1890
May 1891

ISRAEL C. RUSSELL (1852–1906)

WHEN, FROM THE DECK OF HIS SHIP, THE GREAT EXPLORER Vitus Bering first saw the stark white peak towering out of the clouds, he did not immediately name it, although it was the first glimpse any European had ever had of far northwestern North America. Four days later, on July 20, 1741, he sailed close enough to see the coastline. He named the region for St. Elias, or Elijah, whose feast day it was.

For a century and a half the spectacular Mount St. Elias, looming above the glittering glaciers and ranges of southeastern Alaska, was thought to be the tallest mountain on the continent—when it could be seen at all, that is, for proximity to the sea and westerly gales ensured its being perpetually lashed by cloud and storm. It remained a powerful lure, however. In 1886, the New York Times sponsored an expedition to climb it, but the effort was daunted by snow and avalanches. Two years later, the same thing happened to a British expedition.

That year, 1888, the National Geographic Society was established. Among its founders associated with the U.S. Geological Survey was Israel C. Russell. A civil engineer by training, Russell had become an outstanding geologist, working with the Survey's chief, John Wesley Powell, famed explorer of the Grand Canyon, and others who were mapping the West or probing the Alaska Territory. Russell had field experience in both places, which may have led to his being chosen leader of the National Geographic Society's first sponsored expedition, in partnership with the Geological Survey: an exploration of Mount St. Elias and an attempt to reach its summit.

In the summer of 1890 Russell, then 37 years old, and his team of ten men worked their way to the foot of the great mountain, started climbing "Old Eli" itself—and soon began the fight against snowstorm and avalanche. As is obvious from this narrative, which filled an entire issue of NATIONAL GEOGRAPHIC magazine, Russell was a close observer of natural phenomena with a gift for vivid—and dramatic—description.

WE HAD NOW REACHED THE LOWER LIMIT OF PERPETUAL SNOW. There were no more moraines on the surface of the glacier, and no bare rock surfaces large enough to hold a tent. The entire region was

The regions near Mount St. Elias (left) were well mapped by Israel Russell's colleague, Mark Kerr. Yet much else remains blank because it was literally terra incognita, an uncharted sea of peaks and glaciers that is today's Wrangell–St. Elias National Park.

snow-mantled as far as the eye could see, except where pinnacles and cliffs too steep and rugged for the snow to accumulate rose above the general surface. A little to one side of the mouth of a steep lateral gorge we found a spot in which a mass of partly disintegrated shale had fallen down from the cliff. We scraped the fragments aside, smoothed the snow beneath, and built a wall of rock along the lower margin. The space above was filled in with fragments of shale, so as to form a shelf on which to pitch our tent. Soon our blankets were spread with our waterproof coats for a substratum, and supper was prepared over the oil-stove.

Darkness settled down over the mountains, and the storm increased as the night came on. What is unusual in Alaska, the rain fell in torrents, as in the tropics. Our little tent of light cotton cloth afforded great protection, but the rain-drops beat on it with such force that the spray was driven through and made a fine rain within. Weary with many hours of hard traveling over moraines and across crevassed ice, and in an atmosphere saturated with moisture, we rolled ourselves in our blankets, determined to rest in spite of the storm that raged about.

As the rain became heavier, the avalanches, already alarmingly numerous, became more and more frequent: A crash like thunder, followed by the clatter of falling stones, told that many tons of ice and rocks on the mountains to the westward had slid down upon the borders of the glacier; another roar near at hand, caused by an avalanche on our own side of the glacier, was followed by another, another, and still another out in the darkness, no one could tell where. The wilder the storm, the louder and more frequent became the thunder of the avalanches. It seemed as if pandemonium reigned on the mountains. One might fancy that the evil spirits of the hill had prepared for us a reception of their own liking—but decidedly not to the taste of their visitors.

Soon there was a clatter and whiz of stones at our door. Looking out I saw rocks as large as one's head bounding past within a few feet of our tent. The stones on the mountainside above had been loosened by the rain, and it was evident that our perch was no longer tenable. Before we could remove our frail shelter to a place of greater safety, a falling rock struck the alpenstock to which the ridge-rope of our tent was fastened and carried it away. Our tent "went by the board," as a sailor would say, and we were left exposed to the pouring rain. Before we could gather up our blankets they were not only soaked, but a bushel or more of mud and stones from the bank above, previously held back by the tent, flowed in upon them. Rolling up our blankets and "caching" the rations, instruments, etc., under a rubber cloth held down by rocks, we hastily dragged our tent-cloth down to the border of the glacier, at the extremity of a tapering ridge, along which it seemed impossible for stones from above to travel. We there pitched our tent on the hard snow, without the luxury of even a few handfuls of shale beneath our blankets. Wet and cold, we sought to wear the night away as best we could, sleep being impossible. Crumback, who had been especially energetic in removing the tent, regardless of his own exposure, was wet and became cold and silent. The oil-stove and a few rations were brought from the cache at the abandoned camp, and soon a dish of coffee was steaming and filling the tent with its delicious odor. Our shelter became comfortably warm and the hot coffee, acting as a stimulant, restored our sluggish circulation.

We passed an uncomfortable night and watched anxiously for the dawn. Toward morning a cold wind swept down the glacier and the rain ceased. With the dawn there came indications that the storm had passed....

Rising at three o'clock on the morning of August 22, we started for the summit of St. Elias, taking with us only our waterproof coats, some food, and the necessary instruments. The higher mountain summits were no longer clearly defined, but in the early light it was impossible to tell whether or not the day was to be fair. From the highest and sharpest peaks, cloud banners were streaming off toward the southeast, showing that the higher air currents were in rapid movement. Vapor banks in the east were flushed with long streamers of light as the sun rose, but soon faded to a dull ashen gray, while the cloud banners between us and the sun became brilliant like the halo seen around the moon when the sky is covered with fleecy clouds. This was the first time in my experience that I had seen colored banners waving from the mountain tops.

We found the snow-surface hard, and made rapid headway up the glacier. Our only difficulty was the uncertainty of the early light, which rendered it impossible to tell the slope of the uneven snow-surfaces. The light was so evenly diffused that there were no shadows. The rare beauty of that silent, wintry landscape, so delicate in its pearly half tones and so softly lighted, was unreal and fairy-like. The winds were still; but strange forebodings of coming changes filled the air. Long, waving threads of vapor were woven in lace-work across the sky; the white-robed mountains were partially concealed by cloud masses drifting like spirits along their mighty battlements; and far, far above, from the topmost pinnacles, irised banners were signaling the coming of a storm.

We made rapid progress, but early in the day came to the base of a heavy cloud bank which enshrouded all the upper part of St. Elias. Then snow began to fall, and it was evident that to proceed farther would be rash and without promise of success. After twenty days of fatigue and hardship since leaving Blossom island, with our goal almost reached, we were obliged to turn back....

The following day, August 25, after some consultation, it was decided to once more attempt to reach the top of Mount St. Elias. Lindsley and Stamy, who had shared without complaint our privations in the snow, volunteered to descend to a lower camp for additional rations, while Kerr and myself returned to the higher camp in the hope that we might be able to ascend the peak before the men returned, and if not, to have sufficient rations when they did rejoin us to continue the attack. The men departed on their difficult errand, while Kerr and I, with blankets, tents, oil-stoves, and what rations remained, once more scaled the cliff where we had placed a rope, and returned on the trail made the day previously. About noon we reached the excavation in the snow we had bivouacked in the storm, and there prepared a lunch. It was then discovered that we had been mistaken as to the quantity of oil in our cans; we found scarcely enough to cook a single meal. To attempt to remain several days in the snow with this small supply of fuel seemed hazardous, and Mr. Kerr volunteered to descend and overtake the men at the lower camp, procure some oil, and return the following day. We then separated, Mr. Kerr starting down the mountain, leaving me with a double load, weighing between sixty and seventy pounds, to carry through the deep snow to the high camp previously occupied....

Trudging wearily on, I reached the high camp at sunset, and pitched my tent in the excavation previously occupied. An alpenstock was used for one tent-pole, and snow saturated with water, piled up in a column, for the other; the snow froze in a few minutes, and held the tent securely. The ends of the ridge-rope were then stamped into the snow, and water was poured over them; the edges of the tent were treated in a similar manner, and my shelter was ready for occupation. After cooking some supper over the oil-stove, I rolled myself in a blanket and slept the sleep of the weary. I was awakened in the morning by snow drifting into my tent, and on looking out discovered that I was again caught in a blinding storm of a mist of snow. The storm raged all day and all night, and contin-ued without interruption until the evening of the second day. The coal oil becoming exhausted, a can was filled with bacon grease, in which a cotton rag was place for a wick; and over this "witch lamp" I did my cook-ing during the remainder of my stay.

The snow, falling steadily, soon buried my tent, already surrounded on three sides by an icy wall higher than my head, and it was only by almost constant exertion that it was kept from being crushed in. With a pint basin for a shovel, I cleared the tent as best I could, and several times during the day re-excavated the hole leading down to the pond, which had long since disappeared beneath the level plain of white. The excava-tion of a tunnel in the snow was also begun in the expectation that the tent would become uninhabitable. The following night it became impos-sible to keep the tent clear in spite of energetic efforts, and early in the morning it was crushed in by a great weight of snow, leaving me no alternative but to finish my snow-house and move in. A tunnel some four or five feet in length was excavated in the snow, and a chamber about six feet long by four feet wide and three feet high was made at right angles to the tunnel. In this chamber I placed my blankets and other belongings, and, hanging a rubber coat on an alpenstock at the entrance, found myself well sheltered from the tempest. There I passed the day and the night following.

At night the darkness and silence in my narrow tomb-like cell was oppressive; not a sound broke the stillness except the distant, muffled roar of an occasional avalanche. I slept soundly, however, and in the morning was awakened by the croaking of a raven on the snow immediately above my head. The grotto was filled with a soft blue light, but a pink radiance at the entrance told that the day had dawned bright and clear.

What a glorious sight awaited me! The heavens were without a cloud, and the sun shone with dazzling splendor on the white peaks around. The broad unbroken snow-plain seemed to burn with light reflected from millions of shining crystals. The great mountain peaks were draped from base to summit in the purest white, as yet unscarred by avalanches. On the steep cliffs the snow hung in folds like drapery, tier above tier, while the angular peaks above stood out like crystals against the sky. St. Elias was one vast pyramid of alabaster. The winds were still; not a sound broke the solitude; not an object moved. Even the raven had gone, leaving me alone with the mountains.

As the sun rose higher and higher and made its warmth felt, the snow was loosened on the steep slopes and here and there broke away. Gathering force as it fell, it rushed down in avalanches that made the mountains tremble and awakened thunderous echoes. From a small beginning high up on the steep slopes, the new snow would slip downward, silently at first, and cascade over precipices hundreds of feet high, looking like a fall of foaming water; then came the roar, increasing in volume as the flowing snow involved new fields in its path of destruction, until the great mass became irresistible and ploughed its way downward through clouds of snow-spray, which hung in the air long after the snow had ceased to move and the roar of the avalanche had ceased. All day long, until the shadow of evening fell on the steep slopes, this mountain thunder continued. The echoes of one avalanche scarcely died away before they were awakened by another roar. To witness such a scene under the most favorable conditions was worth all the privations and anxiety it cost.

Besides the streams of new snow, there were occasional avalanches of a different character, caused by the breaking away of portions of the cliffs of old snow, accumulated, perhaps, during several winters. These start from the summits of precipices, and are caused by the slow downward creep of the snow-fields above. The snow-cliffs are always crevassed and broken in much the same manner as are the ends of glaciers which enter the sea, and occasionally large masses, containing thousands of cubic yards, break away and are precipitated down the slopes with a suddenness that is always startling. Usually the first announcement of these avalanches is a report like that of a cannon, followed by a rumbling roar as the descending mass ploughs its way along. The avalanches formed by old snow are quite different from those caused by the descent of the new surface snow, but are frequently accompanied by surface streams in case there has been a recent storm. The paths ploughed out by the avalanches are frequently sheathed with glassy ice, formed by the freezing water produced by the melting of snow on account of the heat produced by the friction of the moving mass.

The day following the storm was bright and beautiful; the sunlight was warm and pleasant, but the temperature in the shadows was always below freezing. The surface of the snow did not melt sufficiently during the day to freeze and form a crust during the night. It thus became more and more apparent that the season was too far advanced to allow the snow to harden sufficiently for us to be able to climb the mountain. The snow settled somewhat and changed its character, but even at midday the crystals on the surface glittered as brilliantly in the sunlight as they did in the early morning. Although the snow did not melt, its surface was lowered slightly by evaporation. The tracks of the raven, at first sunken a quarter of an inch in the soft surface, after the first day of sunshine stood slightly in relief, but were still clearly defined....

On the sixth day after separating from my companions, judging that they must have returned at least to the camping place where we had separated, I packed my blankets and what food remained, abandoned the tent and oil-stove, and started to descend the mountain. The snow had settled somewhat, but was still soft and yielding and over six feet deep. Tramping wearily on through the chaff-like substance, I slowly worked my way downward, and again threaded the maze of the crevasses, now partially concealed by the layer of new snow, with which we had struggled several times before. Midway to the next camping place I met my companions coming up to search for me. Instead of meeting three men, as I expected,

I saw five tramping along in single file through the deep snow. The sight of human beings in that vast solitude was so strange that I watched them for some time before shouting. Glad as I was to meet my companions once more, I could not help noticing their rough and picturesque appearance. Each man wore colored glasses and carried a long alpenstock, and two or three had packs strapped on their backs. Several weeks of hard tramping over moraines and snow-fields had made many rents in their clothes, which had been mended with cloth of any color that chanced to be available. Not a few rags were visible fluttering in the wind. To a stranger they would have appeared like a dangerous band of brigands....

On the steep slope now exposed to the full sunshine several avalanches had gone down, and there was great danger of others. Selecting a point where an avalanche had already swept away the new snow, we worked our way downward in a zigzag course and reached the bottom safely, although an avalanche starting near at hand swept by within a few yards. When nearly at the bottom my attention was attracted by a noise above, and on looking up I saw two rocks bounding down the slope and coming straight for me. To dodge them on the steep slippery slope was difficult and dangerous. Allowing one to pass over my right shoulder, I instantly moved in that direction and allowed the other to pass over my left shoulder. They shot by me like fragments of shells, but did no injury....

Nerves probably a bit worse for wear, Russell and his men did make their way safely back to civilization, carrying with them a mass of scientific data. They were the first to spy Mount Logan, Canada's highest peak, hidden in the ranges behind Mount St. Elias itself. Their field determination of Old Eli's height was within a hundred feet of what we know it to be today: 18,008 feet. In 1897, using maps made by Russell's expedition, Luigi of Savoy, better known as the Duke of Abruzzi, arrived at Mount St. Elias and, fighting his way past snow and avalanche, finally reached the summit.

Israel Russell moved on to the University of Michigan, where he taught geology until pneumonia carried him off at the early age of 53. By then Mount St. Elias's glory had also passed. Mount McKinley, or Denali, was considered the highest peak in North America. Though Old Eli has since slipped into fourth place, Wrangell–St. Elias National Park and Preserve is today the largest unit within the U.S. National Park System.

THE VALLEY OF
TEN THOUSAND SMOKES

February 1918

ROBERT F. GRIGGS (1881–1962)

THE VALLEY MUST HAVE BEEN BEAUTIFUL ONCE. FRAMED BY mountains, snow-covered and glacier-riven, it was nearly 15 miles long and 3 miles wide. Caribou grazed its meadows and moose browsed its birch and poplar groves; beavers built dams among its swamps, trout swam in its streams, and wolves lurked in the shadow of its spruce. Ominously, hot springs issued forth here and there, signs of the nearby presence of Mount Katmai, a volcano on the Alaskan panhandle so little explored that for years the river flowing through the valley was unnamed on charts. It was Robert F. Griggs who eventually called it the Unak, after a small settlement near which he once camped. A botanist by training, Griggs would have loved to have seen the valley at its green prime; by the time he first laid eyes on it, it had been transformed forever.

In June 1912 Mount Katmai erupted. The explosions were felt all over northwestern North America; if located in New York City, its plume could have been seen in Albany, its blast would have sounded in Chicago, and its fumes would have tarnished brass in Denver. It was the most tremendous eruption of the 20th century, certainly in North America and probably on Earth—yet it happened in a location so remote that not a human being is known to have perished.

Griggs was one of the first scientists to venture into the blasted region. Between 1915 and 1919 he led a series of National Geographic–sponsored expeditions that struggled across ash-choked rivers and quicksand beds toward the shattered stump of Mount Katmai. On the last day of the 1916 expedition, crossing Katmai Pass to see what lay on the other side, Griggs discovered that unnamed valley—a hellish, seething cauldron of fumaroles, or steam vents. A stupendous panorama, he christened it the "Valley of Ten Thousand Smokes."

He returned in the summer of 1917. Hundreds of miles from any settlement, at a time before radio or airplanes were common, his ten-man expedition faced a prospect both nightmarish and sublime. Strong winds raked the valley, sending sharp pumice flying. Steam vents roared and hissed, and the smell of hydrogen sulfide permeated the air. It was like watching a planet being formed, and Griggs and the other men gazed awestruck before taking their first tentative steps onto the quaking ground.

WHEN THIS YEAR'S PARTY REACHED THE VALLEY, THE EFFECT ON THE men was stupendous. None had imagined anything nearly so wonderful. Every one agreed that no description could convey any conception of its immensity of grandeur.

I found that my matter-of-fact chemist was counting the smokes to see whether I had been justified in asserting that there were ten thousand of them. He soon announced that I was quite well inside the number. There are certainly many times ten thousand to be seen, even on a clear day, and when the weather is moist myriads more appear, for then the smoke from the millions of little holes whose gases ordinarily are invisible condense until there are a thousand times ten thousand.

One member of the party, who having traveled considerably and found many of the sights of the world overdrawn, was somewhat skeptical in advance about the Ten Thousand Smokes. When once he felt its thrall, however, he repeated over and over again, "Why, you couldn't exaggerate it." This statement is perfectly true. While the statistics of length, area, etc., could be falsified, the enlarged figures could no more convey any idea of the immensity of the new wonderland than can the real dimensions.

This is one of the greatest wonders of the world, if not indeed the very greatest of all the wonders on the face of the earth. The valley cannot be described; only after one has spent many days within its confines does one begin to grasp the proportions.... The sensation of wonder and admiration, which came first to all, soon gave way to one of stupefaction. The magnitude of the phenomena simply overcame us. As we moved to any corner of the valley, what we had supposed from a distance to be little fumaroles turned out monster vents, each group more wonderful a spectacle than the whole, seen in panorama, so inconceivably vast is the volcanic region. No amount of experience seemed sufficient to enable us to grasp the proportions of this enormous safety-valve.

For the first few days we were over-awed. For a while we simply could not think or act in the ordinary way. At night I would curse myself, as I lay in my blankets, and make a list of the things I wanted to do the next day; but when the morning came I could not move myself to action. I could only look and gape.

Shipley, the chemist, was easily the most self-possessed of the crowd. But for him we probably would have turned around and come home without any of the scientific material we had gone to collect.

After all, the whole valley is very much of a gigantic chemical laboratory, and perhaps that accounts for his greater command of himself. Yet on the third day he remarked that "he did not feel like monkeying with his little bottles of chemicals."

X-[Griggs tactfully would not name him] was frankly scared to death. He did what I told him, but except when told to do something he sat in a dull-eyed stupor, like one at the funeral of his sweetheart, from which no efforts of ours could rouse him. I can only guess the effort it must have cost him to go up to the fumaroles and get pictures of them. He said himself that he expected to go crazy before he got out again. He had to be relieved and sent down to the lower camp before he regained his nerve, but in the end had as good a command of himself as any of us.

I was utterly unprepared for the feelings which thus overcame me. In 1916 I had not stayed long enough in the valley to get beyond the first sensations of wonder and admiration. I had by no means grasped the situation sufficiently to report it accurately. This region should have been named "The Valley of a Million Smokes," for there are certainly not one, but several million of them all told.

A large factor in my feelings was plain fear. Perhaps I ought in honesty to say cowardice. The spectacle was so much bigger than I remembered it that I was badly scared by the job I had undertaken. The fear which beset me was twofold: fear of cave-ins and fear of the fumes.

As we explored the margin of the valley (the worst place, as we afterward found), we could plainly hear the ground ring hollow beneath the tunks of our staffs, and more than once we felt it shake beneath our blows. What if the ground should suddenly give way beneath our feet and precipitate us into a steaming caldron?

A breath of the steam from a vent blown around us for a moment by a chance breeze gave an uncomfortable burn. We knew that if once a man fell into such a place he would be instantly parboiled.

At first we roped up as for mountain-climbing and spread out, so that if one man went through, the others could pull him out. But when we came better to realize the conditions, we discarded the ropes, for we decided that if a man once goes in it would be more merciful to leave him than to attempt to pull him out.

We had been assured by the best authority that there could be no danger from the fumes, but I had brought along a chemist partly for the express purpose of warning us as to what was not safe. I knew this valley

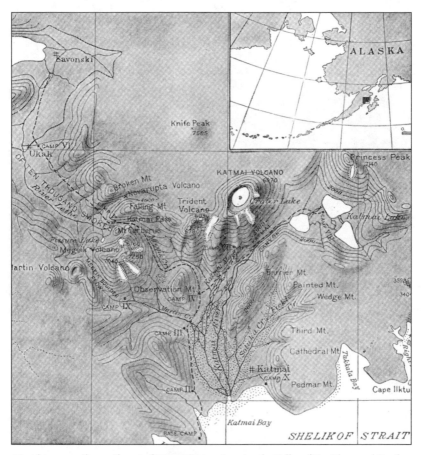

Stretching 15 miles northwest of Mount Katmai's crater, the Valley of Ten Thousand Smokes was blanketed by incandescent ash when that volcano, mightiest on the Alaskan panhandle, erupted in 1912.

to be different from every other place in the world, and reasoned that there could be no real basis for the assurances given me. What I feared was carbon monoxide, that colorless, odorless, tasteless gas, deadly even in concentrations as small as five parts in 10,000. It is usually present in the emanations from volcanoes. There is, moreover, no simple chemical test by which its presence may be detected. What if we should get a dose of that before we were aware of the danger?

But, like practically all the bugaboos which one meets in this world, these were proved by experience to be much less dangerous than our imaginations had pictured. Experience showed that there was always plenty of air to breathe, and we found no insidious gases likely to strike one down without a warning, for our noses always gave us an abundant

*No camera could do it justice: A partial view down the Valley of Ten Thousand Smokes,
depicting but a fraction of the millions of hissing, roaring steam vents,
one of Earth's most awesome spectacles for the few years it lasted.*

notice of the dangerous places, so that we suffered no injury beyond slight headaches and temporary inconvenience.

So also with the cave-ins. As we grew familiar with the conditions we built up a basis of experience that soon enabled us to pick our way with some degree of safety. The deposits brought up by the fumaroles themselves so encrust their throats and the ground round about that a thin roof over a cavern will support a man with safety. The worst places were those where fissures had been bridged over by ash and mud, so as to leave nothing to indicate their presence. After we had been in the valley several days we had some experiences with such places that probably would have turned us back had they occurred when we first arrived.

Several times, when we accidentally put a foot through a thin place in the crust, steam came spouting out of the hole, forming a new fumarole. But it was always one foot only and the owner did not take long to get it out....

We chose our camp well up on the mountain side overlooking the valley, close beside a melting snow-drift. Here, although we were denied the pleasure of a campfire, for not a stick of wood remains anywhere in the valley, we had "all the comforts of home." Fifty yards behind us was our refrigerator, where we could keep everything freezing cold until needed.

Just in front was our cook-stove—a mild-mannered fumarole—into which we hung our pots to cook our food. We were somewhat dubious beforehand as to the feasibility of this method of cooking, because of the noxious gases that came off along with the steam; but the results were more than satisfactory. We never detected the faintest taint in any of our food. Everything was always done exactly right. Since the pots were surrounded by an atmosphere of live steam, just at the point of condensing, nothing ever boiled away, cooked to pieces, or burned, no matter how long neglected or forgotten.

There was only one drawback: while we were in the valley we had to do without our old standbys, bacon and flapjacks, for our stove would not fry. There were, however, many vents in the valley quite hot enough to fry bacon. The vapor from most of the more active ones is so hot that the steam does not condense for some distance beyond the vents. When a stick is poked into these the end is quickly charred, indicating a temperature considerably above the frying point.

Our thermometers did not read high enough to measure the temperatures of these vents, so we were unable to ascertain exactly how hot they were. But we did not think it advisable to try bacon and flapjacks in them, because most of them are a little too vigorous to be altogether manageable. The vapor in many cases comes out with such force that the frying pan would have had to be held down against the rising steam. A sudden puff of wind from an unexpected quarter might, moreover, have blown the steam in the cook's face and inflicted a serious burn.

When we turned in the first night, we were astonished to find that the ground under our tent was decidedly warm. On examination we found that a thermometer thrust 6 inches into the ground promptly rose to the boiling point. This was indeed a surprise, for the place only recently had been vacated by the retreating snowbank behind us.

We put most of our bedding under us to keep us cool! But before long our blankets were as hot as the ground. Close to the snowdrift as we were, and at an altitude of about 2,500 feet, the air was at times quite cold; so while we steamed on one side we froze on the other. We had to keep turning over and over in the effort to equalize the temperature. We did not sleep much the first night, and all expected to "catch our death of cold."

After a few hours we discovered that the ground was not merely hot, but that invisible vapors were everywhere seeping up through the soil. The condensation of this steam from the ground made our bedding first damp and then wet, so that by morning we were in a most curious case. The sensations that greeted us on awakening in these warm, wet beds can in justice be compared only with certain distressing memories of one's childhood days, which they exactly paralleled....

While the smoke from the craters comes out quietly, in vast, rolling clouds, that from the fissures often is emitted under considerable pressure, roaring and hissing. If one tosses pebbles into the mouths of these vents they are so buoyed up by the rising gases that they are either immediately spewed out again or they sink slowly down through the rising steam like feathers settling to earth. Such vents are the hottest places in the valley; the gases from them do not condense for several yards beyond the orifice. They furnished some of the most satisfactory places for the collection of gases for analysis, because of the ease with which the collector could assure himself that his sample was free from contamination with the atmosphere....

Over large areas the ground has been burned to a bright red by the heat. The variations in the intensity of the color produced are extremely beautiful, including, as they do, all shades from orange and brick red to bright cherry reds, purples, and on down to black, with occasional contrasting streaks of blue. This type of coloration is most pronounced in areas originally occupied by small fumaroles which have burned out. In places the ground has the appearance of having been burned with fire for a mile at a stretch.

The snow-fields which surround the valley send trickling rills down the slopes, but these dry up and disappear long before the floor of the basin is reached. From the glaciers, however, comes a considerable stream, which runs, in spite of all obstacles, clear through the valley, dwindling to almost nothing before passing out of the hot area. These waters thus so nearly forget to run that we christened the stream the River Lethe. The appropriateness of this name is increased not only by its course, which lies through the center of Hades, but also because the uncanny waters, full of deep-brown silt from the glaciers, have a most weird aspect as they rush swirling down the valley.

In many places the river cuts straight across lines of volcanic activity, and here we see how close the antagonistic elements—"fire" and "water"—may approach one another without disturbance. The mud, which lines the banks, is so perfect a non-conductor that within a few inches of the cold water the ground is boiling hot. There are places where the steam from the small fumaroles actually boils up through the water of the river! Several good-sized vents are located on the very banks of the river.

Here one could catch a fish in the stream and cook it without taking it off the hook—if only there were any fish, for one can hardly imagine fish frequenting this murky stream. There is, however, no real reason why they might not occur; for, in spite of the fact that the very banks are boiling hot, the waters maintain their glacial temperature of about 48°F throughout the valley....

I can never forget my last day in the valley. We had been lying in our sopping tents for two days, unable to stir outside in the blinding storms. The rest of the work was pressing, for I had already overstayed the time allotted for the valley. In the morning I had announced that we would move out that night, regardless of the weather, and had given orders for the equipment to go down. We started out for some last pictures in rain and mist which made it impossible to find our way around through the steam, but after a couple of hours there came a break.

The atmosphere cleared and disclosed the sun shining out of a blue sky, spotted with big cumulus clouds, with a light that was dazzling bright. I never saw the valley half so wonderful. We exposed our films as fast as we could wind them up, getting within a few hours many of our best pictures. There were a dozen showers during the day, soaking rains, too, but we utilized such intervals to travel from one group of vents to another. We came in at 6 o'clock tired out, but bent on taking out the big photographic outfit for the one grandest panorama of all. But it was too late; because of my own orders we found the camp stripped of everything we needed.

There was nothing to do but follow, so we made up our packs and reluctantly trudged out through the pass and down the other side. I almost wept as I turned for one last look at the marvelous valley, showing off now as never before, for as we came up to the divide, which we were perhaps never to cross again, a magical curtain was unrolled, as a background for the scene, in the most gorgeous sunset I ever saw. The wonderful colors held us almost spellbound for hours, until they slowly faded into twilight, as we rounded the shoulder of Observation Mountain into Katmai Valley....

Not everyone, however, was so affected by these experiences. Griggs quotes one of his topographers, a more exacting if less imaginative man:

"I am not a vegetarian; furthermore, tea cooked in a steam pit is not tea. A tent that never sheds a drop of water is not a tent. A wool comfort placed on the ground which was 110° Fahrenheit in the above tent will steam beautifully. It is a natural phenomenon, but it is not a good bed. I believe I mentioned that I am not a vegetarian. I like bacon in the morning; I like it fried. A steam jet, in spite of its being glorious and a natural phenomenon, will not do this. I am from New England and have decided ideas on baked beans. Again the steam jet fell down.

"I should say the coming of the smokes ruined what might otherwise have been a perfectly good country. My opinion, however, is probably valueless, as being out of tobacco always colors my views."

In 1919, President Woodrow Wilson created Katmai National Monument (today Katmai National Park and Preserve), trusting that the scenic wonderland that was the Valley of Ten Thousand Smokes might then be preserved for future generations to behold.

The Smokes themselves, however, let him down. Within a few years they began dying out. The valley was not acting as a great safety valve after all. Its 40 square miles had instead been blanketed by hundreds of feet of incandescent ash, trapping the considerable water originally present, which then gradually escaped through steam vents.

Though the fumaroles are long gone, the valley remains an impressive place, and today is the most popular destination for hikers setting out from park headquarters. Because the sandlike ash is still inimical to vegetation, the valley's stark, lunar quality also made it an ideal training ground for the Apollo astronauts.

PART NINE

Along old spanish Roads

ALONG THE OLD SPANISH ROAD IN MEXICO

March 1923

HERBERT COREY (1872–1954)

WHEN A CHARACTER IN D. H. LAWRENCE'S NOVEL, THE PLUMED Serpent, *refers to 1920s Mexico as "this high plateau of death," where even flowers "have their roots in spilt blood," she is recalling the Mexican Revolution of 1910–1920, in which upwards of a million people may have been killed. The violence was not confined just to Mexico, for in 1916 the colorful bandit-general Pancho Villa led a raid into the United States. In retaliation, Gen. John J. Pershing led a punitive expedition south of the border, chasing, if never actually catching, the legendary Villa.*

A veteran war correspondent named Herbert Corey accompanied Pershing's column. Reared on the Western frontier, Corey had been a cowboy, stagecoach driver, and sheepherder before turning to newspaper work. During the First World War—when not chasing Villa with Pershing—he was the only accredited correspondent to cover both sides on all fronts. After the 1918 Armistice he was one of the first journalists to enter Germany, where he obtained an exclusive interview with Field Marshal von Hindenberg. This combination of experience made Corey the natural choice when NATIONAL GEOGRAPHIC *looked for a reporter willing to venture into Mexico after the revolution.*

By 1922, after a new regime had stopped the violence, Corey, 49, joined by GEOGRAPHIC *photographer Clifton Adams, 31, traveled across Mexico and observed conditions there. The journey lasted only a few months, but the pair amassed material for four articles. Despite the ruined agriculture, the burned estancias [ranches], and the abundant evidence of summary executions, Mexico cast its spell over Corey. Neither bullfight nor fiesta entranced and amused him, but rather the life he found along the "Old Spanish Road," the oldest highway on the continent, little better than a mule trail in places. For Corey, "The Road" took on mythic dimensions as it wound across the heart of Old Mexico. The following passages display what most impressed him: resiliency, stubborn inborn pride, and sweeping courtesy, even in the face of so much death.*

THE OLD SPANISH ROAD IS AN INCREDIBLE THOROUGHFARE. Once upon a time, according to the people of the countryside, stage coaches ran all the way from Guadalajara to Nogales, in Arizona. Now only a flivver [automobile] or a mule-cart can negotiate parts of it, and the other parts are barely fit for traffic under saddle. It is well laid out, for the Toltecs, and after them the Aztecs, and after them the Spaniards, knew something of surveying.

Everywhere the views are superb of rolling hills and deep-seated valleys. There are patches of vivid green where farmers have held their own and kept the water flowing on the fertile land. Honeysuckle and bougainvillaea and roses and a score of unknown flowers wreathe the walls of black volcanic stone that mark the borders of the great ranches.

The dust was of a talcum lightness and a shoetop depth. Our forewheels threw up a bow wave like that of a fast launch in still water. Behind us rolled a pillar of dust to mingle with the other clouds that were stirred by the feet of peon and burro and horse and mule....

Darkness came on and the passage through the villages became perilous. Mexican cows seem to sleep by preference in the soft dust of the road, and our car had no lights. The driver did not slacken speed. Time after time I was conscious that the tip of a horn had flashed past under my nose, as a cow rose leisurely by the side of the flivver. Sometimes we stopped in a storm of dust, the front wheel actually touching a recumbent beast. The driver said with a curse that he did not like to hit cows; they were so solid that it was always the automobile that broke....

The landlady sat down at the table, a long black cigarette hanging from one corner of her mouth, and alternated gossip with inquiry.

The bandittoes—had we heard, now, that the bandittoes had roasted the feet of another man upon The Road? God's curse on them! And that the patriotas were about to begin another revolution? Curse the patriotas! Could we not have peace? Two of her neighbors, kindly men, with pretty wives, had been made soldiers and killed. One thinks what one thinks, mind you. A pretty wife is a burden. Business was bad, but it might pick up again. No touristas ever came to Santiago. Commercial travelers now and then; but nowadays they are ill-tempered. One prefers not to see them. Poor men. One sorrows for them.

She piled our plates with all manner of tasty but unknown dishes. She spat between her teeth on the stone floor. Of the score of birds swinging overhead among the flowers in the open gallery, one gave out a torrent of clear, crystalline, brittle notes.

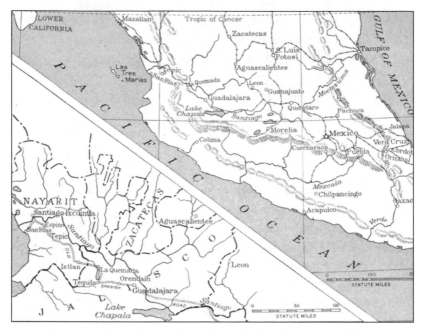

From Vera Cruz on the Gulf to San Blas on the Pacific, the Old Spanish Road, highway to Aztec and Conquistador alike, rolled across the heart of Mexico.

Of course, the floor was bare, for all hotel floors in Mexico are bare, but it was clean. The rough timbers of the tiled roof overhead were clean. The stone steps, worn into hollows by generations of travelers, were clean. The canvas cots, with a single sheet by way of bed clothing, were clean.

We forgave the House of the Black Spider, that hostel which had been in such *mal estancia*, in our gratitude.

I remarked to our hostess that her daughters were more than pretty. They were exquisite.

"How greatly they resemble Madame."

"But certainly," said Madame, aiming at a crack in the floor, "certainly they are pretty. We come from Guadalajara, where all women are beautiful."...

Dust—dust in thick, gummy, greasy clouds—and ruts that jolted the very soul out of one, and sun rays that burned down in white flame. Overhead there was the clear, fathomless, brilliant azure of the Mexican sky, in which little wooly clouds floated, and alongside was the tinkle of running water in the irrigation ditches, and now and then the boughs of great trees arched overhead.

Yet it was the human element that caught and held one's fancy.

It seemed such a very little time ago that Cortez and Fra Junipero and Alvarado the Damned trod this bed of staring yellow sand....

Along The Road, every few feet it seemed were the crosses Mexicans erect where men have been killed. Usually the crosses were but little sticks, rudely tied together, that could not outlast more than a year or so in any climate. Yet there was an abundance of them.

In one deep, narrow cut there were ten crosses newly scratched in the rock of the wall. From the sparkling white of the new graving, they might have been made within the week. Evidently there had been an ambush in this narrow way.

Once, too, there was an Indian merrymaking. A score or more of peons, in their ceremonial clothing of spotless white, the width of their pyramidal pantaloons being so phenomenal that they seemed to taper up to their huge hats, leaned against a rock wall. Inside an adobe hut a jerky accordion was whining.

"Hola, senores," cried one.

He leaped down the stepping-stones that told him the roadway is at times a flood, waving a bottle of tequile. He was evidently something more than half drunk. We explained that we had a long road ahead and had not time to drink, but that we wished him well. He fell back with the grace that is inborn in these people and lifted his mountainous hat and bade us go with God.

We drove on, vainly wishing that fate had provided the Anglo-Saxon with a manner....

"About that little breakfast, now," I said to Tomaso. "You have not forgotten it?"

The muleteer said vaguely that we would, no doubt, eat somewhere along the road. So we started, at half-past 4 o'clock of a frosty morning. The muleteer was dressed in a high, wide sombrero and white cotton shirt and trousers and open-toed sandals.

As soon as we got into the street, having headed off several determined rushes by the mules back into the mesón, he strapped a pair of huge spurs on my feet, giving me somewhat the appearance of an old-fashioned Missouri River side-wheeler, and hit my little horse violently on the tail, and we were off.

The muleteer ran behind. Whenever he got near enough, he snapped my little horse on the rump with his quirt. I objected to this, because each time the little horse leaped about 14 feet; but my objections were overruled.

"Adelante!" said the muleteer.

We trotted savagely up the hill road. Now and then Tomaso hit my little horse on the tail. Doubtless there was scenery on either side, but my memory failed to register it. We passed other trotting mule trains, and sometimes other mule trains outtrotted us. Every one seemed to be in the most desperate hurry.

The dawn came in azure rose and gold. The trunk with which one mule was packed slipped from time to time, and I took occasion of the pauses to work my way further from that flicking quirt.

We came to a town of small adobe houses built flush with the great rock-filled Spanish Road.

"We eat here," said Tomaso.

It was light enough to see things and people. Chickens, pigs, dogs, cats, and babies walked in and out of the open doors. Smoke curled out of the doorways and over the flat, chimneyless roofs. In front of each hut was a little elevated platform of mud and stone on which the residents sat to watch their world go by.

The Indian woman who had been picked as our hostess said she had no food. The hens had not yet laid. A hasty census revealed that no one had any food, and so we waved our hands and were unmannerly, and in return were given coffee. It was, perhaps, the worst coffee in the world, thick with dirty brown sugar of the market-places. We also were given delicious little loaves of brown, crusted, fluffy, sweetened bread.

"Adelante!" said Tomaso.

We adelanted for aching hours. We came to the bad place in the trail of which we had been told. Evidently those who told knew nothing about it, for it was not at all bad. One could have driven a wagon over it, except that to get there a wagon must have been dropped out of a dirigible.

Over the unguarded edge one could easily see the bottom of the ravine when the gray mists swirled away; but it seemed a long time before the sound of a thrown rock came up, muffled by the fog. The worst of it was that the road had given up trying to be a road and was putting on a jazzy imitation of a disorderly stone quarry. No wheeled vehicle had ever been over it, I am sure.

Yet one does not know what the incredible Spaniards may have done with their ox-carts, of which the wheels were of solid ebony. There are carts in operation to-day that are known to be more than 300 years old. The wheelwrights built to last in those days. The pavement was of rocks the size of one's head. Sometimes they had been washed out and the gully had never been filled.

One progressed uphill by a series of surges and dropped downhill in dislocating, neck-snapping bounds. Adams became voluble and injured. He said that his horse was a demon and that his knees were killing him. He paused to confide this to me, and Tomaso snapped at his horse with his quirt.

"Adelante!"

"I won't," yelled Adams. "I will not go another foot." He got off and walked. The *arriero* relapsed into an embittered silence. I gathered that by this act of Adams he had lost a chance to break the world's worst road record with amateurs; also he lost face with his friends. Sometimes he would catch up with Adams and expostulate, but Adams waved him away. He said that he could hike with any man, but that he had been so carefully reared that he did not know how to tell the world about the pain in his knees.

Mule trains passed on the clattering trot, and the drivers said funny things to our driver, which were not appreciated. The riders all wore rifles or revolvers where they could be gotten at easily. This stretch of road had a vile reputation not so long ago.

"Where do we eat lunch?" I asked.

"La Venta," said Tomaso.

From his tone, La Venta seemed to be a Flamingo or Biltmore. I began to plan a menu. We kept on trotting angrily over this road, which no sane American would have even led a good horse over.

We trotted through a village, catching glimpses of pleasant porticoes under which we might have rested had Tomaso been propitious. An old woman was revolving a spindle and her aide, 20 feet away, was holding the end of a hair riata.

Cooking fires were smoking in the streets, by the side of the buildings, near the stream, under rocks on the hillsides. Men stood in the doorway of the village inn with glasses of cool beer in their hands. We kept on adelanting ruthlessly.

At 2 o'clock we came to an Indian shack by the side of a hacienda which had been burned by the bandits. It had been an imposing place. There had been a good-sized restaurant and a store and the offices of the ranch. Inside the great patio were rooms in which the ranch servants and the travelers of the past had slept. The stones of the quadrangle had been blackened by their little fires. There were watchtowers on the walls.

The whole was set in a frame of gray hills, down which tracings of green told of little trickling streams. Under the arched portico which had protected the restaurant's patrons from the sun, five black crosses had been rudely drawn with charcoal.

There was a huddle of bullet-marks on the soft plaster.

A few mules were at fodder near the shack. The arrieros were sleeping in the shadow of a wall. Half a dozen pigs shared the shade with them. In a little shelter near by—just a thatch of grass thrown over sticks—an Indian family had set up housekeeping.

Smoke seeped out through the thatch of the other shack. A naked baby was being awakened from where it slept, with its head on a sow, and was being forced into a shirt. Two or three women peered at us from the shadow of the door.

"Let us eat here," I said.

"What—here?" asked the arriero. He seemed horrified. Then I asked the name of the place, and he said it was La Venta and very villainous.

The Indians, bless their kind hearts, gave us their best. The nests were searched and we had eggs and, of course, tortillas and beans. More than that, we received smiles and kindness and a real desire to please. We got their only chair, and their only box to sit on, and their only two spoons. They had no other furniture except a bowl or two, and the stone on which the women rolled out the paste for the tortillas, and the bit of tin on which they were baked.

A bucket simmered over a smoky fire outside the door, in which more corn was being boiled to make more tortillas. Indian women spend all their time in boiling corn in lime water, in boiling it again in fresh water, in mashing it into paste, in patting it into cakes, and finally in baking it over the fire. They have no time for anything else.

"Adelante!"

The road grew worse and worse. Once we climbed a spiral stairway from which the horses would be rolling yet if they had made a misstep. At the foot of the twist was a rudely built shrine in which a candle burned before a picture of the Virgin.

The road became a mere washout, except that there was no earth to wash, and so the bucket-sized stones had been tossed about by the freshets.

At intervals we crossed long stretches of flat rock cupped by the hoofs of mules which had used this trail for almost four centuries. That gilding of romance on the Old Spanish Road again became visible. One of the innumerable crosses was crowned with an indistinguishable coat of arms and an obliterated date. A grandee of Old Spain had died there....

Looking across the Plaza de la Constitucíon to the cathedral at Vera Cruz, where the Old Spanish Road commenced. West to Guadalajara it was once a broad highway; as the centuries wore on, it became in parts little better than a mule track.

Near La Quemada we met The Romantic Family. Here the road had sobered up from a debauch of tumbled stone that turned under the feet of the little white horse and it had become possible to trot once more. We crossed a stream in which the clear water gurgled around stepping-stones. There were trees overhead and a narrow, fertile valley, and dikes of stone ran up the rounded hills.

I call them The Romantic Family because they look precisely as *hacendados* should look, to be even with pictures and tradition. They were moving up the road at a slapping trot, as though they were anxious, as they might well be, to be safe at home before darkness fell. The two sons rode ahead, 18 years old at a venture—slender, spirited, aquiline—dressed in *charro* costumes of skin-tight trousers and silk shirts under short jackets. They sat on a pair of horses like men who from childhood had ridden rather than walked.

Each nipped his reins delicately in his left hand. His right hand rested on his thigh. Under the knee of each thrust the butt of a carbine. Pearl-handled pistols swung from gold-worked belts, and their spurs gave out a silver jingle in harmony with the tinkling of the bridle bits.

They looked at us politely from beneath the brims of their wide white sombreros, their lips moving in greeting. Behind them rode their sister—dark-eyed, arrogant, beautiful, and somehow appealing. One thought of her as returning from school in New York or Paris to a life of stagnation on a country ranch.

Her mule was an aristocrat, if the god of accuracy will turn a blind eye long enough to permit the concession of aristocracy to a mule. Head up, thin ears twitching, deer-like eyes, it trotted quite as easily as the horses of the cavaliers ahead. She glanced at us and glanced away. Truly there was nothing in our cavalcade to interest her—an American riding a small white horse which was being flicked by Tomaso and a sorrowing American afoot—but she might have looked again out of pure charity.

Then came the elderly mother, slender and dominant, her castellan's eye fierce upon the outlanders who had looked upon her daughter. She was sitting sidewise in a chair on a trotting mule, erect as a grenadier. She catalogued and dismissed us as we passed.

Two pack-mules, nervous and fast, and finally a pair of armed *mozos* bringing up the rear, with rifles and knives and pistols clanging and battering all over them, scowling at all they saw.

That family was a credit even to the Old Spanish Road. Adams climbed back on his horse out of sheer shame. Then he recanted loudly and climbed off again....

BUENOS AIRES TO WASHINGTON
BY HORSE
February 1929

AIMÉ-FÉLIX TSCHIFFELY (1895–1954)

A MAN BORN IN SWITZERLAND AND EDUCATED IN ENGLAND MIGHT seem an improbable candidate for achieving what some have called, without much exaggeration, "the greatest feat ever accomplished by man and horse." Yet A.-F. Tschiffely was always a bit unpredictable. He had been expelled from two schools for his impudent ways, then he up and decided to become a teacher himself. Wanderlust took him to Argentina, where for ten years he taught at a private academy outside Buenos Aires. There, surrounded by the vast stretches of the pampas, the tall, red-haired Tschiffely made increasingly long, solitary camping trips into the grasslands, accompanied only by dogs and horses, whose company he seemed to prefer to that of human beings.

By 1925, the teaching bit wasn't working any more. Perhaps it was boredom; perhaps the prospect of turning 30. Whatever it was, he bought two wild if aging criollo horses, broke them to the saddle, mounted up, and rode from Buenos Aires nearly 10,000 miles to Washington, D.C., an odyssey that lasted two and a half years. His way took him through 11 different countries, and as he crossed mountains, plains, deserts, and jungles his time and route were constrained only by the need to obtain fodder for his horses. Tschiffely himself lived off whatever came to hand: beans, bananas, yucca root stew, monkey meat, wild pig, boiled iguana—and occasionally, it seems, coca leaves.

Thus Aimé Tschiffely became a kind of modern Quixote, a legendary figure among those who love and live with horses. Even during the journey, newspapers everywhere were reporting on his progress. With popular interest riding high, the trip had hardly come to a close before he was writing an article on his experiences for NATIONAL GEOGRAPHIC, from which the following excerpts are taken.

THE CRIOLLO HORSE IS NOT BIG. HE STANDS ONLY BETWEEN 13$\frac{1}{2}$ and 14$\frac{1}{2}$ hands high. His chest is deep; his legs are stocky, and he is well muscled, hardy, and remarkably agile. But with the introduction of the English race horse and others into Argentina, and the consequent cross-breeding, the original criollo became scarce, being crowded out of the big cities and off the ranches.

So the famous riding exploits by pioneers and soldiers in the early days of Argentina, when the criollo pony was popular, came to be looked upon as fables and legendary feats, handed down from father to son beside the ranchhouse fireplace.

It was to find out for myself whether the criollo horse was ever really capable of the amazing feats of endurance claimed for him in Argentine song and story, as when San Martín marched his cavalry over the high Andes, that I undertook this ride. The whole project was absurd and impossible, my friends insisted; but I went ahead with my plans.

Where to get horses was my first problem; for, as I say, today the criollo is very rare. It was by a stroke of luck that I obtained my two mounts from a friend, a horse lover himself, who had just returned from an expedition into the interior of Patagonia, in southern Argentina, where he had met a Tehuelche Indian chief named Liem-Pichun (I Have Feathers). From him my friend bought 30 pure criollos and brought them back to Buenos Aires. From this herd we selected two for my long trip to the United States and broke them to the saddle....

On April 23, 1925, all plans made, I swung into the saddle and pointed my horses' noses toward the United States. Here began a journey that was to carry me through 11 different republics and was to consume nearly 900 days. Both of my horses were named after their colors. One, a pinto, called Manchado (Stained) in Argentina, had his name shortened to Mancha. The other, a dark buckskin, was Gadeado (Cat-colored)—in Argentina, shortened to Gato (Cat).

I rode one horse and carried my pack on the other. At first I had to lead the pack horse; later, when we came to be friends, halter ropes were discarded and we all stuck together. On the first stage of my ride the pack horse had little to carry, aside from a few clothes, some photographic material, and one or two books. Most of the way my literary companion was "Pickwick Papers."...

Heavy rain held me 12 days in Rosario [Argentina]. With clearing weather I pushed on toward the northwest. Here was a prairie land with monotonous roadways, straight as an arrow and reaching to far horizons; long lines of wire fence to right and left across a country flat as a billiard table, its skyline broken now and then by a ranchhouse, a tall steel windmill tower, or a solitary ombu, or elephant tree. Seas of corn, wheat, and oats, vast herds of fine fat cattle—a land of milk and honey, yet, to a horseback rider, tiresome in its sameness.

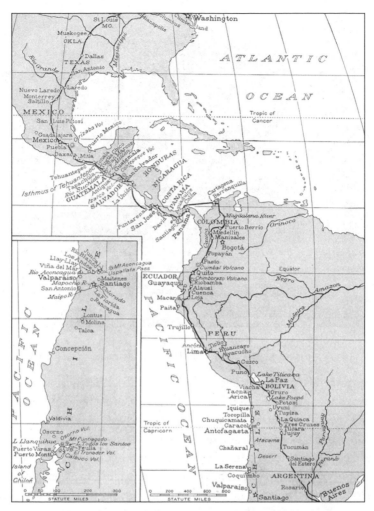

One long ride: A. F. Tschiffely's epic 9,600-mile journey by horseback
from Buenos Aires to Washington is traced across grassland, mountain,
and jungle from one continent to another.

Two hundred miles of this, and then the great salt beds of Santiago de
Estero. Here everything changed. Coarse shrubs and tall cactus took the
place of wheat and corn.

Here we met with fresh difficulty. I say "we," meaning the horses and
me. Among Argentinians one man riding a horse is "I"; accompanied by
two or more horses, the group is "we."...

Halfway up a valley called the Quebrada of Humahuaca [near the
Argentine-Bolivian border] are the prehistoric ruins of Tilcara, standing on
a high, steep mountain, overlooking the river far below. Strange and fasci-

High in the Andes of northwestern Argentina,
Tilcara offered not only panoramic views but also ruins of a pre-Incan civilization.

nating legends cling to this ancient town of the dead. Often treasure hunters have disturbed its slumbers in their arduous quests. Long ago, when the people of Tilcara buried a chief, they covered his face with a golden mask.

I wished if possible to obtain a memento of my visit, so I took a guide, climbed far up the steep trail to ancient ruins, and looked for graves.

Most of the natives hereabout are very superstitious. They will not go near the "dead towns," as they call the ruins; they say that disaster or death may overtake anyone who meddles with ancient graves. With them the fear of such misfortunes is usually above the lure of lost treasures....

In one of these graves, as I was scraping the sand away, I stuck an old thorn in my right hand. The next day blood poison set in. Soon my left hand and face were affected; then my right leg. The credulous Indians, of course, might well have said, "I told you so." There were no doctors, as we know them, within 120 miles—120 miles of terrible trails. Yet there was no alternative for me but to saddle up and make the fight. In pain and misery we passed Tres Cruces, 11,000 feet above sea level—cold, desolate, and wind-swept, surrounded by endless mountain chains.

Among dirty Indians I slept on the floors of little stone huts at night. Fodder for the horses hardly existed. I could only tie them to a rock and leave them out in the cold. I could not turn them loose because hereabout were poisonous weeds.

After six days of scrambling, stumbling, and falling over one of the worst trails imaginable, we finally arrived at the border town of La Quiaca.

Miserable as it is, it seemed a paradise to me then. Although I received medical treatment, my condition did not improve. The physician advised me to return to Buenos Aires at once. This I did not wish to do. I feared ridicule, or that people might think my illness a mere pretext for quitting the journey before striking the main range of the Andes. So, after a delay of four weeks, during which time my condition showed little improvement, I made up my mind to push on and trust to Providence.

I provided myself with guns, ammunition, suitable clothing, and equipment for the next stage of the trip. When I was ready I packed up and mounted, hoping for the best, but expecting the worst. Mountain sickness added to my discomfort. For a few days I bled much at the nose. My right leg was so swollen that I had to discard my boot and wear only a bandage, a thick woolen sock and a sandal. In this condition we pushed on.

In a mountain village I heard of an Indian *curandero*, or herb doctor, of local fame. I sent for him. Through an interpreter, he asked me many questions about my habits and general health. I answered these, and he started dosing me with medicines made out of herbs. In five days the swelling in my leg went down. My fever left me and the sore places on my foot dried up with amazing quickness. For his "professional service" the Indian charged me the equivalent of thirty cents in American money. When I gave him five times that much and a handful of coca leaves he was overwhelmed with surprise and gratitude....

One of the roughest and most tiring mountain stretches I climbed was that between Cuzco and Ayacucho, in Peru. Range after range had to be crossed, and in places the narrow, slippery trails were treacherous and dangerous. Yet these climbs had their compensations. From high up on cold peaks, amazing panoramas spread before me, with summits towering above mist and fog of tropical valleys.

Grand and inspiring as these vistas were, they hardly compensated for the interminable climbs, the painful zigzagging up and up, only to slip and stumble down again for miles into another hot valley, where screeching parrots seemed to protest my invasion and where swarms of gnats and mosquitoes harassed me and my horses.

Going down one such dizzy trail, my pack horse slipped over the edge. Luckily, he struck the only tree in the vicinity, as he slipped, and it broke his slide at the very brink of a deep precipice. With the help of friendly Indians, he was rescued after several arduous hours. Often the trail was so steep and crooked that my riding horse had all he could do to make it alone, without being bothered with a man on his back; so I walked, led one horse, and the other followed....

Because I knew full well what sandy, difficult desert coast lay between Lima and Ecuador, I took every precaution. My heavy mountain clothes I changed for light, cool things, and I modified my pack-saddle, as there would be no more climbing for a long time. I let the horses' manes and tails grow long, as a long mane protects the neck from the fierce sun, and a long tail fights off flies and other pests that tantalize a horse in the Tropics.

The first leg of my ride from Lima was to Ancón, a small seaside resort 22 miles away. Even before reaching it I got a good taste of sand and desert. It was near Ancón that the last battle of the Chile-Peruvian War was fought. Here dead soldiers were buried in the sand, often many in one grave. Winds now have uncovered these graves and skeletons lie scattered about with the hair still attached to many of the skulls....

On this march we had to traverse one desert which was 96 miles across. My horses achieved this almost incredible feat in 20 hours. Part of the time we traveled at night, with a full moon as guide. When I could, I led the march along the sea beach, where the sand was firm and easier for the horses than the soft, hot ground back from the shore, where the animals sank deep with every step.

Contrary to the practice of most travelers in dry regions, I carried no water. For my own use I had a flask filled with lemon juice, sugar, and salt, mixed. This concoction was very stimulating, but tasted so badly that it was never any temptation to drink it all at once. As for the horses, I calculated that the energy wasted by them in carrying water would be greater than the actual benefit derived from drinking it. So they could drink only when we came to water along the trail. I believe my theory was sound; with a light load, we gained in speed and thus came the sooner to where there was water. Only on rare occasions did the horses seem to suffer from excessive thirst....

A rough, mountainous, but much-traveled road connects Loja with Cuenca [Ecuador]; but only saddle and pack animals can travel over it. It is too narrow and rough for vehicles, so the considerable volume of goods and the passengers that move over it are all carried on pack animals. With loud cursing and shouting, the *arrieros*, or drivers, wind their blasphemous way uphill and down.

Regular steps, *camellones*, as they call them, are trodden into the steep trails, where the ground is soft. Because my horses took longer steps than the mules and burros that had made the camellones, they often stumbled at first. Later they got used to the short and tedious way of stepping between these holes worn by thousands of former hoofs.

In some stretches of this road the mud was so deep that the horses sank almost to their bellies. Sometimes they fell down, completely covering me as well as themselves with mud and slime.

Over this bad road, among other freight, heavy things like machinery, pianos, and billiard tables are transported. Articles too big to load on mules are set on a framework of poles and carried by a squad of Indians.

I also saw whole families moving. Children were carried in baskets, two of which were lashed together and swung across a mule. The rest of the family, with pots, pans, parrots, and cats, were all piled on the sore backs of other mules. Meaning no blasphemy, my conception of hell is the life of these so-called "friends of man," the pack animals of the Andes....

The stories I had heard about snakes must have been exaggerations. On the whole trip I had very little trouble with them. Possibly the heavy steps of the horses frightened these reptiles away before I reached them.... I did have trouble with vampire bats, however. In deep, warm valleys, from the north of Argentina to the north of Ecuador, the horses were often bitten at night by these blood-sucking creatures. In the morning blood would still be running from the wounds. It appears that animals do not feel these vampires at all, but the loss of blood makes them very thin if they are bitten several nights in succession. These pests can be discouraged by sprinkling strong Indian pepper on the horses and painting them over with creosote and camphor mixed with garlic....

There is a very good road into the interior of the Panama Republic as far as Santiago; but, unfortunately, in many places it was difficult to find fodder; also, the horses and I were at times literally covered with wood ticks and other insects. I found that a mixture of vaseline, sulphur, and camphor lightly applied to the coats of the horses, especially on the legs, gave excellent results, and I sponged myself every night with creosote diluted with water.

After Santiago, one travels over a narrow trail winding through forest and jungle. Twisted roots and mud made it very dangerous for the horses. They might easily have caught a foot in this veritable network of roots and broken a leg. So progress was slow. Mosquitoes added to our torment. But, as always on my long ride, things happened which took my mind off my troubles. In the jungle now I saw occasional herds of wild pigs, and chattering monkey troops up on the roof of the forest. Beautifully colored butterflies fluttered in and out, especially in forest clearings, and many hummingbirds darted among the flowers....

There is no need to describe my trip through the United States; most of my readers are far better acquainted with conditions here than I am; but it may be of interest to mention my impressions and some of the difficulties I met with—difficulties I never expected to find.

Concrete roads are excellent for motorcar traffic, but they are very tiring and hard on horses; and heavy motor traffic makes horseback riding anything but pleasant.

Today, also, the problem of stabling horses in American towns is not as simple as it once was. Stables have given way to garages in most villages and towns and sometimes even on farms....

I had originally intended to finish this long ride in New York City; but, after two fairly serious accidents, when I was run into by reckless automobile drivers, I decided it would be better to finish in Washington, having ridden from capital to capital. I did not feel it sane to expose my horses to further danger and possibly even to lose them. They had already more than proved their worth.

From Washington I shipped both of the horses to New York. Now, as I write this, they are comfortably housed there, awaiting shipment back to Buenos Aires, where they will enjoy a well-earned pension in a public park. While they live, people will point them out—famous specimens of the historic criollo breed—the only horses that ever traversed the Western Hemisphere from Patagonia to the Potomac.

The trip ended on September 21, 1928, when Tschiffely arrived in New York from Washington and, dressed as a gaucho, rode up Fifth Avenue with a police escort. In 1933 his book, Tschiffely's Journey, was published. It soon became a best-seller and led to many subsequent travels, often on horseback, his lance still tilted at the modern age. Gato and Mancha returned to an estancia on the Argentine pampas, where they lived out their remaining years, reverting once more to a wild and free existence.

PART TEN:

Lost worlds of the
Amazon and
orinoco

EXPLORING THE VALLEY OF
THE AMAZON IN A HYDROPLANE
April 1926

CAPT. ALBERT W. STEVENS (1886–1949)

IN 1914, WHEN THEODORE ROOSEVELT AND WHAT REMAINED OF HIS expedition arrived in Manáos, Brazil, they had just finished two harrowing months of exploring the River of Doubt, a previously unmapped tributary of the Amazon. The journey had virtually killed them; they were emaciated and fever-ridden; Roosevelt never really recovered. It was Amazon exploration the old-fashioned way— by dint of machete and gun and canoe, pushing through a vast, intricate braid of rivers, ensnarled by vegetation, tormented by insects, debilitated by disease.

Dr. Hamilton Rice, founder of Harvard's Institute of Geographical Exploration, had led expeditions into the Amazon since 1910, and reportedly knew "headwaters as some men know headwaiters." Having faced the same kind of challenges Roosevelt had, he was ready to embrace anything that might make the work more fruitful and less daunting. So in 1924, when he returned to Manáos, he had with him two technologies as yet untried in tropical exploration: a shortwave radio and a pontoon-mounted airplane.

As a result, the 1924–25 Rice Expedition became famous for its pioneering achievements. As the boats moved up the Negro and Blanco Rivers, the plane scouted ahead, soaring over and photographing in half an hour territory that would have taken two weeks to traverse. Flying the plane was Walter Hinton, 35, a legendary pilot who had made the first Atlantic crossing. Manning the Fairchild aerial camera was Capt. Albert W. Stevens, 38, of the U.S. Army Air Service, the foremost aerial photographer of his day and a man who lived life, so his friends said, at the highest pitch of "strenuous strenuosity." The reckless gleam in his blue eyes might make any companion pause.

Stevens—who routinely worked 48 hours straight—had learned aerial photography during World War I, directing his pilot to make insanely low passes over the German lines. An inventive genius, he had improved the photomapping equipment for the Amazon. Furthermore, he had a quirky nonchalance, evident in this expedition account that he wrote for NATIONAL GEOGRAPHIC.

OUR EXPEDITION STARTED OFF WITH A BANG—WITH SEVERAL BANGS. On the night following our arrival at Manáos a revolution broke out.

The city looked peaceful enough at the time and most of our party had gathered for dinner in the lobby of the Grand Hotel, when a troop of soldiers marched by, carrying rifles and dragging some light fieldpieces and machine guns. We thought twilight a queer time for a parade, but, after all, it was their country.... During the first course a regular Fourth of July celebration broke loose outside. Frightened hotel attendants slammed doors, banged down windows, and pulled the shades.

The unmistakable spatter and whistle of bullets in the near-by main street made it plain that the explosions were not harmless firecrackers. We were at the ringside of a full-fledged revolution! A hotel employee rushed to close the window by our table. We waved him away. Wild gesticulation and a flood of unintelligible Portuguese had no effect on our determination. For most of us this was our first revolution and we had no intention of missing any of it.

Through the window I looked out upon a street as empty as if a cholera epidemic had decimated the town. Everybody had shut up shop and pulled the curtains. Our hotel was just off the avenue which was being swept with intermittent squalls of musketry and machine-gun fire. Now and then a bullet would carom off a wall into our street.

While we debated whether or not to resume dinner, a man came running into the side street at full speed. He zigzagged back and forth, wildly searching for a place of refuge. The yellow light streaming out of our window caught his eye and he made for it. The window was high, but he threw himself against the wall. He could not reach the sill. Bull and I leaned out, the scared Brazilian gave a big jump, and we caught him by the wrists and pulled him to safety. He collapsed on the floor, his teeth chattering audibly....

The fireworks died down later in the evening, so we decided to venture out to look over the field of carnage. The streets were still deserted, but soon we came to a soldier on guard. Could we go on? He assured us we could. A few blocks farther along another guard let us pass into the public square where most of the fighting had occurred. The police barracks facing the square had been riddled by gunfire. The police had defended Manáos from the unpaid soldiers, but when their barracks fort became too hot all had fled save one—an old police colonel, who held out doggedly against the attackers. His return fire from the barracks finally ceased and the troops closed in.

The old colonel was found inside, down, but not disheartened. In picturesque Portuguese he told his captors that he would still be picking them off if he could, but four bullet wounds through the legs and arms

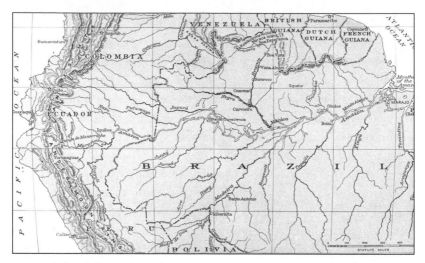

The braid of rivers that is the Amazon Basin: Manáos is located near the center, and from that city the Rice Expedition moved north up the Rios Negro and Blanco into unmapped forests near the Venezuelan border.

had laid him out. With true Latin spirit, the besiegers promptly embraced their prisoner, praised him to the skies for his gallant defense, and then packed him off to the hospital to be patched up.

Manáos had changed hands with not more than a dozen casualties.

One morning a few weeks after the revolution our steamer and hydroplane started up the Rio Negro, and for nine months thereafter we were in, beside, and over the world's greatest forest....

Below us a sea of green billowed away over the low hills to a slender blue-black shore of mountains far to the west. From our elevation the palms scattered through the forest below looked like hundreds of starfish at the bottom of an ocean, their lighter green focusing in strong contrast against the dark tones of the jungle.

At first we could pick out creeks, streams, and rivers, over a tremendous expanse of country, by the lines of thin white vapor hanging a thousand feet or less above them. Three-quarters of an hour later this vapor was burned off by the hot sun; but while it lasted it enabled me to get the compass bearings of many watercourses and to note them on our sketch maps....

It was not until January that we again took the air over the Uraricoera [a river to which the Parima is tributary] on what proved to be a most eventful trip. We swooped down to the surface of the river at a previously selected spot, called Kuleikuleima by the Indians and Kuleikuleima Rocks by us, intending to make further reconnaissance for the location of a supply base. Hinton made a perfect landing and was taxiing toward shore when suddenly there was the sound of splintering wood. The hydroplane careened, hung for a moment at a drunken angle, and then slowly righted herself. We had run onto a submerged pinnacle of rock!

The two layers of wood planking of the hull were only a quarter-inch thick; so that, weight for weight, the hydroplane's sheath was far thinner and more delicate than the shell of an egg. It seemed probable that the plane was mortally hurt, and even if we succeeded in getting the craft to shore, it would be many weeks before our companions could reach us.

It was a time for quick decision. Hinton risked tearing away part of the hull and gave the ship "the gun." We rose from the river and headed toward Boa Esperanca and safety, 150 miles away....

Twilight began to settle as we came to Maraca Island, and Hinton turned the plane full speed down the north *furo* (channel). Darkness comes quickly near the Equator, and we soon realized that if we did not come down in a few minutes we would be flying over a dead-black jungle without a landmark to guide us.

With the prospect of a crash among the trees before us, there was no alternative but to descend. Three small islands came into view, the middle one flanked by a sand bar, and we decided this was the safest place to beach the plane. Down we dived to the river's surface, Hinton driving the plane as high up on the sand as possible.

When the plane came to rest, we climbed out of the cockpit to explore the jungle isle where we were to establish squatter sovereignty for eleven days.

Our "Robinson Crusoe Island" was a mile long and a quarter mile wide, heavily forested with a great variety of trees, and apparently uninhabited. Choosing the most likely spot for a camp, we stretched a cord between two trees for a ridge pole and suspended a canvas over it to make a shelter. Under this we hung our hammocks; for, like true sailors of the sea, navigators of the green jungle always sleep in hammocks. They are the universal Amazon bed for a very obvious reason—only a limited number of crawling insects can walk the two supporting tight ropes in one night. It is a problem of traffic. And we had learned that by creosoting the ropes we could set a "stop" signal on the crawlers.

The first night passed uneventfully, and next morning we started work on the hydroplane. With marine glue, canvas, and mahogany strips, which we always carried in the tail section, we were able to patch up the broken hull, for the damage was not serious. The big difficulty lay in getting the plane into the water again, for the river's level unfortunately had dropped while we were at work. Two men could not possibly move the plane; so there was nothing to do but cool our heels until the river should rise again.

About the middle of the third night on our jungle isle I was awakened by a hoarse whisper from Hinton: "Steve, wake up."

"What's the matter?"

"Something's prowling around camp. Sounds like a great big animal."

Carrunch! Walter was right! A ponderous, a loud, a threatening crunch! Only a fitful light came from our camp fire, which we kept going all night to make the island seem less lonely.

Crunch! Crunch! Crunch!

"Sounds like an elephant," whispered Walter, and I agreed. By light of day both of us knew that elephants are not likely to be roaming about the Amazon Basin; but this was midnight, and big branches were breaking and trees were cracking on the other side of that fire!

We lay still for ages—listening. Then a strange swishing sound could be distinctly heard, as if some large creature were moving through the long grass. Surely no elephant would make a sound like that. It must be an alligator! I remarked as much to Hinton. How far can an alligator reach with his jaws? The disquieting thought spurred me to action. I suggested that we get up and cinch our hammocks farther off the ground.

This we did, and, once on our feet, both courage and curiosity began to assert themselves. I dug out my flashlight and a revolver too small to be useful. Meanwhile a medley of crunching, snapping, and swishing sounds continued to break the stillness of the night. Neither of us was inclined to wait passively to be devoured by some unknown beast, so we decided to meet the monster. Armed additionally with an ax and a machete, we wormed our way toward the noise. I turned the flashlight into the black jungle. We could see nothing, but the sounds grew closer.

All at once a terrific crash resounded in the dark. Trees shivered, limbs gave way, and some large animal made off into the forest at full speed, bumping trees and breaking things right and left in its mad flight. For some time we could hear it tearing through the jungle....

By morning light we examined the scene of our night's adventure and, finding hoofprints much like those of a cow, we came to the conclusion that all the commotion had been caused by a tapir, that queer but harmless animal, with both swinish and bovine characteristics, the largest quadruped of the Amazon jungles, sometimes weighing as much as 500 pounds....

As the cook stands by appraisingly, a 500-pound tapir is brought into camp.
The expedition's principal source of food—and the "elephant" that seemingly menaced Stevens
and Hinton—the harmless tapir, once abundant, is increasingly scarce today.

One night Hinton hung his shirt up on a fish line. The next morning when he started to put the garment on it nearly fell to pieces in his hands, being mostly holes. Investigation showed that during the night a labor battalion of ants had gone up and down the line like a file of coolie coal-passers, cutting the shirt to pieces bit by bit.

Nor was this our only experience with ants. There are ants everywhere in the Amazon, and all kinds of ants—black ants, red ants, and white ants, great ants and tiny ants. They get into everything and eat almost anything. They boarded our plane by the hundreds and flew as stowaways, but fortunately the paint of the wings and hull was not to their taste.

Ants appear in one's food always, whether in settlements or in camp. Often one puts a spoonful of native sugar into his cup, skims off the ants from the surface of a little hot water poured in to dissolve the sugar, and then adds coffee. This method seldom removes all the ants, but after the coffee is added they are not readily seen!

One of the most dreaded insects in the Amazon Valley is the large *tucandeira* ant, whose sting is excessively irritating. Some Indians use it to test the manhood of their boys. When a youth reaches a certain age he must put his arms into a hollow bamboo containing a colony of the insects, and if he endures the grueling test without flinching he is received into the tribe as a man—a quick and certain method of assaying courage.

After three days of rain, on the tenth day of our exile on the island, the river rose and, much to our relief, floated the hydroplane again....

After rejoining the expedition at Boa Esperanca, Stevens and Hinton continued making exploratory flights, including on into the Parima canyon, where they were real pioneers.

The rushing waters swept under us viciously, the hills closed in, and the palm trees began to disappear, for the altitude changed the climate; but the jungle still stretched on all sides, muffling the hills and sometimes even the narrowing rapids in green. We discerned many falls in the river and put them on our sketches for the guidance of Dr. Rice's party.

The river drops 400 feet in 4 miles in one place. High waterfalls were discovered on the short tributaries coming off the mountain slopes. In the midst of the green we would see a thread of silver water, spun from a source lost in the forest, falling over a sheer cliff into an inkwell of blackness hundreds of feet below...

Over the Indian camp sites on the upper stretches of the river we released parachutes, to which were attached beads and trinkets of various kinds. These gifts were peace offerings to show the friendliness of Dr. Rice's party, which was to advance into this country later. None of the ground party was ever molested; so the parachutes may have served a useful purpose.

By this time our gasoline was nearly half used up, so we turned downstream through our newly discovered country. The situation had its ironic side. Here we were, the first white men who had ever penetrated into this corner of the Amazon Valley, discoverers on an old sphere that has been pretty well discovered, charted, and nailed down. Yet we couldn't set foot on our land nor swim in our river. Our eyes were privileged to see magnificent falls, but the swift product of our speedy age whisked us away from the cataracts after a moment's contemplation. From an elevation of 6,000 feet we greeted the inhabitants of this new country with parachutes!

The report we brought back and the maps and photographs of the river were invaluable to the ground party, but obviously the story of De Soto, La Salle, or any of the early explorers would provide not nearly such rich reading today if they had used airplanes....

A JOURNEY BY JUNGLE RIVERS TO THE HOME OF THE COCK-OF-THE ROCK

November 1933

ERNEST G. HOLT

In 1920, when Col. Percy Fawcett, most romantic and deluded of British explorers, returned to seek legendary lost cities deep in the Amazon, he was accompanied by a young American he had met by chance in Rio de Janeiro. Fawcett looked on Ernest G. Holt with a slightly contemptuous eye, yet the pair spent months together chasing will-of-the-wisps in Brazil's remote interior. Holt later wrote that Fawcett "played godfather at my baptism into wilderness exploration." He could not have known it then, but he would be the last man to emerge from a Fawcett expedition alive.

Holt was a first-class ornithologist, but he seemed unable to hold any job for long. When he met Fawcett, he was with the Standard Oil Company; later, in 1925, when the colonel disappeared for good in the Xingú River region, Holt was staff ornithologist with the Carnegie Museum in Pittsburgh. Eventually he would bounce from one conservation-related post to another, along the way befriending Aldo Leopold, a leading light of the 20th-century conservation movement.

In 1930–31, Holt led a ten-month expedition to the highlands along the Amazon-Orinoco watershed, a region almost entirely unknown zoologically. In the wake of the Brazil-Venezuela Boundary Commission, which was surveying the shared border, Holt's party collected thousands of specimens, mostly birds, including some species new to science. He was assisted by Charles Agostini of the Pittsburgh Museum and Emmett R. Blake, a graduate student at the University of Pittsburgh, who also became a famous field ornithologist. The expedition spent as much time on the water as in the forest, voyaging up the Amazon and through a tangled skein of tributary rivers before departing down the Orinoco.

If each traveler to the Amazon is impressed according to mood, as Holt observes in his November 1933 NATIONAL GEOGRAPHIC article, then Holt must have been experiencing a lonely, reflective melancholy, for here water and forest are omnipresent and irresistible, dark and fathomless as night.

OUR BIG FREIGHTER HAD WON HER GAME OF HIDE-AND-SEEK WITH a West Indian hurricane, and now, 13 days out of Jacksonville, she stood against a sullen brown flood from the southwest. She had steamed against it all day long, alone except for occasional native boats, whose sails of brown, blue, or red gave promise of a colorful picture to come. Over the starboard rail there was nothing but muddy sea and night's darker canopy; on the port beam, only a low black line along the horizon. Then the quartermaster put over the helm, the ship slipped to leeward of the end of the black line—and we caught our breath.

The familiar smell of salt spray was gone from the easterly trades. In its stead came a delicate perfume, hauntingly sweet, the entrancing odor of wet earth, of leaves, of blossoms unseen; while above the low black line rose a dull-red three-quarter moon etched with a fretwork of branches. Another turn and the electric lights of Pará (Belém) blinked through the darkness; a startling rattle of anchor chain, a splash, and we had arrived in Brazil....

"There are few situations more intriguing to the traveler," writes another who has ridden at anchor here, "than to be lying at midnight off Nossa Senhora de Belém do Grao Pará.

"Blackness toward the west, and silence. How it calls to the heart of a wanderer! Naked Indians on the shores of the Xingú. Alligators basking in the mud. Birds of gorgeous plumage and strange fruits... It pulls with the force of a primal passion."

Since 1500, when Pinzón filled his casks from a sea of sweet water while yet no landfall was made, and especially since 1543, when Orellana returned to Spain to spread tall stories of female warriors and a golden city of Manoa, this mightiest of rivers had kindled imagination.

A stream that opens its mouth so wide that the Thames, with all the kinks ironed out, would barely reach from lip to lip, gargles an island larger than the Kingdom of Denmark, and every second spews forth 4,000,000 cubic feet of muddy water to stain the ocean for 600 miles, still quickens the pulse. O Rio Mar, the Brazilians call it, the River Sea....

When the day is done, the Pará merchant pulls down the rolled iron shutters of his shop, eludes his business cares in the dark, narrow streets down town, and slips away to the gay neighborhood of the Grande Hotel. Here the young people promenade in the park while the band plays, or meet for the cinema. It is here, too, that one finds the *Americanos*, gathered about little spider-legged tables on the sidewalk beneath fine old mango trees.

But it was not for us to drop into these delightful ways of life. We docked at Pará on a Saturday, but, thanks to the kind offices of United States Consul George E. Seltzer, our supplies and equipment were soon passed through the customs, and we sailed for Manáos next morning on the *Belém*, of the Amazon River Steam Navigation Company. A big, twin-screw triple-decker she was, blunt-nosed and square of stern, perfectly designed in the Netherlands for the comfort of the Amazon traveler. A crowd packed her decks when we came aboard; but a blast from the whistle started an epidemic of back-patting, some tears, and a general rush for the gangplank; and when the confusion subsided we were left with a mere handful of passengers. Here, as at home, the *bon voyage* is a fetish, though with more reason in a region where all travel is by water and cities are days instead of hours apart—where the journey from Pará to Manáos, for example, requires more time than the passage of the North Atlantic....

Just before sunset we entered Breves Strait, one of numerous deep, narrow, winding channels through which the tide ebbs and flows between the Pará estuary and the Amazon proper, which dissect the terrain into a maze of jungle islands. Here we tied up at a small place to take wood for the boilers.

So insatiable are these iron maws that wood stations have become typical institutions of the low country and account for most of the steamer's stops during the first two days. For hour after hour, sometimes far into the night, men and boys with coppery torsos gleaming with sweat run across the plank in endless line to dump 10-stick loads with resounding thumps on the steel deck....

If one boat consumes so much wood, what of the hundreds that have plied this route since the first steamer paddled the Amazon in 1852? Yet clearings, even about the wood stations themselves, make scarcely a break in the green walls that spring from the very water. And the huts of thatch that straggle along the channels stand on piles in the river's edge, as if refused a land hold by the jealous forest. Nature tolerates no bare ground.

Mangroves persist for a time, alternating with rank beds of giant arums and other aquatic plants to form marginal tangles beloved of the anachronous hoatzin. Behind them rise ranks of the graceful assai or the indispensable *miriti* palm, sometimes in immense stands; yet both are but components of a forest of amazing complexity—a forest of figs, Cecropias, rubber trees, hardwoods of a hundred species; little trees and big, whose white boles shine through enmeshing lianas like bleached skeletons entangled in gallows ropes.

Towering above them all, giant Ceibas fling orchid-bejeweled arms wide to the sun. They are monarchs among trees, but, like all the rest, slaves to the vine...

No matter how many travel books he may read, the newcomer to the Amazon is never prepared for the reality. He is impressed according to mood. He may turn his gaze ahead to a distant horizon with no thin hazy line of shore intervening between blue and brown, and let his imagination wander the width of the continent, to where the river takes its source in Andean snow within sight of the Pacific; or he may look into its depths and see only mud. My own impressions are of too much water, too much food, languorous weather, and the inevitable result of the combination. But we never missed the cool evenings on the top deck, or the splendor of sunsets such as only tropics—and deserts—produce.

One does miss the huge snakes, jaguars, monkeys, and brilliant-plumaged birds of which he has read so much. Animals in a forest a mile away might as well be on the moon! In the narrow channels and by-passes one hears the raucous screams of parrots and macaws, but unless the birds happen to fly overhead he sees nothing. And were he to go ashore, the wild creatures would still elude him unless he knew where and how to look—that is, all save the insects! Even the giant waterlilies, with leaves like 8-foot platters, contrive to hide themselves in secluded lagoons....

The Boundary Commission assembled at Manáos, whereupon Holt and party transferred to a small launch and joined the flotilla making its way up the Rio Negro to its confluence with the Rio Cauabury, where the island of Jerusalem served as a base. From there they continued upstream to the tiny Rio Maturacá, near where the boundary was to be run along the crests of the Cordilheira massif.

The Maturacá is no more than a creek, a lowland stream meandering aimlessly between the foothills of the Cordilheira and some outlying spurs. The narrow channel is a succession of hairpin turns, shallows, deep pools, and small but stiff rapids, so choked with logs and fallen branches that it was necessary to keep a gang of axmen ahead of the boats.

If on the Cauabury we had voyaged overland, here we navigated the woods! Overhead the tree tops almost meet, and huge moss-covered stones replace the naked boulders of the sunny Cauabury. But the gloom gave immediate respite from the clouds of piums [bloodsucking gnats] that had pursued us all the way from Jerusalem. Just within the mouth of the Maturacá we came upon the only sign of wild Indians found on the trip—an old bridge of saplings thrown across the stream.

Following my custom of making the most of the lunch stop, I went

*Portrait of an expedition leader: In an improvised jungle lab, Ernest Holt
measures birds collected along the Brazil-Venezuela frontier
prior to labeling them for the Smithsonian's Natural History Museum.*

ashore at noon one day to hunt in the fine forest of the right bank. Soon I located one of those mixed bands of birds whose erratic presence constitutes such a contrast to the normal stillness of the tropical forest and gave my full attention to keeping it in sight, following it up quickly as soon as the specimens shot could be retrieved.

When at length I had secured as many birds as could well be prepared during the remainder of the day, I started back to the boat—and suddenly realized that I did not know which way to go.

For one of long woods experience to get lost in broad daylight was absurd, but the situation was not funny then. Though the low terrain was crisscrossed with streams, I felt that I could recognize the Maturacá all right, but it was so crooked that there was no assurance of reaching it by walking in any direction other than exactly that whence I had come. And should I stand again on its banks, which way should I turn? There might be ax marks to indicate the passing of the Commission; there might not. But what would tell me whether our own boat lay upstream or down? And if I failed to find the right river, what then? The nearest *caboclo* house was at least 50 miles away—a journey impossible of accomplishment through a pathless, swampy jungle, even if I had had a compass to guide me, which I had not. The Commission, I was sure, had long since moved on; and, having left no broken twigs along my trail, I knew that my own small party could never track me.

. I had no matches with which to raise a smoke, even could it have been seen. I did fire a signal with my gun, but knew as I did so that I was too deep in the forest to be heard.

As I quartered back and forth in an effort to pick up my trail, I found myself increasing my pace, and realized that my breath was coming faster and faster, and my mouth getting dry. To avoid panic, I forced myself to sit down.

I detail this for the benefit of those who may never have paused to consider what it means to be lost, with no traffic policeman handy to direct the way. The conventional terrors of the jungle—ferocious wild beasts, huge snakes darting swiftly from ambush to crush out one's life in their relentless coils or to deal a slower, more horrible death by poison—meant nothing to me, for I knew them to be dangerous only in the imagination of fanciful writers.

But I also knew what a cold and cheerless bed the sodden forest floor would make. I knew the heartbreak of trying to force a way through tangled jungle with hunger gnawing at one's stomach, and the growing weariness that comes when one no longer feels the pain. I knew as utterly vain the popular idea that the tropical forest abounds with edible fruits, ready to be plucked by the hungry. Fear of the Macús never crossed my mind. Death by their swift arrows would be like a sudden accident, nothing to contemplate with dread. But to starve, to become gradually weaker until not strength enough remains to brush the ants from one's mouth and eyes—panic lies on the road of such thought.

Of course, I ultimately found my way back to the river, recognized a spot we had passed that morning, and followed up the stream until I reached the boat. There were no rents in my clothing, no telltale scratches on my hands and face, and I threw down my bag of birds with a nonchalance that fooled even our keen-eyed Indians. I hope they never learn to read....

The Commission's task was to locate the key hill from which the international boundary follows the watershed of the Cordilheira, then survey and mark the divide. To determine where it lay, among the maze of detached peaks, hills, and separate mountains springing from a seemingly level plain, was indeed an undertaking. Exploring parties were immediately sent out to open trails to the Cordilheira, and we, of course, were right at their heels. But it was not until the engineers had felled the trees on a mountain top to set up their astrolabes that we got any conception of the terrain.

Stretching away interminably to the northeast, the rugged peaks and shoulders of the Cordilheira rose in rank after rank until lost on the horizon under masses of cloud, an unknown land for hundreds of miles. In the opposite direction, a flat-topped mountain and a number of hills and ridges lay here and there, as if thrown from the Cordilheira like fragments from a shattered column.

Fifty miles to the northwest the granite boss of the Piedra del Cucuy rose to accentuate a limitless plain. But most impressive of all was the vast, unbroken blanket of forest extending in every direction as far as the eye could reach—and beyond—obliterating every feature save the mountains, humped beneath it like brickbats under a carpet.

On my very first climb to the engineers' lookout I got my biggest thrill of the expedition. I had bagged a yellow-and-black tropical finch (named *canadensis* by some misguided ornithologist) and was stalking a big, slate-colored grosbeak with coral-red bill when sheer amazement froze me in my tracks. But snapshooting at strange things had made my trigger finger automatic, and as the crash of my gun startled me back to my senses, an unbelievable creature fell to the ground. I hesitated, hardly daring believe that an ambition of twelve years had come so suddenly to fruition, then stopped to pick up the most beautiful bird in the world. I had shot the cock-of-the-rock, a marvelous fowl resplendent in a coat of flame, with a double crest sweeping from tip of bill to occiput, like the ridge of a Roman helmet. That is, the male is so colored. The female is demure and brown and its crest is reduced to a mere suggestion of its mate's.

It is a shy bird and has chosen for its haunts the occasional isolated hills and the lower mountain slopes of the Guiana highlands—a region little disturbed by white men and only thinly populated by Indians. We obtained several additional specimens, and found one nest, very much like a robin's, fastened to the bare face of a huge split boulder; but it was empty....

It is good management for an expedition to obtain locally as much as possible of its food supplies. In Amazonia, therefore, farinha at once becomes a staple to rank with beans and rice, and monkey meat is accepted as a matter of course. But ... we were majoring in ornithology, so to speak, and rare blends of parrot and toucan, or a tinamou stew flavored with a dash of ant-thrush, naturally became the order of the day. In fact, the body of almost any bird large enough to yield a morsel of food found its way into the pot as soon as its skin was preserved, for we utilized as fully as possible everything collected....

One day a hunter brought in a tiger cat [jaguarundi], a handsome little jungle animal, that fell to Agostini to prepare. Now, when I skin a specimen and perforce inhale odors that might well give point to some

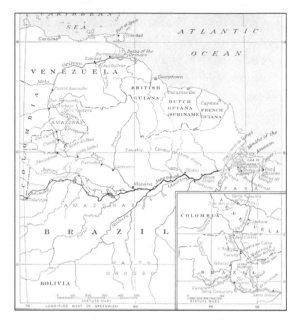

After arriving in Pará, Brazil (right), Holt's expedition proceeded by steamer to Manàos, then north up the Rio Negro, through a skein of jungle rivers, to the Orinoco (upper left), collecting natural history specimens along the way.

modern advertisements, my thoughts seldom dwell on the next meal; least of all do they picture the carcass before me as it might appear on the dinner table. But evidently Agostini was intrigued by the animal's firm white flesh, and much to my amazement suggested that we have it for dinner. My refusal was prompt and unequivocal. Nevertheless he wheedled until I gave in. But our Brazilian cook almost mutinied. The day was a busy one, and we were all hungry when at dinner the cook served an enticing sauté. I had eaten to repletion when I remembered the cat!

Revenge was both sure and swift. We enjoyed the luxury of a mud hut at Sao Gabriel, and I had been interestedly watching some Indian children under my window catch giant sauba ants as they issued from their burrows to launch upon their nuptial flight, and drop them into a squirming mass in an earthen pot. Either embarrassed by my question, or not understanding it, the children told me that the ants were to be used for fish bait, and disappeared. Not long after, an Indian entered and, with the hospitality of the true woodsman, proffered a calabash of food. I smilingly accepted—to find the calabash half filled with fried ants! The wings were gone, but every leg was intact.

Our Indian neighbor out of the kindness of his heart had brought us a delicacy, so it must be eaten. What could be more appropriate than that my experimentally inclined assistants should enjoy a new dish? In fact, I insisted that they do so. Each put a single sauba—an enormous thing more than an inch long—gingerly into his mouth and began to chew. Agostini chewed slowly and meditatively, and, finally, removing the debris and injecting a judicial tone into his voice, said: "It might be all right, but it's just a trifle too acid to suit my taste." Blake, on the other hand, unceremoniously spat forth a tangled mass of legs and chiton and exploded, "Well, I'll be honest about it, it's just too much ant for me!"....

Ultimately we had reached Ciudad Bolívar, on the lower Orinoco, and, with our specimens safely stored in the hold, we were steaming downstream toward Port-of-Spain and home.

Entering one of the mouths of the Amazon, we had voyaged 3,000 miles of continuous inland waterways through the greatest jungle on earth, and would soon depart by one of the 36 mouths of the Orinoco.

We had traversed the length of that strange artery, the Casiquiare Canal, that links the Amazon and the Orinoco like Siamese twins and makes the Guiana highlands the largest island on earth save Greenland. We had stood upon rain-drenched mountains where never white foot had trod. Now we were leaving it all.

The other passengers had gone to bed. Only we three remained on the darkened deck to stare over the rail into the night, reluctant to miss even the remnant of the river on which we had journeyed so long.

But there was little our eyes could see. No moon rode the heavens, and even the stars, usually so near and so lustrous in these tropic skies, were now obliterated by a pall of smoke drifting seaward from the annual burning of the delta plantations. Over the sides was only blackness; straight ahead, only the dull silver of the channel, flanked by two inky lines of half-submerged mangroves. The immaculate egrets and flashing scarlet ibises, like most of the passengers, were asleep, and the watch was kept by the frogs and caymans, and the hordes of fiddler crabs swarming over the mangrove roots.

Noiselessly the steamer swept on. Out past the farthest point attained by the boldest of the mangroves, wading tiptoe against the tide, she slipped from the Orinoco, to be met instantly by angry whitecaps. Flat of bottom and wide of beam, she began to pitch and heave like something possessed, and the cargo of steers, thoroughly frightened, set up a terrible bawling, as if suddenly sensing their imminent doom in the slaughter pens of Trinidad.

The low fringe of mangroves receded into the general blackness of the tropic night, and, our last tie severed, we turned sadly into our bunks.

JUNGLE JOURNEY TO THE WORLD'S HIGHEST WATERFALL
November 1949

RUTH ROBERTSON (1905–98)

RUTH ROBERTSON LEARNED AS A WORLD WAR II CORRESPONDENT in Alaska that frontier regions made for good stories. So given a chance to profile American pilots in Venezuela, Robertson quit a dead-end job with the New York Herald Tribune and moved to Caracas. Most Americans, she realized, knew little or nothing about Venezuela, so she might eke out a living by selling stories from there. It was frontier, too: five hundred miles south of Caracas lay the largely unexplored Gran Sabana, cloaked in tropical forest except where huge, mist-wreathed mesas soared to over 8,000 feet, crowned by plateaus that inspired Sir Arthur Conan Doyle's The Lost World, where they were home to remnant populations of dinosaurs and cavemen.

Soon Robertson heard tales of a mile-high waterfall cascading off a cliff somewhere in that lost world. Many people discounted the stories, but then she met legendary bush pilot Jimmy Angel, who told her how, while flying on a gold-prospecting mission, he had seen a magnificent waterfall, tumbling over the rim of a vast tableland into a mysterious canyon. Her photojournalistic instincts perked up, but not until she herself, from the window of a little plane, glimpsed the falling silver ribbon dissolve into rainbow-hued mist did she resolve to photograph it—only not from above, "looking condescendingly down," but rather from below.

Thus Ruth Agnes McCall Robertson of Peoria—barely five feet tall, 44 years old, dark hair streaked with silver—planned and led the first expedition to the foot of Angel Falls and proved it to be the highest waterfall in the world. She set off in April 1949, accompanied by Alejandro Laime, a guide who had recon-noitered part of the route; Enrique Gómez, a government-supplied radio operator; Ernest Knee, a movie cameraman; Perry Lowrey, a surveyor; and ten Pemon Indians who held Auyán-tepuí—Devil Mountain, the massif from which the falls cascade—in such awe that they had never penetrated the Churún River canyon below. As this excerpt opens, the expedition, having already paddled up the river, is breaking trail to the foot of the falls.

THE SECOND DAY ON THE TRAIL LEFT ME INEXPRESSIBLY WEARY. It seemed I just couldn't lift myself and light backpack over one more log or rock. The rains stopped for a while, and the sun filtered through the jungle in little cracks here and there. The heat was oppressive. I found that oftener and oftener I had to stop for a breathing spell.

We crossed innumerable streams fed from the many waterfalls off the canyon walls. The water from these streams was icy and sweet and a little flat-tasting, but at the moment of a rest stop along the trail no nectar could have tasted better.

Our lunch stop was in a rock shelter which seemed to be some animal's also. At least it was a dry place. I wrung my socks out and hung them over a bush in one of the rare sunny spots, where they steamed but did not dry. Laime insisted I take some sugar, and I did, hoping to derive some energy from it.

Laime was getting discouraged by our slow progress. He himself was a human dynamo. His energy never seemed to let up, and at the end of a day he was still fresh.

We knew that we were getting close to our goal, because the canyon walls on both sides were narrowing. And once, in a clearing, I could see a rounded curve ahead that I recognized from the aerial photographs I had taken of the falls. In distance it couldn't have been very far, but by trail it was a tortuously slow process making our way over centuries of deadfall and landslides. Enrique and I exchanged private confidences that day and decided that the next time we made a trip into this canyon it would be over a concrete highway!

And then, just when it seemed I could not go another step, a shout went up ahead. The first view of the falls!

We had rounded the curve and there, in the distance, was our goal. There's no describing what it did to our spirits. We didn't have a front view, but rather a profile from the northeast side, and an outcropping of rock hid the lower part from view. Nevertheless, the sight was stunning. Now we knew we could actually get there. We were all for going closer, but Laime wisely advised us to make camp and scout ahead the next day to see if there was a better place for the camp.

Little was done the rest of that afternoon. It was too wonderful to walk out on the rocks of the Churún and stand and gaze at the majestic sight, so different from the 10-second views I had had from a plane.

The Indians set to work making another hut for the night. A welcome sound, the ringing of their machetes, the pounding of poles in soft earth, and the whack-whack as they cut down palms and other big leaves for a roof. Soon we would have a fire and I could dry my clothing.

I was stiff and sore from the long trek. Moreover, I was bruised and scratched, and my slacks were torn in a dozen places and filthy from scooting over rotten logs and tumbling headfirst into leaf mold.

Rafael, our Indian, who wore nothing but a bright-red loincloth, came to me just after we arrived with a bad slash in the bottom of his foot. I put sulfa cream in the wound and Perry taped it tightly. The Indian woman, too, came with smaller cuts on her bare feet, and we gave her the same treatment.

For all our weariness we stayed up late that night. We took our cups of tea from the campfire and went to sit on rocks by the water. As if on cue, an orange full moon came up about 7 and turned the dark mass of the canyon wall into half-light, with the falls a shimmering silver streak down the middle. Whatever hardships we had endured on the trip this particular moment seemed to make worth while. Perry said we were about two miles away from the falls. Enrique sent out our message that night, telling those who were listening that we were in sight of our goal.

It was noon on May 12 when I finally climbed the last rocks of the promontory in front of the base of Angel Falls.

For hours we had been struggling over tremendous rocks which had fallen off the top, almost a mile above us. We could hear the roar of the falls, but could see nothing because of the jungle growth.

Finally, around 11, I caught a glimpse of the top of the falls pouring off near the rim. I plunged into the dense growth again and climbed upward in that direction.

The rock promontory in front of the base of the falls seemed to be made solely to observe the magnificent spectacle before us. Plunging through jagged rocks a few feet below the canyon rim, more than half a mile in the first unbroken drop, roared the falls. They deafened every other sound, and whirled in spirals as the wind caught them and sent them out over the valley below. Often they swirled out to the rocks we were sitting on and drenched us.

Behind the waterfall is a tremendous amphitheater, providing a spectacle beyond description. So far as I can learn, we were the first to see this sight from the promontory. The rocks overlooked not only the falls but the whole valley up which we had come. We could see the deeper green winding line of the Churún and even the rocky little beach about two miles back where we had made our camp.

After one quick look Perry hurried off to begin the job of measuring the falls. Laime disappeared to help Perry in finding spots for the base

Angel Falls, the world's highest waterfall, tumbles 3,212 feet from the edge of a flat-topped mesa, Auyan-tepui, cloaked in jungle and located so deep in the Venezuelan hinterland that no expedition made its way to the foot of the falls until 1949.

line. I sat fascinated on the rock. Old Reya sat cross-legged nearby, his impassive face bent over a reed mat he was making for me.

Before we had taken off from camp that morning, the Indians had come to me all painted with red paste. They brought a small piece of it and a mirror over to me and asked if I would also "make myself invisible to the spirits." Obligingly I had painted circles and dashes over my face.

Finally we took leave of our box seat and headed down in another direction to explore the secondary falls and the small river which joins them to the Churún....

"Anybody superstitious?" Perry wanted to know the next morning. It was Friday, May 13. Both Perry and Laime set off early on the surveying job with enough Indians to cut a base line for his chain tape. Since it looked too rainy for pictures when they took off, I dawdled around camp,

Night in the jungle: The campfire was always welcome after long, rain-soaked days of clambering through wet vegetation. Expedition members, basking in its glow, could dry their shoes and wait for coffee to boil.

luxuriating in the realization that we had achieved our goal. With that achievement there had come a letdown and, after breakfast, for the first time I went back to my hammock for another couple of hours.

Friday the 13th brought only two untoward incidents. A large stinging ant climbed on one of my socks, but I got it off without getting bitten. At noon, a huge tarantula crawled to within striking distance of Enrique as he sat on the ground eating. Laime and I saw the horrid thing at the same time as it came out of the jungle and headed rapidly toward Enrique to get up. Enrique literally rose from the ground in one swoop, never spilling a drop of his soup. After Laime had killed the tarantula with a stick from the campfire, Enrique put aside his soup. He'd lost his appetite, and I didn't blame him. I made a mental note to stop wearing string sandals around the camp.

There was one more day's work for Perry, measuring angles from every conceivable spot in the canyon floor. It was ticklish business, wading the swift Churún to get to the opposite side with his heavy theodolite and all the other necessary instruments.

Messages of congratulation came in on the morning broadcast time. We sent out word to have the little airplane ready at the advanced airstrip within two days. More than ever I realized how valuable to the success of the expedition was the radio equipment, which could make such arrangements from as isolated a spot as this "lost world."

On Sunday, May 15, we were up at 5 and ready for the trek out of the canyon. It was Ernie's birthday. While the Indians and Laime were breaking camp and packing everything in the backpacks, I decided on the plan I'd made the day before. I told Laime I was going on ahead alone. I explained that this would give me a head start.

I left camp blithely at 6, sure in the knowledge that the rest of the group would be along within a few minutes. The trail was not too difficult to follow, and the few times I did get lost for a moment I would simply make a small circle and find the blazed bushes. I had not been out more than half an hour, however, when the realization of being alone in the jungle descended on me with crushing force. The light drizzle of rain and wet leaves had me soaked to the skin.

How weird the jungle seems when there is no one else around! The sudden sounds and crackles; the momentary terror at passing a lair where animals have bedded down; the unmistakable odor. I wondered if the beasts were still watching me through the underbrush. I hesitated to go forward, and I didn't want to go back to join the group that *must* be somewhere behind.

I wondered whatever in the world had possessed me to start out without a machete or a knife or *something!* Finally, reasoning overcame terror. Nothing visible moved except a bird resembling a chicken and a few lizards.

Laime and Enrique caught up with me a little after 8. We were determined to make the main camp in one day, but Laime was frankly gloomy at the prospects of my endurance on the long trip. Although impatient over the time that would be wasted, Laime agreed that we would take five minutes each hour for a rest period.

The last few hours were sheer torture for me. I kept getting slower and slower. How Enrique and Laime kept such a pace I simply couldn't see. They would patiently wait for me at the more difficult places, and often, at a riverbank, shout encouragement or point out the safest rocks or logs to pass over. Somehow we made the main camp late in the afternoon. I have a dim memory of the last hours, the fording of the last stream, the last bog to drag my waterlogged jungle boots through, the last wet, slippery log to climb over, and, finally, voices in the distance.

Camp! I dropped my pack, hunted out my damp and dingy towel, and disappeared down to the Churún to wash off the perspiration and bits of bark, moss, and earth. This time the icy water was too much. I went back to camp and hung my hammock, crawled into the damp blankets, and wrestled with the chill that had enveloped me. Later, though, a huge aluminum tin of thick steaming soup and a cup of tea worked miracles.

Getting out the rest of the way was easy. The Churún had risen very high during the last few rainy days and the dugouts rode easily. It was downstream all the way now, through the Churún in the canyon and out the Río Carrao to where the new airstrip was. The sun came out, and we gazed with awe at the many waterfalls coming off the mesas....

Perry Lowrey's calculations, made those May days in 1949, still stand: the total plunge of Angel Falls is 3,212 feet (979 meters), making it the highest waterfall in the world.

Ruth Robertson found herself in the headlines for a while. In the long run, however, she was happier behind camera and typewriter, and spent a total of 13 years freelancing in Venezuela. She then went to Mexico, where she was editor-in-chief of Amistad *magazine, before ending up on the Gulf Coast of Texas.*

Today Angel Falls is a top tourist draw in Venezuela's Canaima National Park, and the more adventurous visitors retrace Robertson's journey up the Churún valley to the promontory in the amphitheater, where they, too, behold what some are now calling the "eighth wonder of the world."

PART ELEVEN:

seas and islands

ROUNDING THE HORN
IN A WINDJAMMER
February 1931

ALAN J. VILLIERS (1903–1982)

BLUFF AND BRAWNY, WITH BEEFY HANDS, A RUDDY FACE, AND DEEP blue eyes, Alan Villiers looked the part he was born to play, that of the vanishing square-rigger sea captain. Since childhood, when masts crowded the harbor of his native Melbourne, he had loved sailing ships, and at the age of 15 the young Australian ran away to sea—"the best university I struck." A hard school, but it taught well, and when barely past 30 Villiers skippered a windjammer 58,000 miles around the world for the roving hell of it. He sailed the Indian Ocean in Arab dhows and to the Grand Banks with Portuguese "Captains Courageous" fishing fleets. During World War II his command of landing craft at Anzio and Normandy won him a Distinguished Service Cross. His life was burnished by wind and spray; he even refused to turn a wheel on land—his wife had to do all the driving.

Villiers was one of the great nautical writers of his time. Son of a poet, he dabbled in journalism. By the age of 20, he was writing the first of his 40 books, which captured in word and picture the lost Age of Sail. He was also the NATIONAL GEOGRAPHIC's master mariner, as it were, writing no less than 30 articles for the magazine, the first being "Rounding the Horn in a Windjammer," the story of the voyage of the Grace Harwar.

A Finnish-owned, three-masted, full-rigged ship, Grace Harwar *was the ideal vessel in which Villiers, then 25, and his journalist friend, Ronald Walker, might document the windjammers that still worked the Australian grain trade, carrying wheat to Europe by way of Cape Horn and battling some of the stormiest seas in the world. The two signed on as sailors, and in April 1929* Grace Harwar *weighed anchor and departed the Australian port of Wallaroo; 138 days later she limped—barely—into Cobh, Ireland, after a grueling, tragic, and nearly disastrous voyage. Seamen are always superstitious, and the crew should have known that things might go wrong, since they embarked with 13 hands before the mast ...*

WE BEGAN THE VOYAGE WELL. WE KNEW THAT IT WAS COMING ON winter then and prayed for a quick run to the Horn. The Horn is bad enough in summer, and we did not want to prolong our passage of the west winds getting there. In six days we passed to the south of Tasmania.

That was good. We had a strong west wind the whole time, with a big sea. It was piercingly cold and the little *Grace Harwar* was inclined to throw the sea about her decks a lot. We blew out a sail or two. The first night out the mizzen-topgallantsail blew out of its boltropes, and we set no sail upon that yard thereafter because the ship had none....

We did not mind the cold. We did not mind the ceaseless wet at the cold wheel, the seas that slopped over us at brace and buntline, the teeth-chattering peril of the work aloft. We laughed at the big seas and thought it a joke when a larger one than usual fell aboard with a shock that made the whole ship tremble and threatened to do her serious damage. What did we care, while the wind was fair and we came quickly toward Cape Horn?

From Wallaroo to Cape Horn is, roughly speaking, about 6,000 miles. If we ran nine knots before the strong west winds, we should make it in 30 days—say, 35 or 38, allowing for some spells of lesser winds and maybe some days hove to, when there was too much wind to use. We went that way, as all sailing ships do, in the hope of getting strong west winds, in order that if we had to suffer acute discomfort, and cold and wet, and ceaseless work, at least it would not last long and we should be quickly round. The sailing ship does not mind strong wind, so long as it is fair. We had nothing to fear from westerly gales, which would help us on; it was wind from the east we feared.

The wind came from the east. It hauled around to southeast and hurled itself upon us with all the sting of the Antarctic ice, in its frigid and unwelcoming blast. We could do nothing with the strong east wind. We shortened down and hove to. This was in the southern waters of the Tasman Sea, between Tasmania and New Zealand, across which we had been making to pass to the south of New Zealand on our way to the Horn. The Tasman Sea is storm-lashed and furious in winter time. We knew that, but we expected at least that we would have west wind....

The east wind continued, with no slightest sign of ever giving up. Gale succeeded gale. Constantly the open decks of the old full-rigger were awash; one had to look lively to the lifelines going to the wheel. At night the lookout man could not go on the forecastle head, for the seas came over there green, and if he had gone there he would have been drowned. We began to notice how short-handed we were, with six in one watch and seven in the other.

In the end, Captain Svensson got fed up with the east wind and put up the helm to run for Cook Strait, that separates the two islands of New Zealand, intending to pass through that way into the South Pacific

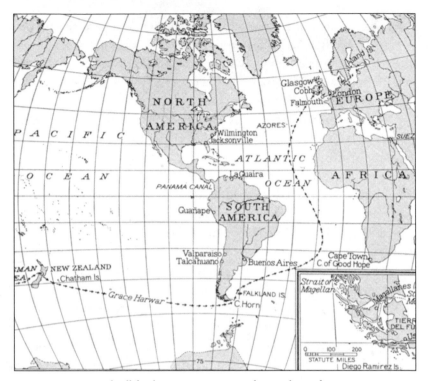

The ill-fated Grace Harwar *voyaged across the Pacific from Wallaroo in Australia, around stormy Cape Horn, and up the Atlantic to Cobh, Ireland.*

beyond, if the east wind would not allow us to pass south of that Dominion. We reached Cook Strait after three weeks at sea, and then it fell calm and we could not get through. Four days we lay there, wallowing stagnantly, with Mount Egmont on the one hand and the rocky northern shores of the south island on the other. We were about to up helm and stand on northward to pass right round the northern extremity of New Zealand, when a west wind came at last and saw us through.

We saw the lights of Wellington, capital of New Zealand, and reported the ship all well. The west wind kept with us for a day or two and saw us clear of Chatham Islands. We began to think it meant to stay, and that we would come to the Horn without further undue misery. But then the wind faltered and stopped again. When it returned it was from the east, with fog and rain and gale in miserable succession. Day succeeded day in sodden gale and cold misery. We went out to so many alternate watches on deck, hoping that while we slept the wind had changed, and were disappointed, that we gave up hoping any more. We accepted what was in store for us with sullen indifference.

Oilskins were long since useless; there was no dry spot in the ship, nor dry rag. The hutch of a forecastle was washed out time and time again by great seas that swept joyously through the inefficient doors. When the forecastle doors were shut, the atmosphere was stifling. When they were open, the sea swept in. We kept them shut, preferring to die of suffocation rather than exposure.

There was often no warm food. The seas put the galley fire out, and because the water stormed so incessantly across the main deck, where the fresh-water pump was, we could not work the inefficient pump for fear of mingling salt water with the fresh, and went thirsty. We were cold, wet through, and hungry. There is no heating system in a full-rigged ship. The very cockroaches and the bugs in the bunks retired from active service and might all have died, for all we saw of them....

On the 38th day Walker was killed at his work in the rigging.

It was very simple. Just one of those ordinary everyday accidents that nine hundred times kill nobody and on the 901st wreak vengeance on some innocent for their previous failings.

We were setting the fore upper topgallantsail, which had not been loosed since its getting in, described in his diary. The wind, which for so long had been from something east, had at last something of west in it, and we were giving the ship a little more sail to help her on—not that the fore upper topgallantsail would make much difference, really, but the psychological effect was not to be scorned.

Walker, with a small boy named Finila, went up to loose the sail. It was a little after 4 o'clock in the morning, the worst time of the day. We had so few in a watch that it was bad to send two men into the rigging: but there were reasons for that. We had coffee at 5:30, and the tradition of the sea is, that if there is any work afoot and it is not finished before the coffee bells, then whatever time is taken up with finishing the work is lost. The coffee hour is not extended merely because some of it has been given up to the ship's work. A good mate will see that his watch receives its coffee time unbroken.

That was why our second mate sent both Walker and young Finila to loose the fore upper topgallant that fateful morning. It was very securely made fast with many gaskets to stand against the Cape Horn gale. Since it had been made fast it had become sodden with rain and the canvas had swollen. Ice had formed in the gaskets, and any sailor knows it may take an hour to get a sail loose in such conditions. With the two of them at it, they managed in half an hour, and then we on deck—five of us with the second mate—began the painful process of heaving the yard aloft by the capstan. When it was halfway up, the second mate saw that a gasket was foul on the weather clew. The sail would not hoist properly. He yelled aloft to Walker, through the rain, to go out on the lower topgallant yard to clear the gasket. Walker went and cleared it. He called down to us that everything was clear. We began to heave again. The halyards carried away and the yard came tumbling down.

It fell on Walker, beneath it, and killed him there.

We did not know that he was dead when we rushed up the mast and found him unconscious between the yards. We thought he was merely senseless. There was no sign of wound, save for some blood oozing slowly from his mouth.

It never occurred to us that he was dead; we were too much concerned with bringing him to and getting him to the deck that we might see the extent of his injuries and what we could do about them. I tried to bring him to with cold water that had been brought from the deck. I did not know how hopeless it was. We wanted to restore him to his senses in order that he might help us with the difficult task of getting him, from high on that swaying mast, to the deck. It was not easy to bring a senseless body down that slippery and pitching rigging.

But he did not come to. We rigged a gantline and lowered him down, gently, carefully. When we got to the bottom, Captain Svensson took one look. "He is dead," he said.

Dead! The shock was stunning. We did not, could not, believe it. Nowhere is the awfulness of death more painfully apparent than at sea. Ashore there are diversions; one forgets. There are other people to see, other people to talk to. One is not missed so much. But at sea, in a full-rigged ship, there is only the one little band, and always the wind moans in the rigging and the sea rolls on. When one is gone, no one comes to take his place; there are no diversions; nothing happens to deaden sorrow and make up for the loss of the one who is gone.

We buried him from the poop next day, with the Finnish ensign at half-mast and the crew white-faced and deeply moved. I do not know of anything more moving than sea burial—not the committal of some poor corpse of a steerage passenger from high on the steamship's promenade deck, in the dead of night, lest the saloon passengers be put off their dancing for a moment, but the last sad rites over a shipmate's bier in a Cape Horn windjammer.

Grace Harwar, a three-masted, full-rigged windjammer, was a vanishing sight on the high seas even during her heyday in the early 20th century. By then the remaining windjammers worked the grain trade between Australia and Europe, staging "races" to make the fastest passage.

We all had known him so well. At sea, like that, you see the utmost "innards" of a man—what he is made of. No subterfuges, no pretense of city life, no masking of real intents and real character, will pass here; you see all. We knew poor Walker and we liked him well. And this was his end!

The captain said some prayers; we sang Swedish and English hymns. There was a short address. The ship was hove to, sadly wallowing, with the moan of the wind in her rigging now quieted by her deadened way, the surly wash of the sea about her decks now softened. We carried him to the rail, tilted the hatch; there was a dull "plop" and it was over.

We put the ship before the wind again and sailed on.

It was the 57th day before we came to the Horn. It was June then. We had a gale from the west, and though the sea ran huge and the cold was almost overpowering, the old ship ran on and we were glad.

We wanted to come round the Horn now more quickly than ever, that we might forget something of the tragedy on the other side of it. Death is a worrying thing at sea, especially when its cause is bad gear that might have killed another of us. At the wheel, on the lonely lookout, aloft on the yards, sleeping in the wet, cold forecastle, we remembered the one who had died, turned the details of that tragedy over and over in our minds until it was not good for us longer to remain in that saddening belt of the wild ocean. A boy screamed in his sleep; he had dreamed of Walker's wraith coming in the forecastle to call us.

The ship began to leak in the height of a gale; the pumps jammed; the water seeped in, and we could do nothing about it. Through a night of storm and snow-squall fury we were huddled on the poop, not certain that the ship would live to see the morning.

The next day one of the boys was swept overboard by a big sea, and there were no falls rove off [no ropes attached] in the lifeboats to try to save him. What could we do? Many had gone like that, and the wind ships could only run on.... It seemed futile to try to save him. We jammed the wheel hard down and brought her, shivering and groaning, into the wind. We rove off new ropes into the lifeboat tackle blocks with mad speed. One of us was aloft in the mizzen-top, seeing where the floating figure had gone. It was coming on nightfall then, with rain squalls and gale in the offing. We saw he had grasped a life buoy flung to him, and still lived. But for how long?

We got the boat over and six volunteers quickly leaped into it, the mate in charge. Nobody was asked to go; nobody hung back.

We dropped astern and the boat seemed a futile thing, rising and falling in the big seas. It was queer to see the green bottom of the old ship, when we rose on a crest, lifted almost bodily from the swirling water. When we dropped in a trough her royal yards swept wild arcs through the gray sky, and we saw little else. Soon we could not see her at all, when the boat sank deep in the valleys between the big seas. We had no idea where the boy was. We could not see him. How could we? We could see nothing there, not even the ship. Maybe it was madness to look.

We pulled this way and that, hopelessly; yet we could not go back. It began to rain heavily. None of us had oilskins. Frenchman was in his underpants, just as he had come from his bunk. (It was our watch below.) Sjöberg, from Helsinki, had been laid up with neuralgia. But now he pulled at his oar, coatless, wet through, hungry and tired, yet not noticing any of those things and intent only on the saving of this second life. We did not want to lose one more. One was enough to give to Cape Horn—more than enough.

The mate, at the steering oar in the stern sheets, swept the sea with his sharp eyes, this way and that. There was a chance we would not find the ship again, if the squall came down heavily and shut her out. That had happened with the Swedish bark *Staut*, in much the same circumstances. She put out a boat to save a man fallen into the sea from the main yard, and a squall came down and she lost everybody—man overboard, those who went to rescue him, boat, and everything. We remembered that. There was nothing in the boat to sustain life. We had thrown the water cask and the bread barrels out to lighten her.

Then, in the moment of light, we saw him. It was a sea miracle, if ever there was one. He was on the crest of a sea, only three seas away from us! We had been on the point of giving up. We lay to heartily and soon had the boy back aboard. We pulled him in over the stern and went back to the ship, which had been watching us and now ran slowly downwind toward us. The boy was unconscious and nearly frozen to death, but he lived. He was among the lucky ones...

But it was not a lucky voyage. Soon afterward the second mate lost his mind and had to be confined to quarters; then the ship was becalmed in the South Atlantic and food supplies were exhausted. Yet after finally berthing in Ireland (the 138-day voyage was long even by square-rigger standards), and after Villiers had left her, the Grace Harwar loaded another cargo, turned back to sea, and sailed on.

SAILING FORBIDDEN COASTS

September 1931

IDA TREAT (1889–1978)

SHE HAD SUCH FREEDOM AND ADVENTURE, SHE WOULD MAKE A FINE feminist role model today, someone who knew her once said of Ida Treat. "But she wouldn't like that very much. She was always too independent for playing roles."

A writer and Vassar English professor, Illinois-born Ida Treat arrived in Paris just before World War I. By 25, she had earned a doctorate in letters from the Sorbonne; 15 years later, she held a second doctorate, in paleontology. She lived in France for many years, going through two marriages along the way. Husband number one was leader of the Communist Party faction in the French Chamber of Deputies, and husband number two would be a Free French naval commander in World War II.

She wrote prolifically and traveled extensively. Her articles appeared in The Saturday Evening Post, Harper's, The Nation, *and* Paris-Vu, *and she published several books. Her wanderings took her to China, the Soviet Union, Tahiti, and, in the late 1920s, Djibouti, chasing a story on the clandestine Red Sea slave trade. There, as she leaned over a steamship rail, she caught her first glimpse of Henri de Monfreid, known in those waters as Abd el Hai, sailing past in his boat, the Altair.*

Thus began an association that eventually resulted in Treat's Pearls, Arms, and Hashish, *the first book to tell of de Monfreid's adventurous life. While gathering the material, and disguised as a sailor, she made a monthlong cruise with the old sea wolf, exploring the Dankali coast of French Somaliland (today's Djibouti). Officially that was forbidden territory: Colonial authorities believed the Danakil despised Europeans for disrupting the profitable slave trade. It might be extremely dangerous to land there—so of course they did.*

De Monfreid we shall get to know better in the next selection. Ida Treat went on to publish numerous short stories in The New Yorker. *"She was an attractive writer," said William Shawn, its legendary editor. That quality is everywhere apparent in "Sailing Forbidden Coasts," her article for* NATIONAL GEOGRAPHIC— *fresh and surprisingly modern, full of sly humor and understated irony.*

"YOU WILL NEVER GET PERMISSION TO TOUCH ANYWHERE ON THE Dankali coast. With the exception of Obock, perhaps, it has been taboo for years."

"But that is where I want to go," I protested.

The master of the *Altair* smiled quizzically. "And that is where I intend to take you. Only you will have to travel as contraband. If you were a man, it would not be so easy. Already here in Djibouti you would have had several large-footed and mustached gentlemen prying into your affairs. But they are not used to ladies embarking on any such wild cruise. For the comforts of the *Altair*–!" He grinned. "It is no private yacht! So don't worry. You will slip through the hands of my official countrymen like a letter in the mail."

As he spoke, the little car chugged sturdily south over the hard red earth of the desert. We had left the lights of Djibouti behind us—the European town with its white facades and empty avenues, and the crowded Bender Djedid, humming with life in the stagnant heat and smelling of incense, wood smoke, and goats. Before us, the Somali coast stretched south and east along the Indian Ocean, and rose to the right in a long incline toward the heights of Ethiopia. At the "oasis," with its burnt gardens among spiky palms, we had left the trail leading to Zeila, and for an hour we had rolled through the bush, zigzagging among stones and scrub mimosa, tilting across waves of hard-packed sand, and all the while following the sea that glowed dimly in the blackness at our left under a sky spangled with stars.

"Why is the Dankali coast taboo?" I asked.

"Oh, for a lot of reasons. Chiefly because the Danakil have a deep-rooted aversion to white skins. And a nervous hand on the trigger. They have never taken kindly to colonizing. And, given the climate and the country—a sizzling desert, if ever there was one—the French have never made a very serious attempt to turn them into docile colonials. Dijibouti is important merely as the terminus of the Franco-Ethiopian Railway and the only seaport for Ethiopia. As for the Dankali country, it serves as a convenient hinterland; it keeps the Italians out of harm's way up in Eritrea.

"The Residence at Djibouti maintains a species of armed truce with the Danakil—a you-leave-me-alone-and-I-won't-bother-you sort of agreement. That's why the Government at Djibouti isn't keen on letting any white man wander off into the Dankali bush. In case he should meet with a stray bullet, there would have to be reprisals, punitive measures, and a lot of unnecessary trouble stirred up all around."

"But you? After all, you have a white skin."

"*Si peu.*" The master of the *Altair* gave a short laugh. "I am one of the dark family, so to speak. I have sailed with the Danakil for years..."

Djibouti to Obock, across the Gulf of Tadjoura, takes a night's sail, if the wind holds. Our boat, an 18-foot *boutre* [small coasting vessel], the little sister of the *Altair*, spread its lateen sail full overhead and slid out of the black harbor. We were loaded to the gunwales with provisions for the bigger boat, coils of rope, and *tanikas* [earthenware jugs] of oil for the auxiliary Diesel, and we carried one passenger, neatly disguised in a sailor's outfit of rusty-red sailcloth topped incongruously by a turban. Somewhat superfluous, that disguise, I thought, as we had met only a handful of black men on the pier—fishers from the *sambuks* moored along the mole. However, it was well to be prudent, it appeared.

We had papers for Obock. Afterward, destination uncertain. Abd el Hai, when I inquired, gave a vague gesture that swept the horizon from Tadjoura Gulf to the eastern limits of the Bab-el-Mandeb. It depended chiefly on the wind. For the moment it held.

Behind us, the lights of the coast disappeared. All about us, the wave crests rose and fell, tipped with phosphorescence. A hand dipped in the sea let fall a shower of silver drops. Beneath the rudder, a slanting ray of green light streamed down into the blackness below. The three Danakil— our crew—had stripped off their "city clothes" (the shirt worn flapping outside the close-wrapped *fouta*), and their bare torsos made dark triangles against the sail.

"Djoch!" (Luff!) The big yard climbed the mast, rotated around it, and we veered northeast. The lights of the twin islands, Maskali and Moucha, slid past to starboard; and ahead, the long white beam of the Ras Bir Light swept the horizon at regular intervals. Not a sound but the hiss of water along the keel and now and then a mighty splash, as a big skate flopped in the darkness off our bows.

At dawn we were in sight of the Dankali coast, a silvery white line, and behind it the lavender shadows of the Mabla Mountains. The wind dropped and we floated aimlessly, the sail hanging in lifeless folds from the yards. Our Danakil got out the oars, timing their stroke to a litanylike chant:

Benat' a Bérbera … Benat' al Bérbera.
Reh chamálo … Reh chamálo.
Reh halbár … Reh halbár.
(The girls of Berbera.
A north wind.
A land wind.)

The colony of French Somaliland (today the independent republic of Djibouti) curved around the Gulf of Tadjoura, a blue bight in the unrelieved African brown. The north shore, backed by stony desert, was the Dankali coast.

To the rhythm of the song, we moved slowly over the glassy water. By 8 o'clock we rounded the reef at Obock and entered the little bay where the *Altair*, a 15-ton sailboat, built like an Arab and rigged like a cutter, rode at anchor....

"Not much hope for a breeze before dawn. In the meantime, I'm going to turn in." The master of the ship disappeared down the ladder into his cubbylike cabin. A sailor spread a grass mattress for me aft, in the narrow deck space between the cabin roof and the bulwarks. Above my head a second figure crouched on the steering bench, the tiller between his knees—a turbaned statue black against the stars.

The creaking of the boom and a familiar voice giving sharp commands in Arabic wakened me. We were under way. In the half light, I made out the master of the *Altair*, one foot on the steering bench, his body braced against the bar. He had discarded European clothes and was wearing the costume of the coast—torso bare and a fouta wrapped tight about the loins. In the bow, the cook's fire flamed yellow. Beside it, Aden, the boy, was preparing the day's provision of firewood, accompanying each crash of splintering wood with the customary cry, to show that it was not the rigging that had given way.

Over in the east the sky grew gold. A disk of metal slid up from the horizon. The lines of the *Altair* lost their vagueness and stood out distinct against the blue overhead and the paler blue of the morning sea. As its master had said, the *Altair* was no yacht, but a 40-foot sambuk, sturdily built of Indian teak, with the after-deck—the skipper's quarters—raised a foot or two above the rest. Nothing gleaming white about the deck—a coating of fish oil, spread to protect the planks from the blistering sun, had in time formed a dark crust, gummy in spots, but for the most part so slippery that only bare feet could cling to it in safety. Prudently I discarded my sandals.

Abdi, the Somali mate, lean and black, with shrewd, fine features always puckered in a smile, seven sailors, and the boy formed the crew. Seven Danakil and one Sudanese, expert seamen all of them, from Kassem, the slender Arabian Nights' prince I had seen the evening before at the tiller, to stalwart Hamid Baket, the Sudanese....

Her canvas taut, the *Altair* skimmed through the morning wind toward the Gulf of Tadjoura. Out by the horizon, a host of triangular black fins pricked the surface and dozens of dark bodies flashed in gleaming arcs above the water. *Abou Salaam* (He-who-says-good-morning)—the porpoises. They headed toward us in an immense triangle, leaping and splashing. In a few minutes they were all about us, darting past, swift as torpedoes, diving under the keel, dashing ahead just where the prow cut the wave.

A rifle gleamed at my elbow. "Watch Abdi," came the voice of the *Altair's* captain. The Somali crouched on the low bulwarks, the end of a rope in his hand. There was a sharp report. In a flash Abdi dived overboard, carrying the rope. An instant later, while the steersman brought the boat about, I made out his dark body thrown here and there, alongside a threshing, struggling mass in a circle of pinkish foam. "Pull!" he shouted from the water. "*Obess!*" (Harder still!) The men then dragged the porpoise, still quivering, a rope about its body, to the deck, while Abdi clambered after.

"That is the only way to bring one aboard. Otherwise they sink like stones," the Frenchman explained.

A red pool spread on the deck. Abdi dipped his hands in the blood, rubbed his breast, arms, and legs with it, and dived overboard again.

"The blood of Abou Salaam makes you young. Abdi is getting old." (He was perhaps forty.) This from Ibrahim, a Dankali sailor, already at work slitting the tough hide of the porpoise. An hour later the forward deck was festooned with strips of dark-red flesh hung to dry in the sun. The death of the porpoise had not been, as I first thought, merely for sport. It meant meat for the crew. Ibrahim cut open the animal's stomach, hoping to find freshly swallowed calamaries, a great delicacy, he assured me. But we had killed Abou Salaam too late in the morning. The squid were already partially digested. They could only be used for bait....

The first night out from Obock, we moored in the lee of a cape on the south shore of the gulf. The men slid the dugout into the sea and Kassem paddled me across to a strip of glistening sand that bordered the cliff. One of the rifles went with us, for this was Issa country and the Issas and the Danakil have quarreled for centuries along the vague frontier that separates the tribes. When an Issa meets a Dankali unarmed, he kills him on sight, Kassem told me, adding a precise and shocking description of the type of mutilation that follows the killing. Dankali women meet the same fate, he assured me, with special refinements if the victim happens to be pregnant.

"And you, if you met an Issa?" I inquired.

Gengle Kassem, the Arabian Nights' prince, gave a savage smile and flourished his big curved knife significantly. "The Issas are all devils," he replied succinctly.

While Kassem and his rifle dodged among the mimosa bushes hunting for sea birds' eggs on the sand, I strolled along the beach strewn with rainbow-colored shells—big pink conchs, pearly sea snails, and twigs of red and white coral. Armies of hermit crabs, like shoals of moving pebbles, slid along the hard sand by the water's edge; and little spirit crabs—green, yellow, and rose pink—pattered sidewise on absurdly long legs. A shout from Kassem brought me back to the dugout. He had gathered a dozen eggs in a fold of his fouta. When we had covered half the distance

"I am an old man. I have traveled much," declared Sheik Issa, venerated as a saint among the Danakil, as he climbed aboard the Altair *on its voyage to Arabia. His word alone often sufficed to maintain peace.*

out toward the *Altair*, he laid the paddle across his knees and pointed back toward the cliff. Two little figures showed black against the sky, Issas armed with the customary lance and round shield of hippopotamus hide.

"You ran no danger, of course," the master of the *Altair* reassured me, "though it is just as well to avoid such encounters. Had you not been there, Kassem might have felt tempted to try out the range of his rifle.".....

Long before sun-up the next morning, four of us went ashore—the master of the *Altair*, Abdi, with the rifle, Kassem carrying the water jar, and I wearing a mammoth turban (Abd el Hai refused categorically to land with anyone topped by a sun helmet) and a big, curved knife called a *djembia* buckled horizontally at the waist, so long that its brass hilt and sheath interfered with my arms as I walked.

We climbed a sandy trail along the flank of one of the peaks and soon the *Altair* lay far below us, like a fly on a black-rimmed mirror.

The droppings of camel and gazelle dotted the sand, but of the animals themselves, tame and wild, we saw no sign. But a strange smell hung about the mimosa clumps and oozed from between the rocks, a smell I had always associated before with zoos and circuses—the smell of the bush and the jackal and the panther—its unseen inhabitants.

Climbing steadily, we reached a bare region of sand and rock where even the mimosa no longer found a foothold. To the left, hundreds of feet below, in a deep pocket, lay a curiously crackled plain—a lake of dried volcanic mud—and all about us, heaped in chaotic masses, lava, rock, and ash—a congealed eruption. Instinctively one looked for the active crater, but the only flame visible blazed down from the sky overhead, and the hot blast that stung and suffocated was the desert wind sweeping over the dead landscape.

Stopping every few yards for breath, we reached the pass. Before the horizon that opened inland, one had the feeling of looking down on an uninhabited world, another planet seared with fire, or the earth after the cataclysm. Peak and plateau and, far below, a stretch of blue water, the great salt lake Assal, with its beaches of glistening crystals, lying in a ring of black cones like a jewel guarded by dragons.

"You are doubtless the first white woman to look down on that." The voice of Abd el Hai came like a shock in the tremendous silence. It was as if a jinni had spoken....

Long before we reached it, the Dankali capital [Tadjoura] showed a distant white strip along the gulf. We dropped anchor at sunset. A row of sambuks, their bows painted with stripes of green, black, and white, lay beached on the sand. Beyond them the white cubes and arcades of houses built in the Arab style rose against the hill, and to our right the ogival roofs of brush huts crowded close together, each with its high fence of branches and palm mats.

The master of the *Altair* draped his bare shoulders in a *chamma*, I put on a stiff Arab gown, and Abdi and Kassem paddled us ashore.

"*La Illaha illa Allah!*" The call of the muezzin from the mosque echoed across the water. Crossing the beach, we entered a narrow street, the Frenchman striding ahead, I at his heels, and Abdi and Kassem with their rifles—for purely ornamental purposes—bringing up the rear. We passed groups of Danakil who greeted my companion with courteous salaams, women carrying water from the oasis in goatskins, little boys, their heads shaven except for a scalp lock, and girls whose dozens of tiny braids stood out stiffly, smeared with butter and yellow earth. The children trotted at our heels until a word from Abdi sent them tumbling and giggling to the shelter of a gate.

Here there was none of the cluttered filth of European towns. The sand between the two rows of fences, stirred into choppy waves by passing feet, was clean as a beach, and smelled of incense, sheep dung, and wood smoke that filtered blue through the roofs overhead....

Toward dawn a storm broke over Khor Ali. Immense black clouds shot with lightning tumbled up from the horizon, blotting out Orion, and the morning star hung like a lantern above the rim of the plateau. With an explosion of thunder, the clouds burst, letting down the rain like a cascade. The deck ran with water. Part of the crew took refuge in the hold, the others in the captain's cubby, where we spent an uncomfortable hour, shivering in our wet clothes and dodging little waterfalls that dripped through the uncalked roof. In an hour it was all over and the rising tide floated the *Altair* over the reef into the gulf....

All day long we beat north against the wind, passing Obock and the tall column of the Ras Bir Light. Toward afternoon, the wind shifting, we set in close to shore, a low white cliff, eaten in hollows by the sea, with here and there a cave which the Danakil assured us were filled with bones of men the jinn had eaten. Beyond the cliff rose the flat highlands of the Table Mountains and the silhouette of the Djebbel Ghin, a strange stone figure like a turbaned warrior.

Shoals of flying fish, shuttles of silver, fled in startled bounds from our bow. A swordfish shot into the air, lunging back into the sea as if the arc of its trajectory had snapped at the summit. Out by the horizon, what looked like a fleet of slender sails glistened and disappeared—a band of cachalots, *Soltan al Bahar*, the King of the Sea, were blowing water jets into the sun....

PEARL FISHING IN THE RED SEA
November 1937

HENRI DE MONFREID (1879–1974)

PEARL FISHERMAN, GUNRUNNER, HASHISH SMUGGLER: HENRI DE Monfreid was all of these and more. A renegade Frenchman, his lean and sinewy form clad in sandals, a loincloth, and a turban, was recognized up and down the Red Sea, where in the first quarter of the 20th century he was considered to be the "most remarkable figure from Suez to Bombay."

De Monfreid grew up in a family that was both bourgeois and bohemian. His wealthy father, an Impressionist painter and one of the artist Paul Gauguin's closest friends, lived in Paris and also had a house near the Mediterranean. That's where the son first felt the tug of the sea. As a young man, though, he spent ten fruitless years engaged in failing business ventures before, at the age of 30, he changed tack. In 1910, he sailed from Marseille to Djibouti, where he promptly went native, learned Arabic, and built a shallow-draft boat rigged with a lateen sail.

For the next two decades he coursed the reef-strewn, pirate-infested waters between Africa and Arabia, a sea rover for whom pearl fishing was just one of many possibilities for profit. Nearly shipwrecked by a sudden storm, he vowed to his Somali crew that he would embrace Islam if Allah would save them. Thus de Monfreid duly became Abd el Hai, "Slave of the Life-Giving." To the authorities, however, the "sea wolf" remained a freebooting smuggler. Ethiopia's Haile Selassie tried to have him assassinated, though Mussolini was a great admirer.

For de Monfreid, smuggling was just another face of the quest for perfect freedom. Risks and trials alone formed character: Cast off the trammels of civilization, act as an individual, and destiny will guide you. He took flights into mysticism, identifying with "the sea, the wind, the virgin sand of the desert, the infinity of far-off skies in which wheel the numberless hosts of the stars." By the 1930s he began writing what would amount to more than 40 volumes of autobiography. That's when editors at NATIONAL GEOGRAPHIC decided to introduce this singular adventurer to a broad American audience. The following excerpt relates one of his more typical exploits.

AFTER STAYING A FEW WEEKS IN THE DAHALACH ISLANDS, I decided to go to the archipelago of Farasan, near the Arabian coast, where the [pearl] beds are less worked over. As we neared the slightly hilly island of Harmil, we saw in one of its most elevated parts a man waving a long cloth on the end of a pole. We approached the shore with a sandy bottom beneath us.

"Luff!" By putting the tiller hard over, I avoided the remains of a wreck whose timbers were too near the surface; it had been a fairly large boat. Once anchored, I saw the man who had been making signals hurrying down toward the sea. My divers knew him and showed him great respect. He was a Sudanese nakhoda [skipper of a pearl fishing boat] of Massaua. The wreck we had just encountered was that of his boat, which had sunk after taking fire that same morning.

But before going into details he led me to the shade of a half-vaulted rock, raised a covering of tattered cloth, and I saw the still form of a man, another Sudanese. He opened his eyes, seemed to look at us, and then closed them again to withdraw into a sort of savage loneliness. The poor fellow was dying from a rifle wound in the lower part of the abdomen. I went to get a restorative, but when I returned the old nakhoda said simply: "It's all over."

As the sun was sinking into the calm evening and the noisy gulls were wheeling round and round above us, in silence we covered the warm, dead body with sand still burning hot from the sunlight. Two stones set upright marked the spot, and the immense peace of its solitude gave a poignant grandeur to this primitive tomb. We returned on board. The nakhoda then told us of the drama which had taken place here a few hours before. To him it was banal enough, a mere incident that is one of the risks of the job, like being drowned or snapped up by a shark.

While his craft lay at anchor after a season's fishing a big Zaranik zarug [a light, swift vessel, much favored by pirates and smugglers, sailed by members of an Arabian coastal tribe] came just before dawn and surprised them. They plundered everything, even taking the rigging of the boat, which they set on fire and sank at its moorings.

The nineteen Sudanese who made up the crew were carried off to be sold as slaves. The man now dead had been shot accidentally while trying to make use of the only gun on board. One of the attackers set it off in trying to snatch it out of his hands. As for the nakhoda, he escaped because he had slept on shore to go fishing with a dragnet at dawn.

When the zarug had gone, he found his companion fainting on the beach. He had been thrown into the sea for dead, but had had strength enough to drag himself to the shore and hide behind a rock.

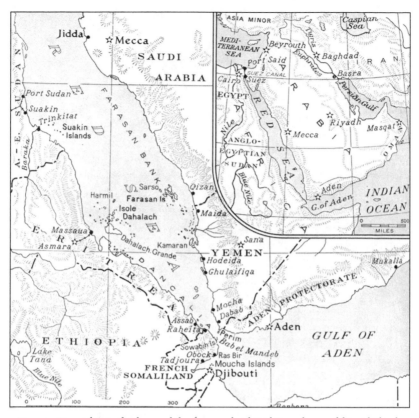

For years Henri de Monfreid coursed the clear, coral-rich Red Sea, where reef-fringed islands like the Dahalachs and Farasans attracted pearl divers, pirates, smugglers, and slavers.

I was outraged by this raid and my first thought was to give chase to the pirates; I had six guns on board and, in addition, a few dynamite caps which I used for fishing. But the nakhoda was resigned; he would rely on Allah, who had permitted this thing, to give him whatever retribution was just. However, my Somalis were eager to do something. The old hate of the African races for the invading Arabs awoke.

The nakhoda had seen the zarug scudding along toward the east and its sail had disappeared only a short while before. All the afternoon it had been becalmed. At the most it could have reached Sarso, the only anchorage possible on the edge of the reef of the Farasan Bank. Moreover, the crew would suspect nothing, believing all the survivors to be aboard the zarug. "What did you have on board?" I asked.

"A few sacks of sadafs [mother-of-pearl shells], but in my box the pearls of our entire trip, and they are worth more than 10,000 rupees."

A rakish zarug—a slim, swift, lateen-rigged Arab fishing vessel—quickly transformed into a smuggling craft, was a favorite with those pirates who lurked in the shoals, coral banks, and islands of the Red Sea.

I discounted the exaggeration; nevertheless, the sudden raid had been very fruitful.

The breeze was holding and gave hope that it would last all night. We decided to attempt the adventure. If the bird was in the nest we should surprise him in turn at the approaching dawn.

The decision was welcomed with cries of joy from all the Somalis. In ten minutes we were outside the island, the mainsail bellying. Night had come and I set the course by the compass toward the open sea. We had to cross the central part of the Red Sea—about 90 miles to make before dawn.

I certainly had no desire to see any of my men killed or wounded for an affair which, after all, was none of my business. But, all said and done, I was certain we were running absolutely no risk if we surprised the zarug during the night. I knew enough of the native's habits to foresee their reaction to the type of attack I had in store for them. I made a packet of three dynamite caps, one of which was primed and furnished with a fuse calculated to burn for 20 seconds. This improvised torpedo was fastened to the end of a long boat hook. If everything went as I foresaw, this would suffice to avoid anything approaching a fight; but we had to get there in time.

The island was mountainous. We could see it in the night. It was 2 a.m. and all eyes were fixed on the horizon. Not even the cabin boy slept.

With the aid of a night glass I guided us closer and Ali pointed out to me an isolated black point in the sea to the south of the island. It was a zarug moored to the edge of the reef.

Our rifles were quickly loaded with five cartridges each. I had only 50 all told. Then the ax, a jumper bar, and a big iron hammer were put in battle order as if we were going to board. I was in a state of nervous irritation caused by all these preparations. But the die had been cast; I could no longer retreat.

We were half a cable's length from the sleeping zarug when the old Sudanese recognized it. I put the helm up, and as the sail fell we drifted to within a few yards of our quarry. Forms stretched out under the sails began to stir. I called the usual "Hooooo" as if we were an innocent boat coming there by accident, though this was a very unusual hour to drop anchor.

Meanwhile I had lighted the fuse with my cigarette. The little light from the jet of flame passed unobserved and the black fuse smoked on ominously in the dark. I plunged the long boat hook into the sea as if about to anchor, but held the bomb under the vital parts of the boat. I carefully counted the seconds up to ten. Then I cried to the nakhoda, who was ready: "Call your men." All together we shouted to the men in the zarug to jump into the sea if they could.

The Zaraniks awoke; the breech of a rifle clicked; I continued to count—18, 19 ... Then a greenish flame spurted from the center of their boat as the dynamite exploded. I had held the explosive under the mast, where there are usually no sleepers. The mast crashed down, and a few seconds later stones rained on all sides—the pebble ballast had been blown sky-high. By a miracle nobody was knocked senseless.

The zarug sank in a few seconds and men floundered in the water. There were wild shouts. The Sudanese swam heavily by their arms, as they were chained two and two by the legs. The Zaraniks fled toward the island in small boats. The panic was complete.

I lighted a big torch of gasoline, which illuminated the scene. The zarug had disappeared, but a multitude of objects floated on the placid water. The Zaraniks were paddling off in three boats, bailing out the water meanwhile. I fired in their direction while my Somalis gave chase. With the men who remained on board I hauled in the Sudanese and with considerable difficulty removed their heavy iron shackles.

Day was breaking and soon we could see through the transparent water the hull of the sunken zarug, the bow resting on a big rock and the stern hanging in the deep-blue water.

One of the rescued Sudanese, a Hercules with rather thin legs, took one end of a rope and dived. I saw him climb over the wreck, feeling each object, his arms stretched out, the soles of his feet pointing to the surface. With a supple movement of his back he turned up again and came straight to the surface, blowing streams of bubbles through his nose as he rose. He had made fast the rope and told us to haul on it. A box came up; we pulled it aboard. It was the coffer of the Zaranik nakhoda, ornamented with inlaid copper figures. I opened it by forcing the padlock.

The Sudanese swore the pearls were inside. But we searched the contents in vain. There were silk garments, the dyes of which had run; and a thousand other things, soaked with sea water, that had been wrapped in paper. In a silk handkerchief were 50 thaler, two pounds sterling in gold, and some Turkish money. I deciphered the name engraved on the inside of the lid— Mohammed Omar—the name of the nakhoda, the prisoners told me.

So the nakhoda must have the pearls on his person! But there was still hope because two boats were chasing them....

Sounds of firing came from behind the island and soon our two boats hove in sight. With a glass I could see two Arabs in each, surrounded by my men; they were bringing back prisoners. The nakhoda was there with three others. Two were absolutely naked and immediately demanded a loincloth; the feeling for modesty is very strong with the Arabs.

The nakhoda was a man of 35, his face brown with the tan of the sea; a short beard that covered his entire face gave him a noble air which would have impressed me had he not been my prisoner. He carried a string of black beads and seemed scarcely interested in the events which had brought him before me in my simple boat. He wore at his waist the sheath of the dagger my men must have taken from him when they captured him.

The other three were young, between 20 and 30. In the morning's ducking they had lost the little baskets which usually serve them as headgear. Their long, curly hair fell on magnificent bronzed shoulders, and a bracelet of silver encircled their arms just above the elbow.

As he came on board the nakhoda said a salaam from habit, as if he had come to visit, and it would have needed but little to make him shake hands all round. Nonchalance comes very naturally to the Arabs because of their fatalism.

Yesterday these men had been put in irons by him; today it was the other way around. Such is luck. So whatever may be the circumstance, they maintain a sort of quietude that would become a disinterested spectator. Moreover, they don't feel at all guilty. That feeling simply does not exist. They win or lose.

Rapidly my Somalis told me that two other boatloads had gone out to sea. They had frightened this one into stopping by rifle shots. I ordered the four prisoners put into the irons I had recently opened. They suffered this with the indifference they would have shown a shoe merchant. There were a few protestations, but only because Abdi made one of the rings too tight around the nakhoda's foot.

"Be quiet, Mohammed Omar, and keep your complaints for the knot which in a few minutes will squeeze your neck."

"As Allah wills. But how do you know me?"

I did not reply, wishing to create an air of mystery. The prospect of hanging seemed to ruffle the affected serenity of the bandits.

I say bandits, but that is incorrect. They were Zaraniks—Arab sea rovers. To seize a boat, for example, is for them something less cruel than hunting; a boat can always defend itself, but an animal cannot. At Djibouti many of them live honestly according to the rules of society.

In any case, I did not intend to carry things so far. I was trying to create a psychology of fear so that I might learn where the pearls were. While we were deliberating, I saw the nakhoda examining the coffer we had fished up with an attention and persistence that were not warranted by such a simple box. I gave the order to remove his irons and to bring him to me.

"You know what awaits you according to the law of the sea?"

"Allah is mighty and let what is done be done according to his will! If you wish to kill me I cannot go against you. However, I wish to point out that I have killed nobody."

"And he whom you threw into the sea at Harmil; is he living?"

"Allah alone knows."

"And I, also, since I buried him." He shrugged his shoulders and kept silent. "However, I know you even if you don't know me, and all your tribe shall know that you are dead, hanged like a thief, and that your severed head was thrown to the sharks. For you don't think I am going to give you a sepulture—you who toss wounded men into the sea. Your soul of a dog shall wander until the day of fire."

"As Allah wills."

"However, I give you a way to save yourself, and to save those who are with you if you give the pearls to this man."

"I don't have them."

"I'm not asking that. I want to know where they are."

"I don't have them, I tell you. Search me." And he tore his clothes apart.

"No good making fun of me. I know you don't have them on you; but I also know where they are. I only made believe to all these men who want your death"—I added in a low voice—"that you told me where they were so as to be able to save you."

In saying this I looked by turns at the copper-inlaid coffer and at his shifty eyes. The interest he had shown in the coffer suggested the idea of a hiding place, and I dropped the hint without being too sure of anything. But I was on the right track.

After a long silence, with lowered head, he spoke in a subdued voice, like a man who surrenders: "Bring my box; they are there."

A hole had been bored the entire length of one of the mountings that formed the base of the coffer, and closed with wax. From this he drew a little bag; I gave it to the Sudanese, who opened it. "But some are missing!" he exclaimed.

"What do you expect?" replied Mohammed Omar. "I had to put some in another packet I entrusted to the *serinj* [agent or broker], so that nobody knew of the existence of these. One must be careful, and I have experience."

"All right," I said. "I believe you." And, turning to the Sudanese, I added, "As for you, thank heaven you have recovered the most beautiful pearls, for the serinj must have the worst." I ordered the three Arabs set at liberty, as it was mealtime; they joined the sailors to eat the traditional bowl of rice as if nothing extraordinary had happened. But what was I going to do with them now? While I was thinking, two boats appeared on the horizon, coming toward us. It was the rest of the Zaranik crew. I called to them to stay at a distance; one [of them] was sufficient to explain....

They had thought that at sea, without water or food, death was certain. It was better to try to arrange things, for in the Orient everything is arranged. They threw themselves on our mercy, lamenting their lost boat. There was a chorus of supplications. The devil had deceived them in leading them to the island of Harmil. Moreover, they had only wanted water, and it was because of the rifle shot fired by the Sudanese that the fight began. Etc. In the story of the hunter it was the rabbit who began it!

"Where is the serinj?" I asked at once.

"We don't know. He must have been drowned when the boat blew up, for nobody has seen him since. You killed him with your powder."

I thought at once of the prudence of the nakhoda, who knew how to steer clear of the terrible danger which covetousness can become at a time when it is impossible to enforce authority. This packet of pearls given to the serinj had singled him out as the holder of all the treasure, and without doubt he had paid for that honor with his life. The nakhoda's look crossed mine as if to exchange the same thought.

I did not want all those men to come aboard, for in such big numbers they were dangerous, although unarmed. I had them searched, and on the third we found the packet of pearls which had cost the serinj his life.

I made out I did not know its origins; I was not there to render justice. I was above all in a hurry to get away from the whole band of them and I did not want to keep them on board. We were already twenty too many and I should never have enough water or food for more.

I had four empty kerosene tins filled with water, to which I added a big packet of dates, and, abandoning all the Zaranik crew to its lucky star in two pirogues, I advised them to make for the steamer routes and be picked up by a philanthropically minded captain.

Some time later I met the former pirate nakhoda, this time on a peaceful merchant boat. He told me that a Norwegian cargo ship bound for Aden had picked them up. Making themselves out to be real castaways, they had been cared for by the English authorities....

Those English authorities arrested de Monfreid in World War II for collaborating with the Italians, and they sent him to a prisoner-of-war camp in Kenya. Soon released, he lived in a hut in the forest and survived by hunting. Returning to France after the war, he bought a 17th-century house in the Loire Valley and settled down to write and paint—and, it seems, cultivate opium poppies in his garden, for which he narrowly avoided prosecution. He mortgaged the family collection of Gaugin paintings; which only later were found to be fakes. The old sea wolf had a trick or two up his sleeve still.

Henri de Monfreid lived a long life, and when he died at the ripe age of 95 he had become, unsurprisingly, a cult figure in France.

TURNING BACK TIME
IN THE SOUTH SEAS
January 1941

THOR HEYERDAHL (1914–2002)

THE QUEST FOR PARADISE MUST BE THE OLDEST OF TRAVELER'S dreams, and no place, since Captain Cook's voyages to the South Seas, has seemed more alluring a paradise than the palm-fringed islands of Polynesia. In particular the Marquesas, as faraway as any islands on Earth, have had an especially romantic appeal. There Herman Melville lived among the friendly cannibals; there Paul Gauguin painted once Tahiti became too civilized. And there, on ravishing Fatu-Hiva, Thor Heyerdahl began his extraordinary career.

From youth, Heyerdahl had dreamed of escaping the modern world. At the University of Oslo the young Norwegian met Liv Torp, who shared his love of the outdoors. They married on Christmas Eve, 1936. The following day they departed on a classic South Seas idyll to Fatu-Hiva, the place to make a leafy home, live on coconuts, and dwell blissfully with nature. This "first attempt to find paradise," as he later called it, did not succeed. Not serpents but mosquitoes chased them from the garden: They carried elephantiasis, which was ravaging the island population.

Their failed experiment might be unremarkable were it not for Heyerdahl's maverick ideas and subsequent adventures. On Fatu-Hiva he discovered plants and stone artifacts he believed to have come originally from South America. It was but one—admittedly large—step toward his premise that Polynesia was settled from that continent and not from Asia, as universally believed. In 1947, defying those who scorned his ideas, he climbed aboard a balsawood raft in the Peruvian surf and, three months and 4,300 miles later, crashed into a reef in the Tuamotu Islands of Polynesia. The daring and dramatic voyage of the Kon Tiki made Thor Heyerdahl a household name.

That triumph, however, was undreamed of in 1937. Thor was 22 and Liv 20, and it was paradise they were hoping to find. The narrative of their Fatu-Hiva experience, published in NATIONAL GEOGRAPHIC *when he was still a complete unknown, gave Heyerdahl his first broad exposure to an English-speaking public.*

EVEN BEFORE WE COULD SEE ITS LAND, WE CAUGHT THE WARM AND living scent of earth and growing things wafted to us over the salt seas.

And when we sailed into the shadow of the island, where the blue ocean turned to green like the jungle creeping downward from the hills, we knew we had chosen a land of unsurpassed beauty....

Slowly the schooner crept along the steep coast, where deep valleys passed in review, opening their rocky gates to disclose their lush beauty. Red rocks shut out the sight of waving palms, a sunny beach, and the white foam of breakers until the steep mountain wall opened on the next valley.

Where to land? This was our present problem. Luckily a young native lad on board had been born in Fatu-Hiva. He alone knew the place from within, for even our captain had never been there.

As the valleys succeeded one another, he described where the natives lived, where drinking water was to be found. And finally, under his guidance, we were in the lifeboat, our hearts hammering with excitement, while natives rowed us toward the island. The roaring breakers rose and burst into snow-white foam before they reached the shore.

Riding in a furious race on the tumbling crest of the green wall of water, we were thrown amid dancing foam far up on the soft black lava sand. Overhead the trade wind ruffled the fringed leaves of coconut palms. Green hills rose around us. The air was heavy with a haunting, tropical scent.

The natives climbed back into the boat and rowed toward the schooner. Soon the white sails of the *Tereora* melted into the horizon.

We stood alone with our trunks that contained the clothing we had worn during the voyage, and with nothing else save the materials I had brought for scientific research on this little-explored island. A strange feeling of loneliness assailed us.

What to do next?

With a mutual impulse we turned to our trunks and began to drag them toward the shade of the trees....

Far into the valley, across the river, and up the hill we went, until we found the site we wanted for our first home. It was a royal site, literally, for once the king of the inner valley had chosen it for his residence. Now the jungle had recaptured the clearing.

Exploring the thicket, we discovered a cold, clear spring with the remains of a bathing pool built of huge stones. Nearby, platforms and terraces of equally big rocks had been built into the hill.

The dense vegetation entangled itself over our heads, shutting out both sunlight and any view of the surrounding country. But here was good water, and if the site had suited a king, who were we to find fault?

I cut a piece from a bamboo tree, pierced the joints with a stick, and thrust the cane between the stones of the pool. The water came through the bamboo clear and cool, and never did water taste better than this.

Without wasting time we started to clear. Our Tahitian machete cut the thick green banana stem as if it were an onion. Even the mighty breadfruit tree fell crashing to the ground. Liv tore away brush, creepers, giant leaves and ferns, and soon a faint breeze together with sunlight reached the old ruins.

Before long we were able to look out upon a marvelous view. Below was the green roof of the palm forest, with here and there a glimpse of blue stream. Above was the mighty mountain range where white dots marked the presence of mountain sheep.

Before nightfall we had cleared sufficient space to erect our little tent against mosquitoes and poisonous centipedes, and I had cut some red mountain bananas which we roasted before we retired to our bed of palm leaves. We slept to the soughing of the palms and sounds like distant shots that marked the falling of coconuts.

Strange noises pierced our slumber. Was that a boar or a wild dog, or maybe a wild cat jumping for a fruit rat? The gay song of small birds awakened us next morning, with a larger blue and yellow bird making a deep bass to their melody. Flitting about in the palms, this beautiful creature sounded his deep *hoo* that carried for miles.

After a dip in the clear waters of our pool, we breakfasted on coconut, finishing with a few ripe oranges hooked down from a tree. We laughed for sheer joy.

What a country! What a life!

It took us three days to free the old plateau from the grip of the jungle. Around the site we cleared a sunny garden of coconuts, bananas, papayas, mangoes, oranges, lemons, and breadfruit, and of many of the less-known wild tropical fruits. Except for the breadfruit and mangoes, which ripen in regular season, many of the bushes and trees carried blossoms and green and ripe fruit at the same time all year round.

The red mountain bananas, or *fei*, so difficult of access in Tahiti, where they grow on precipices, were abundant in the Omoa Valley forest. This fruit was on our daily menu. Being inedible raw, it was roasted over our open fire and eaten with the white oil of the grated and squeezed coconut kernel.

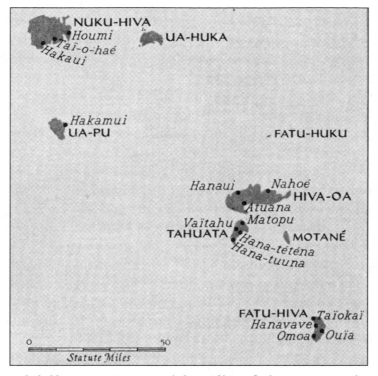

The lushly romantic Marquesas, with their surf-beaten flanks, craggy gorges, and luxuriant vegetation, were part of French Polynesia and administered from Tahiti when Thor Heyerdahl arrived on Fatu-Hiva.

Equally important on our daily bill of fare were the big green breadfruit, which also had to be cooked. We placed them in the center of a small fire and left them until the rind was burned black and cracked loose from the delicious white meat inside. It was a starchy and heavy dish, tasting like a cross between fresh-baked bread and potatoes.

But down in the swampy soil below the spring we found our real potato field. Here grew the taro root with its big, heart-shaped leaves.

These foods, with bananas and coconuts, formed our staple diet. We never tired of coconuts, which we had for breakfast and for our evening meal, and the cool milk of the young green nut was always on hand. Orange and lemon juice with squashed sugar cane were also favorite cold drinks, while for hot beverage we had a sort of tea boiled from withered leaves of orange trees.

But we discovered more than food as we cleared the site for our home. Among the old ruins we found utensils of stone, shell, and bone—true collectors' pieces.

When our clearing work was completed, we called on the friendly natives to help raise our cabin atop the ruins. Where once a king's castle stood, we reared our modest home, six feet by twelve when the framework of strong branches was completed....

Our little home received us with the freshness of spring, and we never tired of the beautiful color which changed as the bamboo aged. The plaited walls turned from green to reddish brown and yellow. We made a bed from branches and covered it with piles of palm leaves. Then I made a little shelf, a table, and two crooked stools. Our plates were giant mother-of-pearl shells, which we gathered on the beach. For glasses and spoons we used bamboo joints, while coconut shells were our cups and bowls....

When the sea was tolerably calm, we went fishing in dugout canoes with a couple of the natives. Since there are no coral reefs around the Marquesan islands, the heavy seas that roll across thousands of miles of open ocean thunder on the coast of Fatu-Hiva. Yet for days and nights the vast Pacific may lie like a shining mirror around the island. Such nights, when the moon was full, we would go fishing for flying fish.

Two or three dugout canoes, with outriggers, slipped out on the black velvet water. Behind us lay the torn silhouette of the islands against the tropic sky, and before us, in the bow of each canoe, was a flaming torch of dried canes. Blazing and sparkling along the water, the torches attracted the flying fish from the black depths and they would come shooting through the air like torpedoes. Sitting in the bottom of the low canoes, we tried to catch them with big nets. It was immense fun. With the speed of arrows the fish shot around the canoes.

They hit us on the head, in the stomach, and on our sides, and several flew right into the canoe, where they floundered helplessly about, unable to take off except from the water. When the torches burned down, the fish disappeared, and we, with our palatable catch, would start deep-sea fishing in the moonlight.

We never knew what we would find on the end of our lines. Sometimes it was a shark or a giant deep-sea eel of the moray family, with sharp and dangerous teeth; sometimes a fish with a beak like a parrot's or with a needle-covered body. We caught fish of all sizes, shapes, and colors, for the waters around Fatu-Hiva are a vast aquarium.

Most of our time, however, we spent alone in the jungle, often wearing only native garb. We went on our little expeditions for ripe fruit or pandanus kernels, or we made our way along the river bed, trapping the delicious fresh-water shrimp with chewed coconut as bait.

Our enjoyment of life was deep. It was as if our senses, dulled by the noise and speed of civilization, had awakened from a substitute of life to actual living.

Back with our loads from a hard day in the open, we flung ourselves in the fresh mountain stream and relaxed in its clear, cold water before enjoying our main meal. Having no watch, we ate when our stomachs said it was mealtime and slept and rose with the sun.

We learned there were two man-made things we could not do without in our new life. One was a pot in which to cook many of the fruits and roots which were inedible raw, and the other a knife to open the thick outer armor of the coconut....

To picture the South Sea islands as a perfect paradise would be untrue. The lavishness of nature and her beauty probably give this part of the world more claim to the title than any other. But the snake has entered Eden. Although unafflicted with poisonous reptiles, these islands are filled with the danger of disease from insects and even from the jungle mud. One must, in honesty, mention this.

The tiniest cuts or scratches, particularly on our feet or ankles, had to be guarded against. Once there they did not heal, but grew and spread. Often our troubles started as boils that left growing wounds. We tried old native remedies of leaves and flowers, and sterilization with boiling water, but nothing gave lasting help.

As months passed and no schooner called at Fatu-Hiva, our situation became serious. For weeks we could scarcely crawl from our cabin in quest of food. Then we made a desperate decision. On the beach near the native village lay a decrepit lifeboat, discarded long since by some schooner. Urged by my insistence, the natives patched this up, fitted it with sails, and stocked it with provisions.

Finally, one day Liv and I, with a crew of eleven rowers, set out from our island. Brisk winds soon carried us from sight of land, and with no compass or other instrument we set our course, old Ioane [a native sailor] steering by means of an oar toward the neighboring island of Hiva-Oa, hidden beyond the horizon....

Hiva-Oa, main island in the south Marquesan group, has a Catholic mission, a French policeman, an English shopkeeper, a Norwegian copra planter, a few Chinese, and several hundred natives. One of the natives, who

First evening in Paradise: Still innocent, with all still before them, young Thor Heyerdahl carries red bananas that he and his bride will roast for their simple meal.

had studied in the Papeete hospital, acted as doctor for the island. He quickly opened our wounds and dressed them, and a month later, when they were completely healed, we were ready to return to Fatu-Hiva by schooner.

We found our bamboo cabin had been eaten by insects and overrun by ants, poisonous centipedes, and giant spiders, while our little clearing was once again in the grasp of the jungle. Therefore, with the aid of a few native friends, we moved to the Valley of Ouia, on the eastern side of the island, where an ancient native lived with his adopted daughter....

It was a strenuous trip over the interior highland, through dense bamboo forests and thickets of fern trees, but a warm welcome awaited us. From his cabin between the palms, the old chief Tei Tetua came running to greet us. Breathless for a moment, he finally began to gasp out in his native tongue: "Come and eat. Eat pig. No more pig, eat chicken."

Next morning our friends departed, leaving us with Tei Tetua and the little girl, Tahia Momo.

Down near the beach, where the refreshing trade winds swept away the mosquitoes and the evils of the jungle, we built our new home on high poles with one wall open and no furniture save a heap of leaves for our bed.

We felt we were living in a bird's nest. When a storm swept in from the open ocean, or when wild boars, roaming the valley, stopped to scratch the poles of our home, it swayed like the palm tops outside.

Old Tei Tetua came running in protest when I went to seek porous crack-proof stones to form Liv's cookstove. "You guest in my valley. You eat my food," he said. And he grasped our single pot and went away.

In the months that followed we did not cook a meal. Every day Tei Tetua came climbing the ladder to our doorway with big wooden bowls filled with strange but palatable food. His specialty was a dish consisting of small edible-shell crabs boiled in coconut milk, and boar that had been baked in leaves between hot stones and dipped in a piquant sauce, all served with heaps of boiled taro root.

Together with old Tei, who was strong and wiry, I spent most of my time seeking fruit and edible roots, or exploring old caves and ruins for carvings of the early days.

Unforgettable were the evenings we four spent together around the campfire, old Tei telling us of days gone by. Our own world was far away. Nothing existed save us four around the glowing fire, with the moon cutting a patch over the dark ocean and lighting the top of the palms up the valley where the world ended in a wall of dark precipice.

Sometimes we spoke to Tei of big cities and of modern marvels like airplanes, but even in the telling we found ourselves wondering: "Is it really true?"

Perhaps the music Tei blew on his bamboo flute by means of his nostrils was crude and monotonous, but it fascinated us and interpreted the spirit of the jungle night. When he sang the old native story of Creation, we marveled that it was our own religion with other names for Adam and Eve and Jehovah.

We often shuddered as Tei told stories of cannibalism and of cruelties during tribal wars, but we felt our own civilization was none too advanced in spite of superior knowledge.

Still to be seen at an old tribal meeting place was an oven where once enemies of war were roasted and eaten by the medicine man in honor of Tiki, one of the characteristic Marquesan gods. Cannibalism seldom occurred among the common people, though Tei, with great respect, mentioned that his father, Uta, preferred the old but sweet man meat—which they called "long pig"—to anything else....

Several months after we first met Tei and his little adopted daughter, we bade them a regretful farewell. Alone we managed the exciting climb over the mountains and down to the other coast to make our final home on the island in a cave in the wild cliffs at Tahaoa beach. Here we lived for a few weeks, collecting our food from the shallow water between the rocks, always watching the blue horizon for the white sails of the little schooner.

When it came, and we clambered over the gunwales from the rope ladder, we almost frightened the native crew by our wild appearance.

"Monsieur," said a polite Tahitian native in French, "you look like a real savage."

As our ship moved out to sea, Liv and I stayed by the gunwale to catch the final glimpse of our island, a blue torn shadow disappearing into the ocean.

"Fatu-Hiva," I said to Liv, "certainly was the right place. But you can't buy a ticket to paradise!"

THEY SURVIVED AT SEA

May 1945

LT. CMDR. SAMUEL F. HARBY (1908–94)

SAM HARBY WAS A RESOURCEFUL MAN. THE RUGGED OUTDOORS
type, he knew how to take care of himself in the woods. Once, while traveling
around the world, he cadged meals by performing gymnastic tricks at Siberian
train stops. He had a flair for communication, writing books on tumbling and on
his experiences supervising Civilian Conservation Corps camps in New York. This
combination of resourcefulness and storytelling came together in World War II,
when Harby, an officer in the U.S. Navy, directed the production of training films,
arriving on still-smoking battlefields to document such activities as field hospital
operations. In the Pacific theater he filmed native survival techniques for military
personnel who might find themselves lost or trapped in remote jungles or on lone-
ly atolls. He was a spellbinding lecturer, and wrote articles for such magazines as Life,
Look, Pageant, Reader's Digest, *and, of course,* NATIONAL GEOGRAPHIC.

"They Survived at Sea," published in the May 1945 issue, was described by
Vilhjalmur Stefansson as "one of the most notable articles of your notable maga-
zine." This was impressive praise, for Stefansson, one of the great Arctic explorers
of his day, had once lived for nearly six years foraging off the ice of the far North.
He knew a thing or two about survival.

Two of Harby's stories follow. Navy propaganda or not, his work is
riveting reading, making clear that survival is roughly three parts luck, one part
resourcefulness, and one part sheer dogged determination to live.

THE CASE OF LT. (JG) GEORGE H. SMITH WAS ONE IN WHICH THE PILOT
had the new-type equipment, retained it all, and put it to the severe test of
20 days afloat.

On July 14, 1943, Lieutenant Smith, flying a Grumman Wildcat, was
en route to Munda from Guadalcanal. His flight encountered a series of
thunderheads and was forced to take the long way around to avoid
trouble. Smith was eventually separated from the rest of the flight and,
as he had an unreliable compass and almost no fuel left, he was forced to
make a water landing in the dark on a rough sea.

After the belly of his plane hit the water, the plane went forward 15
or 20 feet, then nosed down for Davy Jones's locker.

Smith, well trained, had prepared in advance for a quick getaway. An extra canteen and an extra emergency kit were tied on his parachute harness; his shoulder straps and safety belt were drawn tight. When the plane stopped its forward motion, he disengaged the safety harness, kept the parachute buckled on, gave a hard push with his legs, and went about five feet up to the surface. Split-second timing was essential to get out alive. This feat accomplished, the next thing was to pull the cord on his Mae West and inflate the life jacket; then, with this support, break out the rubber raft. His raft was the one-man seat-pack type attached to his parachute harness.

Inflating the rubber boat took Smith about five minutes. It consisted of jerking the pin and turning the valve on the CO_2 cylinder, a difficult operation to figure out in the dark, but one easy to perform if practiced in advance. Smith followed instructions exceptionally well, even saving his unopened parachute, which was to come in very handy later.

The sensation of riding such a small craft in a vast ocean was thrilling and fearsome. His water-soaked equipment was weighty and, with his own bulk, crowded the raft. He felt as though the least move would upset the tiny craft and leave him to the mercy of the sea. Therefore, as soon as he was rested, he moved cautiously to trim ship and lash down its loose gear, so that if his raft capsized his precious gear would not be lost.

Cold winds blowing through Smith's wet clothes spurred him to open his parachute and use the silk as a blanket. The huge canopy proved cumbersome; so he cut off the top half and about a dozen shroud lines, bundled up the rest, secured this to the boat with a line, and cast it overboard to drag along aft in the water, where it helped the sea anchor steady the craft. He used the shroud lines to secure his gear further, then tucked the silk about him and tried to sleep. There was little sleep that first night, but later on he learned the trick and could sleep at least several hours a night despite the bobbing of his floating leaf.

The worst thing was the pounding of the waves on the bottom of the raft, or rather on his own bottom, as only a thin sheet of rubberized cloth separated him from the sea. That was nerve-racking and nearly drove him mad. Three times, at night, he resorted to the morphine syrettes of his first-aid kit for relief. They seemed to soften the pounding and induced much-needed sleep.

The days were hot, the nights were cold, and the waves were merciless. Smith wisely kept on all his clothes, including shoes, helmet, and goggles. Being blond and particularly subject to sunburn, he fashioned a mask of parachute silk and so protected his whole face.

Having an extra canteen and a week's rations, he did not immediately worry about subsistence. The first 24 hours he fasted, then used the stored rations sparingly. His equipment included a fishing kit, a sheath knife, and his .45 automatic strapped about his waist.

In the weeks which followed he hooked not a single fish, but shot nine birds. He did find an 8-inch mackerel in the sea anchor one morning. He ate it, and he managed several times to dip up minnows with his mosquito head net. Sharks got his lines early in the voyage, but, though he shot them, they sank out of reach.

His biggest excitement over marine life came when two huge sperm whales appeared. One of the giants came up to his boat, nudged it with his nose, and slid gracefully under. Smith was scared stiff, but he sat still and lost only about ten years' pleasant dreams.

Another time he saw a desperate struggle between a marlin and a mackerel. The marlin was about seven feet long, with an 18-inch spike, and was apparently trying to catch the 30-inch mackerel. The two fish came directly toward the boat and finally splashed out of the water within three feet of Smith, who was petrified for fear the marlin would pierce his rubber raft and leave him on the ocean without a seat. But luck was with him, and nothing happened.

On July 20, his sixth day, he sighted the first of many Japanese planes he was to see, as he was now drifting on a 300° course deep into enemy waters. A few of these planes passed directly overhead, as low as 500 feet, but failed to see him. From then on he sighted planes almost every day. He would wait until they were close enough to identify and, if friendly, would signal excitedly with tracer bullets, a mirror, or sea-dye marker. However, not until August 1, his 18th day, did he succeed in attracting the attention of a plane. This was a New Zealand land-based Lockheed Hudson, which passed very close.

The tail gunner saw Smith's sea-marker dye on the water; the plane turned, made a wide circle, and flew down close to the raft. Smith said of this incident later: "For the first time in my life, and I hope the last, I cried for joy. I was afraid they would check my position and leave without dropping supplies and, frankly, I was getting pretty hungry and thirsty. I put on my rubber paddles, leaned back in the raft, and signaled in semaphore the letters E-A-T."

The plane made another wide circle and then dropped an inflated life jacket with supplies attached.... He paddled to it and found Army-type emergency rations, a canteen of water, a map marking his position, ammunition for the .45, a waterproof flashlight, first-aid equipment, a Very pistol, and other useful items. The New Zealanders flew by once more, wobbled their wings, and headed for home.

The 20th day was overcast and dreary. The wind still blew in squalls. It was not a day to expect rescue. But just before noon three Navy Catalinas hove into view. Smith jumped with excitement and spread a sea marker. Two of the Cats passed within half a mile but failed to see him. The third came directly overhead, saw his signal, dropped a smoke bomb, and then called the others back.

Waves and swells were 10 feet high, and the three flying boats circled as they considered the risk of landing on such a rough sea. Two of the planes lowered their retractable wing floats in an attempt to land, but both pilots decided not to chance it. The third pilot was more daring. He knew that, as the weather was closing in, if one of them didn't set down on the water in the vicinity, they would probably never find this castaway again. So the pilot dropped his depth charges and about 800 gallons of gas to lighten the ship and made a power-stall landing on the water.

The Catalina managed to retrieve Smith, but the ocean was too rough to take off, and so the plane stayed on the water all that afternoon and night.

Smith was indescribably grateful for companionship and, despite the precarious plight of the Catalina, he felt he was in the lap of luxury. He drank two tumblers of grape-juice, a couple of cups of coffee, ate two big steaks and a large dish of peas. It's a wonder he didn't die from this extravagance alone; but he was the only one who remained well. The rough sea got the best of the others....

The castaway was taken back to a field hospital on Florida Island, where he spent only three days recuperating. Despite meager rations he had been able to keep his body in fairly good condition for the 20 days afloat. He lost a total of 20 pounds, suffered from salt-water sores on elbows, back, and buttocks, and for a few hours after rescue was unable to move from the waist down because of sitting so long in a cramped position. These difficulties, however, did not last, and he was soon ready for the long trip home....

The story of Poon Lim, a Chinese sailor who survived 133 days afloat—and alone—has been described as the "story to end all raft stories." The raft he used was of a variety common to warships of the time: It looked like a large wooden pallet, equipped with a footlocker on one end in which provisions had been stocked. Each ship had a certain number of these rafts for emergency use.

Poon Lim had signed up with the British Merchant Marine in Hong Kong when the Japanese incursion began to threaten his island home. In 1942 he was working as a steward aboard the S.S. *Benlomond* when she received two torpedoes, 15 days out of Capetown, en route to South America.

Lim was in his cabin when the first torpedo struck. It was high noon and a clear day. Rushing on deck at the shock of the explosion, he grabbed a life jacket and made for his abandon-ship station. But that was where the torpedo had struck, and his raft was gone.

Quickly he made for the bridge station, hoping to get on a raft there, but before he could reach the bridge, the ship settled under and he was engulfed in a torrent of green water, swirling and sucking him down.

It seemed hours before he came up, but his life jacket finally brought him to the surface. Being only a fair swimmer, he looked about for something to hang onto. A plank from the hatch cover was near by; so he secured this and hung on for dear life. Now was a chance to wipe his face, to get the oil out of his eyes, and to look around.

Men were all about him in the water, but two hundred yards away was a raft with five seamen on it. As he made for the raft, a submarine surfaced, painted white with green Italian fasces sketched on its conning tower. The sub approached the raft. Some of the British seamen were taken aboard for questioning. Lim was in the line of its course when it got under way again. As it approached, he called out, "Save me, or I drown!" The men on the bridge heard and looked him over quite dispassionately, but the only answer he got was a jesting "Goodbye!" shouted back in broken English.

After an hour in the water he sighted an unoccupied raft, probably one blown free when the first torpedo struck. It was a long, hard swim to reach it, but once aboard Lim found provisions which would last him about 50 days. By this time all his companions were out of sight, and he was so exhausted that he immediately fell asleep.

The first week afloat was uneventful. Lim studied his situation and used his supplies frugally. Having lost all his clothes except shirt and vest before he reached the raft, he made a skirt from a burlap bag in

Poon Lim, who survived for 133 days on the open ocean, reenacts his raft ordeal for the benefit of future sailors. Around his neck is a replica of his makeshift knife.

which the bottle of lime juice had been wrapped and fashioned a knife from a piece of tin off a pemmican can. [His total stores consisted of six large boxes of hardtack, two pounds of chocolate, ten small cans of pemmican, one bottle of lime juice, five cans of evaporated milk, and ten gallons of water.] There were also four poles and a tarpaulin, a long strip of canvas for a bulwark and a smaller piece to cover the well, two paddles, some signal flares and smoke pots, a can of massage oil, a flashlight, and some rope. There was no fishing equipment, no first-aid kit, and not a tool except an iron key to the water tank, which Lim later used to pound out other tools necessary for survival.

At the end of the first week, he sighted a ship and used his smoke pots to attract attention. He was apparently observed, for the ship changed course and came within half a mile of his raft, but did not pick him up. He was uncertain whether they saw him and used up all his signaling devices to make sure. This failure to pick up a survivor can be explained only by the possibility that the people aboard thought Lim was a decoy, and, being in submarine-infested waters, didn't care to take the risk. There may be circumstances that warrant such a drastic decision, but they are rare. Lim, however, accepted the matter stoically. He had decided from the first that if his number were up, he would die; and if not, he would come through all right.

He kept reminding himself that China had been able to stay in the war against Japan for almost six long years, and that if China could survive so long in the face of such tremendous odds, then he likewise could survive until help should come. This philosophical attitude, born of centuries of struggle, undoubtedly enabled Poon Lim to hang on to his sanity where other men would have gone stark, staring mad. Lim swears that at no time did he get delirious or have hallucinations, or in any way go out of his head.

The approximate location of the torpedoing was 00.30°N by 38° 45'W. This is above the easternmost tip of South America and about 750 miles from the mouth of the Amazon. The weather is warm in this region and there is plenty of rain, as well as an abundance of marine and bird life.

Poon Lim did not attempt to fish until the rations with which the raft had been stocked originally were consumed. Then he fashioned a small hook from the wire spring in his flashlight. This he pounded to a bent point on one end and a ring on the other, using the metal key to his water tank as a hammer. He unraveled strands of rope and twisted to these into a fish line, then baited his hook with pemmican and tried his luck.

The pemmican bait would disintegrate on contact with the water and drop off the line. Looking around for something better, he discovered a barnacle on the side of the raft. This was promptly attached to his line and, presto—he caught a minnow! But he wanted bigger game and set to work making heavier tackle. He pounded the deck of his raft with the metal key until he literally dug a large nail out of the planking. Not wishing to risk the loss of the nail overboard, he completed the extraction by pulling it out with his teeth. Then, like the smaller hook, this was hammered to a point and bent into shape. A strong line was twisted and braided directly on the nailhead, and the new gear was ready for use.

At first Lim's luck with the large hook was poor. The big fish seemed very cagey, and it was not until he used live bait that he really became "of age" as a fisherman. His practice was to catch a small fish on the small line and transfer it to the larger one, putting the big hook through its tail in such a way that the minnow could still swim.... He regularly pulled in big 20-pounders, and what he could not eat at one sitting was carefully cut into strips and hung in the sun to dry....

On the 100th day afloat, he sighted a formation of six airplanes and signaled them as best he could, waving his flag and canvas. One came down to investigate and dropped a smoke bomb to mark the spot, but since the sea was rough, it did not land. Words are inadequate to describe the feelings of a man when, after drifting for 100 days, a would-be rescuer passes him by. This was Lim's second great disappointment, and he was destined to carry on alone for another month before help should come.

Help finally arrived in the form of a small fishing boat manned by half a dozen native Brazilians. They spoke only Portuguese, but where the need is great men can usually make themselves understood. Lim got along very well with these people, actually a family, including a woman and a girl. They cruised for another three days before putting him ashore at Salina, in the state of Pará, Brazil. An incident occurred on the second day with these people which proves that our castaway must have been in good condition when they found him. The father asked Lim if he would like to marry the girl, his daughter....

Poon Lim's experience is a wonderful example of how a rugged physique and resourcefulness of mind will extend the limits of human endurance beyond all expectations.

Though we hope no human being will have to undergo such privation again, we have learned from Poon Lim, and others like him, never to give up hope. Survival is an all-or-none proposition; the alternative is death. The secret of success here, as elsewhere, lies in having good equipment and knowing how to use it.

PART TWELVE:
New worlds to explore

FROM LONDON TO AUSTRALIA BY AEROPLANE

March 1921

SIR ROSS SMITH (1892–1922)

BY 1919, ONLY A DECADE AFTER LOUIS BLERIOT WAS LIONIZED *for having flown the 21 miles across the English Channel, men were attempting truly long-distance flights. In June, British pilots Alcock and Brown flew a Vickers Vimy bomber, a speedy twin-engined biplane, nonstop across the Atlantic. They won Lord Northcliffe's £10,000 prize for being first to do so. Winston Churchill wasn't sure which to admire more, their "audacity or their good fortune."*

Both were needed to win the next aviation purse. Australia had never yet been reached by air, so its government backed another £10,000 prize for the first flight by Aussie aviators from England to their home continent in 30 days or less. Six aircraft entered the competition; one plane made it. The others either crashed, killing their crews, or were disabled along the way—an indication of the dangers involved in the untried route. Even the winning plane just barely made it: Another Vickers Vimy, it almost dropped from the sky, fuel tanks empty, at the end of 28 days.

Lifting off from Hounslow Aerodrome near London on November 12, 1919, the plane crossed Europe, the Middle East, India, Southeast Asia, the East Indies, and Timor before arriving in Darwin—nearly 10,000 miles. It accomplished nearly 20 hazardous takeoffs and landings in stump-filled fields and swamps. At the helm was Capt. Ross Smith, 27, a highly decorated officer of the Australian Flying Corps who had once been Lawrence of Arabia's pilot. His brother, Lt. Keith Smith, a former RAF flight instructor, served as navigator. Two mechanics, Sgts. Jim Bennett and Wally Shiers, also flew along, for obvious reasons.

Landing nearly halfway around the world, the four were acclaimed heroes, the Smith brothers knighted. In March 1921, NATIONAL GEOGRAPHIC published a long, triumphant account in which Sir Ross not only described their hairbreadth escapes from makeshift fields but also the anxiety and enchantment of cloud flying, the intoxication of flight, and the sheer exhilaration of being aerial pioneers. As Sergeant Shiers put it, it was fine to flit through air that had "never smelt a blanky exhaust."

THE AEROPLANE IS THE NEAREST THING TO ANIMATE LIFE THAT man has created. In the air a machine ceases indeed to be a mere piece of mechanism; it becomes animate and is capable not only of primary guidance and control, but actually of expressing a pilot's temperament. The lungs of the machine, its engines, are again the crux of man's wisdom. Their marvelous reliability and great intricacy are almost as awesome as the human anatomy. When both engines are going well and synchronized to the same speed, the roar of the exhausts develops into one long-sustained rhythmical boom-boom-boom. It is a song of pleasant harmony to the pilot, a duet of contentment that sings of perfect firing in both engines and says that all is well....

[*Above France*] So we climbed steadily in a wide ascending spiral, until we reached an altitude of 9,000 feet, and were then just above the clouds. Below us the snowstorm raged, but we had entered another world—a strange world, all our own, with bright, dazzling sunshine.

It might have been a vision of the polar regions; it undoubtedly felt like it. The mighty cloud ocean over which we were scudding resembled a polar landscape covered with snow. The rounded cloud contours might have been the domes of snow-merged summits. It was hard to conceive that that amorphous expanse was not actual, solid. Here and there flocculent towers and ramps heaved up, piled like mighty snow dumps, toppling and crushing into one another. Everything was so tremendous, so vast, that one's sense of proportion swayed uncontrolled.

Then there were tiny wisps, more delicate and frail than feathers. Chasms thousands of feet deep, sheer columns, and banks extended almost beyond eye-reach. Between us and the sun stretched isolated towers of cumulus, thrown up as if erupted from the chaos below. The sunlight, filtering through their shapeless bulk, was scattered into every conceivable gradation and shade in monotone. Round the margins the sun's rays played, outlining all with edgings of silver.

The scene was one of utter bewilderment and extravagance. Below, the shadow of our machine pursued us, skipping from crest to crest, jumping gulfs and ridges like a bewitched phantom. Around the shadow circled a gorgeous halo, a complete flat rainbow. I have never seen anything in all my life so unreal as the solitudes of this upper world through which my companions and I were now fleeting.

The cold grew more intense. Our hands and feet lost all feeling and our bodies became well-nigh frozen. The icy wind penetrated our thick clothing and it was with greatest difficulty that I could work the machine. Our breaths condensed on our face-masks and iced up our goggles and our helmets.

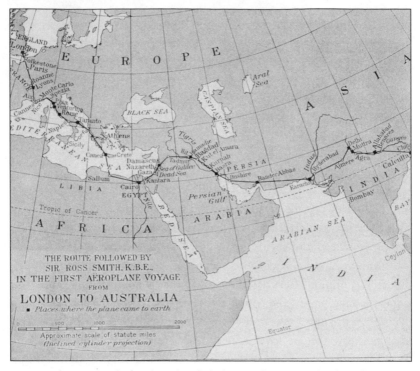

As part of its route on the first, hazardous flight from London to Australia, the Vickers Vimy successfully flew across the Mediterranean, the Middle East, and northern India.

Occasionally immense cloud barriers rose high above the lower cloud strata, and there was no circumventing them; these barriers were invariably charged with snow, and as I plunged the machine into them, the wings and fuselage were quickly armored with ice. Our air-speed indicator became choked, and we ourselves were soon covered white by an accumulating layer of driving snow. Goggles were useless, owing to the ice, and we suffered much agony through being compelled to keep a lookout with unprotected eyes—straining into the ninety-miles-an-hour snow-blast....

Ahead loomed up a beautiful dome-shaped cloud, lined with silver edges. It was symbolical; and when all seemed dark, this rekindled in me the spark of hope. By the side of the "cloud with the silver lining" there extended a gulf about two miles across. As we burst out over it, I looked down into its abysmal depths.

At the bottom lay the world. As far as the eye could reach, in every direction stretched the illimitable cloud sea, and the only break now lay beneath us. It resembled a tremendous crater, with sides clean cut as a shaft. Down this wonderful cloud avenue I headed the Vimy, slowly descending in a wide spiral. The escape through this marvelous gateway, 7,000 feet deep, that seemed to link the realms of the infinite with the lower world of mortals, was the most soul-stirring episode of the whole voyage....

[*Across the Riviera*] Nature's great map was no longer obscured. It lay unrolled below, an enlarged edition of our own tiny charts, on which we checked its features. Picking up the River Durance quite easily, we crossed it and passed above the city of Aix; then swung east, heading for the coast and Cannes—across the famous Riviera.

Soon we caught sight of the sea. Five thousand feet below us the Mediterranean was laving the cliffs of innumerable little bays and inlets, embroidering a thin white edging of surf round their rugged bases—a narrow, white boundary-line separating green-topped cliffs from deep-blue waters.

Nice soon lay below us. The city, with its fine buildings and avenues of palms, encircled by high hills, rests on the shores of a sea of wondrous blue. It is a place of ineffable charm and peace.

A large crowd had collected on the Promenade des Anglais to witness our flight and cheer us up. We flew low enough to distinguish the doll-like figures, and though we could not return their greetings we appreciated them none the less. Then onward again with a following breeze, white-cresting the blue sea that stretched away from beneath us to the southern horizon. We circled above Monte Carlo and the famous Casino, admiring the wonderful terraces and gardens, which looked like a skillfully carved and colored model rather than a real palace and its garden....

[*Over Egypt*] We took off from Heliopolis aerodrome with the cheers of my old war comrades sounding above our engines. For 50 miles we followed the Ismailia Canal to Tel-el-Kabir. The banks were bordered by a patchwork of densely cultivated and irrigated lands; beyond, arid barrenness, sand, and nothing.

On the canal the great white lateen sails of dhows and feluccas in large number resembled a model yacht regatta. It was all very beautiful and wonderful. Northward the waterways, canals, and lakes of the Nile delta stood out like silver threads woven around the margins of patches in a patch-quilt, for the sun had now burst through the clouds, and all the world sprang into life and light. From aloft, without the sun, the world is a gloomy-looking place, doleful and dead....

And soon to Ismailia and the canal that links north with south—a straight cut of deep-blue water, running to the horizon transversely to our course—and ahead the gray desert sands, only limited by the blue sky.

Below, a P. and O. steamer, heading south, passes down the Suez Canal. Perhaps she is bound for Australia; she will call in at Adelaide, my home and destination! With a smile, I contrasted the old and the new methods of transportation, and a throb of exultation thrilled us all. Still, we wondered—unspoken thoughts—who would reach Australia first....

[A *mirage*] I now headed the Vimy northeast for Damascus and climbed up to 5,000 feet. Occasional cloud patches passed below us, but the landscape for the most part was drear and featureless, save for a line of snow-clad summits that lay away to the north, Mount Hermon and the Anti-Lebanon Mountains....

Then once more joy filled our thankful hearts when our straining eyes picked up Damascus, a miraged streak on the horizon of a desert wilderness. The streak became irregular. It grew into a band assuming height and breadth, minute excrescences, and well-defined contours. Color crept in; details resolved, developed, enlarged; a city arose from out of the waste of sands, an oasis, glorious, magical, enchanting—this was Damascus. A city almost ethereal in its beauty, rearing a forest of slender minarets and cupolas, surrounded by dense groves and woods, had sprung into being as if by magic, from the Syrian desert....

[*India*] There was great excitement at the aerodrome next morning. While we were taxiing to the far end, preparatory to taking off, a fine bull broke on to the ground, and as we swung round to take off he charged head on toward the machine. The position, though ridiculous, was extremely hazardous. No doubt, to quote the celebrated railway engineer, it would have been "bad for the coo," but a collision would also have been extremely "bad for the Vimy."

I frightened him for the moment by a roar from the engines. Evidently he took the roar for a challenge, and stood in front of the Vimy, pawing the ground and bellowing defiantly. At this point a boy scout rushed out from the crowd to move the monster, and, much to the amusement of ourselves and the crowd, the bull changed his intention and turned on the hero. Our brave toreador retreated to the fence, pursued by the bull.

We took advantage of the diversion and made a more hurried ascent than usual. What became of the scout I do not know, but as we circled above I noticed that the bull was still in sole possession of the aerodrome....

[*Over Siam*] The clouds rested down to 4,000 feet, and we were flying just beneath them. Somewhere ahead lay the mountains that had to be crossed, rearing their summit another 3,000 feet higher. Our maps indicated a pass which we tried to find, and so we started off along a deep valley.

An angel's-eye view of St. Peters Cathedral in the Vatican:
Early pioneers of flight were thrilled with the new perspectives opened on the world.

At first it looked hopeful, but after five minutes' flying the cliffs narrowed in, and fearing I might be trapped in a tapering dead end, I turned the Vimy about. There was just sufficient room in which to effect this maneuver.

After a consultation with my brother, we agreed that our safest course was to climb above the cloud-mass or at least to an altitude sufficiently high to clear the mountain tops, and barge our way through the mist. At 9,000 feet we emerged above the first layer; but eastward the clouds appeared to terrace up gradually, and in the distance there extended still another great wall, towering several thousand feet higher....

At first all went well; but, while turning to check over an engine, I apparently and unconsciously, with the natural movement of my body, pushed one foot, which was on the rubber bar, slightly forward. This turned the machine off its course, and when next I looked at my compass I was ten degrees off course. I then kicked on the opposite rudder to bring the machine back; but, as the Vimy is much more sensitive to respond than the comparatively sluggish compass-needle, I found that I had put on too much rudder. The result was that when the compass-needle started to swing it did so through an angle of forty-five degrees. In my attempt to correct the course and bring the needle back on to its correct reading, I glanced at the air-speed indicator and found it registering over one hundred miles an hour—twenty-five miles above normal flying speed. This meant that I must have pushed the nose of the machine down. The inclinometer indicated that the machine was not flying laterally correct; in fact, we were flying at an inclined angle of forty degrees. I realized that the machine was slipping sideways, and that if I did not get matters righted at once, the machine would get out of control and go spinning down to earth.

It is useless attempting to describe how I acted. A pilot does things instinctively, and presently my instruments told me that we were once more on our course and on an even keel.

All this took but a few seconds; but they were anxious moments, as a single mistake or the losing of one's head would have been fatal. This happened several times, and at the end of what seemed hours I glanced at my watch and found we had only been in the clouds for twelve minutes! Perhaps my nerves were a little ragged, owing to staring and lack of sleep during the past fortnight; but I felt at last that anything would be better than going on under these tense and nerve-racking conditions.

It was now an hour since we first started across the clouds, and both Keith and I concluded that we must surely be across the mountain range. So I decided to take the risk and go lower and "feel."

Shutting off both engines, we glided down, and I held up the machine so that we were going as slowly as possible—only about forty miles an hour. The sensation was akin to the captain navigating a vessel in uncharted shoaling seas—expecting every moment to feel a bump. Lower and lower we went—ten, nine, eight thousand feet—and then we both anxiously peered over the sides—straining for a glimpse of hidden peaks.

As we approached the 7,000-foot level, which I knew to be the height of the range, we huddled together and held on tight, in anticipation of the crash! I noticed a small hole in the cloud, with something dark beneath. It was past in a flash, but instantly I pulled the throttle full open and flew level again. At first I thought it was the top of a dreadful peak, but on further consideration I remembered that in my brief glance the dark patch had looked a long way down.

Once more I shut off and went lower, and as we had not hit anything by the time we reached 4,000 feet, I concluded that the range had been crossed.

A few minutes more and we burst out into a full view of a glorious world carpeted with trees, 1,500 feet below. The sudden transformation was stunning. It was an unspeakable relief—the end of an hour that was one of the veriest nightmare experiences I have ever passed through.

Before our bewildered gaze there stretched a dark-green forest, only limited by the distant skyline. Here and there the dark green was splashed with patches of bright-colored creeper, and in spite of the fact that there was not the vestige of a possible landing place, it was beautiful and a welcome relief. Later, the Siamese told us that all this country was unexplored....

[Java] The hazy contours of the mountains marking the western end of Java soon began to show up to starboard, and ahead a scene of rare enchantment began to resolve itself upon the bosom of the tropical sea.

The sea was a glorious mirror almost as rippleless as the canopy above, and scattered broadcast lay a thousand isles, each one beautiful, and all combined to make one of the most beautiful sights I have ever looked down upon. Many of the islands are heavily grown with palms extending to the very water's edge; others, sparsely cultivated, fringed with a narrow ribbon of beach; but around each is a setting of an exquisite shade of green, marking a sand-girt shallow; then deep-blue and depth. Myriads of tiny white fisher-sails passed through the channels, gleaning their harvest from the sea.

Reluctantly we turned from this glimpse of fairy-land, and bearing for the Garden Island of the East, soon reached Batavia, the city of canals and beautiful avenues.... With beautiful weather favoring us, we sped rapidly over fertile tracts of this amazing island, charmed by the unsurpassable beauty that unfolded below. Java impressed me as one vast bounteous garden, amid which rise the immense, shapely cones of volcanic mountains.

Perhaps one of the most striking sights was the "paddy" country. From our height, the whole expanse of the land appeared to be inundated by irrigation water—all contained in miniature, cell-like squares, that gave the effect of a mighty grid, stretching away to the mountains on our right. Even there the irrigation did not cease, but climbed up the mountain sides in a system of stairlike terraces.

Here and there native villages nestled beneath the shelter of the palm groves or among the verdant green of sugar plantations. Always in the background, subdued by tropic haze, rose the chain of peaks, practically all quiescent, and far away to the left that faint blue line which marked the Pacific horizon....

[Journey's end] In front of us rose a chain of high hills, and, as the atmosphere was hot and we climbed very slowly, we made a detour to avoid them.

Still flying low, we approached the coast and pulled ourselves together for the final lap—the jump across the sheet of blue Indian Ocean that lay between us and Port Darwin.

Keith took all possible bearings, noted wind direction, and made numerous calculations of ground speeds. Then we set compass course for Darwin, and with a "Here goes!" we were out over the sea. All our hearts were beating a little quicker; even our fine old engines seemed to throb a trifle faster.

Our watches registered 11:48 when Keith nodded ahead, and dead on the line of our flight, we made out a faint smoke haze that soon resolved itself into the smoke-plume of a fighting-ship. It was the *Sydney*, and we knew now that, whatever might befall, we had a friend at hand.

We swooped low, and exactly at twelve minutes past noon passed over the vessel, seeing plainly the upturned faces of the sailors and their waving hands. It was a cheer of welcome quite different from anything that we had experienced on the long journey. Perhaps it is not to be wondered at that the result of our snapshot was blurred through the shaking of the camera....

An hour later both of us saw ahead and to port what appeared to be haze, but which we hoped was land, though neither dared express his hopes. They were justified, however, ten minutes later, and hailing Bennett and Shiers, we pointed joyfully to Bathurst Island lighthouse.

It was just 2.6 p.m. when, as our diary prosaically notes, we "observed Australia." At three o'clock we not only observed it, but rested firmly upon it, for, having circled over Darwin and come low enough to observe the crowds and the landing-place, we settled on Terra Australis on December 10th, 27 days 20 hours after taking off from Hounslow.

Two zealous customs and health officials were anxious to examine us, but so were about 2,000 just ordinary citizens, and the odds of 1,000 to 1 were rather long for those departmental men, and our welcome was not delayed.

The hardships and perils of the past month were forgotten in the excitement of the present. We shook hands with one another, our hearts swelling with those emotions invoked by achievement and the glamour of the moment. It was, and will be, perhaps, the supreme hours of our lives....

Not long after those words were printed, Sir Ross Smith was killed. He had been testing a Vickers Viking amphibian, hoping eventually to fly it around the world, when it spun out of control and crashed. In 1923–24 a team of U.S. pilots, in a months-long odyssey, accomplished what Sir Ross gave his life attempting: the first around-the-globe flight.

THE CONQUEST OF
ANTARCTICA BY AIR

August 1930

REAR ADM. RICHARD E. BYRD (1888–1957)

"I MUST CONFESS THAT I LIKE ADVENTURE AND THE FAR PLACES," Richard E. Byrd *once admitted, understating the case, for history has wreathed him with the icy mantle of Antarctica, the farthest of all places, called the last continent of adventure.*

Dick Byrd had glittering good looks and Old Virginia charm, but he was also ambitious and competitive. Though small and slender, he played both tennis and football with intensity. An ankle injured at Annapolis never healed properly, and for the rest of his life he walked with a slight limp. Permanently sidelined from active sea duty, he became a naval aviator, specializing in the Arctic. In 1926, accompanied by Floyd Bennett, Byrd was the first to fly over the North Pole—or so he claimed. He was showered with ticker tape and draped with a Medal of Honor, yet some doubts lingered. Many experts believed that, inadvertently or not, he actually fell 100 to 150 miles short.

If so, he redeemed himself on the opposite end of the globe. In 1928–30 he led his first expedition to Antarctica. Two ships crossed the seas to deposit 41 men, 94 dogs, a Ford snowmobile, and three airplanes on the vast Ross Ice Shelf. Byrd was a superb organizer, and soon "Little America" took shape. Living quarters, mess hall, hangars, even a gymnasium were sunk deep in the snow; 70-foot radio towers loomed above, connecting to the distant outside world. Nestled in those burrows, the men were the first ever to endure the unremitting cold and dark of an Antarctic winter.

When the sun returned, the men emerged and parties began exploring the edge of the continent. Byrd prepared to undertake the first flight over the South Pole, unseen since Scott's ill-fated 1912 expedition dragged itself over that ice. On November 28, 1929—late spring—Byrd joined three companions in a Ford tri-motor: the Floyd Bennett, named after his late friend, recently killed in a crash. The Pole was over 700 miles away; and the tiny plane would need to clear the massive ramparts of Queen Maud Range to get to it.

OUR FLIGHT TO THE POLE WAS DIFFERENT FROM MOST OTHER LONG flights, in that it was absolutely essential we have clear weather. The flight would not be profitable from an exploration standpoint without good visibility. Under certain types of visibility which frequently occur in the Antarctic, flying is not possible. Bad weather would make it impossible for us to get over the high mountains that encircle the Polar Plateau. Many of these are 15,000 feet high, and we would reach them with a heavy load....

We were to fly into an unknown country of changeable weather, sudden blizzards, and extraordinary light conditions which often mark the surface of the snow. "Landing fifty feet up," as aviators say, is a constant danger there....

On the morning of November 28 the geological party reached a point about 100 miles from the foot of the Queen Maud Range, and flashed weather reports to Haines. One of the reports from Gould said conditions over the plateau were favorable. Haines had a tremendous responsibility. "They could be more nearly perfect," he said, "but you had better go now; another chance may not come."

We took off on the flight to the Pole at 3:29 o'clock (10:29 p.m. in New York time) that afternoon. Clouds partly covered the sky at the base. Our concern, however, was the weather at the mountains.

The last thing we put in the plane was a stone that came from Floyd Bennett's grave at Arlington. We weighted it with the American flag, to be dropped at the Pole. This flight he and I had planned together, as we had planned the transatlantic flight. Fate sidetracked him from both. But he was not forgotten.

As the skis left the snow I saw my shipmates in the white bowl beneath us, dancing, jumping, shouting, throwing their hats in the air, wild with joy that we were off for the Pole. I got the same kick then that I got when I looked down upon an exactly similar scene in 1926 as Bennett and I left the snow and headed toward the North Pole. These fellows had given us our great opportunity and they were unselfishly glad.

My planemates were Bernt Balchen, Harold June and Captain Ashley McKinley. Balchen was pilot.... We began our climb while the mountains were still 100 miles away. Before us lay the great uncertainty.

George Black, our supply officer, had weighed everything aboard the ship. The total was a trifle less than 15,000 pounds. By measuring our consumption of gasoline and oil we could tell at any moment what our weight was. This was one of Harold June's many jobs.

McKinley was "fighting" with his camera all over the plane. I was navigating. June was sending radios, dumping gas from cans to tanks, estimating gas from six tanks, and between times taking pictures. Later he

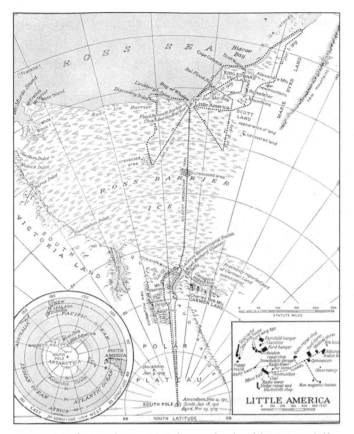

Fanning out from Little America, its base on the edge of the Ross Ice Shelf,
the Byrd Antarctic Expedition of 1928-1930 explored the frozen continent by dogsled and airplane, making the first flight over the South Pole on November 28, 1929.

took his turn at the controls. McKinley and I could take our turns at
piloting only when there was no photographing or navigating to do. This
opportunity probably would come on the return from the Pole. Our activity was in violent contrast to the stillness of the lifeless white spaces below.

We were heading for Axel Heiberg Glacier. Amundsen had reported
that the highest point of the pass was only 10,500 feet. He also noted
towering peaks on both sides.

To the right loomed another huge glacier. We had sighted it on our
base-laying flight and it appeared wide enough for air passage. We were
more than a mile high when we passed our little cache of food and
gasoline—too high to see it.

The sun on the bare, vertical rocks sent up warm currents which
struck the cold air above and formed some fog. Balchen and I conferred.

Should we tackle Axel Heiberg, altitude known, but width and air currents unknown? The bordering peaks might be so high that the currents they created would dash us to the ground, hovering as we were near the absolute ceiling of our plane.

Or should we take the unknown glacier, which looked feasible? Beyond the wider pass there might be mountains to block us.

We had to choose now—and the choice would be irrevocable because we did not have enough gasoline to enable us to fly up a glacier and back again and try another. And we had to choose quickly—we were heading into the mountains at a speed exceeding a mile a minute in spite of our angle of climb.

We chose the unknown glacier.

The peaks and their formations now in view were majestic—colossal shapes carved into amazing jagged and rounded forms by untold centuries of creeping ice. When we had alighted on our base-laying flight the east-west mountain ridge four miles south of us loomed up from the snow as a large mountain. Now, from the air, the towering peaks behind it made our base mountain seem a pygmy.

We realized anew how little the foot traveler sees.

McKinley was elated, snapping picture after picture, panting from wielding his huge camera at high altitude. Harold June was cranking his movie camera, dashing over to the radio to report our position and checking gasoline consumption. The air bumps were throwing both men about.

The critical time had come. The moment of a thousand discussions. How about our gasoline consumption? Enough left to reach the Pole? And not too much to prevent us from climbing over the hump? Czegka had installed a dump valve. We could drop 100 gallons of gas at a moment's notice.

Tranquil now, in a critical time, June examined the gauges of the five gas tanks in the great wing. Then he unscrewed the cap of the fuselage tank and measured that with a stick. He cut open several of the sealed five-gallon tins, dumped the gas into the tank, and threw the tins overboard.

Each can weighed only a pound, but every pound counted now.

He figured on a pad and handed me the result. Then he looked at the engines.

Balchen was fighting to get altitude. The glacier loomed a long way ahead; the lowest point in the pass was still above the nose of the plane.

At times the mixed air currents jostled and tossed the plane about like a cork in a washtub.

Wind sweeping up from a 9,000-foot peak to the right helped us, we thought. To the right opened up deep gorges, which meant more turbulent air. Bernt eased off to the left. Ahead lay a long, fairly smooth slope. The air was not so rough, but down currents resisted our struggle for altitude.

Suddenly the ailerons failed to have any effect; the wheel turned loosely in Bernt's hands.

Above the roar of the engines Bernt yelled, "It's drop 200, or go back!"

June jumped to the dump valve of our fuselage tank. A slight pressure and 600 pounds of gasoline would go overboard. But if we did that we would not have enough gasoline to reach the Pole and get back to base. That was the story Harold's slip of paper told me.

The alternative was to drop food. Would that be fair to these men? It is doubtful whether we could have gotten off the plateau if we were forced to land. Food we would need most of all.

"A bag of food overboard!" I yelled to McKinley.

Over went a 150-pound brown bag.

I might have been wrong in that decision. The effect was instantaneous. A plane hovering near its ceiling is as buoyant as a balloon. Bernt smiled. The influence on the controls was marked.

But we were not yet high enough. Mac was still taking pictures. If I had told him to throw overboard his beloved camera, I felt that he would have preferred to go with it.

Slowly we went higher. Again the wheel turned loosely in Balchen's hands. "Quick! Dump more!" he shouted.

I pointed to another bag. Mac nonchalantly shoved it through the trapdoor. He watched it hit the glacier. More than a month and a half's supply of food for four men lies out there on the ice.

Again the plane responded. No more food should go. I had 500 pounds left. Loss of gasoline meant missing our goal. Would we have to dump more weight? It seemed so.

Those were the slowest minutes we ever spent. Amundsen had described the grandeur of the eastern end of Mount Nansen, which we could see to our left. To our right were even more majestic mountains no one had ever seen.

Finally we reached the pass. We ambled over—a few hundred yards to spare.

Bernt let out a yelp of joy. No mountains ahead. A clear route to the Pole, dead ahead over the horizon!

Our next thought was our engines. The plateau was so high that the stopping of one engine meant landing in the snow. We had to "ride the engines"—all three of them—to the Pole.

The starboard engine sputtered. June rushed to the gas tank valves. Even McKinley hesitated in his mapping. Balchen manipulated the wheel. The gasoline had been made too lean in our effort to conserve it. The motor sang again.

We had time to look around. The Polar Plateau, at last! Ahead was limitless, level, white. To the left mountain masses towered above the floor of the plateau 10,000 feet above sea level. Some of these peaks must reach 17,000 feet. McKinley's photographs tell the story of those mountains.

I looked to the right and got one of those kicks that attract a man to places like Antarctica and make his going worthwhile.

A mountain range emerged from the horizon far to the right—a new feature to put on the map of the world. The crests of the peaks did not seem to be high, although they must have been to stand out so prominently above the plateau. They extended to the southward as far as we could see. Mountains, I thought, as I looked around, must surround the entire plateau. They constitute the mighty dam that will encase this vast bowl of ice until future geological ages mark the passing of Antarctica's ice era. Then the ice will melt, and run through the outlets, leaving behind, perhaps, the world's largest inland sea. This is speculation—as yet we can only guess at what is beneath that mammoth ice cap and how deep is the ice. The Polar Plateau is still one of the mysteries of the world we live in.

The plateau surface we traversed ranged from about 7,000 to about 11,000 feet. We saw several small scattered new mountain peaks projecting through the snow. It was hard to believe that they were the tops of mountains about 9,000 feet above sea level. Rather they seemed fragile outposts of the unmarked goal toward which we were heading....

The wind held us back somewhat. We were making only about 90 miles an hour. It would take us longer to reach the Pole than we calculated. However, these contrary winds we knew would give us a boost on the return flight. The character of the plateau changed constantly. To the left a magnificent glacier running down the mountains came into view; chaotic masses of crevassed ice shone blue against the white snow.

We passed clusters of haycocks—small, rounded domes of snow that conceal deep pits. We saw sastrugi—hard, wind-formed snow-ridges, with knifelike edges—with a brighter glitter than that of snow surfaces. These showed the area to be one of at least occasional violent winds. The mountains Amundsen had reported were fading out of view to the southeast, just as he had seen them disappear as he approached the Pole. McKinley made many overlapping photographs of them....

June was piloting and Balchen came aft to report the air was not very clear ahead. Clouds were approaching. We thought we could beat them back to the mountains. Did they bring strong winds with them? It now appeared certain we should have to race the clouds back to our pass through the mountains. If we lost, our retreat would most likely be cut off and we might have to face the uncertainty of a landing 10,000 feet above sea level, perhaps on rough snow.

Our time showed us that the barrier side of the mountains was four hours back; and from there it is 300 nautical miles from the Pole! No wonder my companions thought I was flying beyond the Pole. The wind had slowed us up.

But the big moment had come!

That imaginary point—the aloof and lonely bottom of the earth—was beneath us. I handed June a message to radio to Little America!

"My calculations indicate we have reached the vicinity of the South Pole. Flying high for survey. Soon turn north."

Perhaps the last sentence was superfluous. We could fly in no direction other than north.

We opened the trapdoor and dropped the American flag, weighted with the stone from Bennett's grave. We saluted our country's flag and the spirit of our gallant comrade.

We turned right, and flew three or four miles, then circled and flew left for an equal distance, then back to our original line of flight on a diagonal course. After we had gone about six miles beyond the point where we turned right, we turned back.

We flew over the Pole at an altitude of about 2,500 feet above the snow. This was about 11,500 feet above sea level. The temperature had dropped meanwhile to 15 below zero. Visibility was good, but not perfect. Clouds obscured the horizon in several places.

In the vicinity of the Poles one must adopt a new conception of time and direction. To try to think in terms of north and south, noon or midnight, or even to-day or to-morrow, is to become hopelessly involved in meaningless, contradictory phrases. At that theoretical point from which all directions are north, the meridians converge....

At the South Pole we are at all meridians; therefore we can consider correctly that it is any or all times of day at any given instant. If we fly in an arc of a small circle around the Pole, we can go from to-day into to-morrow in a very few minutes, or we can reverse our course and fly back again to yesterday.

Directions are just as meaningless. Near the Pole we can start flying on a straight line to the southeast, and in a few minutes that straight line will have changed in direction ninety degrees to northeast.

We were in an infinitely restricted area where we had to abandon the usual methods of navigation and depend solely upon the bearing of the sun.

The immortal Scott lost his life to reach that spot—the South Pole—which lay beneath us. His superhuman struggle showed that things of the mind and heart, the intangible spirit of a man, can have a far more enduring effect than the material results of his struggles. In honor of this hero we carried the British flag beside the American.

We turned back at 1:25. A job lay ahead of us. Later, we saw patches of drifting snow beneath us. Like hawks, we watched for the sun-compass and drift indicator; for we must hit that mountain pass. We must find our base at the foot of the mountains.

Time now seemed to crawl. The mountains which had been clear were now partly shrouded by clouds. We aimed our course a few degrees right with the intention of descending Axel Heiberg Glacier. We wanted to reach the barrier east of the point where we had flown over it, in order to get a better view of Carmen Land and photographs of it.

Suddenly Balchen gave voice to one of his happy shouts. To our left was the pass through which we entered the plateau; Axel Heiberg Glacier was slightly to the left of our course. We swung a bit to the left, then to the right, to have a look at a glacier to the eastward. Then we turned left again and soon we were sliding down a pass into Axel Heiberg Glacier, down which we flew. It was rough going in the pass, but the plane was light. A few minutes later June, who had landed there before, brought the plane down upon the ice-hard sastrugi at our mountain base.

We took aboard 200 gallons of gasoline and left 350 pounds of food for Gould's party. This would enable the party to remain longer at the mountains. In an hour we were off again.

We landed at Little America at 10:10 a.m., Antarctic time, 5:10 p.m., New York time, having covered 160,000 square miles in 15 hours and 51 minutes. Peary, in planting the American flag at the North Pole, was out of touch with civilization for 429 days, and Amundsen, on his journey to the South Pole, for seven months.

We were deaf from the roar of motors, tired from the strain of the flight, but we forgot all that in the tumultuous welcome of our companions.....

For this accomplishment, Byrd was promoted to rear admiral and was awarded the Navy Cross, the Founders Medal of the Royal Geographical Society, and the Special Gold Medal of the National Geographic Society.

No one laid eyes on the South Pole for another 17 years, when Byrd flew over it again. By then he was leading a succession of ever larger and more sophisticated expeditions, involving thousands of men surveying millions of square miles, most of which had never been seen before. Such massive, technologically complex efforts changed forever the nature of Antarctic exploration.

Yet Byrd never repudiated the myth of the heroic individual. He once spent five winter months alone in a snowbound weather hut, 123 miles from Little America, and nearly died from carbon monoxide fumes emitted from his stove.

As has often been noted, he was both the last of the old-time explorers and the first of the new.

FLYING AROUND
THE NORTH ATLANTIC
September 1934

ANNE MORROW LINDBERGH (1907–2001)

FEW EARLY FLYERS CAPTURED THE PUBLIC IMAGINATION THE WAY Charles Lindbergh did when in 1927 he flew alone across the Atlantic Ocean. Nothing he did thereafter escaped public notice or newspaper headlines, certainly not when the tall and lanky "America's darling" married pretty, petite Anne Morrow, daughter of an ambassador to Mexico and a future U.S. Senator. As her books attest, Anne's gifts were more literary than political or mechanical. Still, Charles taught her how to fly, navigate, and operate a shortwave radio, and Anne became his copilot, radio operator, navigator, and constant companion.

In the early 1930s, this glamorous couple flew many thousands of miles, charting potential aviation pathways. Most routes over the continents had already been mapped, but not reliable sky trails across the oceans. So in July 1933, the Lindberghs climbed into their seaplane and lifted off from Flushing Bay, New York, on a six-month circumnavigation of the North Atlantic, surveying potential routes and bases. He was 31, she 27; they left one baby to a nurse's care, though they still suffered from the traumatic kidnapping and murder of another.

The Lindberghs flew a Lockheed Sirius mounted on pontoons so heavy that the plane always needed a good, stiff breeze for takeoff. They dubbed their craft Tingmissartoq, Inuit for "one who flies like a big bird," a name they picked up in Greenland where, out of radio contact, they were reported as crashed and killed. Huge crowds greeted them wherever they touched down, and the press eagerly followed their progress, including stops in Iceland, the British Isles, Copenhagen, Stockholm, Moscow, Paris, Geneva, and Lisbon.

In the sky, however, they were alone, accompanied only by clouds and crackling radio transmissions. That is what Anne Morrow Lindbergh captures in the account she wrote for NATIONAL GEOGRAPHIC. *As the following excerpt opens, the couple has arrived at the Cape Verde Islands off the coast of Africa. They are preparing to cross the ocean to Brazil, although conditions do not bode well.*

THIS HOT, DRY TRADE WIND BLEW STEADILY ALL THE TIME we were there. We went to sleep listening to it. As we lay in our plane, baked hot by the unrelieved sun, I would wait in vain for the long roar to break, like a wave on a beach. But there was no relief from it. Every morning we woke and looked out to sea, hoping for a calm day. Always, the heavy swell and the wind. It seemed to make everything harder work, on the plane or climbing up the hill to the radio station—as if one were pushing against it all the time. I had the feeling sometimes that we must be on the prow of a ship, steaming forward. Motion only could create that constant wind. And sometimes, as though it were not an outward physical force but an inward illness, a fever, a pressure on my temples.

"Is it never calm here?" we asked. We had stationed our fuel at Porto Praia and hoped to take off for South America from this point.

"Yes, it is sometimes calm—but never this time of year. It will blow like this for six months."

"And no change? No storm or change in the wind?"

"Never—always like this."

We began to realize that, as we could not take off from these rollers with sufficient gas to reach South America, we would have to go back to Africa and start from there, even though it would be 200 miles farther.

On the morning of November 30 we left Porto Praia, bouncing several times as much as ten feet in the air, striking one roller after another. Each time I thought we were off we would come down again with a worse spank than before. Finally, stalling off, we headed for Bathurst.

Originally we had planned to go to Dakar, but after being warned of the yellow fever epidemic and quarantine there, we changed our plans and obtained authority to land in British Gambia. After about three hours' flying, we saw Cape Verde, stretching out to sea ahead of us, then the flat green shores of British Gambia.

In the early afternoon we landed on the muddy river at Bathurst....

The greatest problem was the time of take-off. We had only a little over 13 hours of daylight to count on for the trip. If we went as fast as possible, we could perhaps accomplish the whole trip, including take-off and landing, by daylight. But we would have too small a reserve of fuel in case we encountered strong head winds or found it necessary to detour storm areas.

We abandoned the possibility, although it was attractive with its shorter hours. We must have that extra margin of safety. The speed for greatest fuel economy was about 100 knots. At that rate it would take us about 16 hours to reach Natal, the nearest point in South America....

After a day or two of preparation we were ready. The plane was refueled; radio schedules with the Pan American stations on the South

American coast, with Bathurst, and our friend at the French seaplane station at Porto Praia were already arranged. We had also asked for daily weather forecasts from Pernambuco (Recife) and Pará (Belém) on the South American coast. The encouraging word came back, "Weather Pernambuco—Pará—always good—never fog."

We decided to try to take off at daybreak, the time of most wind, with all fuel tanks full, part of which we could unload if necessary and still have a safe reserve. The morning of December 3 we taxied out into the bay, the pontoons almost submerged under their heavy load, the plane heaving bulkily from side to side as we taxied across the wind and waves. After several hopeless attempts to take off—the spray sluiced down over the wings continually and we never got up on the step—we turned back to the mooring. Unloading our extra gasoline, we tried again. But the wind had dropped by then, and though this time we got up on the step we could not get off the water. We decided to go back and wait for a wind....

"What was the matter, Colonel?" asked a friend who had kindly stayed to watch us.

"Overload, that's all," answered my husband. "We've taken off with that much before (in Greenland). But it's different down here in the Tropics; different air...."

My husband spent the day inside the plane, cutting out an unused gasoline tank, piece by piece, with tin snips. It was very hot with the sun beating down fiercely on the outside of the ship, and the fumes from the empty tank were suffocating. He was tired at the end of the day, but much more cheerful at the thought of the saved weight. We decided not to try until the next night. Although the moon was waning, a good sleep seemed more important.

By the next evening we had cut out even more weight: some emergency chocolate (there was still enough food and water left for a month); the anchor; the rope; the tin bucket: a great many tools; the flying suits; the sleeping bag; all our clothes, except the ones we wore; our duffel bags, and many other things—a total of about 150 pounds.

The day seemed unusually calm, the tops of the palms hardly stirring. At sunset, when I walked out on the pier, there was not enough wind to lift a handkerchief. The moon rose about nine, reddish and grown lopsided since the night before. "It's certainly the last night we can use that," I thought.

"We could still take off at daybreak, couldn't we?" I asked my husband.

"No," he answered. "You see, the moon rises later every night—and it wouldn't be light enough when we reach the other side to land by."

There was never any wind at sunset; this seemed to be our last chance as far as Bathurst was concerned.

We left Government House at 10:30, local time, carrying only what we wore, some lunch, and two sun helmets. It took us a long time to get started after we reached the plane. First we pumped out the pontoons. They were loaded so heavily that the back ends had to be lifted out of the water by a rowboat under the tail. Next, we sealed up the anchor box in the pontoons with putty, to prevent water from leaking in during taxiing. "There's about a five-mile wind right now," said my husband cheerfully to the Captain of the Port, who had come out to help us.

Our friend held up his hand. "You air folks must look at it differently," he replied.

"Why? What would you call it?" my husband queried.

"Almost a dead calm."

We all laughed. My husband took off the lantern and the plane's mooring bridle and handed them to the Captain.

"If we come back we'll want these; otherwise"—he stopped for a moment and then—"we'll have another try, anyway"—and off we went.

I looked back in the tail to be sure that everything was securely lashed; sat on my extra shirt; stuffed the lunch into the map case; put the radio bag in the seat beside me, and fastened the belt.

The lights of the town were on our left and, above them, the palms were outlined quite plainly in the moonlight. Out in the bay there was more wind. We turned, slowed up, throttled down. A pause for breath.

"All set?"

"Yes, all right."

Then the roar—the spray. I watched it over the wing and looked down at my watch. The spray stopped. We were spanking along—up on the step—a good deal faster than before. Sparks from the exhaust. We're going to get off! I thought in a flash of realization. But how long it takes! We're off? No—spank-spank-spank-spank—but almost—.

I held my breath. We're off! No more spanks. I looked at the watch— just 2:00 G.M.T.

The Lindberghs called their small Lockheed Sirius seaplane Tingmissartoq, *"one who flies like a big bird," an Inuit name they picked up in Greenland, one of their many stops on a 30,000-mile odyssey charting skypaths around the North Atlantic.*

Yes, we're off—we're rising. The engine smoothed out into a long sigh, like a person breathing easily, almost like someone singing, ecstatically. We turned from the lights of the city. The plane seemed exultant, then, even arrogant. We did it—we did it! We're up above you—we were dependent on you, just now, River, asking you for favors, for wind and light. But now, we are free of you; we are up—we are off. We can toss you aside—you, River—there below us, a few lights in the great, dark, silent world that is ours—for we are above it.

My husband switched on the cockpit lights to check the instruments and our compass course. Then, quickly, off again. We were flying quite low over the strip of land between the river and the ocean. I decided not to turn on my lights until we were over the water. They might make it harder for my husband to see. Still very excited, I wrote down by moonlight my first message, "Left Bathurst 2:00 G.M.T."

Looking at it on the top of the bare sheet of paper, I realized that there was no reason to feel so elated. We had the whole trip ahead of us. This was just the beginning.

I called an African station and, hearing no reply, sent out this first take-off message "blind." Then I began to call the Pan American stations on the South American coast, not hoping to get any answer so early on our trip, but because we had arranged a schedule each hour on the hour as soon as we were in the air.

At three o'clock, however, I heard a reply. The static was very bad, but in the welter of sounds I heard my name—KHCAL, friendly and comforting, across the ocean and through the dark. The first radio contact. What was it? PVB, Bahia (Sao Salvador), down the coast of Brazil. Right on the watch—good for him! I thought. I poked my husband excitedly and passed forward a note: "I have Bahia! Any message?" We were over the water now and I switched on the light to send our first position.

"Posn 03:00 G.M.T.—12°17' north—17°50' west—course 224° true."

From then on, through four hours of darkness, I stayed bent over in front of the dials, straining to hear through the crashes of static, sending the position reports every hour, and picking up a few words of the weather reports sent back to me from Brazil— "Visibility good."

Only once, looking out, I saw the lights of a ship far down below us. But without looking, I knew the weather was good, for the moon lighted the cabin dimly. After four hours the radio began to be much better. I could hear Rio now, and, relaxing, began to realize that we had really taken off and were on our way to South America.

About 5:30 G.M.T. we began to hit clouds. Flying under them we lost the moon for periods. The periods became longer. I could still see a kind of horizon where water met clouds, a difference in darkness. Then we lost the water and flew blind. I turned off the light quickly to avoid any reflection in my husband's cockpit.

Now we were out again. There were holes below us through which one could see the dark water, and holes above us through which one could see the dark sky. More blind flying. But day was coming—it must come soon. I tried to figure it out. It should be day in an hour, anyway. We were climbing up through the clouds. I could not see to receive, but continued to send, "QRX (Stand by), QRX—going through clouds—min pse (Please wait a minute)."

More clouds ahead. More blind flying. It began to get cold. We must be quite high. I put on my extra shirt and sent again, "QRX, QRX—all OK." Then, after about an hour of this flying, my husband handed back a message for me, for Rio: "8/10 overcast—scattered squalls—visibility three miles—daybreak."

Daybreak! I had not realized that the clouds were now distinguishing themselves, more and more, from the water and the sea. The night was over. When the sun actually rose, we were still flying through black thunder clouds, but there was better weather ahead. "Visibility unlimited outside of squalls."

The radio was good. I received intact (after repetition) a long message from Rio about the landing arrangements in Natal. It seemed very strange to be taking down the practical details of landing when we were still so far away—a whole ocean away.

"PAA [Pan American Airways] barge at Natal (Would we ever really get there?) located on river at southwest edge of city (It is hardly daybreak yet) between city and large Aeropostale hangar and ramp (As though finding it would be any difficulty!). Caution tall radio masts at Aeropostale hangar (Caution! Radio masts in full daylight—caution!—after that moonlight take-off!) Few spare parts available on barge." (They sound as though they really expect us.)

This anticipation of arrival gave me a feeling of confidence. The very attention to detail took for granted our safe arrival. I ate one of my sandwiches and felt refreshed.

At 8:06 G.M.T., I heard another note coming over the radio, a new loud voice calling me, "KHCAL-de-WCC—answer 54 or 36 (meters)." I could not quite believe it and looked up in the call-book to make sure—Chatham, Massachusetts, calling me!

It seemed very unreal, but the whole night had been unreal. So I answered rather casually on 54 meters (the wavelength I was using), not bothering to change frequencies. He answered immediately, the notes coming in very loud and clear, every word intact. I did not need his triple sending, but hardly dared interrupt.

Chatham—think how thrilling! The sentence dribbled out slowly on the page: "Would-you-answer-answer-answer-few-few-few-questions-questions-questions-first-radio-radio-radio-interview-interview-interview-from-from-from-airplane?" Newspapers here, too! Out in the middle of the ocean. It made the whole trip more unreal than ever. I sent back my answer: "Sorry too busy here—must get weather—from PVJ."

No matter how thrilling a contact with Chatham, Massachusetts, might be, we certainly had enough to do without giving interviews. I was relieved to get PVJ (Rio) again, this time on 36 meters.

"Posn 09:00 G.M.T—05°00' north—23°40' west—course 224° true—2/10 overcast at 1500—9/10 overcast at 8000—visibility unlimited—sea calm—wind 0—altitude 1200."

There was also the drift meter to use, sighting down carefully at the water through the eye-piece; and at this point, for we were nearing the halfway mark, the sun was high enough in the sky for my husband to take sights. I had to fly the ship and missed some of my radio schedules. It was very refreshing to sit up straight after the cramped position over the dials, and to look out at the clouds and sea.

I would have enjoyed it if I had not been trying to read the results of the sextant in my husband's expression. He did not look satisfied. In between the sights, I tried to recover the lost contacts. But, incredibly stupid and slow, I could not seem to make anything work.

My back was stiff from bending over the dials and my ears hurt from the clamp of the phones. I sent with closed eyes. And yet none of these things were very hard in themselves; they could easily be overcome, with a little will power. But when one is very tired it does not seem worth the effort. Nothing seems worth the effort.

My husband was taking the sextant to pieces in the front cockpit. What was the matter? Had the sights turned out badly? We were over halfway across and it was more necessary than ever to keep radio contact. Roused from my lethargy, I reached for the canteen. A drink of water, a little on my face, and another sandwich refreshed me. I continued calling constantly.

Our first answer came back from the African side, although much farther from us than South America. It was CRKK, the French station at Porto Praia we had tried to get when we left Bathurst.

"Posn 12:00 G.M.T.—01°30' north—28°20' west—4/10 sky overcast—visibility unlimited—sea light."

After losing contact with CRKK, I began to send a CQ (General Call), signing not only with our call sign, KHCAL, but also adding "Lindbergh Plane." This had worked before. Stations absolutely deaf to KHCAL sometimes answer "Lindbergh Plane." It was like changing the fly on the end of one's fishing rod.

We very quickly had a bite. "Lindbergh—Lindbergh," came back the answer, "S.S. *Caparcona*—bound Rio." A boat off the coast of Brazil—I was delighted. Everything began to be easy after this. They very kindly said they would relay our position to the stations on the coast of South

America. The sextant was intact again, and my husband evidently satisfied with the sights.

"Posn 13:00 G.M.T—00°15′ north—29°25′ west—1/10 overcast—visibility unlimited—sea light—wind 135°—10 miles—altitude 800."

At about 14:00 we saw our first boat on the South American side. We had not seen one since the lights below us off Bathurst, eleven hours before. A tiny white speck to our right, it looked comforting as the first sight of land to me.

At 14:20 we passed over a freighter, the *Aldebaran*. From 13:55 to 15:30 we were in contact with the *Westfalen*, the German catapult ship, which had passed Fernando de Noronha that morning. After hearing our position report at 14:00 G.M.T., they said we were going to pass very near them and gave us our radio bearing from the ship. We turned slightly off course and flew over them at 15:20 G.M.T.

In the excitement of diving down, I remember only the white wake surging behind the ship, all arms waving from the deck, and, on top, their plane and catapult. They gave us a bearing to Fernando de Noronha and to Natal and signed off with "Xmas wishes and Happy New Year."

After passing the *Westfalen*, I felt we had reached the other side. We had been right on course; we were sure of our position; and the skies were "unlimited" ahead of us. I felt very happy. Only the noise of the radio in my ears was a constant annoyance. I was now in contact with Ceará (Fortaleza), Pan American station north of Natal.

I knew he was just as tired as I was, after listening for my signal all night. In fact, he was much more tired. I did not realize it until afterwards, when I found out that practically all the Pan American stations from Miami to Rio had been on 24-hour duty for almost a week during our attempted take-offs. They were on constant watch for us, not being certain when we were going to leave Bathurst.

We passed Fernando de Noronha soon after we left the *Westfalen*. Flying by a huge, round volcano, which sticks up straight on one side of a bare island, like a long French roll, we set our course for Natal. I received again from Ceará the message I had heard ten hours earlier from Rio, while we were still in the dark on the other side of the ocean.

"PAA barge at Natal (The coast of South America spread low and green in the slight haze ahead) located on river at southwest edge of the city (We came to it very quickly, following the coast only a few minutes) between city and large Aeropostale hangar (My husband looked back and signaled with his hand, 'Five minutes more!'). Caution tall radio masts—(There they were—we were circling)—Few spare parts available on barge." (I could see it now—a small square barge in the river, crowded with people.) "Landed Natal 17:55 G.M.T."

After touching down in steamy Brazil, the Lindberghs wrapped up their long trip, returning to the United States via Trinidad, Puerto Rico, and the Dominican Republic, finally landing in Flushing Bay on December 19, 1933. They had flown nearly 30,000 miles. Today, Tingmissartoq may be viewed in the Smithsonian Air and Space Museum.

A ROUND TRIP TO DAVY JONES'S LOCKER

June 1931

A HALF MILE DOWN

December 1934

WILLIAM BEEBE (1877–1962)

NOTHING IN HIS YEARS SPENT STUDYING JUNGLE PHEASANTS *prepared William Beebe for what he saw when he donned a diving helmet and slipped beneath the surface of tropic seas. The bizarre coral formations, waving sea fans, and extraordinary variety of creatures so entranced the New York Zoological Society naturalist that he felt he was gazing on another world.*

Soon Beebe shifted his interests from ornithology to marine science. After setting up a research lab on Bermuda, he began trawling nets through the ocean, the standard method for sampling the life of the depths. Although he hauled up many curious species, he realized it was no better than if a spaceship dredged blindly through a Manhattan street, expecting the catch to represent the city. Beebe decided to go down there himself—in a deep-sea observation chamber.

Thus was born the bathysphere, designed by engineer Otis Barton. The two-ton steel cylinder featured a cramped interior crowded with dials and gauges, a porthole made of fused quartz, and a spotlight—all suspended from a very thin steel cable. Another cable supplied electricity and telephone connections. Into this chamber crawled Beebe and Barton, and a crane on a barge lowered them into the deep.

No scientist had dared do this. Although pushing his mid-50s, Beebe had the stamina and drive of a man half his age and a flair for the dramatic. From the moment the bathysphere splashed into mile-deep waters off Bermuda, in 1930, it captured the public imagination. Millions listened to the first deep-sea radio broadcast, as Beebe described vast pastures of luminous creatures in the blue-black water. Over 30 descents were made, and by 1934, the last season, Beebe and Barton descended half a mile, literally reaching the end of their tether. They were what astronauts would be to a later generation, the first explorers to venture into an alien realm and return alive. From "A Round Trip to Davy Jones's Locker:"

FINALLY WE WERE ALL READY AND I LOOKED AROUND AT THE SEA and sky, the boats and my friends, and not being able to think of any pithy saying which might echo down the ages, I said nothing, crawled painfully over the steel bolts, fell inside and curled up on the cold, hard bottom of the sphere. This aroused me to speech and I called for a cushion. Otis Barton climbed in after me, and we disentangled our legs and got set.

I had no idea that there was so much room in the inside of a sphere four and a half feet in diameter, although the longer we were in it the smaller it seemed to get. At Barton's suggestion I took up my position at the windows, while he hitched himself over to the side of the door, where he could keep watch on the various instruments. He also put on the ear-phones.

Miss Hollister on deck took charge of the other end of the telephone, while Mr. Tee-Van assumed control of the deck crew. I gave the word and the four-hundred-pound door was hoisted into the air and slipped into place with a clang of cold steel. The nuts were screwed down and then hammered home, the terrific reverberations almost deafening us inside.

We were now fastened in tight with only a four-inch opening left in the center of the door. At last this great bolt was screwed down and we were completely isolated from the world of sun and air, and from human beings except for the comforting words which slipped up and down the telephone wires.... Like the lightest of airplane take-offs we rose from the deck and swung out over the side. Here we dangled for a short time and then slowly began to sink.

As we submerged I realized for the first time the tremendous weight and terrific strength of the sphere: we were lowered very gently, yet we struck the surface with a splash which would have crushed a rowboat like an eggshell. Within, we hardly noticed the impact until a froth of foam and bubbles surged up over the glass and the chamber was dimmed to a pleasant green.

While the two cables were being clamped together to prevent twisting, we revolved once and the hull of the barge came into view a few yards away. It was covered with a magnificent coral reef growth—waving banners of seaweed, long, tubular sponges, jet-black blobs of ascidians and tissue-thin pearl shells. Word came down. I sent up an answering order and the hull passed slowly upward and out of sight.

This was the last visible link of the upper world; from now on we had to depend on distant spoken words for knowledge of our depth, or speed, the weather or the sunlight, or anything to do with the world of air on the surface of Mother Earth....

"Two hundred feet" was called down to us and we stopped with a gentle jerk while another clamp was attached, and soon we were sinking again. We were now very far from any touch of earth; ten miles south of the shore of Bermuda and one and a half miles from the sea bottom....

In two minutes more we were at four hundred feet; then five hundred and six hundred came and passed. Here the electric searchlight began to be effective, the yellow shaft cutting through the dark blue with great intensity.

Ever since the beginnings of human history, when first the Phoenicians dared to sail the open sea, thousands upon thousands of human beings had reached the depth at which we were now suspended, and had passed to lower levels. But all of these were dead, drowned victims of war, tempest, or other Acts of God. We were the first living men to look out at the strange illumination. And it was stranger than any imagination could have conceived.

It was of an indefinable deep blue quite unlike anything I have ever seen in the upper world, and it excited our optic nerves in a most confusing manner. We kept thinking and calling it brilliant, and again and again I picked up a book to read the type, only to find that I could not tell the difference between the blank page and a colored plate. All our remarks were recorded by Miss Hollister and when I read them later, the repetition of our insistence upon the brilliance which yet was not brilliance was almost absurd.

As we began our further descent I found that Barton and I had the same thought; we were waiting breathlessly for the sudden elimination of all light. It seemed from moment to moment that it would soon become absolutely dark, and the fact of the terrible slow change from dark blue to blacker blue was the most impressive thing about the descent. Then the thought came that this was not night because there had never been any day....

"Eight hundred feet" came down the wire and I called a halt. Half a dozen times in my life I have had hunches so vivid that I could not ignore them, and this was one of these times. Eight hundred feet spelled bottom and I could not escape it....

[*Going deeper*] The lanternfish (*Myctophids*) came close to the glass and were easy to call by name. Only instead of having half a dozen scales left, like those caught in the nets, these fish were ablaze with their full armor of iridescence. Twice I caught the flash of their light-organs but only for an instant. An absurdly small and rotund puffer appeared quite out of place at this depth, but with much more reason he probably thought the same of me.... At five hundred feet I had fleeting glimpses of black fish nearly two feet long, and here for the first time I saw strange, ghostly dark forms hovering in the distance—forms which never came nearer, but reappeared at deeper, darker depths.

Flying snails passed in companies of fifty or more, and small squids balanced in mid-water. I hoped to see some of the larger ones, those with orange, bull's-eye lights at the tips of their arms, or the ones which glow with an indescribable glory of blue, yellow and red light-organs. None came close enough, however, or it may be I must wait until I can descend a mile and still live, before I can come to their haunts....

Again a great cloud of a body moved in the distance—this time pale, much lighter than the water. How I longed for a single near view, or telescopic eyes which could pierce the murk. I felt as if some astonishing discovery lay just beyond the power of my eyes....

Here and at eight hundred feet a human being was permitted for the first time the sight of living silver hatchetfish (*Argyropelecus*). I made Barton look quickly out so he could verify the marvelous sight. At eight hundred feet where the water was blackish-blue, I saw groups of lights moving along slowly, or jerking unsteadily past, and the searing beams of the searchlight revealed these as silver hatchetfish, gleaming with tinsel, but with every light quenched, at least to my vision, until I switched off the electricity or until the fish moved out of its path, when their pyrotechnics again rushed into play....

At twelve hundred and fifty feet several more of the silver hatchets passed, going upward, and prawns became abundant. Between this depth and thirteen hundred feet not a light or an organism was seen; it was fifty feet of terrible emptiness, with the blue of some wholly new color term—a term quite absent from human language.

It was probably sheer imagination but the characteristic most vivid was its transparency. As I looked out I never thought of feet or yards of visibility, but of the hundreds of miles of this color stretching over so much of the world.

Life again became evident around thirteen hundred feet, and mostly luminous. After watching a hundred or more firefly-like flashes, I turned on the searchlight and saw nothing whatever. These sparks, brilliant though they were, were kindled into conflagration and quenched in the same instant upon invisible bodies. Whatever made them were too small to reach the eyes, as was almost the host of copepods and other tiny crustaceans through which we passed now and then....

At 10:44 we were sitting in absolute silence, our faces reflecting a ghastly bluish sheen. I became conscious of the pulse-throb in my temples and remember that I kept time to it with my fingers on the cold, damp steel of the window ledge. I shifted the handkerchief on my face and carefully wiped the glass, and at this moment we felt the sphere check in its course—we felt ourselves press slightly more heavily against the floor and the telephone said "Fourteen hundred feet."

I had the sensation of a few more metres' descent and then we swung quietly at our lowest floor, over a quarter of a mile below the surface.

I pressed my face against the glass and looked upward and in the slight segment which I could manage I saw a faint paling of the blue. I peered down and again I felt the old longing to go farther, although it looked like the black pit-mouth of hell itself—yet it still showed blue.

I thought I saw a new fish flapping close to the sphere, but it proved to be the waving edge of the Explorer's Club flag—black as jet at this depth. My window was clear as crystal, in fact clearer, for fused quartz is one of the most transparent of all substances and transmits all wavelengths of sunlight. The outside world I now saw through it was, however, a solid, blue-black world, one which seemed born of a single vibration—blue, blue, forever and forever blue....

As fish after fish swam into my restricted line of vision—fish, which heretofore I had seen only dead and in my nets, as I saw their colors, and their absence of colors, their activities and modes of swimming and clear evidence of their sociability or solitary habits, I felt that all the trouble and cost and risk were repaid manyfold.

After these dives were past, when I came again to examine the deep-sea treasures in my net hauls, I would feel as an astronomer might who looks through his telescope after having rocketed to Mars and back, or like a paleontologist who could suddenly annihilate time and see his fossils alive....

At the very deepest point we reached I deliberately took stock of the interior of the bathysphere; I was curled up in a ball on the icy-cold, damp steel, Barton's low voice relayed my observations and assurances of our safety, a fan swished back and forth through the air, and the ticking of my wrist-watch was like a strange memory sound of another world.

Soon after this there came a moment which stands out clearly, unpunctuated by any word of ours, with no fish or other creatures visible outside. I sat crouched with mouth and nose wrapped in a handkerchief to prevent condensation, and my forehead pressed close to the cold glass—that transparent bit of Mother Earth which so sturdily held back nine tons of water from my face.

There came to me at that instant a tremendous wave of emotion, a real appreciation of what was momentarily almost superhuman, cosmic, of the whole situation; our barge slowly rolling high overhead in the blazing sunlight, like the merest chip in the midst of the ocean, the long cobweb of cable leading down through the spectrum to our lonely sphere, where, sealed tight, two conscious human beings sat and peered into the abysmal darkness as we dangled in mid-water, isolated as a lost planet in outermost space.

Here, under a pressure which if loosened, a fraction of a second would make amorphous tissue of our bodies, breathing our own home-made atmosphere, sending a few comforting words chasing up and down a string of hose—here I was privileged to sit and try to crystallize what I observed through inadequate eyes and interpreted with a mind wholly unequal to the task.

To the ever-recurring question "How did it feel?" etc., I can only quote the words of Herbert Spencer, I felt like "an infinitesimal atom floating in illimitable space."

From "A Half Mile Down:"

[*Deeper still*] It is strange that, as the blue goes, it is not replaced by violet, the end of the visible spectrum. That has apparently already been absorbed. The last hint of blue tapers into a nameless gray, and this finally into black; but, from the present level down, the eye falters and the mind refuses any articulate color distinction. The sun is defeated, and color is banished forever, until a human at last penetrates and flashes a yellow electric ray into what has been jet black for two billion years....

At 1,900 feet, to my wonder, there was still the faintest hint of dead gray light, 200 feet deeper than usual, attesting to the almost complete calm of the surface and the extreme brilliancy of the day far overhead. At 2,000 feet the world was forever black. And this I count as the third great moment of descent, when the sun, source of all light and heat on the earth, has been left behind. It is only a psychological milepost, but it is a very real one. We had no realization of the outside pressure, but the blackness itself seemed to close in on us.

At 2,000 feet and again on the way up I saw at the very end of our beam some large form swimming. On earlier dives I had observed this and had hesitated even to mention it, for it savored too much of imagination backed by imperfect observation. But here it was again. The

Snug within the huge cyclopean eyeball that was the bathysphere,
William Beebe (left) and Otis Barton (right) are framed by the porthole
from which they gazed wide-eyed at the wonders of the deep.

surface did not seem black, and what outline came momentarily to view was wholly problematic. But that it was some very large creature or creatures, of which we had glimpses five separate times on dives separated by years, we are certain....

Suddenly I leaned forward. At a moment of suspension came a new and gorgeous creature. I yelled for continuance of the stop, which was at 1,900 feet, and began to absorb what I saw: a fish almost round, with long, moderately high, continuous, vertical fins; a big eye; a medium mouth; and small pectoral fins. The skin was decidedly brownish.

We swung around a few degrees, and from the vantage thus gained I saw its real beauty. Along the sides of the body were five unbelievably beautiful lines of light, one equatorial, with two curved ones above and two below. Each line was composed of a series of large pale-yellow lights, and every one of these was surrounded by a semicircle of very small but intensely purple photophores.

The fish turned slowly, showing a narrow profile. If it had been at the surface and without lights I should, without question, have called it a Butterfly-fish (*Chaetodon*) or a surgeonfish (*Acanthurus*). But this glowing creature was assuredly neither, unless a distant relative adapted for life at 300 fathoms. My name for it is *Bathysidus pentagramus*, the Five-lined constellation fish. In my memory it will live throughout the rest of my life as one of the loveliest things I have ever seen....

[*The deepest dive*] A very large, dim, but not indistinct outline came into view at 2,450 feet for a fraction of a second, and at 2,500 feet a delicately illumined ctenophore jelly throbbed past. Without warning, the large fish returned, and this time I saw its complete, shadowlike contour as it passed through the farthest end of the beam. Twenty feet is the least possible estimate I can give to its full length, and it was deep in proportion.

For the majority of the "size conscious" human race this marine monster would, I suppose, be the supreme sight of the expedition. In shape it was a deep oval; it swam without evident effort, and it did not return. That is all I can contribute, and while its unusual size so excited me that for several hundred feet I kept keenly on the lookout for hints of the same or other large fish, I soon forgot it in the (very literal) light of smaller but more distinct organisms....

Now and then I felt a slight vibration and an apparent slacking off of the cable. Word came that a cross-swell had arisen, and, when the full weight of Bathysphere and cable (nearly four tons at this depth) came upon the winch, Captain Sylvester let out a few inches to ease the strain. There were only about a dozen turns of cable left upon the reel, and a full half of the drum showed its naked, wooden core. We were swinging at 3,028 feet, and would we come up? We would....

The only other place comparable to these marvelous nether regions must surely be naked space itself, out far beyond the atmosphere, between the stars, where sunlight has no grip upon the dust and rubbish of planetary air, where the blackness of space, the shining planets, comets, suns, and stars must really be closely akin to the world of life as it appears to the eyes of an awed human being in the open ocean a half mile down.

Although Beebe and Barton's half-mile descent established a depth record that stood for 15 years, their bathysphere was never again used. The cost was prohibitive, and technology soon outstripped it. But it did give rise to a whole fleet of later submersibles, which have been indispensable in revealing the mysteries of the deep. Beebe himself, restless as always, soon left his ocean explorations and returned to studying the ecology of tropical forests, settling in Trinidad, where he died in 1962.

EXPLORING THE STRATOSPHERE
October 1934

MAN'S FARTHEST ALOFT
January 1936

CAPT. ALBERT W. STEVENS (1886–1949)

ALBERT STEVENS COULD NOT GET HIGH ENOUGH. THE WORLD'S greatest aerial photographer was by the early 1930s chief of the Army Air Corps photography lab. When not at his workbench, he was usually up on the air some- where, making photographs, though it was anyone's guess how he might come back down. Often he just walked away from plane crashes. Once he returned with his eyeballs frosted, having removed his goggles in the upper atmosphere. And sometimes he sailed in by parachute, once leaping from a plane at 24,000 feet—an unofficial record—for the sheer exhilaration of it.

Stevens had flown in airplanes to their ceiling, well under seven miles. Several balloons had reached the edge of the stratosphere, however, between seven and thirty miles up—and he intended to top them. In 1934–35 he persuaded the Army Air Corps and the National Geographic Society to sponsor two stratosphere balloons, the Explorer and Explorer II, which achieved a new height record and paved the way for the Space Age.

The launches were proto-NASA events. There was the launching pad—the "Stratobowl"—in the Black Hills of South Dakota, surrounded by a vast tent city—the "Stratocamp"—complete with sawdust roads, plumbing, and a weather station. And there were the balloons, as tall as 26-story buildings. Specially made gondolas, ringed with portholes and hatches, were crammed with scientific instruments. There was a zany, hold-onto-your-hats quality that mirrored Albert Stevens's personality. The aeronauts even wore leather football helmets borrowed from a high school. The first launch attempt was nearly a disaster. On July 28, 1934, veteran balloon pilots Maj. William Kepner and Capt. Orvil Anderson joined Stevens in the gondola of the Explorer. Soon the vast hydrogen-filled bal- loon lifted off the Stratobowl; the men hoped to rise 15 miles into the sky. Everything went exceedingly well ... for a while.

From "Exploring the Stratosphere:"

To look back, we were indeed in a strange predicament. We were imprisoned in a stout metal shell, hanging from a huge balloon, more than 11 miles above the earth. Yet we had at arm's length two hatches we had only to open to be free.

One of the hatches had a lever to facilitate prying it open. But no one made a move toward the lever. To have opened it would have meant almost instant unconsciousness from change of pressure. Our tissues would have expanded suddenly, somewhat as would those of certain fish drawn hurriedly to the surface from ocean depths, and the results would have been both distressing and disastrous.

Our lofty prison was a very livable place. We were perfectly familiar with every square inch of it, for we had been in and out of it dozens of times daily for many weeks. It was airtight; it resisted all the strains of the heavy load it carried; it was almost comfortable, certainly much more so than we had expected.

The inside walls were painted a glossy white, and on them shone bright rays of sunlight streaming through the glass ports above our heads. All around us were scientific instruments, and their subdued clatter, ever increasing as the balloon ascended, had been music to our ears. With earphones on our helmets and microphones in front of us, we could talk, allowing a few minutes for necessary connections, to practically anyone in the United States. We were neither hungry nor thirsty, and the artificially prepared air we breathed was surprisingly good.

Suddenly and without warning there came a great rent in our balloon! A glance above us just a few minutes before and all had been well; soon we were dropping—bag, gondola, instruments, and men. As long as things held together reasonably well, there was hope. But if too many breaks in the fabric developed the gondola would go hurtling through space, and we with it.....

The crew had reached 60,613 feet—11 miles—only a thousand feet short of the altitude record. Fortunately the ripped balloon acted like a big parachute, slowing their otherwise rapid descent. Yet its hydrogen mixture was extremely explosive, making the return an excruciating ordeal.

We had worn our parachute harnesses constantly during the flight, and when things began to look bad we had each put on the detachable portion, or parachute proper. We were all set to leave, but we wanted to stay with the balloon as long as possible to avoid being distant from it when we landed.

At 10,000 feet we really should have left the balloon, but we did not wish to abandon the scientific apparatus. So we stayed on. At 6,000 feet we again talked the matter over and decided we had better leave. The last altimeter reading I gave was 5,000 feet above sea level.

Since this part of Nebraska was 2,000 feet above sea level, we were in reality only a little more than a half mile from the ground.

In the meantime Captain Anderson, atop the gondola, had been having difficulty with his parachute. The release handle had caught on something and the parachute pack had come open. It was a situation that might have been disconcerting to a less cool head. There was only one thing to do—that was to gather the folds of silk under one arm preparatory to leaping.

While getting the fabric together, Anderson stepped down until both his feet were in the hatch from which I planned to leap. Andy is a big man, but never before had I noticed that his feet were large. Now, looking up at the opening partially blocked by his pedal extremities, I shouted:

"Hey, get your big feet out of the way! I want to jump."

Whether Anderson heard me or not does not matter. Things started to happen fast. The feet disappeared, and I knew he had leaped. As he jumped, the balloon exploded. The pressure suddenly became too great all over, and the fabric burst at once in hundreds of places.

The gondola dropped like a stone.

Twice I tried to push myself through the hatch of the gondola, but wind pressure around the rapidly falling sphere forced me back. So I backed up and plunged headlong at the opening. I managed to hit it fairly, and went out in a horizontal position, face down, with arms and legs outspread like a frog. By that time we had fallen 1,500 feet and were descending so fast that the wind pressure held me practically even with the gondola. In other words, I was not falling away from it, but moving downward at the same rate of speed. I turned over a half revolution and, as I came right side up, pulled my rip cord. The parachute opened instantly. The jerk was like that made when one jumps from an airplane at 80 miles an hour. The folds of white silk opened in a large circle—and then a portion of the balloon fabric above the gondola fell on top of my parachute.

For a second it looked as if the balloon would take my chute with it. The fabric covered it to the very center of the silk. And then luckily the parachute slid out from under and worked itself free.

How about Kepner and Anderson? I looked around and saw the other two parachutes in the air and knew they were safe. Directly below me, I heard the gondola hit with a tremendous thud, and saw a huge ring of dust shoot out. Forty seconds later I hit—fortunately with a much lighter thud—and the parachute dragged me a few feet on my face through the black dirt of a Nebraska cornfield.

In a very few minutes, Major Kepner, Captain Anderson, and I had rolled up our parachutes and hastened to the spot where the gondola had struck; already a score of people were present, seemingly rising out of the very ground, and in a few minutes hundreds more were coming across the fields to the wreck.... It then appeared that hundreds of local people had been trailing the balloon by automobile. Soon the place swarmed with spectators.

The crowd of sight-seers lent willing assistance in rolling up the main section of the balloon fabric into a pile. But, like people the world over, they became relentless souvenir hunters. Numerous small fragments of balloon had fallen like snowflakes all over the farm field, and probably nearly every member of the crowd had picked up a small strip of the rubberized fabric.

Major Kepner and I went to the farmhouse of Mr. Reuben Johnson, on whose field we had landed, to telephone and send some telegrams. For some time I had been conscious that it was nearly 100 degrees in the shade (with no shade), and that I still wore two suits of heavy woolen underwear and a light canvas flying suit; so in the farmhouse I asked permission to use a room to shed some clothing.

In a few minutes I was dressed only in the canvas suit, and I took the two suits of underwear outside and hung them over a fence. Then I went inside to get my messages off by telephone.

When I came out, I found that souvenir hunters had taken my underwear! I have not seen it since. Perhaps by this time it has been cut into small squares. Maybe, like pieces of balloon cloth that have been received by mail, some of it may be sent in with the request that it be autographed!

That was no note to conclude on. The instruments were smashed and the data lost. So they tried again the following year. On November 11, 1935, using helium instead of volatile hydrogen, an even larger balloon lifted a new gondola, Explorer II, with Anderson and Stevens inside. They rose a few feet, then started to settle back down. Things didn't look too promising.

From "Man's Farthest Aloft:"

As Anderson sensed the fall of the balloon, he shouted to me, stepped on the electrical switch, and turned the handle that controlled the 40 sacks of ballast, totaling 3,000 pounds in weight, that hung outside the gondola. In less than three seconds he had tripped ten of these sacks, dropping 750 pounds of ballast.

I lifted a sack of ballast from the floor, held it out of a manhole, and pulled the pin from its bottom. The contents fell in a spray of fine lead directly on the head of a man who was already running from the rim of the bowl to get from beneath us. As the shower of fine lead struck him, he shouted, ducked his head, and seemed to run even faster, if that were possible!

We were now about 50 feet above the tree tops. To the right and left the dense crowd was scattering in a frantic attempt to get away from the towering structure that apparently was about to wreck itself and fall on the heads of many of them, who probably visualized themselves trapped under acres of rubber-coated fabric.

But the balloon stopped its descent and started upward again. It was fortunate that we had available the electric ballast discharge built for quick emergency, and tested over and over again on the ground to insure that it would operate without fail. When we had wired these sacks into place before the take-off, we had provided that as the handle, operable from either inside or outside, was turned, from contact point to contact point, sacks would be exploded by dynamite caps and be dumped from opposite sides of the gondola.

Therefore, as Andy turned the handle that controlled the 40 sacks, lead shot spilled from ten 2-inch openings almost equally spaced around the gondola.... I have often wondered since how many scores of people were sprayed by those streams of fine shot...

Many people think it must have been extremely dangerous for us to walk around on the slippery surface on top of a gondola hanging in space. Actually, there was no sensation of danger whatever. We climbed in and out, up and down, like monkeys, always having a handhold and a foothold.

The ten 1-inch ropes that suspended the gondola from the rope load ring, six feet higher, were stretched taut and were practically as rigid as iron bars. Each of these ropes carried nearly 1,000 pounds of weight. Together, they formed a cage through which it would have been difficult to fall, unless one really tried to fall....

Of the many items of apparatus, none functioned more perfectly than the radio apparatus of the National Broadcasting Company.... The

Rising as high from its moorings as a 26-story building, the stratosphere balloon Explorer
*prepares to carry the aeronauts in its pressurized gondola up toward the shores of space.
Its successor,* Explorer II, *set a manned height record that stood for 15 years.*

transmission and reception were faultless; the outgoing speech level was
kept constant by an ingenious "gain control" installed this year by Mr.
Morris. Substantially, this device had the effect of making the micro-
phone less sensitive when one was near it and more sensitive when one
was farther away. It was largely because of this feature that listeners with
short wave radio sets could hear us working and talking in the gondola
even when we had no intention of addressing the public.

If any difficulty existed, it was in reception, because I was sometimes
careless in tuning in or in the use of the volume control on the receiver.
Sometimes the clatter of instruments made repetition necessary.

Even at 10 miles above the earth Andy, the married member of the crew, was not beyond his family's voice. Mrs. Anderson, in the National Broadcasting Company tent at the Stratobowl, asked her husband, "How is everything? Where are you now?"

"Very good, Muddy," was the reply.

"Where are you?"

"I am up in the air," said Andy, dryly, adding that our altitude was about 54,000 feet and that we were on the way to our ceiling.

"Fine, and best of luck!" said Mrs. Anderson, far below us, completing a call that had been put through as readily as a telephone call to the corner grocery.

Again I was amused when I overheard the instructions, given on short wave, of an eastern announcer to his fellow announcers.

"Don't play up this record business, boys, until we are sure that they have gotten down safely," he suggested. "There is still plenty of chance for them to crash and they have to come down alive to make it a record."

We made the record anyway, topping out at 72,395 feet, or nearly 14 miles, nudging the edge of space. Observations of the earth and sky were made at the tip of the flight, 13.71 miles above sea level.

The earth could be seen plainly underneath through the lower porthole and hundreds of miles in every direction through the side portholes. It was a vast expanse of brown, apparently flat, stretching on and on. Wagon roads and automobile highways were invisible, houses were invisible, and railroads could be recognized only by an occasional cut or fill. The larger farms were discernible as tiny rectangular areas. Occasional streaks of green vegetation showed the presence of streams.

Here and there water could be seen in the form of rivers or lakes, especially if the sun was reflected from the water's surface. No sign of actual life on the earth could be detected. To us it was a foreign and lifeless world. The sun was the one object that commanded our attention; we were temporarily almost divorced from Mother Earth.

Overhead, the great balloon blocked out our view of the sky above us. How I wished at this time that we could have a central tube in the balloon through which we could look at the zenith! I am sure that the sky would have been so dark directly overhead that we could have seen the stars at noonday. As it was, we could see the sky, beyond the sides of the balloon, at an angle of about 55 degrees above the horizon.

The horizon itself was a band of white haze. Above it the sky was light blue, and perhaps 20 or 30 degrees from the horizon it was of the

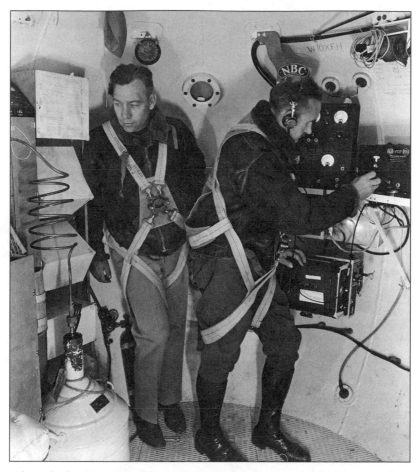

The inside of Explorer II's gondola was crammed with dials, gauges, electroscopes, spectographs, cosmic ray counters, and other gadgets. Orvil Anderson (left) checks the nitrogen-liquid oxygen flask while Albert Stevens (right—wearing cavalry boots) fiddles with the radio gear.

blue color that we are accustomed to. But at the highest angle that we could see it, the sky became very dark. I would not say that it was completely black; it was rather a black with the merest suspicion of very dark blue.

In the rigging hung a new flag of the United States. This flag was in full sunlight and I compared the blue of the field of this flag with that of the sky. Now the blue of our regulation flag is quite deep in shade, but it appeared a much lighter blue than the blue of the stratosphere sky.

We remained at our ceiling for an hour and a half, our instruments clicking away as if to make the most of their unique opportunity. Then Captain Anderson opened one of the valves to start the balloon into descent. Nothing happened at first, and he valved again and again. Finally the balloon started into positive descent.

This time the descent was uneventful, and reporters were free to splash the news of a new height record across the headlines. Anderson and Stevens, now household names, were showered with honors and awards and congratulated by President Franklin D. Roosevelt. They had brought back unprecedented photographs and a wealth of data about cosmic rays, radio waves, the distribution of ozone, and the dispersal of spores in the upper atmosphere. Furthermore, the flight helped spur developments in vertical aeronautics—the technological reach toward space. Much was learned about how to protect humans in the alien edge of the vacuum, about pressurized cabins, heat suits, radio communication, and so on.

Albert Stevens, one of its fathers, never saw the U.S. space program, for he died in 1949. Too bad: It is obvious from the conclusion of his 1936 Geographic *article that he would have loved the idea of plunging through Earth's atmosphere in a space capsule:*

To get still more altitude, the balloon may be flown to a maximum ceiling by dropping all ballast, and saving none for descent; the gondola may be cut away at the top of the flight on a large parachute, leaving the balloon to go still higher with light automatic instruments while the gondola floats to earth with the men and the major portion of the scientific apparatus. The fall of such a gondola on a parachute in the extremely thin upper air of the stratosphere would be for tens of thousands of feet before the parachute would really retard it. That *would* be a ride!

CAMERA UNDER THE SEA
February 1956

I FOUND THE BONES OF THE BOUNTY
December 1957

LUIS MARDEN (1913–2003)

*"THOSE WERE HALCYON DAYS," LUIS MARDEN RECALLED, "WHEN THE
undersea world was new and lay all before us, waiting to be discovered. Every dive
was like a visit to a new planet." The former chief of the GEOGRAPHIC's foreign
editorial staff was remembering one of the great adventures of his globetrotting life,
a celebrated voyage he made in 1955 on the Calypso with Jacques-Yves Cousteau.*

*Cousteau—in the early 1950s he was an unknown French naval officer
espousing a new kind of diving. Coinventor of the Aqua-Lung, the first self-
contained underwater breathing apparatus (scuba), Cousteau had made obsolete
the tethers, hoses, helmets, and lead shoes with which men had been staggering
across the seafloor. The Aqua-Lung opened all the sunlit regions of the ocean to free-
swimming exploration in a way never possible before.*

*Marden was a talented photographer determined to capture the otherworldly
beauty of coral reefs on color film. He eagerly agreed to accompany Captain Cousteau
on a voyage to the Red Sea and Indian Ocean. As the Calypso team filmed an underwater documentary, Marden worked with such legendary divers as Frédéric Dumas
and Albert Falco, and he got to know the slim, blue-eyed, and utterly captivating
Cousteau. The two men forged a friendship that lasted the rest of their lives.*

*It proved a memorable voyage. Cousteau's film, The Silent World, won both an
Academy Award and the Palme d'Or at Cannes and is probably the most influen-
tial underwater documentary ever made. Marden's pictures, published in the
February 1956 NATIONAL GEOGRAPHIC, revolutionized the art and
technique of underwater photography. At remote Assumption Island, near the
Seychelles, they discovered a coral reef, an undersea Garden of Eden. Through
Marden's descriptions we may glimpse the rapture of diving at the dawn of scuba.*

I LIKE FISH. IT IS WELL THAT I DO, BECAUSE DURING FOUR MONTHS in
the Red Sea and Indian Ocean I literally rubbed fins with them
as I swam in the depths of their blue-lit improbable world.

Eight years ago in Paris I heard of Capt. Jacques-Yves Cousteau and his little group of submarine pioneers, but it was not until much later that I met the fearless captain in the United States. In my copy of his book, *The Silent World*, he wrote: "With the conviction that we shall have the occasion to work together some day."

Last spring this prophecy came true: I sailed from Toulon with the captain and his crew aboard *Calypso*, the diving-research vessel that has become legend to undersea explorers all over the world. I was the expedition's underwater still photographer, specializing in color....

We found an ideal place for color photography at a small dot in the monsoon-whipped immensity of the Indian Ocean—Assumption Island, 240 miles from the northern tip of Madagascar. Only a handful of humans were living in the low islet, and above water the white sand and scrub did not look inviting. But *Calypso* moved slowly in toward shore and anchored over the mottled yellow-brown shadows of a vast coral reef.

Seamen rigged the diving ladder, and Frédéric Dumas and Albert Falco descended to look around. In a few minutes they popped to the surface like seals and, removing their mouthpieces, cried out "*Extraordinaire!*"

It was indeed extraordinary. Compared with *Calypso's* veterans, I am a novice, but all my diving has been on coral reefs. Yet never have I seen so magnificent a sight.

When I dropped backward off the diving ladder, I sank for a few feet, then doubled up and rolled over, to drive straight downward with strokes of my rubber-finned feet.

Thirty feet below me a low jungle of corals glowed with soft yellows, pinks, blues, and purples. Stunted trees, umbrellas, convoluted domes, and crooked fingers unrolled and gradually faded into the blue of distance.

The luminous transparency of the warm water bathed me in light. Fish, corals, even my own body, were outlined with a soft lunar effulgence; I seemed to hang suspended in the heart of an enormous liquid sapphire.

The reef pullulated with fish. Small fish of green, yellow, red, blue, and black flashed by or hung motionless in solid, tree-shaped schools. Bigger fish swam with the deliberation of aldermen among the crowds of nervous small fellows.

As I flipped downward, solid walls of fish parted and streamed round me like air smoothly diverted round an airfoil, then closed again when I had passed. Near the bottom little fish came up and peered inquisitively into my mask.

I straightened and came to rest with a gentle bump on a big coral boulder. Standing on my rubber-shod feet among the living polyps that covered the dome with a coat of gently waving fingers, I seemed to rest on a curving carpet of deep translucent pile, yet an inch below the polyps' deceptive softness, razor-sharp coral lay ready to draw blood at a touch.

On a level with my eyes a colony of sea anemones waved their lethal fingers, disclosing as they rippled gracefully in the strong tidal current occasional flashes of deep magenta from their fleshy bodies.

Two small orange fish glowed like hot coals among the beckoning fingers. They lived there, secure in the knowledge that, in some strange fashion, the anemone recognized them as friends and carefully curled its stinging tentacles away. In return the little fish share their captures with the sedentary animal. I made a photograph of the anemones, and bent over my camera to change bulbs. Diving masks permit the diver to see straight ahead but not far on either side, and when I looked up I nearly jumped out of my Aqua-Lung.

Not one foot from my eyes, a nightmare face stared at me. From a blotched and mottled head, bigger than my own, with thick, turned-down disapproving lips, two popping eyes gazed insolently at me.

My leap backward off the boulder was cushioned by the thick medium of water, and I floated down to the sand floor slowly, while the 60-pound grouper beat its thick tail and followed me.

I have already said that I like fish. I now became convinced that fish like me. Everywhere that Marden went, that fish was sure to go. The grouper swam slowly after me, studying everything with its swiveling pop-eyes, and even nuzzling the gleaming flash-bulb reflector. I am convinced that the reflector attracted fish as does a fishing spoon, by sending moons of light glancing through the water.

Cousteau calls the big groupers the intellectuals of the sea. Certainly they have more curiosity than any other fish I have known. You can almost hear the ponderous workings of their minds as they swim toward you, stop, then turn one broad flank to look you over with an eye that swivels drolly in its socket. Intellectuals they may be, but they also have something of the air of the country bumpkin who stands in uncomprehending fascination before some complicated mechanism.

From that day onward the big grouper always accompanied us on our undersea tours. Though it did not have very big teeth and seemed friendly, it was rather disconcerting to see the fish appear unexpectedly from

Jacques Cousteau (left) and Luis Marden (right) on the deck of the Calypso
during the 1955 cruise to the Indian Ocean.

behind. I had the uncomfortable feeling that it was always just out of sight, in the mask's blind spot. I could now understand the bit of stable lore about never approaching a horse suddenly from behind. I did not like it, either.

Someone named the grouper Ulysses. When a diver startled him by making a sudden movement, the big fish would take off in a spurt, making audible thumps—*boomp, boomp, boomp*—as he beat the water with his tail. Gradually he grew tamer, until at last I could stroke his side gently. Whenever I did this, Ulysses would roll over with pleasure like a dog.

Ulysses grew to be a nuisance. It was hard even to make a picture of him. I would set the lens for three feet, then press my mask against the viewing port to focus. The big blunt head would swim into the field and then, before I could trip the shutter, bump softly against the porthole of the camera. My diving companions would knock themselves out laughing at my attempts to back away to keep the grouper in focus. They said he was *cabot*—a lens louse, who mugged the camera and had to be kept out of range.

On Assumption's reefs the fish lived in an underwater age of innocence. Never having seen a man, they had almost no fear of us. At first they stayed just out of reach. After a few days, when they saw that we did them no harm, most of the fish around our anchorage accepted us.

Only once was I actually able to catch a fish with my bare hand. When a slow-moving trunkfish, whose Brazil-nut-shaped body is encased in bony armor like a turtle's, took refuge in a coral crevice, I picked it up gently.

I have heard few fish utter any sound under water, so I was startled when my little trunkfish began to squeak. He creaked like an old gate until I opened my fingers and let him sail off, erratically sculling with fins and tail like a small surrealist galley worked by disorganized oars.

Calypso's cook was the only one to whom Cousteau had issued a fishing permit. Even he was required to use a very small hook, lest he catch one of our movie stars. When I was swimming under the ship one day, I saw the cook's thin nylon line coming down out of the blue. I gave it a tremendous yank, having first carefully got out of the way of the upward jerk I expected. Nothing happened. When I came on deck, Hanen turned a pale-blue Alsatian eye on me and said, "I have caught my share of divers. I'm looking for fish."

Most of the fish we saw under *Calypso* were reef fish, bottom dwellers that usually stayed pretty much in the same place. But amidships of the anchored vessel the reef dropped off into 150 feet of water, and frequently schools of pelagic fishes would streak in from the open sea. These were the hunters—bold, swift fish, streamlined as torpedoes, with the thin lunate tail of the high-speed swimmer. Staring-eyed jacks, flat and compact and glistening like molten silver, would circle us as we swam over the corals. Once a big jack of 30 pounds or more flashed from behind me, hit my flash reflector with a loud clang, and arched back over my shoulder in a streak of light. I nearly spat out my mouthpiece, because I had only glimpsed it and feared it might be a shark or barracuda. I turned and circled to try to tweak its tail, but it was no use. It was in its element, and I was out of mine, and I never touched it....

Whenever I swam over the sudden dropoff of the reef, I looked down into a subtly changing blue that shaded from turquoise just below me to an intense cobalt as the depth increased. Even the clearest sea water holds myriad minute particles in suspension, and the scattered light reflected from these makes the water itself appear to be luminous. It is this light haze that marks the limits of visibility in very clear sea water; objects at a distance do not so much disappear into cloudiness as dim and vanish in a bright-blue glow of light.

Sea water is a mysterious substance. Cousteau says, "People are apt to think of clear tropical sea water as being like the chemist's distilled water, a liquid cleanliness, an absence of matter. Nothing could be more wrong. It is a living soup, a broth made up of millions of microscopic particles of living animal and vegetable matter, and, as living organisms will, it changes from time to time."...

Calypso's divers made at least three dives per day, and on many occasions we made five. At such times, however pleasant it had been below, the draining fatigue of continued deep diving had a telling effect, particularly at the moment when emerging from the buoying water onto the diving ladder. Then the triple steel cylinders on our backs and the lead-weight belts would seem to weigh a ton.

Once on clambering up the ladder I saw the long birdlike figure of Cousteau standing, spread-legged and arms akimbo, sucking on his broken-stemmed pipe, watching the returning file of divers with brooding eyes. As I shrugged off the heavy cylinders and sank to the hot deck planking, gratefully stretching out in the sun, I remarked to Cousteau, "Underwater photography is the bunk. If God had wanted man to dive, He'd have given him gills." Dumas, who lay supine on the hatch cover, answered without opening his eyes, "Il y a longtemps que j'en suis c onvaincu—I've been convinced of that for a long time."...

One day we filmed a scene for *The Silent World* at 144 feet. Nine divers took part, including actors, lamp carriers, and cameramen. At a signal from director Cousteau we jackknifed and swam down as rapidly as possible, through the squeeze of increasing pressure, into the dark blue of deep water.

Near the base of the reef cliff rose a spire of coral to a height of 10 feet. On this column I saw specimens of nearly every kind of invertebrate marine life of warm seas: scarlet and yellow sponges, small fibrillate yellow sea fans, platelike pearl oysters, and, crowning the pinnacle, a magnificent plumed bush of black coral. Amid this miniature jungle of animal growth flitted darting blue wrasses, nervous round damselfish of black and yellow, and a majestic pair of butterflyfish which peered into each mask in turn.

We took up our stations around the coral head for the scene: the light carriers suspended in water halfway up the coral head, and I kneeling on

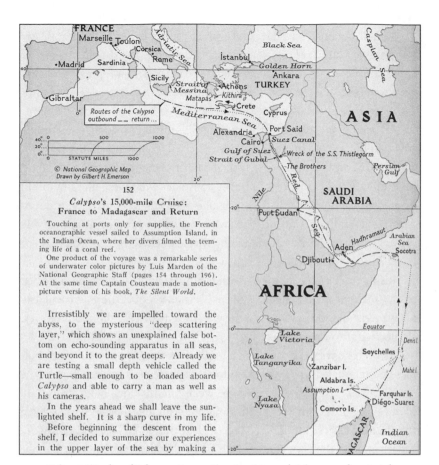

Between March and July 1955 Jacques-Yves Cousteau and Calypso made a storied 15,000-mile cruise from France to the Seychelles, Aldabras, and tiny Assumption Island, producing the underwater film classic The Silent World.

the sandy bottom, gently controlling my sinking into position by exhaling so as not to raise a cloud of sand. The cloud of animal life looked uniformly blue to us, and then Cousteau signaled and the floodlights switched on.

What a transformation! Hot oranges, reds, and mustard yellows glowed in the fan-shaped cones of light from the dazzling incandescent lamps. Fish in somber blue and black darted into the white cone of light, instantly appeared in vivid orange and yellow bands, then swam out of the light to snap quickly back into the world of blue....

I had raised my twin-bulb flash camera, when suddenly there was a dull concussion and a heavy blow knocked me on my back. The implosion of 20 flash bulbs had bowled me over and momentarily stunned me.

Something must have brushed against the net bag of bulbs that floated upright like a bunch of toy balloons on a line tied to my shoulder. The glass lamps, already strained by the pressure of five atmospheres pressing against the vacuum inside the globes, had simultaneously collapsed. Bits of glinting metal foil settled like silver rain about me as I struggled to my knees.

All round me the ghostly laughter of my eight good companions sounded hollow as a dream sequence recorded in an echo chamber.

"My friends!" I muttered through teeth clenched round my rubber mouthpiece; then I grinned up at my comrades, who were literally rolling over with laughter. That is the advantage of submarine mirth; you can do rolls, spins, and slow outside loops while enjoying yourself. You must take only one precaution: do your laughing with clenched teeth, or you may spit out the mouthpiece that feeds you air....

Rising from a deep dive is like something in a dream. With hardly a beat of our fins, we rose in a cluster. Relieved of the weight of the air we had used up, we were slightly lighter than the water we displaced, and mounted gently, head first, toward the surface.

As we rose, we were bathed in a tingling froth of the myriad silver bubbles of our exhaled air. It was like taking a bubble bath in champagne.

Because of the lessening pressure, we felt lightheaded as we neared the blue ceiling of the surface. The limpid blue the diver sees when he looks toward the surface through 100 feet of clear water I have seen in only one other place—in the 13th-century stained-glass widows of Chartres....

Diving with Cousteau was only one of Luis Marden's many achievements. So various was his long career that it has been widely considered the epitome of the NATIONAL GEOGRAPHIC spirit. He helped pioneer 35-mm color photography and discovered a new orchid species in Brazil. He covered the early space program and flew his own ultralight well into his 70s. He skippered his own ketch across the Atlantic and replotted Columbus's route. He taught himself five languages, and Webster's dictionary quoted his precise English usages six times. His book-crammed house was designed by Frank Lloyd Wright, and other acquaintances included Arthur C. Clarke, Thor Heyerdahl, Orville Wright, and the kings of Tonga and Jordan.

Pressed to tell what he considered the greatest moment in his career, Marden would have begun by recalling the day in the mid-1950s when he strolled through a Fiji Island museum and noticed the remains of a wooden plank marked, "Rudder, Bounty." He had stopped, transfixed. He had always considered the story of Fletcher Christian's mutiny against tyrannical Captain Bligh to be among the great sea sagas. Here was an artifact from the actual ship, grappled out of the sea at Pitcairn Island, the lonely outpost where the mutineers, believing themselves beyond the reach of British justice, had burned and sunk the Bounty.

No one had searched for further remains of the ship. Marine archaeology hardly existed, and the island was so far away. Yet the notion of doing so held a quixotic appeal—and for Luis Marden, that was enough. He was the right man at the right time and that distant corner of the world was the right place. In late 1956, therefore, when he was nearly 45 and cresting life's wave, he stood on the rolling deck of a freighter and watched the cliffs of Pitcairn heave into view.

THE *RANGITOTO* STAYED ONLY AN HOUR; THEN I SAID GOODBYE TO MY SHIPboard acquaintances and climbed down the swaying Jacob's ladder. When the last islander had taken his place in the boats, the ladders were pulled aboard the *Rangitoto* and someone called out, "A song for Captain Pilcher and the ship!"

A man began to sing, one by one the others joined in, and then 70 voices of men and women rose in clear harmony, singing the hymn "In the Sweet Bye and Bye." High above us the rails were white with waving handkerchiefs; as the last strains died away our boat captain called out, "Cast off!" and we moved slowly away from the ship. I turned toward shore. The sun had set behind the rocky heights of Pitcairn, and blood-red streaks, like rents in a blast furnace, slashed across the darkening sky.

A voice sang out, "Tillah, tillah! Anybody bin see ah tillah?" The heavy tiller was passed over my head. Then a dozen hands raised the mast, made fast the shrouds, and hoisted our jib and gaff-rigged mainsail.

"H'ist hah shrodes higher!" called the captain, and the men hauled on the shrouds to tauten them.

Left to themselves, the islanders conversed in Pitcairnese. Though difficult for an outsider to understand at first, this was not nearly so unintelligible as I had expected. They used many nautical terms, and the accent was somewhat like that of parts of the West Indies.

As we drove toward the island, with the lee rail well down, my neighbor on the crowded thwart said: "It's darking."

Night does not really fall; it rises, starting at the water's edge and suffusing upward like ink creeping up a blotter.

The man thumped a crate of my air tanks.

"I heardsay you gwen dive in Bounty Bay."

I admitted it.

Native Pitcairners both looked and spoke like the Bounty mutineers who were their ancestors. Once called the world's finest surf boatmen, they lived on an island where waves crash relentlessly against its rugged flanks.

"Man," he said, "you gwen be dead as hatchet!" Why a hatchet should be deader than a doornail, or anything else, I never found out, but it signifies utter extinction....

One of my chief objectives in coming to Pitcairn had been to find, if possible, the resting place of the *Bounty*. I questioned the islanders about any visible remains. Everybody knew that a clutch of iron ballast bars lay in the surf, almost on shore, but no one could tell me anything of the actual ship.

"It-sa gone," they all said. "Nothing left." Everyone knew, of course, that she had gone down in Bounty Bay. The question was, exactly where?

I soon found in going over the area with a waterglass, and later in diving to the bottom, that no "wreck," as such, remained. The burning, the fishing up of timbers more than a century ago, and, above all, the relentless pounding of the Pacific combers had demolished the *Bounty*. The most one could hope to find would be metal fittings....

Len [Len Brown, a Pitcairner] said to me one day: "I can show you one copper bar. My father first see it 'bout 15 years ago. I dive down to it and touch it, but it's stuck to the bottom."

This was the first word I had had of anything definite that might mark the site; so on the first calm day we got Len's canoe and paddled out to the place where Len had seen the copper bar.

Fifty yards offshore Len stopped paddling and turned to take bearings. He sighted over one shoulder at the soaring rock spire of Ship Landing Point, then looked up at The Edge.

"She right here," he said.

I lifted the waterglass over the side and pressed its glass bottom into the heaving sea.

"See it?" Len asked.

I shook my head. Len peered over my shoulder and pointed. Deep in a fissure I saw a short, gray-green bar, too straight to be a natural growth. Little yellow wrasses flickered unconcernedly over it, indifferent to the encrusted fragment of history.

I shrugged into the harness of my Aqua-Lung, put on rubber flippers and face mask, and fell backward, diver-fashion, into the sea.

Turning over, I flutter-kicked my way down into the miniature valley, past flowerlike small corals, until my hand closed on the bar. It was cemented firmly to the bottom. Directly above, Len's face peered through the disk of the waterglass. I made a hammering motion. The face disappeared, and a hammer and cold chisel were slowly lowered to me on a cord.

I stood on my head in the cleft in which the bar lay. Down there my head and shoulders were in comparative calm, but every few seconds the surge would slam into me and my wildly kicking feet were then powerless to hold me vertical. Helplessly I would crash against the coral fingers that clung to the rock and feel the stings that meant the sharp fingers were scoring crimson lines on my legs.

For a quarter of an hour I chipped away around the sides of the two-inch-thick bar. When I had cut a trench in the limestone bottom all the way around it, I inserted a steel rod, heaved, and the bar came away.

In the boat we turned the bar over and over. It tapered slightly to a rounded and eroded point and the upper end was irregular; it was evidently a pintle that had broken off from the rudder strap which held it. I think this is the second of four pintles shown on the Admiralty plan.

Parkin [Parkin Christian, Fletcher Christian's great-great grandson] had pointed out from The Edge the spot where he recovered the rudder; that was only a dozen yards from the rocky embrasure that held the pintle we recovered, but though Len, Tom, and I searched the area minutely in the calm days that followed, we found no other trace of the *Bounty*. Obviously, the main body of the vessel lay elsewhere.

"I think," I said to Len, "that as the ship drove ashore, the following seas broke off her rudder. The pintles dropped in the sand, and the *Bounty* drove aground some distance beyond. What do you think?"

"Sounds reasonable," said Len.

"Well, then," I said, "where did the ship itself go down?"

We talked it over. The thing is relatively simple, we thought: The *Bounty* was about 100 feet long; the ballast bars are over there in the surf; the rudder and pintles were found out there; all we have to do is draw an imaginary line between the two places, cruise along this line on the bottom, and we are bound to find some trace of the ship.

Cruise we did; every day of reasonable calm we filled the air cylinders and dived. We nearly plowed furrows with our chins in the bottom. But we found nothing.

Then, late one afternoon nearly six weeks after my arrival on Pitcairn, I took Chester Young out to show him how diving was done. By this time we were losing hope, but we paddled out to near where we had found the pintle.

Len helped me on with my Aqua-Lung, and I dived first. While waiting for Len, I took my bearings on the big rock under which the pintle had lain and cruised slowly over the animate carpet of undulating seaweed, scrutinizing the cove bottom closely. Big jacks swam round me, watching curiously. On a bed of weed I saw a crescent-shaped object.

Thrusting my face closer, I saw it was an oarlock. Unlike the standard U-shaped oarlock, this one had one arm markedly longer than the other, forming a tilted crescent that looked strikingly like a new moon or the symbol of Islam.

As I watched, 14 Moorish Idols, bizarrely shaped black-and-yellow reef fish, swam in echelon over the crescent—Moorish fish maneuvering over a Moorish crescent. Fantastic coincidence that only the sea can produce!

Then I came unexpectedly on a long, sandy trench. The end nearest me was covered with white limestone secreted by calcareous algae—lithothamnion, a stonemaking plant—and I could see little squiggles in the surface, a curious marking that resembled petrified worms.

I thrust my face closer, almost touching the bottom. My heart gave a jump. The squiggles were encrusted sheathing nails, Bounty nails—dozens of them. I looked up for Len. He was just above me, staring questioningly. I reached up my hand for his, pumped it violently, and pointed. He looked up grinning and nodding, and we shook hands again.

We had found the resting place of the Bounty.

Beyond, two other trenches stretched toward the spot where the ballast bars lay in the yeasty surf. I had been searching too far to the eastward. Apparently, prevailing winds and currents had veered the ship as she went ashore. The bow had pivoted on the shore, and the stern had swung round to the west.

I began to chip away at the layer of nails. At each blow of the hammer a puff of black "smoke" arose—carbonized wood of the Bounty, still clinging to metal fastenings. It was extremely difficult to hold a position on the bottom. Ever and again, the sea would bowl us over completely or carry us shoreward sprawling on our backs.

Near the nails I came on a long bolt, partly uncovered. I carefully chipped down both sides until it came free. Swinging up to the bobbing canoe, I thrust the bolt over the side. Len and I saw enough to convince us that we had found the line of the keel, or at least one of the main strakes of the hull, though we saw no planks or ribs. Everything was covered by a hard, limy growth.

As we dug deeper, we came upon fragments of the copper with which the Bounty had been sheathed, in good condition and almost an eighth of an inch thick. Deeper digging should bring up larger pieces of the ship.

That night I polished and buffed a bronze sheathing nail until it shone like gold. A piece of the original Bounty! The burnished gold surface caught the light with a mesmerizing effect.

As I stared and dreamed, I seemed to see the shipyard at Deptford, with the Bounty on the stocks and the shipwrights swarming over her. I heard the ringing hammer blows, the "chink, chink" of the caulking irons, and the "chid, chid, chid" of the adzes paring away the solid English oak. I smelled the winy odor of new timbers oozing sap in the hot sun, the resinous smell of pitch, and the clean astringent scent of Stockholm tar in the rigging.

A leather-aproned workman, perched in the scaffolding, drives another nail into the copper sheathing, and says to his mate:

"Off to Otaheite and the Great South Sea! Damn my eyes, Sam'l, I've 'alf a mind to ship myself."...

ACKNOWLEDGMENTS

Compiling an anthology such as this is a challenging undertaking. Not only must an editor sift through the thousands of articles published in NATIONAL GEOGRAPHIC between 1888 and 1957, he must also select only fifty—something less than one per cent—to represent the wide range of people and places and voices and experiences found in the magazine during those years. Those fifty—or, more accurately, extracts from 54 of them—must then make interesting or amusing reading today. Furthermore, paring down stories that may originally have been published at eight, ten, or twelve thousand words is not without its hazards. Altogether it is a tricky business to pull off, and if the result is not always successful you have only this editor to blame.

Nevertheless, this volume is in many ways a joint endeavor, reflecting also the efforts of my two longstanding associates in the National Geographic Society Archives. Cathy Hunter marched beside me most of the way, dodging the brigands, joining the caravans, and tactfully employing her editing pencil. Renee Braden, our chief, has been for many years my closest colleague, the proverbial fox to my poor hedgehog, and throughout this project I plodded daily to her office, seeking her wise counsel. I also wish to thank Renee's good friend, Simon Winchester, for his encouragement, his characteristically generous remarks, and his evocative foreword, and Lisa Thomas, my editor, whose idea gave birth to this book

In addition to the archives, other Society offices proved indispensable to this undertaking. In an age of electronic information sources there are still things that can't be found anywhere else but in old books, and I happily plundered the Society's superb library and exquisite rare book room. My thanks also go to Suz Eaton, keeper of the clippings files, for cheerfully hunting down obituaries and obscure articles. These numerous separate collections, including the archives, are today grouped together under the rubric Libraries and Information Services, and all have profited from the energetic leadership of its director, Susan Fifer Canby, whose fostering of innovation and willingness to support venturesome projects have made her a respected figure both at the Society and throughout her profession. I'm grateful for the opportunities she has given me.

André Sobocinsky of the Bureau of Medicine and Surgery and Ali Hamodi of Baghdad and Wyoming assisted in various ways, which I here acknowledge. Susan Tyler Hitchcock and Jane Sunderland lent their valuable editorial skills to the project, as did Cindy Kittner and Lauren Pruneski. Dana Chivvis researched and edited the photographs and maps that accompany the text, and Teresa Tate proved invaluable in clearing the rights. Melissa Farris and Cameron Zotter executed the marvelous design. Melissa Krause transcribed the text. People everywhere expressed their interest or gave me their support, and only space precludes me listing them as well.

Finally, my gratitude goes to my mother, who taught me the love of reading, and to my late father, whose ordered ranks of NATIONAL GEOGRAPHICS could not repose quietly upon a shelf but I made havoc of them, always forgetting to pick them up and put them back. Having now toiled through thousands of old articles, I can see him smiling: poetic justice has been served.

INDEX

ILLUSTRATIONS CREDITS

Page iv, Dr. Robert F. Griggs; 3, Charles Scribner's Sons; 7, Cuninghame/Charles Scribner's Sons; 15, Carl Akeley; 22, Edgar Alrich; 30, Edward Keith-Roach; 37, A. M. Hassanein Bey; 46, H. T. Cowling; 51, Ernest B. Schoedsack; 60, George Kennan; 67, Elsworth Huntington; 70, Elsworth Huntington; 83, Vladimir M. Zenzinov; 91, Roland Woods; 99, Rev. Gabriel Bretocq; 106, D. Van Der Meulen; 116, Owen Tweedy; 121, Stephen H. Nyman; 126, Maynard Owen Williams; 134, Dr. Joseph F. Rock; 143, Dr. Joseph F. Rock; 147, Morden-Clark Asiatic Expedition/courtesy American Museum of Natural History; 158, Owen Lattimore; 164, Maynard Owen Williams; 172, James B. Shackelford; 181, General William "Billy" Mitchell; 191, Lt. Col. Ilia Tolstoy; 199, F. Kingdon-Ward; 213, Charles Wylie/Royal Geographical Society; 225, Cabot Coville; 235, Dr. T. C. Lau; 240, Melvin Hall; 250, Nieuvenhuis; 257, Clifford A. Davidson; 274, Robert Griggs; 287, Clifton R. Adams; 292, A. F. Tschiffely; 303, Albert W. Stevens; 309, Ernest G. Holt; 318, Ruth Robertson/Harry Ransom Humanities Research Center, The University of Texas at Austin; 327, Alan J. Villiers; 336, Ida Treat; 342, Henri de Monfreid; 354, Thor Heyerdahl; 362, US Navy official; 371, Press Illustrating Service; 388, Charles and Anne Lindbergh; 400, Dr. William Beebe; 407, Richard Hewitt Stewart; 409, Richard Hewitt Stewart; 414, Pierre Goupil; 420, Luis Marden.

TEXT CREDITS

"Triumph on Everest" by Sir John Hunt and Sir Edmund Hillary is reprinted with the permission of the Royal Geographic Society; "Buenos Aires to Washington by Horse" by Aimé-Félix Tschiffely is reprinted with the permission of Basha O'Reilly; "Turning Back Time in the South Seas" by Thor Heyerdahl is reprinted with the permission of Gylendal Norsk Forlag; "They Survived at Sea" by Samuel Harby is reproduced with the permission of Rebecca Tran.